Theory for Today's Musician's carefully considered musical examples, drawn proportionately from "classical" and popular genres, clearly demonstrates the theoretical concepts students struggle to understand. Turek and McCarthy's entertaining writing encourages even the most reluctant student to read the text. The text encourages students to think creatively and actively. As a result, students learn to use their ears and then understand the "rules" of music theory. This should be the standard among theory textbooks.

—**David Hanan,** *University of Central Oklahoma*

Theory for Today's Musician is indeed apropos for today's music student. The book offers a logical and thorough presentation of music theory concepts, leaving no stone unturned. Musical examples are drawn not only from the standard classical repertoire, but from musical theater, popular music, traditional tunes, and jazz, so the book is relevant for any musician, regardless of specialization.

—**Eric Alexander,** *University of Northern Colorado*

Theory for Today's Musician's engaging writing style sparks the imagination and curiosity of students and encourages them to read on their own. It approaches music theory in such a way that the concepts and terminology covered may be applied equally well across a wide range of musical styles, and its well-placed examples demonstrate over and over again how useful these concepts can be to understanding and performing music, regardless of whether that music is by Bach, Beethoven, Bartók, or Brubeck.

—**Matt Santa,** *Texas Tech University*

Theory for Today's Musician

Theory for Today's Musician, Third Edition, recasts the scope of the traditional music theory course to meet the demands of the professional music world, in a style that speaks directly and engagingly to today's music student. It uses classical, folk, popular, and jazz repertoires with clear explanations that link music theory to musical applications. The authors help prepare students by not only exploring how music theory works in art music, but how it functions within modern music, and why this knowledge will help them become better composers, music teachers, performers, and recording engineers.

This broadly comprehensive text merges traditional topics such as part writing and harmony (diatonic, chromatic, neo-tonal and atonal), with less traditional topics such as counterpoint and musical process, and includes the non-traditional topics of popular music songwriting, jazz harmony and the blues. The accompanying companion website provides interactive exercises that allow students to practice foundational theory skills. Written by experienced authors, both active classroom teachers for many years, *Theory for Today's Musician* is the complete and ideal theory text to enable today's student to accomplish their musical goals tomorrow.

Updated and corrected throughout, the Third Edition includes:

- Expanded coverage of atonality and serialism, now separated into two chapters.
- Broadened treatment of cadences, including examples from popular music.
- Substantially rewritten chapter on songwriting.
- Interactive features of the text simplified to two types, "Concept Checks" and "Review and Reinforcement," for greater ease of use.
- New and updated musical examples added throughout.
- Charts, illustrations, and musical examples revised for increased clarity.
- Audio of musical examples now provided through the companion website.

The accompanying Workbook offers exercises and assignments to accompany each chapter in the book. A companion website houses online tutorials with drills of basic concepts, as well as audio.

Ralph Turek is a theorist, composer, author, jazz pianist, Professor Emeritus at The University of Akron, and a veteran of 35 years of teaching in the music theory classroom.

Daniel McCarthy is a familiar name in contemporary American music. As a composer, he has received distinguished faculty research/creativity awards at Indiana State University and The University of Akron, where he is Chair of the Composition and Theory Section in the School of Music.

Theory for Today's Musician

Third Edition

Ralph Turek

The University of Akron

Daniel McCarthy

The University of Akron

Routledge
Taylor & Francis Group

NEW YORK AND LONDON

Third edition published 2019
by Routledge
52 Vanderbilt Avenue, New York, NY 10017

and by Routledge
2 Park Square, Milton Park, Abingdon, Oxon, OX14 4RN

Routledge is an imprint of the Taylor & Francis Group, an informa business

First edition published by McGraw-Hill 2006
Second edition published by Routledge 2014

Library of Congress Cataloging-in-Publication Data
Names: Turek, Ralph, author. | McCarthy, Daniel William, 1955– author.
Title: Theory for today's musician / Ralph Turek, Daniel McCarthy.
Description: Third edition. | New York ; London : Routledge, 2020. |
Includes index.
Identifiers: LCCN 2018028285 (print) | LCCN 2018029575 (ebook) |
ISBN 9781351246262 (ebook) | ISBN 9780815371717 (hardback)
Subjects: LCSH: Music theory—Textbooks.
Classification: LCC MT6.T918 (ebook) | LCC MT6.T918 T47 2020
(print) | DDC 781—dc23
LC record available at https://lccn.loc.gov/2018028285

ISBN: 978-0-8153-7171-7 (textbook hbk)
ISBN: 978-0-8153-7172-4 (workbook pbk)
ISBN: 978-0-8153-7173-1 (textbook + workbook pack)
ISBN: 978-1-351-24626-2 (textbook ebk)
ISBN: 978-1-351-24622-4 (workbook ebk)
ISBN: 978-1-351-24614-9 (ebk pack)

Typeset in Galliard and Swiss 721
by Florence Production Ltd, Stoodleigh, Devon, UK

Editor: Genevieve Aoki
Senior Editorial Assistant: Peter Sheehy
Senior Production Editor: Katie Hemmings
Project Manager: Tamsyn Hopkins
Text Design: Susan R. Leaper
Cover Design: Jo Griffin

Visit the companion website: www.routledge.com/cw/turek

Printed in Canada

Contents

Detailed Contents

Preface

TO THE INSTRUCTOR

Theory for Today's Musician was, in the year 2000, intended as a bridge across the chasm that separates the Classical repertoire from the jazz and popular repertoires in the minds of many students entering college music programs. The goal remains: To engage students on familiar ground through the music that inhabits their daily lives—popular music, jazz, rock, the music of TV and film—and guide them toward the magnificent body of art music that comprises our Western music heritage. The challenge for a textbook that addresses vernacular music in any meaningful way is to balance durability, quality, and usefulness in the selection of musical examples. And the larger challenge is to strike the perfect balance in amount of the attention parsed to vernacular and art music.

This third edition remains true to the three original premises:

1. The highest purpose of music theory is the illumination of music; the highest purpose of music is *not* the validation of music theory.

2. The book should be written in an engaging way that can be understood by the average *interested and motivated* music student.

3. Today's musician is likely to be a multi-tasking individual who may well be required to teach, perform, compose or arrange, and produce music at some point. This book should provide basic preparation for such a multifaceted career.

In this third edition:

1. We've retained our conversational style that avoids traditional "academic-speak" and theoretical jargon while yet speaking in precise, articulate prose.

2. We've updated and added examples and retained our practice of drawing "first examples" from popular and traditional song literature and jazz. We continue to draw parallels between present and past practices.

3. We've improved the look and clarity of the charts and illustrations and we've sought greater uniformity in the notation of the musical examples.

4. We've reordered topics within chapters as deemed necessary (but have not changed the basic ordering of chapters).

5. We've occasionally augmented an analysis with some basic Schenkerian concepts.

6. We've addressed errors and oversights that we've discovered or that have been brought to our attention.

7. We've divided the chapter on serial and non-serial atonality into separate chapters and expanded out coverage of both.

8. We've substantially rewritten what is now Chapter 34, "Shaping a Song."

9. We've simplified the interactive features of the text into just two basic types: "Concept Checks" (which provide an immediate test of understanding) and "Review and Reinforcement" (which tests retention).

10. We've retained other organizational features that have received a favorable reaction: "preludes" and/or "codas" for most chapters to set the table and bus it, so to speak; a list of "Terms to Know" that conclude most chapters; a Glossary of Terms; and indices by both topic and composer/composition.

Part One: In Lieu of Fundamentals

Most of the fundamentals remain situated in two Appendices. Formatted as regular chapters, complete with examples, illustrations, and workbook assignments, they differ from the other chapters only in their location in the text. *They are chapters to be accessed as needed.* Necessary but not very exciting, these chapters are at the end of the book because we'd rather the first topics to meet student eyes be ones that engage their curiosity, whet their appetites, and plant the idea that music theory can be an intriguing adventure. This includes selected information on notation and acoustics that usually fascinates students, most of whom unknowingly have had close encounters with phenomena of the acoustic kind, such as equal temperament and the harmonic series. It also introduces modes, which inject a fresh and interesting perspective on the hoary topic of scales and which turn up often enough in popular music and jazz to warrant their early attention. (Instructors who wish to do so may ignore the corresponding exercises in the Workbook at this time and treat Chapter 1 as purely informational.)

Part Two: Diatonic Harmony

Seventh chords are introduced early and reinforced continually. (It is difficult to treat jazz and popular music without them.)

Lead-sheet chord symbols and figured bass reside in the same chapter to promote and facilitate their comparison. We've subsequently accorded lead-sheet symbols a more thorough treatment and more consistent reinforcement than is customary, with the goal that students be not merely cognizant of the system but proficient in its use.

We've broadened the treatment of cadences to include some found in today's popular music that cannot be explained as authentic, plagal, or any of the standard half cadences. The perfect–imperfect distinction "played" better to past generations than to this one. We've opted not to belabor it at this point in the belief that students can better appreciate its usefulness when phrases and periods are discussed.

Part Three: Melody

Part Three moves from general to specific, first dealing with basic melodic features, including large-scale tonal phenomena such as the step progression and large-scale arpeggiation and Schenkerian concepts such as prolongation, then moving to embellishing tones, and finally to phrasing. This first look at melodic form does so from the vantage point of the only three choices available to a composer at any point in the compositional process—to create, to vary, or to repeat.

Part Four: Voice Leading

Four-part voice leading is approached through a chapter that deals only with the soprano-bass framework (simultaneously an introduction to two-voice counterpoint). Our pared and prioritized part writing guidelines reflect today's practices. For example, we've avoided the academic distinction between close and open spacing, since acceptable spacing— whether close, open, or hybrid—automatically follows when the upper adjacent voices are kept within an octave of one another (the important goal, after all). Instead, we've encouraged students to maintain a distinct, mutually exclusive "corridor" for each voice of the texture. We've given a context to consecutive perfect consonances—absent from Baroque common practice, but present in Copland's "Fanfare for the Common Man" and rock music's "power chords."

We've introduced all important voice-leading concepts—melodic principles, chord spacing and doubling, and chord connection—in a single chapter (Chapter 11), using a popular music model. We've done this to establish voice leading's relevance immediately, but the overview can also suffice as a circumscribed study of the topic for instructors who prefer to spend more time elsewhere. Each topic presented in Chapter 11 is covered in depth in the three ensuing chapters.

Part Five: Basic Chromatic Harmony

Secondary function is covered in two chapters, the first (Chapter 15) a more or less traditional presentation, the second (Chapter 16) focusing on jazz and popular styles. This leads naturally into the first of two chapters of modulation (Chapter 17).

Part Six: Counterpoint

Chapter 18, "The Art of Countermelody," is a generalized and condensed species approach. In it we've tried to sweep aside the academic dust that seems to settle over this topic in the student mind by lacing the chapter with examples of counterpoint found in vernacular music before plunging into Bach's Two-Part Invention, no. 6. Chapter 19, "The Fugue," takes a closer look at Bach's art.

Part Seven: Advanced Chromatic Harmony

This five-chapter tour of nineteenth-century harmony is conducted in roughly chronological order—mode mixture, altered pre-dominants, altered dominants, embellishing diminished seventh chords, advanced modulation, triadic extension, and linear harmonic processes. Knowing that chromatic harmony is normally challenging to students:

- We've pared the topics. If our search for a musical example came up lean, we took this as a sign that perhaps a particular topic does not warrant discussion, at least at this level.

- We've kept it simple where it *can* be simple. With altered dominants, after all, we're talking about raising or lowering the chord fifth of a V (or V/V), which then moves up or down accordingly—only this and nothing more.

- We've used creative analogies where appropriate to illuminate matters.

Part Eight: Form

Chapter 25 deals with the root causes of form. By developing sensitivity to the musical processes—thematic, transitional, developmental, and cadential—that create affect, we hope to equip students to comprehend on some level the structure of any piece they hear. We've applied these concepts to small binary and ternary forms, which we've presented as outgrowths of the three composer—choices—repeat, vary, create—introduced earlier. Chapters 26 and 27 introduce sonata form and rondo. We've presented them as larger-scale manifestations of the same musical processes and choices while still addressing the tonal design that is commonly held to define these forms.

Part Nine: Music in the Twentieth Century and Beyond

On the concert music side are Debussy, Bartók, Stravinsky, Schoenberg, and Webern. On the vernacular side are the harmonic principles in jazz and blues, and the shaping of a popular song. The dilemma for theory today is how to add new topics without increasing the total time (four semesters) allotted to the course. This led to some scaling back of twentieth-century concepts in the first edition. Although we're still mindful of space and time limitations, we've included in this edition a more generous look at the analytical tools for the analysis of non-serial atonality, including the interval vector and the Z relationship.

Jazz harmony, the blues, and song writing, of great importance for today's musician, remained largely untouched by general theory texts. These, our final chapters, go well beyond a mere nod and are likely to include concepts new or enlightening even to budding jazz majors. They reflect our belief that no music student should stride across a stage to receive a diploma without a working understanding of jazz harmony and procedures and the ability (however modest) to set a line of lyrics to music.

More about the Musical Examples

One well-chosen musical example is worth more words than we can muster. For this reason, *Theory for Today's Musician* is "example-intensive." In selecting and treating the examples, practicality and relevance have been guiding beacons. Lines and/or octave doublings have been omitted from some few Classical examples to render them more easily playable on the keyboard. Most jazz and popular examples are presented in a style likely to be heard in clubs and on television, although some original arrangements have been retained to give a proper sense of the composer's style. Many of the examples might have been presented in diluted renditions that bleach out musical interest on the altar of simplicity. We've opted, rather, to keep the music authentic-sounding and interesting, instructing students to disregard this or that, noting that such and so will be addressed later, and so on. If this is the price of greater student interest, it's probably a good buy, since a challenged and motivated student is more teachable than a bored and indifferent one.

Arrangements original with this text are indicated "Arr. R.T." We realize and respect the fact that scholars of popular music may find the use of arrangements objectionable, and we offer this apologia:

Much popular music is recorded first and notated after the fact. Transcriptions often sound nothing like the recorded version, due in part to the inability of our notation system to capture the inflections and rhythmic nuances of the performance. In fact, those nuances might be viewed by the transcriber as performance inaccuracies in need of "correction." Also, the use of arrangements in popular music and jazz has been thoroughly sanctioned by practice. This repertoire is routinely "covered" by many artists, invariably differing in the details. In fact, a particularly popular rendition may become, over time, the "definitive" version, more recognized and emulated than the "authoritative" original. Most fake books (now called "real books") contain only the most basic harmonization of a tune, which is routinely embellished by recording artists. The prefaces to these books acknowledge this and often indicate one or more important recordings that deviate from the notated version therein. All of this is because popular music and jazz are improvisational and spontaneous forms of music that invite widely divergent interpretations.

While we've tried to retain the character of the original music, we've enhanced some selections in keeping with current harmonic practice so that the music sounds fresh and up-to-date. We've done this out of no disrespect for the music or its composers but out of a desire to make the examples as useful, interesting, and informative as possible for the student.

About the Sources

Examples from the jazz and popular repertories come from three sources: published editions, transcriptions of recorded performances, and arrangements. Passages transcribed by the authors bear a note to that effect. To the best of our knowledge, they accurately reflect the recorded performance. We take full responsibility for any inaccuracies, which are unintended and purely the result of less-than-perfect ears. Original arrangements are labeled as such. We've classified as "arrangements" even those melodies for which we've expanded the lead-sheet chord symbols or made substitutions. We made such changes either to illustrate a harmonic concept or to present the music in the way it is most often played by today's musicians.

A final word on the musical examples: Permission to use popular music is both restrictive and expensive. If an example seems to end in an odd place (a measure before a natural cadence, for example) or to be too short, it is likely due to a copyright restriction. Your understanding is appreciated.

Proposed Use

Theory for Today's Musician is a 2-year study encompassing the topics most often taught in a comprehensive course:

First Year
    First Semester:
        Part One: In Lieu of Fundamentals
        Part Two: Diatonic Harmony
        Part Three: Melody
    Second Semester:
        Part Four: Voice Leading
        Part Five: Basic Chromatic Harmony

Second Year
    First Semester:
        Part Six: Counterpoint
        Part Seven: Advanced Chromatic Harmony
    Second Semester:
        Part Eight: Form
        Part Nine: Music in the Twentieth Century and Beyond

The ordering of topics in this 2-year plan is not inviolable. You are welcome to reorder as you see fit, and we've tried to write the book in such a way that this is possible. Suggestions for reordering are given in the Instructors Manual.

The Workbook assignments for each chapter correspond to divisions within the chapter, facilitating immediate reinforcement of concepts. We've also included within the chapters ample opportunity for students to apply the information as soon as it has been presented

These opportunities are termed "Concept Check" or "Review And Reinforcement." In the earlier chapters, where students are most likely to need it, "webwork" is indicated. Here students are referred to online self-help.

Jazz Studies majors are an increasing segment of the music student population. If you have jazz piano majors in your classes, you might call upon them frequently to play the jazz and popular examples. This always adds interest to a class. Otherwise the companion website contains the bulk of the musical examples over four measures long in the text and practically all the examples in the Workbook.

Instructor's Manual

The Instructor's Manual follows the organization of the textbook. It provides notes on each chapter, suggestions for additional ways to use the examples and Workbook assignments, solutions to selected assignments, chapter quizzes, course plans and sample syllabi, and recommendations for additional musical examples.

A Final Word

Our hope is that this text will help to: 1) ignite students' interest in the theory behind the music they play and hear; and 2) provide students with the skills they need to function effectively in today's musical milieu.

We invite you to be creative in your use of the book, to amplify and condense as you see fit. We hope your need to *clarify* is minimal.

Ralph Turek and Daniel McCarthy

TO THE STUDENT

Why Music Theory?

Music has probably always come easily to you. If it has, then you may have difficulty understanding how utterly mysterious it can be to others. The fact is, the special mix of physical and mental attributes that translate into musical talent is a gift given to relatively few of the more than six billion inhabitants of this planet. It makes you a member of a special group that sees and hears in music the things most others do not. Your decision to further your study of music indicates your desire to cultivate these insights and share them with others.

Music engages us physically (muscle memory and coordination are necessary to sing or to play an instrument), mentally (we read music, we memorize it, we compose it), and emotionally (it can make us happy, sad, lonely, nostalgic, and so on). Music theory aims to deepen our mental involvement. That's necessary because to communicate all that you hear and feel in music, you need to understand it on many levels. A deeper and broader understanding will make you a more effective ambassador, whether as performer, teacher, or recording engineer.

Musically, much has changed since the time of Bach and Handel, Haydn and Mozart, and Beethoven and Brahms. But much has not. For example, a minor-key melody can still make the soul weep; rapid rhythms and loud dynamic levels can excite, while slow rhythms and soft dynamic levels can soothe; music with harmonies or multiple lines usually engages us more fully than single-line melodies; songs usually begin and end in the same key, often on the same harmony and so on. Music theory explains these things and much more.

Finally, we offer this observation about the music profession today: It's a jungle out there. Jobs? Never before have so many competed for so few, whether the position be an orchestra chair, a college or public school teaching job, an arts management position, or a sound engineer in a club or studio. In the music jungle, the fittest survive, and adaptability counts. Only a select few musicians today have the luxury of specializing in one kind of music, or of being only one kind of musician, whether a violinist, a composer, a conductor, or a music teacher. To join that select group, you need to be uncommonly proficient, and a little luck doesn't hurt either. Generally speaking, though, the more complete your musicianship, the better today's marketplace will treat you.

Using Theory for Today's Musician

Think of this textbook as one element in a triple alliance that also includes your instructor and you. How well the alliance works will determine the measure to which the study benefits you.

1. The book: we've written it in what we hope is a clear and engaging manner.

2. Your instructor: He or she will likely amplify and clarify and bring additional insights to bear.

3. You: You are the third and most variable part of the triple alliance. Without your efforts, the book and your instructor will be of limited value. With this in mind, permit us to suggest the following:

    •   Don't wait until material is presented in class and then rely on the book for clarification. A better plan is to study the assigned material *before* class, and rely on your instructor to fill the gaps and answer questions you may have. By doing this, you enter the classroom familiar with the topic and better able to assimilate all that takes place.

    •   Read thoughtfully, not quickly. Theory textbooks are not meant for speed-reading. Do all the exercises provided within the chapters for added practice; and in the Workbook, do more than just those assigned. It's through the exercises that you apply the knowledge you gain, and it's through application that knowledge gains utility and meaning.

- Don't wait until the evening before an assignment is due to begin it. Instead, make it your practice at least to try out each of the assigned drills *prior to* the class before the due date. This leaves you time for clarification if something confuses you.

- Use the various features of the text to your best advantage. These features are described in the paragraphs that follow.

The Musical Examples

Most of the musical examples in the text and Workbook are available on the companion website. LISTEN to them. Several times. Most are given in keyboard versions that are not too difficult to play. TRY to play them, no matter how slowly. These examples come from all musical periods and from both Classical and popular styles. *All* are relevant to today's musical world.

Concept Checks, and Review and Reinforcement

In reading the text, you'll frequently come upon these interactive features. They punctuate the flow of information and contain suggested activities or questions related to the topic under discussion. Don't ignore them. Use them as talking points with classmates or as ways to gauge your level of comprehension. Answers to the questions posed and/or further discussion can be found at the ends of the chapters.

Online Drills and Reviews

You'll find numerous references directing you to interactive online sites where you'll find pertinent drills and reviews. Avail yourself of these as necessary.

Do You Know These Terms?

This question is asked at the end of each chapter. The terms introduced are listed in alphabetical order. Each term is defined in two places—within the chapter, and in the Glossary. Make it a practice to formulate your own definition of each term once you've completed the chapter. Then compare it to the definition in the Glossary. Don't worry if your definition differs slightly. *Do* worry if it differs greatly, in which case you should re-read the part of the chapter where it is introduced.

Glossary

The Glossary contains all terms introduced in the text, along with their definitions.

Indexes

The Subject Index provides quick access to the initial presentation of every topic or term. The Composer/Title Index guides you to examples listed by composer and by title.

Index of Musical Examples

The music contained in the book is listed by example number and page number.

A Final Word

The insights you gain from your study of music theory will time and again prove useful and relevant to your personal musical goals. In the world of professional music, there is no substitute for solid musicianship. This book is designed to assist in providing that foundation.

The Authors

Acknowledgments

Daniel McCarthy would like to acknowledge the following people for their contributions to this publication. Thanks go to Siobhan McCarthy who sang the female "pop" vocal tracks on the companion recordings for the text and workbook examples. Thanks go also to Rick Jacobi for his guitar tracks on "He Said, She Said" and to Dave McCarthy for the contribution of his song, "Close Your Eyes."

McCarthy would also like to thank the following persons for their constant support and encouragement throughout the completion of this project: his family, Marcia Szente-McCarthy, Daniel II, Alannah, and Siobhan; Dr. Rachel Sternberg of Case Western University, and to "The Fellowship of The Bean" at Angel Falls Coffee Company, Akron, Ohio. Thanks go also to Grand Masters Jeon Gyeong Ho (Akron, Ohio) and James Adkins (Traverse City, Michigan) for their constant inspiration.

Ralph Turek would like to thank the users of previous editions of *Theory for Today's Musician* for their insights and helpful suggestions on ways to improve the text and for the confidence they display through their continued use of this newest edition. We hope to prove that their confidence is well placed.

In Lieu of Fundamentals

PART ONE

THE FUNDAMENTALS, MUSIC, AND YOU

You probably know something about them. You may have learned about them through your private music lessons, or through your high-school band, orchestra, or chorus. Perhaps you picked them up on your own or have taken a preliminary college music course that dealt with them. And if you're not familiar with them, then the time has come. Today, as in the past, no one can hope to become a musician without a thorough grounding in the so-called **music fundamentals**—pitch notation, the treble and bass clefs, intervals, major and minor scales, key signatures, and the basics of rhythm.

But we need to define a term. A **musician** is someone who creates or recreates music. Right? Well, yes. And this would necessarily include any 5-year-old who can sing "B-I-N-G-O." However, we normally reserve the designation "musician" for those who have attained a higher level of musicianship.

If you've chosen to pursue a college degree in music, the road to this higher level will lead you through the study of theory and music history, added years of music lessons, and courses that develop your communication skills. That's for openers. For mere survival in today's musical environment, a musician needs more and better preparation than at any time in history.

You'll find most of the fundamentals in Appendix A, "Pitch," and Appendix B, "Rhythm." Your instructor may wish to devote some weeks of class to them. In any case, be advised: *If you are not completely fluent with the basics of pitch, notation, and rhythm, then your proper starting points are Appendix A and Appendix B.* Because there is no substitute for an intimate understanding of that material, we'll repeat ourselves, rather boldly:

The fundamentals are covered in complete chapters with explanations, drills, and Workbook assignments. These chapters are titled Appendix A ("Pitch") and Appendix B ("Rhythm").

ABOUT PART ONE

We've chosen to begin with some "appetizers," selected topics to whet your appetite—things you'll likely find interesting, things you might not be aware of, things that are often never fully explained.

A few of these topics are merely further insights into certain aspects of the fundamentals. Others relate to musical **acoustics**—the science of sound. And still others amount to historical perspective. However, one fundamental topic—intervals—is presented in greater detail in Chapter 2. This is because intervals are the most important and basic of the musical building blocks. Fluency with them is necessary for chord recognition, which is a prerequisite to harmonic analysis, a necessary component of musical analysis. Finally, it is generally true that every student of music can, at the beginning of his or her college study, benefit from a greater command of the skills involved in recognizing, spelling, and hearing intervals.

CHAPTER ONE

Assorted Preliminaries

PITCH MATTERS

Who came up with this system—five lines and four spaces on which to plant 12 pitches that fit within an octave and have only seven letter names? Our notational system is a little like a mansion that has been built over many years. As each owner adds to suit special needs, it grows into an architectural and functional monstrosity. If only we could start over!

Back in notation's infancy, seven letter names were quite sufficient to represent the music. And the **staff** was merely a gleam in the eye of Guido of Arezzo, a Benedictine monk of the eleventh century. Guido recommended first one, then two, color-coded lines as visual guides against which his choristers could gauge the highness or lowness of the symbols, called "neumes," then used to indicate voice inflections when chanting.

The Staff and its Clefs (See also Appendix A, p. 647)

The idea worked so well that more lines were added and the colors discarded in favor of the Gothic letters G, F, or C—now our **clef** signs—placed at the beginning of the staff to show the location of those particular notes.

These early clef signs:

Evolved into these present-day symbols:

Over time five lines became standard. Eventually, staves were stacked, each with its own clef, to accommodate multiple parts and an expanded range. Our **grand staff** is the residue of that practice. Today's treble- and bass-clef staves are separated by an imaginary eleventh line that is home to middle C, a pitch that appears as a **ledger line** on either staff.

EXAMPLE 1-1 The Grand Staff

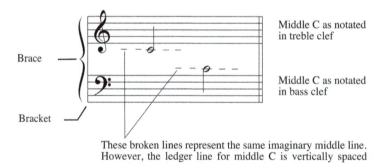

These broken lines represent the same imaginary middle line. However, the ledger line for middle C is vertically spaced according to the staff above or below which it appears.

▶ *For more information on clefs, turn to Appendix A.*

Solmization

Besides being "the father of the staff," Guido was the great popularizer of **solmization**—assigning syllables to pitches as an aid to sight singing. For syllables, he drew upon the hymn *Ut queant laxis*, in which each phrase begins a step higher than the preceding one.

EXAMPLE 1-2 *Ut queant laxis* (LU 1504)

The Hexachord System

The six syllables—*ut-re-mi-fa-sol-la*—were applied to three interlocking **hexachords** (six-note scales):

EXAMPLE 1-3

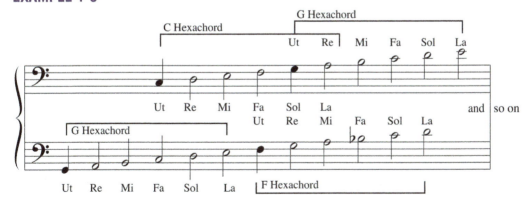

This served as a pedagogical aid to the choirs of Guido's day and remains the basis of our solmization system today. (The word "solmization" was coined from the syllables "sol" and "mi.")

Accidentals

Notice that the hexachords on F and G used different forms of the pitch B. The F hexachord used a "soft B," symbolized "♭." The G hexachord used a "hard B," symbolized ♮.

From these symbols came our signs for the flat and natural, called **accidentals**, which eventually shed their exclusive association with the pitch B.

➤ *For assignments on pitch, turn to Workbook Appendix A.*

MODES, SCALES, AND EVOLUTION

For this discussion to be meaningful, you should be thoroughly familiar with the major and minor scales and the concept of transposition. If you are not, turn to Appendix A.

Church Modes

The hexachord system provided only an accounting of the pitches available to medieval musicians. The actual basis of their music is suggested by the **church modes**, seven-note patterns involving **half steps** (the distance between E and F, and between B and C, our smallest musical interval) and **whole steps** (the distance between all other adjacent letter names, equal to two half steps). Both the hexachord system and the Church modes were theoretical constructs. The former organized the pitch gamut for purposes of solmization. The latter was an attempt to classify the pitch basis of the chants of the Catholic liturgy.

EXAMPLE 1-4

Whole note = **final**: the most important pitch of the mode, typically a chant's point of departure and return.

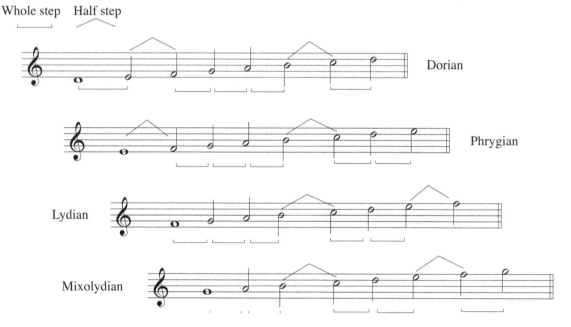

Notes:

1. Each mode is a unique arrangement of whole steps and half steps. Dorian mode can be viewed as the notes of Guido's C hexachord beginning on Re, Phrygian as beginning on Mi, Lydian as beginning on Fa, and Mixolydian as beginning on Sol.

2. The half steps occur *between the same pitches* but *at different points* within each mode.

3. The modes are shown as originally used—involving only what would be the "white keys" on a piano or organ.

Example 1-5 shows the modes transposed to begin on C. Notice how they relate to present-day major and natural minor scales.

EXAMPLE 1-5

a. Modes closely related to the major scale:

Ionian mode (major scale)

Lydian mode (major scale with raised fourth degree

Mixolydian mode (major scale with lowered seventh degree)

b. Modes closely related to the minor scale:

Aeolian mode (natural minor scale)

Dorian mode (natural minor scale with raised sixth degree)

Phrygian mode (natural minor scale with lowered second degree)

Musica Ficta

Although we can best understand the modes by relating them to our present-day scales, it was the modes that begat our scales, and not the reverse. The evolutionary process was gradual over a hundred or so years. It happened through **musica ficta**—a practice in which performers altered pitches according to conventions of the day. Most important were the creation of half steps leading to the final in the Mixolydian and Dorian modes and between the third and fourth notes (mi-fa) in the Guidonian F hexachord.

Example 1-6, though simplified, shows the effect of these rules.

EXAMPLE 1-6

a. Lydian becomes major by using "soft B" for "fa:"

b. Mixolydian becomes major by raising the seventh degree, creating a half step to the final:

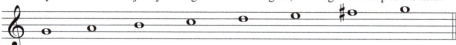

c. Dorian becomes minor by raising the seventh degree, creating a half step to the final:

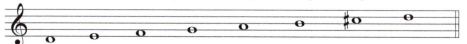

↻ BACK TO BASICS 1.1

Mode Construction and Identification

Today the term "mode" is used to refer both to the Church modes and the major and minor scales and their associated keys. We speak of music being "in the major mode," or "changing from major to the parallel minor mode," and so on.

➤ *For assignments on modes, turn to Workbook Chapter 1, Assignments 1A–1F. For drills on major and minor scales, turn to Workbook Appendix A.*

METER MATTERS

This discussion presupposes your understanding of our proportional system of rhythmic notation, accent and its role in creating meter, and the differences between duple and triple and between simple and compound meters. If any of these concepts are unclear to you, you should log some hours with Appendix B.

Meter

Meter is the grouping of a steady succession of pulses into patterns of accented and unaccented beats. The feeling for it dates to antiquity. Throughout history, two basic types of meter have been favored—binary and ternary. Which do you suppose is older?

You might guess that binary is the older. After all, the rhythms of life and nature are binary. We inhale and exhale; the heartbeat is two-part; we walk by alternately putting forward the left foot, then the right; we exert only two muscular forces—the push and the pull; what goes up comes down; tides rise and fall; night follows day.

Despite all this, ternary appears to have been the older meter. This is because our notational system and the music it enabled had its origins in a profoundly religious culture. And to the medieval mind, the number three was rife with significance (the Trinity).

The Dot

Let's start with the dot. In medieval music notation, it was called *signum perfectionis* (the sign of perfection). Its function was to "perfect" any note it followed by making it equal to *three of the next smaller division*. That function is unchanged today.

Likewise, any note without the *signum perfectionis* was imperfect—divisible into only two parts.

The dot originated as a tiny circle, which stood for closure, or completion, another manifestation of perfection. Philippe DeVitry, in his fourteenth-century treatise *Ars nova* ("The New Art") used the circle and half circle to reflect the perfect and imperfect grouping (*tempus)* and division (*prolation)* of beats.

Early Meter Signatures

EXAMPLE 1-7

Perfect tempus (beats grouped three to a bar), major prolation (beat divided into three parts)

Today's equivalent meter: $\frac{9}{8}$

Example:

Perfect tempus (beats grouped three to a bar), minor prolation (beat divided into two parts)

Today's equivalent meter: $\frac{3}{4}$

Example:

Imperfect tempus (beats grouped two to a bar), major prolation (beat divided into three parts)

Today's equivalent meter: $\frac{6}{8}$

Example:

Imperfect tempus (beats grouped two to a bar), minor prolation (beat divided into two parts)

Today's equivalent meter: $\frac{2}{4}$

Example:

The sole survivor of these fourteenth-century meter signatures is the use of **c**, which today represents not $\frac{2}{4}$, but its close relative, $\frac{4}{4}$.

Hypermeter

Beyond the two- and three-part division and grouping of **beats**, there was what today we'd call a two-and three-part grouping of **measures**, called *modus.* This was indicated by either two or three vertical lines in front of the symbols shown in Example 1-7. For example:

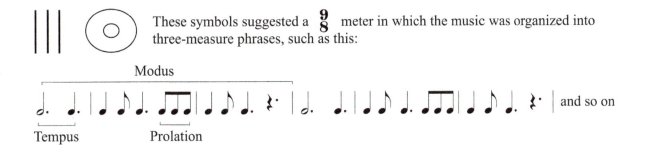

These symbols suggested a $\frac{9}{8}$ meter in which the music was organized into three-measure phrases, such as this:

After the fourteenth century, composers turned their attention back to pitch, and this higher level of metric organization was generally not pursued. Still, theorists today speak of **hypermeter** when the measures of a work exhibit regular accentual patterns the way the beats do.[1]

EXAMPLE 1-8 Harry Dacre: "Daisy Bell"

Notice how beats (quarter notes) divisible *into two eighth notes* (♩ = ♪ ♪) are *grouped into measures of three quarter notes* (𝅗𝅥 = ♩ ♩ ♩) that form larger units, each comprising four measures. The four-measure unit (the *modus*) is a **hypermeasure**, in which measures 1 and 3 are strong relative to measures 2 and 4. This can be better seen through a transcription. In Example 1-10, each four-measure group—each hypermeasure—has been turned into a single measure. Each former measure is a beat in this larger unit.[2]

---

1 Hypermeter is fully explained by William Rothstein, *Phrase Rhythm in Tonal Music* (New York: Schirmer Books, 1989), pp. 3–63.

2 This discussion and the use of this example owe much to Ken Stephenson, *What to Listen for in Rock: A Stylistic Analysis* (New Haven and London: Yale University Press, 2002).

EXAMPLE 1-9 Harry Dacre: "Daisy Bell"

SOUND

Note: If you're unfamiliar with octave designations, see Appendix A.

Sound—the most fundamental of fundamentals—what do you really know about it? We'll wade just far enough into the mysterious waters of musical **acoustics**—the science of sound—to persuade you to take a deeper dip if you have the opportunity.

Sit at a piano, and silently depress C3—the octave below middle C (which is C4). Now, while holding C3 down, sharply strike the octave below it (C2) and release immediately. (Keep C3 depressed.) Listen carefully to the after-ring. Can you hear the depressed note resonating? Now depress G3 (the G below middle C) and strike C2 again. Do you hear G3 resonating? It's quite soft. Now silently depress this chord

and repeat the experiment. Can you hear the chord ringing?

Overtones

What you're hearing is the sympathetic vibration of these other piano strings. They're vibrating in sympathy with the **overtones** of the **fundamental**, C2. Most sounds consist not only of a fundamental tone, the frequency that gives a sound its basic pitch, but also its overtones. These additional frequencies are usually so soft that we don't consciously hear them (like the vibrating strings in our experiment). Yet they're what *color* the sound and impart its **timbre**. In part, they're what make a flute sound different from a flugelhorn, and a flugelhorn sound different from an oboe. Stripped of their overtones, every musical sound would resemble that of a heart monitor, which elicits **sine tones**—pure fundamentals. (How unpleasant would *that* be?)

Harmonics are overtones whose frequencies form whole-number ratios with the fundamental (2:1, 3:1, 4:1, and so on). **Inharmonics** are overtones that are non-integral multiples of the fundamental (for example, 2.7 : 1, or 3.9 : 1). The presence of inharmonics often makes us think a sound unmusical or noisy. Most "musical" tones are richer in harmonics than inharmonics.

The complex of harmonics present in musical tones is called the **harmonic series**. Here is the series above C2.

EXAMPLE 1-11

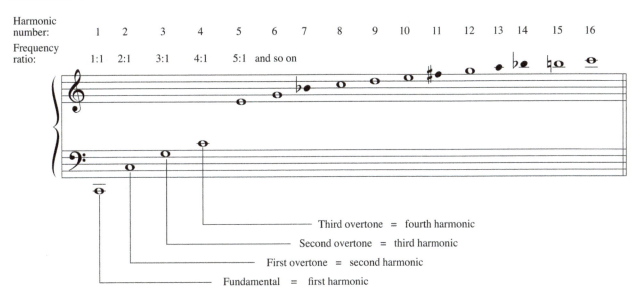

| Harmonic number: | 1 | 2 | 3 | 4 | 5 | 6 | 7 | 8 | 9 | 10 | 11 | 12 | 13 | 14 | 15 | 16 |
| Frequency ratio: | 1:1 | 2:1 | 3:1 | 4:1 | 5:1 | and so on |

Third overtone = fourth harmonic

Second overtone = third harmonic

First overtone = second harmonic

Fundamental = first harmonic

Notes:

1. The fundamental is the *first harmonic*, so the *first overtone* is the *second harmonic*, and so on.

2. Quarter notes indicate pitches that can be only approximated by our notation (more on this shortly).

3. The harmonic numbers correspond to the frequency ratios of the pitches.

    For example, our "tuning A" (A4),

    at 440 cycles per second (cps), has its second harmonic A5

    at 880 cps (a 2:1 ratio) and its third harmonic (E6)

    at 1320 cps (a 3:1 ratio).

Every pitch on your instrument is a fundamental tone that contains its own harmonic series. If you play a brass instrument, you can play the harmonic series above any **pedal tone** by keeping the same fingering (or slide position) and simply adjusting your embouchure. (Most pedal tones are below the standard playing range.) If you play a string instrument or a guitar, you will eventually learn how to play the open strings' harmonics by lightly touching them at appropriate points.

Equal Temperament

Overtones 15 and 16 represent the only *acoustically pure* half step in the overtone series. (Half steps are discussed in Appendix A. See p. 650) You'd think that 12 of these, stacked one atop the next, would span an octave. But they actually exceed the octave by a quarter tone (half of a half step). This is visually represented thus:

EXAMPLE 1-13

```
s
s          ┌─────  Exceeds the octave
s
s     O
s
s     C
s
s     T
s
s     A
s
s     V
s
s     E
s
```

s = semitone (16 : 15 half step)

So how can each octave on the piano, for instance, be in tune with the one above or below it? The solution is **equal temperament**. To fit 12 16:15 half steps into a perfectly in tune (2:1) octave requires that each half step be tempered (made slightly smaller). That's what equal temperament does, and it's how pianos are tuned today (although the actual process involves detuning fifths rather than half steps). As a result, the only perfectly in tune intervals on a piano keyboard are the octaves.

What effect does this have? Well, after a couple hundred years, we're used to it. But cultures not attuned to equal temperament might find our beautiful music rather discordant. You've probably addressed the problem in your own music making. In fact, if you've played to the accompaniment of a piano, you've *certainly* dealt with it. You've had to make minute adjustments on your wind instrument, which produces pitches in tune with the harmonic series, or on your string instrument, which is tuned in Pythagorean (pure) fifths, in order to play "in tune" with the piano. And if you play in a brass ensemble, you're no doubt frustrated when you play a note *exactly the same way as before*, but the note's now part of a new chord, and your director tells you you're slightly flat. Now, doesn't just knowing there's a good reason for these things help?

By the way, we're not totally locked into equal temperament. When a string quartet plays, they have the luxury of tuning to each other, and they play differently than when playing in a piano quintet. Likewise, barbershop quartets and doo-wop groups, being *a capella* (unaccompanied), often produce perfectly in tune harmonies. And orchestras generally strive for something better than equal temperament. In general, though, our musical heritage is an uneasy accommodation to "the tuning problem." We've combined instruments constructed on a variety of tuning principles, and we've adjusted our ears accordingly.

⊕ CODA

Much of this chapter has concerned notation. Many of the peculiarities and apparent inconsistencies in our notational system exist because it and the music it represents *evolved*. If we could start from scratch today, we could probably simplify many things, but the conversion would be painful. So, the beast goes on.

Meanwhile, music notation has become increasingly inadequate to present-day demands. Blues and rock vocalists sing pitches that often fall somewhere between adjacent keys or frets. Likewise, jazz players spend a lot of time in the "rhythmic cracks." This is why transcriptions of jazz solos look incredibly complex, yet give but a mere notion of the music, which is represented accurately only through audio recordings.

Still, for all its problems, an intimate understanding of our notational system remains an indispensable tool of today's practicing musician.

▶ *For additional drills on the material presented in this chapter, see Workbook Appendix A, Pitch.*

DO YOU KNOW THESE TERMS?

- accidentals
- acoustics
- Church modes
- equal temperament
- fundamental
- gamut
- grand staff
- half step
- harmonic series
- hexachord
- hypermeter
- ledger line
- meter
- musica ficta
- pedal tone
- solmization

CHAPTER TWO

Intervals

PERSPECTIVE: FIVE WAYS TO EXPRESS AN OCTAVE

An **interval** is the difference in pitch between two tones. That difference can be measured in many ways. For example, the interval between tuning A—with a frequency of 440 Hz (Hertz, or cycles per second)—and the octave higher (880 Hz) can be expressed as:

1. 440 Hz

2. 1200 cents (The cent is a measurement used by acousticians. An equal-tempered half step contains 100 cents)

3. Six equal-tempered whole steps

4. 12 equal-tempered half steps

5. Eight scale steps ("octave" means "eight")

If you can construct a major or minor scale on any pitch, then you know at least two intervals—the whole step and half step. And from Chapter 1, you know that the equal-tempered half step is the smallest interval on the keyboard and the smallest commonly used in our music. It's time to learn more.

KEY CONCEPTS IN THIS CHAPTER

- Interval Measurement and Designation

- Intervals in the Major Scale

- Inversion

WHITE-KEY INTERVALS

The most common way musicians identify intervals is through a two-part designation consisting of a numeric value and a qualifying term. The numeric value indicates *the number of letter names spanned*. Interval a in Example 2-1 is a third because it spans three letter names (G, A, and B); interval b is a fifth because it spans five letter names (A, B, C, D, and E); and so on. *Notice that both notes comprising the interval are included when counting letter names.*

EXAMPLE 2-1

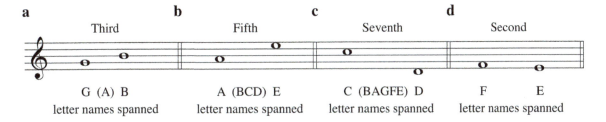

a	b	c	d
Third	Fifth	Seventh	Second
G (A) B	A (BCD) E	C (BAGFE) D	F E
letter names spanned	letter names spanned	letter names spanned	letter names spanned

But that's not enough. Because all letter names are not a whole step apart—E–F and B–C are half steps—intervals that span *the same number of letter names* may span *a different number of half steps*. Interval **a** in Example 2-2 is *not* the same size of third as interval **b**.

EXAMPLE 2-2

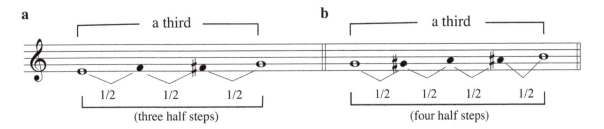

To describe an interval's size more precisely, a qualifier is added to the numeric value. Five qualifiers are used:

Major (M)
Minor (m) ⎤ apply to seconds, thirds, sixths, and sevenths (m2, M2, m3, M3, m6, M6, m7, M7)

Perfect (P)   applies to unisons, fourths, fifths, and octaves (P1, P4, P5, P8)

Augmented (+)
Diminished (o) ⎤ can apply to any interval (+2, o5, and so on)

One way to understand how these descriptors work is to visualize an octave on the piano, an image you should engrave in your mind's eye.

White-key intervals span from 0 to 5 black keys. Major intervals (M2, M3, M6, and M7) all span one more black key than their minor forms (m2, m3, m6, and m7). In Example 2-3, compare the major intervals (above the staff) to their minor conterparts (beneath the staff). The black keys spanned by each interval are shown as stemless quarter notes.

EXAMPLE 2-3

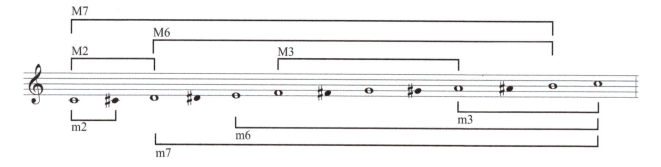

This leaves only the perfect fourth (P4) and perfect fifth (P5). The P4 spans 2 black keys and the P5 spans 3. *All* white-key fourths and fifths are perfect except the ones formed by B and F. The fourth formed by these two pitches is augmented (spanning three black keys rather than two) and the fifth is diminished (spanning two black keys rather than three).

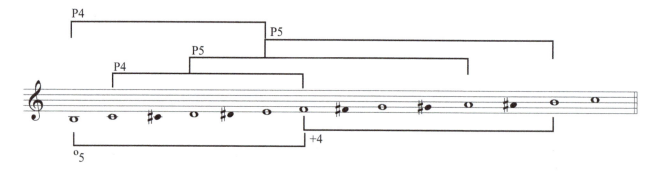

CONCEPT CHECK

Using the method just described, answer these questions about white-key intervals:

1   How many seconds in a white-key octave are major? Minor?

2   How many thirds are major? Minor?

3   How many sixths are major? Minor?

4   How many sevenths are major? Minor?

5   Identify each interval in the following melody. Use "M" for major, "m" for minor, "P" for perfect, "o" for diminished, and "+" for augmented, and follow the symbol with a numeric value, as shown.

EXAMPLE 2-4 Paul Gordon and Jay Gruskal "Friends and Lovers"

➤ *Assignment A on Workbook p. 12 can be completed now.*

If *both* of an interval's pitches are altered *in the same direction by the same amount*, its size remains unchanged.

EXAMPLE 2-5

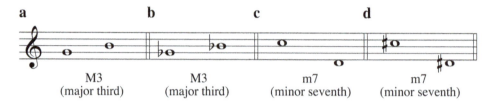

M3   M3   m7   m7
(major third)   (major third)   (minor seventh)   (minor seventh)

Notes:

1. In **a**, the third is major (it spans two black keys instead of one). In **b**, *both* pitches are lowered by a half step, so the interval is unchanged.

2. In **c**, the seventh is minor (it spans four black keys instead of five). In **d**, *both* pitches are raised by a half step, so the interval is unchanged.

However, if *only one* of an interval's pitches is altered, the interval's size changes as follows:

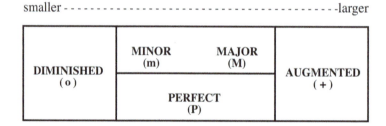

smaller -larger

DIMINISHED (o)	MINOR (m)	MAJOR (M)	AUGMENTED (+)
	PERFECT (P)		

For example, a m6 expanded by a half step becomes a M6. If expanded by another half step, it becomes an +6. If contracted by a half step, a m6 becomes a o6.

Notice that perfect intervals cannot become major or minor, nor can major or minor intervals become perfect.

↺ **BACK TO BASICS 2.1**

Interval Recognition and Spelling

CONCEPT CHECK

Using the preceding chart, name the interval in Example 2–5 that would be created in a: by lowering B one half step; in b: by raising G♭ to G♯; in c: by lowering C one half step; in d: by lowering D♯ one half step.

➤ *Assignments 1A through 1D on Workbook pp. 12–13 can be completed now.*

INTERVALS OF THE MAJOR SCALE

Another method for spelling and recognizing intervals is to compare them to the intervals of the major scale, measured above or below the tonic.

EXAMPLE 2-6

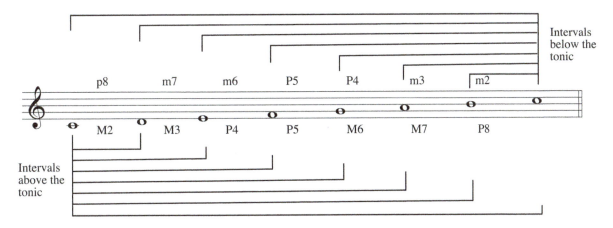

Notes:

1. All intervals *measured from the tonic up* are either major or perfect (M2, M3, P4, P5, M6, M7, P8).

2. All intervals *measured from the tonic down* are either minor or perfect (m2, m3, P4, P5, m6, m7, P8).

Question: What is this interval?

Answer: Intervals measured below the tonic in the major scale are either minor or perfect. Spelling the E♭ major scale downward brings us to G. G is the sixth scale step *below* the tonic E♭, and thus a *minor* sixth below E♭. But the note in question is G♭. This makes the interval a half step wider. A minor interval expanded by a half step becomes major. E♭ down to G♭, then, is a major sixth (M6).

You can work this in either direction, of course. If you're more comfortable spelling scales upward, you can count up the G♭ major scale to its sixth degree, E♭. Measured *above* the tonic, sixths are major, meaning the interval is a major sixth. Different approach, same result.

CONCEPT CHECK

Use the major scale approach to name the following intervals: A up to C; D♭ down to E; F♯ down to B; G♯ up to B. Now use any approach you like to name the intervals in the following melody.

EXAMPLE 2-7 Schumann: "Träumerei" from *Kinderszenen*, op. 15 🔊

▶ *For assignments on intervals of the major scale, turn to Workbook pp. 12–13.*

RELATED MATTERS

Inversion

The right-hand part of Example 2-4 is reprinted in part in Example 2-8a. Observe how the lower pitch in mm. 1 and 2 becomes the higher pitch in mm. 3–4.

EXAMPLE 2-8 Gordon and Gruska: "Friends and Lovers"

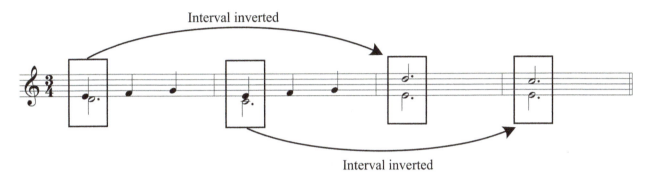

Inversion of an interval involves octave transposition of either pitch so that the higher pitch becomes the lower and vice versa.

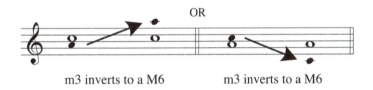

If you look again at Example 2-6, you'll notice that the interval formed by any pitch of the major scale *below* its tonic is the inversion of the interval it forms *above* the tonic. Notice further that:

- Major intervals invert to minor and vice versa.

- Perfect intervals remain perfect.

- The numeric sum of an interval and its inversion is 9.

These intervals	invert to these	and change quality like this:
2nds	7ths	M → m, m → M
3rds	6ths	M → m, m → M
4ths	5ths	remain P

and vice versa.

Not shown in Example 2-6 is the fact that augmented intervals invert to diminished and vice versa. For example:

o7 inverts to +2 and vice versa.

Smaller intervals are usually easier to recognize and spell than larger ones. If you are uncertain what a large interval such as this is,

try inverting it:

BACK TO
BASICS 2.2

Interval
Recognition
and Spelling

The smaller interval is a m2. Because the inversion of a second is a seventh and minor intervals invert to major, the larger interval must be a M7.

Enharmonic Intervals

Intervals having different numeric values and qualifiers can sound identical. That is, they can comprise an identical number of half steps. We call these intervals **enharmonic equivalents**.

All three are enharmonic equivalents, containing two half steps.

EXAMPLE 2-9a All three are enharmonic equivalents, containing two half steps

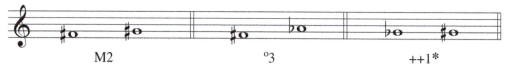

M2   o3   ++1*

* Doubly augmented unison--a unison made larger by two half steps.

EXAMPLE 2-9b All three are enharmonic equivalents, containing nine half steps

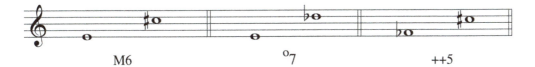

M6   °7   ++5

Does it really matter which way an interval is spelled? Well, yes it does. Recall from Chapter 1 that enharmonic intervals are truly identical only on equal-tempered instruments, like the piano. For instruments not constrained by equal temperament, such as a violin, a chromatically raised pitch (i.e., C♯) is likely to be played slightly sharper than a chromatically lowered one (i.e., D♭). Another way of saying this: Chromatically altered pitches are adjusted slightly *in the direction of their chromatic inflection*.

Intervals can have the same numeric value and quality and yet be spelled differently. Example 2-10 shows a P4 involving *the same two pitches*, spelled two ways.

EXAMPLE 2-10

⟳ BACK TO BASICS 2.3

Enharmonic Intervals

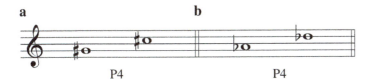

a   b

P4   P4

Here both *pitches* are spelled enharmonically without altering the size or quality (or designation) of the *interval*.

CONCEPT CHECK

For the given intervals, write an enharmonic equivalent that has a *different* numeric value:

EXAMPLE 2-11

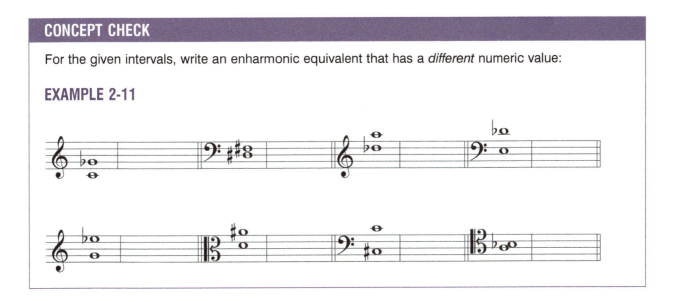

Simple versus Compound

Intervals are classified in ways other than numeric value and quality. A **simple interval** is one that is an octave or smaller, whereas a **compound interval** exceeds the octave. Compound intervals are traditionally reduced to simple intervals for ease of reference. This is easily accomplished by either raising the lower pitch by an octave or by lowering the upper pitch by an octave.

EXAMPLE 2-12

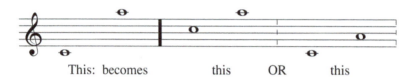

This: becomes   this   OR   this

Diatonic versus Chromatic

Diatonic intervals are those formed by only the pitches of a given key. For example, in E♭ a diatonic interval can be formed by any of the following pitches: E♭, F, G, A♭, B♭, C, D. **Chromatic intervals** are those in which one or both pitches of a diatonic interval have been altered by a flat, natural, or sharp or have been respelled enharmonically. For example, if in the key of E♭, A♭ is respelled as G♯, then the half step from G to G♯ would be a *chromatic* half step rather than a diatonic half step (G-A♭).

Consonance versus Dissonance

Intervals may also be classified as consonant or dissonant. **Consonance** refers to sounds that suggest a feeling of stability or repose. **Dissonance** denotes sounds that suggest tension or unrest. Intervals were classified by the theorist Franco of Cologne in the thirteenth century. We still use his classifications:

> **Perfect consonances**: P1, P4,* P5, P8
>
> **Imperfect consonances**: m3, M3, m6, M6
>
> **Dissonances**: m2, M2, m7, M7, and all augmented or diminished intervals

*Although an acoustic consonance, the P4 has been traditionally treated as a dissonance in musical settings.

> ↻ **BACK TO BASICS 2.4**
>
> Intervals

Are you wondering why thirds and sixths—the harmonic basis of so much music—were considered "imperfect?" Recall that today's equal temperament "spreads the dissonance around" equally, so that the octave is the only pure interval. Franco's system was not so egalitarian. In it, fourths and fifths were more pristine, to the detriment of thirds and sixths, which were somewhat more dissonant (harsh sounding, hence "imperfect") than their modern-day counterparts.

➤ *For additional assignments on intervals, turn to Workbook p. 17.*

⊕ CODA

The ability to recognize and spell intervals underlies most of the advanced harmonic analysis and writing you'll do. Different approaches work for different people. For some, a combination works best. Two methods have been advanced in this chapter—the "white-key method" and the "major scale method." One additional approach, which might be called "the additive method," is given here:

The Additive Method of Interval Construction

This interval	contains:	which equals:
Perfect unison (P1)	0 half steps	
Minor second (m2)	1 half step	1 half step
Major second (M2)	1 whole step	2 half steps
Minor third (m3)	M2 + m2 (or P4 − M2)	3 half steps
Major third (M3)	2 M2 (or P4 − m2)	4 half steps
Perfect fourth (P4)	M3 + m2	5 half steps
Augmented fourth (+4)	P4 + m2 (or P5 − m2)	6 half steps
Diminished fifth (o5)	P4 + m2 (or P5 − m2)	6 half steps
Perfect fifth (P5)	P4 + M2	7 half steps
Minor sixth (m6)	P5 + m2	8 half steps
Major sixth (M6)	P5 + M2	9 half steps
Minor seventh (m7)	P8–M2	10 half steps
Major seventh (M7)	P8–m2	11 half steps
Perfect octave (P8)		12 half steps

You should find what works best for you, then spend the time necessary to build a solid foundation for your later work.

DO YOU KNOW THESE TERMS?

- chromatic interval
- compound interval
- consonance
- diatonic interval
- dissonance
- enharmonic equivalent
- imperfect consonance
- interval
- inversion
- perfect consonance
- simple interval

Diatonic Harmony

PART TWO

One of the features that distinguishes our Western music heritage from that of Eastern cultures and others is its harmonic system. Part Two examines that system.

The chords used by Johann Sebastian Bach (1685–1750) and his contemporaries remained fundamental to the music composed throughout the eighteenth and nineteenth centuries, and they persist even today in many styles. Still, composers constantly seek out new sounds and new ways of using the existing ones. Thus, both the types of chords—**harmonic vocabulary**—and the way they are used with respect to one another—**harmonic syntax**—are factors that help to create style differences, whether between Mozart and Brahms, Debussy and Wagner, Quincy Jones and Dave Brubeck, or Paul McCartney and James Taylor. A complete musical training includes the ability to understand such differences.

CHAPTER THREE

Basic Harmonic Structures

TRIADS

Harmony and Chord

The word **harmony** can refer generally to the effect of two or more musical lines in combination or specifically to the sound produced by three or more pitches (not counting octave duplications) sounding together. The latter is usually called a **chord**. Implicit in the concept of harmony is "agreement" of some sort among the tones, although ideas about what that means differ somewhat from style to style and from person to person. Herbie Hancock's jazz classic, "Maiden Voyage," relies largely on chords deemed dissonant by earlier musical standards. Yet, while these may not be the harmonies of Bach, Beethoven, and Brahms, they're filled with the same building blocks—thirds and fifths.

EXAMPLE 3-1 Herbie Hancock: "Maiden Voyage" (from Herbie Hancock: *Maiden Voyage*—Blue Note 4195)

Harmonies constructed of thirds are called **tertian**. We'll begin with the simplest tertian structure, called the **triad**—a chord containing three discrete pitches (excluding octave duplications) *that can be stacked as a third and a fifth above one of the notes.* When so stacked, the lowest note in the stack is the triad's root. Only one note in a triad can perform this function.

EXAMPLE 3-2

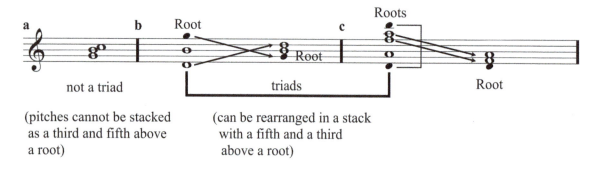

not a triad	triads	
(pitches cannot be stacked as a third and fifth above a root)	(can be rearranged in a stack with a fifth and a third above a root)	

Note:

Octave doublings are not considered to be additional chord tones in determining whether a chord is a triad. The notes of any triad can either be placed on adjacent lines (as in b) or in adjacent spaces (as in c).

➤ *Assignment 1A in Workbook Chapter 3 can be completed at this time.*

Basic Triads

In Chapter 2 you learned that thirds (and other intervals) can be major, minor, augmented, or diminished. However, the four most common types of triad contain only major and minor thirds. A fifth—perfect, augmented, or diminished—is formed by the root and top note in this stack.

EXAMPLE 3-3

Triad Type   /   Symbol - Example on the Root **G**

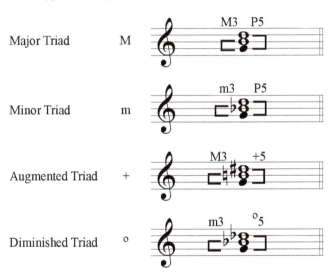

Although it is admittedly difficult to express the sound of an isolated chord in words, major and minor triads are often described as "bright" and "dark" respectively. Augmented and diminished triads are considered more dissonant and "restless" sounding. These and other subjective terms are no doubt associative, based on the way the chords have been used. But an acoustic reason exists as well. Any chord root and its first five overtones form a *major* triad. (Refer to Example 1-10.) Minor, augmented, and diminished triads contain thirds and/or fifths that clash with the overtones of the chord root, making them dissonant in varying degrees.

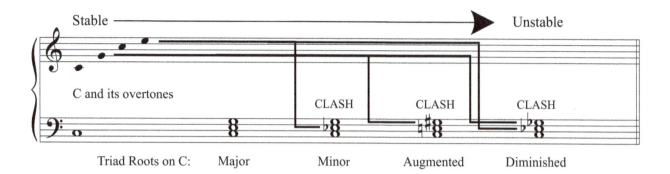

Stability and Color

Major and minor triads sound more harmonically stable than do diminished and augmented triads. This is due to the **perfect fifth** (a perfect consonance) that is part of their construction. While the perfect fifth provides *harmonic stability*, the third provides the *harmonic color*, giving the chords their respective **major** or **minor** sound. Augmented and diminished triads get their names from the quality of their respective fifths. Since the quality of these fifths is dissonant, the sound of the augmented and diminished triad is unstable.

In Example 3-4, augmented and diminished triads each appear once (they are identified for you). Major and minor triads are more abundant (one of each is identified).

EXAMPLE 3-4 "Prayer of Thanksgiving" (traditional Dutch air) 🔊

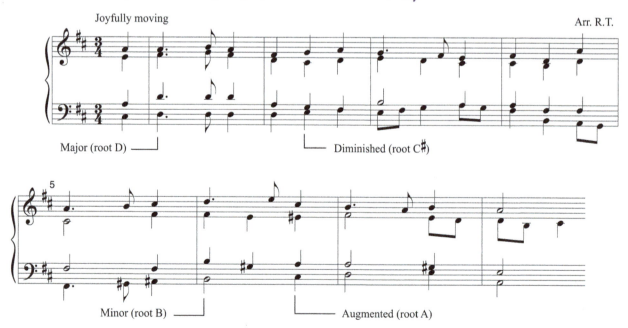

CONCEPT CHECK

Identify the other major and minor triads in Example 3–4. Every measure contains at least one. *The root may not be the lowest-sounding note.* To determine the triad type: (1) identify the root, (2) measure the interval formed by the other pitches above it, and (3) assess the chord's structure. Using the first chord as an example: The only pitch above which the others can stack as a third and fifth is A. C♯ is a M3 above, and E is a P5 above. The triad, therefore, is major.

↺ BACK TO BASICS 3.1

Triad Identification and Spelling

➤ *For assignments on triads, turn to Workbook Chapter 3, assignments 1A–1E.*

CHORD INVERSION

Inversion and Bass Line

In addition to the four triads identified for you, Example 3-4 contains 15 more, including a triad on every beat through m. 4. Example 3-5 is a reprint of the bass from Example 3-4. The numbers indicate whether the bass note is the root (R), third (3) or fifth (5) of the triad.

EXAMPLE 3-5

Note:

In m. 7, the chord on beat 1 is not a triad.

In seven of the chords, the bass note is not the root. In the next example, those seven bass notes have been changed so they are now the chord roots. Sing or play Examples 3-5 and 3-6. Which bass line sounds more tuneful? Which is easier to sing? Why might that be?

EXAMPLE 3-6

If you prefer Example 3-5 to Example 3-6 it's probably due to its more stepwise character. Stepwise motion usually sounds more "melodic" than relentless movement by leap. In fact, this is one reason to use inversion—to enhance the melodic character of a bass line.

Determining Chord Inversion

Chord inversion places a chord member other than the root in the lowest position. Triads can appear three ways.

EXAMPLE 3-7

Black notehead = **root**

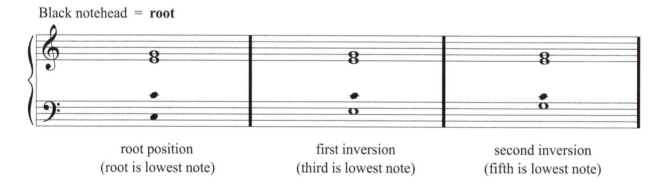

root position	first inversion	second inversion
(root is lowest note)	(third is lowest note)	(fifth is lowest note)

It makes no difference how the other chord members are distributed above the bass. Inversion is determined *solely by the lowest pitch*. Example 3-8 shows the opening of Tchaikovsky's famous Overture-Fantasy, "Romeo and Juliet." The F♯ minor triads that begin measures 2 and 3 are both in first inversion, even though the fifth is the highest note in the first chord and the root is highest in the second.

EXAMPLE 3-8 Tchaikovsky: *Romeo and Juliet*

REVIEW AND REINFORCEMENT

Which mode seems to be implied by the melody of Example 3–8? Which note sounds like the final? (Refer to Example 1–4.) Identify the root, triad type, and inversion for each of the chords. Disregard the chord enclosed in the box. Which triad types do not appear in the excerpt?

Notice that only root-position and first inversion chords appear in Example 3-8. *Second inversion is rarely used as a substitute for root position the way first inversion is* and in fact is traditionally the least common triad inversion.

➤ *For assignments on inversions, turn to Workbook Chapter 3, assignments 2A–2E.*

↺ **BACK TO BASICS 3.2**

Triad Inversion

SEVENTH CHORDS

A jazz pianist like Michele Legrand or Keith Jarret might begin "A Prayer of Thanksgiving" this way:

EXAMPLE 3-9 "A Prayer of Thanksgiving" 🔊

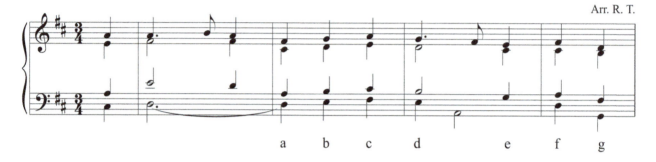

The more contemporary sound is due to the use of seventh chords at the points numbered "a" through "g." A **seventh chord** is formed by stacking an additional third above the fifth in a triad, which is the same as adding a seventh above the chord root. Here, for example, is the chord at letter "a" in its root-position form:

EXAMPLE 3-10

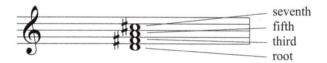

Classification of Seventh Chords

A seventh can be added above any triad type. The seventh—measured above the root—can be major, minor, or diminished (augmented sevenths are enharmonic duplications of the root). Seventh chords are classified according to the triad type and the quality of the seventh. The chord of Example 3-10 is a major-major seventh chord (symbolized MM7) because it consists of a major triad with a major seventh above the root.

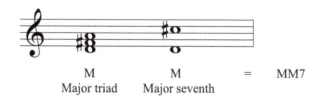

CONCEPT CHECK

Identify the two other MM7 chords in Example 3–9.

The three remaining seventh chords in Example 3-9 are of two other types. They are shown in Example 3-11.

EXAMPLE 3-11

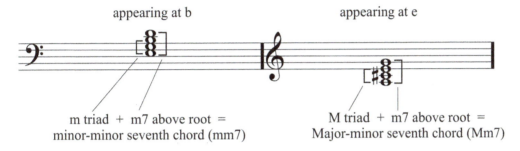

appearing at b

appearing at e

m triad + m7 above root =
minor-minor seventh chord (mm7)

M triad + m7 above root =
Major-minor seventh chord (Mm7)

Although seventh chords are used pervasively in jazz and popular music, they are by no means unique to those styles. In fact, seventh chords were used freely from the high Baroque era (ca. 1680) on.

EXAMPLE 3-12 J. S. Bach: *Brandenburg Concerto No. 2* (first movement)

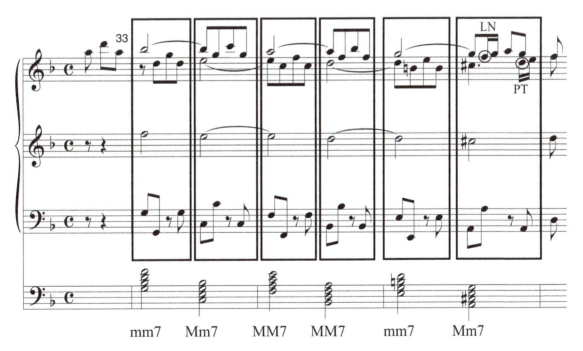

mm7   Mm7   MM7   MM7   mm7   Mm7

* Some lines have been omitted from this piano reduction to facilitate performance.

The seventh chords in Example 3-12 are shown in root position beneath the music. The same three types found in Example 3-9—major-major seventh (MM7), minor-minor seventh (mm7), and major–minor seventh (Mm7)—appear here. Two other types are among the most common seventh chords:

EXAMPLE 3-13

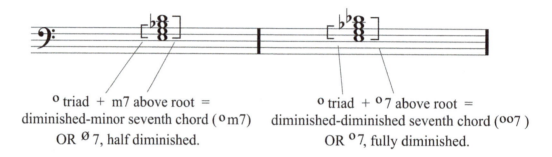

^{o} triad + m7 above root =
diminished-minor seventh chord (^{o}m7)
OR $^\emptyset$7, half diminished.

^{o} triad + ^{o}7 above root =
diminished-diminished seventh chord (^{oo}7)
OR ^{o}7, fully diminished.

Example 3-14 shows the five common seventh chord types built on the *same* root. The common name for each chord is shown below it. Play and observe the sound of each.

EXAMPLE 3-14

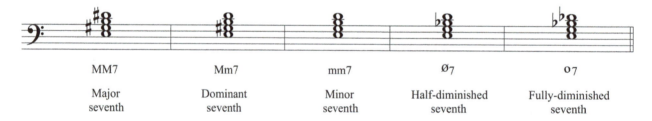

MM7	Mm7	mm7	$\emptyset$7	o7
Major seventh	Dominant seventh	Minor seventh	Half-diminished seventh	Fully-diminished seventh

↻ BACK TO BASICS 3.3

Constructing Dominant Seventh Chords

For a while, we'll focus only on the two *most common of these chords*—the minor seventh and the dominant seventh.

➤ *Assignment 3A in Workbook Chapter 3 can be completed at this time.*

Inverted Seventh Chords

The seventh chords you've seen so far have been in root position. As with triads, they can be used in inversion to enhance the melodic character of a bass line. However, seventh chords contain an additional possibility—third inversion. Again, the sole determinant of inversion is the chord member that is in the bass.

EXAMPLE 3-15

Black note = **root**

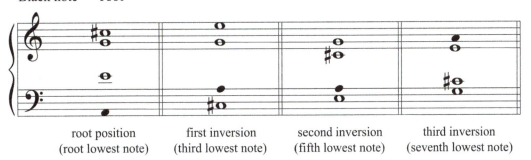

| root position (root lowest note) | first inversion (third lowest note) | second inversion (fifth lowest note) | third inversion (seventh lowest note) |

The next example contains seventh chords in all positions except second inversion.

EXAMPLE 3-16 J. S. Bach: Prelude No. 1 (from *WTC*, Book I) 🔊

CONCEPT CHECK

Notate each of the seventh chords in Example 3–16 on a single staff, first in root position, then in each of the three possible inversions. Then identify each seventh chord type.

Seventh Chords in Inversion

If the prelude in Example 3-16 has a familiar ring, it may be because the nineteenth-century Parisian, Charles Gounod, used it as the harmonic basis for his "Ave Maria," a setting of this text heard frequently at Christmas time. The beginning of his song follows, transposed from its original key of D. Sing or play the melody against Bach's prelude.

EXAMPLE 3-17 Charles Gounod: "Ave Maria"

▶ *For assignments on seventh chords, turn to workbook Chapter 3, assignments 3A–3G.*

⊕ CODA

Chords can be built from stacks of intervals other than thirds. However, triads and seventh chords form the harmonic basis of the vast bulk of our concert music, popular music, and jazz. Fluency in recognizing and spelling the four basic triad types and five basic seventh chord types is—next to interval spelling and recognition—the most fundamental skill you can cultivate. This is because it underpins the analysis of so much music. The exercises in the Workbook will help you acquire these skills. But don't stop there. On your own, practice building triads and seventh chords on random pitches, 20 or so chords at a time. On another day, practice identifying the chords you've constructed. As with your instrument, the most rapid progress comes from *daily* reinforcement. The time you spend now will pay dividends with each subsequent chapter.

DO YOU KNOW THESE TERMS?

- chord
- harmony
- inversion
- root
- root position
- seventh chord
- tertian
- triad

CHAPTER FOUR

Musical Shorthand

Lead Sheets and Figured Bass

Complex harmonic practices lead to abbreviated methods of symbolizing them. Throughout history, systems have arisen to meet the needs of the time, but two are particularly relevant for today's musician: the lead-sheet and figured bass notation. The former is a common way of notating popular music and jazz, whereas the latter is integral to a working knowledge of Baroque music—the music of Vivaldi, Bach, Handel, and their contemporaries.

LEAD-SHEET NOTATION

A **lead sheet** provides the melody (and lyrics if present) on a single staff, with chord symbols above the staff. A keyboardist or guitarist interprets the chord symbols and improvises an appropriate accompaniment based on them. The style is up to the player, and it can be varied to suit the purposes of the group.

Example 4-1 shows lead-sheet notation in its simplest form.

EXAMPLE 4-1 Wayland Holyfield and Bob House: "Could I Have this Dance?" (from *Urban Cowboy*)

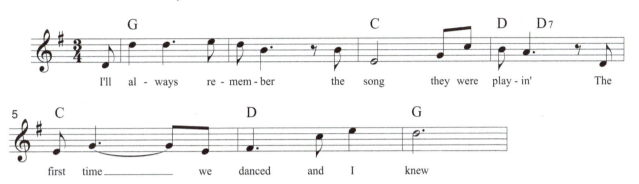

Note:

Chord changes are placed where they occur in the music. A given chord remains in effect until the next change occurs.

Lead-Sheet Chord Symbols

Lead-sheet symbols show a chord's root and quality. Because it has evolved over time, the system is inconsistent. Performers, composers, and arrangers need to be aware of the various ways a chord can be symbolized. Example 4-2 shows the more common symbols.

EXAMPLE 4-2a Triads

EXAMPLE 4-2b Seventh Chords

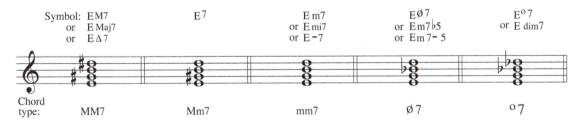

Consult Appendix C for a complete table of lead-sheet chord symbols.

A good way to familiarize yourself with the sound and spelling of the seventh chord types symbolized in Example 4-2b is to play the chords in the order presented in a variety of keys—for example, GM7–G7–Gm7–Gø7–Go7. Cycling through the pattern in this way involves changing only one pitch at a time.

► *Assignments 1A–1E in Workbook Chapter 4 can be completed at this time.*

⟳ BACK TO BASICS 4.1

Lead-Sheet Symbols— Triads and Seventh Chords

Lead-sheet symbols serve well in styles where a bass player "walks" through the chord changes in a largely stepwise fashion, or plays alternately the chord roots and fifths. In these styles, it's often unnecessary that the notation indicate chord inversions. Yet the bass line often is the second most important melodic element in a piece. We discussed in Chapter 3 how the bass can subtly alter the character of a given set of harmonies. It can also rescue a lackluster melody. For these reasons, it is often desirable that chord symbols reflect the bass note.

Example 4-3 is a solo piano rendering of Example 4-1. Notice that the lead sheet (see Example 4-1) offers an incomplete view of the actual bass line. Yet the enhanced bass line adds much to the song.

EXAMPLE 4-3 Wayland Holyfield and Bob House: "Could I Have This Dance?" 🔊

Expanded Symbols

The chord symbols added in mm. 2, 5, and 6 help. They show both the chord (left of the slash) and the bass note *when different from the chord root* (right of the slash). In this way the symbol can indicate chord inversion and thus reflect more accurately (though still not completely) the bass line.

EXAMPLE 4-4

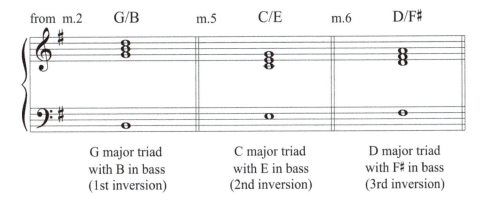

↺ **BACK TO BASICS 4.2**

Lead-Sheet Symbols— Inverted Chords

| G major triad with B in bass (1st inversion) | C major triad with E in bass (2nd inversion) | D major triad with F♯ in bass (3rd inversion) |

CONCEPT CHECK

Show the lead-sheet symbols that would completely describe the chords (chord type and bass note) at the indicated points in Example 4–5. Be sure to factor in all tones that are sustained at the given points.

EXAMPLE 4-5 Mann Curtis and Gilbert Becaud: "Let It Be Me" 🔊

➤ *For assignments on lead-sheet notation, turn to Workbook Chapter 4, assignments 1A–1I.*

MORE ON CHORD INVERSION: THE NUMBERS GAME

For all their precision, numbers can be confusing. Recall from Chapter 3 that every triad, whether major, minor, diminished or augmented, has a "root," a "third," and a "fifth." When a third (3rd) and fifth (5th) are placed above a given pitch, that lowest pitch is called the root. Recall, too, that when we change the chord member that is on the bottom, we invert the chord.

In the process of inversion, *something remains constant and something changes.* Remaining constant are the *chord member names:* root (R), third (3rd), and fifth (5th). No matter how we rearrange the notes, *the chord member names remain unchanged.* Following is a C major triad in root position. Arrangements are also shown with the 3rd and the 5th on the bottom. No matter what inversion we use, the chord member names of "root," "3rd," and "5th" remain:

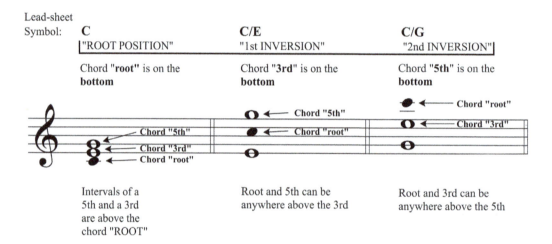

Notes:

1. Chord members derive their names from the intervals they form above the *root.* They retain those names (Root, 3rd, 5th) in all inversions.

2. First inversion places the 3rd of the chord on the bottom of the stack. It doesn't matter where the root and 5th are placed, so long as they appear above the 3rd.

3. Second inversion places the 5th of the chord on the bottom of the stack. It makes no difference where the root and 3rd are placed, so long as they appear above the 5th.

Upon inversion, the chord member names remain the same but the *intervals they form against the lowest pitch (which is no longer the root) change.* These intervals are shown beneath the staff for the triad in each of its positions.

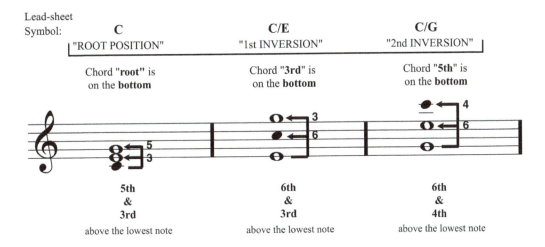

Notes:

1. In first inversion, the root (C) is a *sixth* above the lowest pitch, and the 5th (G) is a *third* above the lowest pitch.

2. In second inversion, the root (C) is a *fourth* above the lowest pitch, and the 3rd (E) is a *sixth* above the lowest pitch.

As you can see, the chord members get their names from root position and *only in root* position are the intervals above the lowest pitch the same as the chord member names. The numerals appearing beneath the staff in Example 4-5b above form the basis of another shorthand notation system known as the figured bass.

FIGURED BASS NOTATION

Ours is not the only time in the history of music when improvisation has played an important role. During the Baroque era (ca. 1600–1750) a shorthand system of notation, consisting of a bass line along with numbers below the notes to indicate the intervals to be added above, provided the information necessary for the harpsichordist, organist, lutenist, or (mostly in Spain) guitarist to improvise an accompaniment. Similar in concept to today's lead sheet, the system specified the bass line more precisely. Known as the **continuo**, the part was played (**realized**) by a performer who fleshed out the harmonies according to his or her musical taste and skill. Example 4-6 shows elements of the system. The bottom staff contains the bass line with its accompanying figures, the part the performer would have seen. The small staff above it shows one possible way—a rather basic way—to realize this **figured bass**.

EXAMPLE 4-6 J. S. Bach: "Ich steh' mit einem Fuss im Grabe" (from *Cantata* 156) 🔊

* beats one and two contain
figures yet to be discussed

Although the points that follow relate figured bass to chord inversion, it's important to know that composers and performers of the time thought in terms of intervals only—not chord inversion, a concept unknown to all but the last generation of figured bass composers.

Realizing a Figured Bass

1. The numbers indicate intervals to be added *in any octave* above—*never below*—the bass notes.

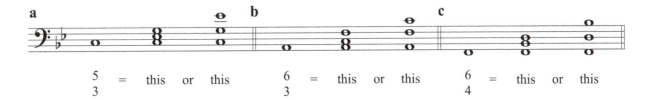

2. The intervals to be added are diatonic—that is, found within the key. Chromatic pitches are never added or subtracted unless the figure so instructs.

3. A $\frac{5}{3}$ indicates a root-position triad (as shown in 1a). However, this figure was normally omitted; therefore, a bass note with *no* numbers beneath it signifies root position.

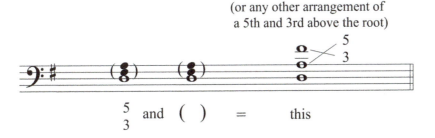

Also see Example 4-6: m. 1, beat 1 and m. 4, beat 3.

4. A 6 (short for $\frac{6}{3}$) indicates a first inversion triad.

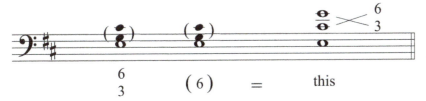

Also see Example 4-6: m. 1, beat 3 and m. 5, beat 1.

5. A $\begin{smallmatrix}6\\4\end{smallmatrix}$ indicates a second inversion triad.

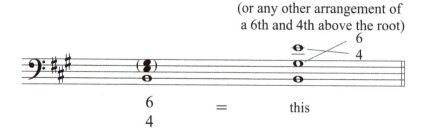

6. An accidental alone always refers to the *third above the bass note.*

Also see Example 4-6: m. 6, beat 4. (The natural refers to the third above G.)

7. An accidental preceding or following a number indicates a chromatic raising or lowering of the pitch to which the number refers. Raised pitches are also indicated by a plus sign or by a diagonal stroke through the number.

These figures all mean a raised sixth (along with the diatonic third) above B.

These figures all mean a raised sixth (along with the diatonic third) above C.

8. The figures for seventh chords are the following:

	Root pos.	First inv.	Second inv.	Third inv.
usual symbol: (abbreviated)	7	6 5	4 3	4 2
complete symbol:	7 5 3	6 5 3	6 4 3	6 4 2

See Example 4-6: m. 3, beat 4; m. 6, beat 3; m. 6, beat 4.

9. A dash beneath a bass note indicates that the chord is unchanged. The bass note is quite possibly not a part of the chord (a nonchord tone).

Also see Example 4-6: mms 3, 4, 5, and 6. In which of these measures is the bass note a passing tone?

Note that a missing dash in the previous illustration would prompt a harmonization of the second bass note.

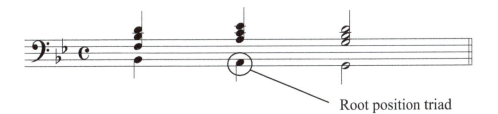

Root position triad

↻ BACK TO BASICS 4.3

Constructing Chords from a Figured Bass

10 A 9, 7, or 4, usually indicates a tone that is not part of the chord. A number showing the pitch to which it moves (8, 6, or 3) often follows, that is, 9–8, 7–6, 4–3. See Example 4-6: m. 6.

CONCEPT CHECK

In the blanks beneath the music in Example 4–7, add figures to the bass line consistent with the realization shown on the reduced staff.

1 Where a chord is in root position, leave the blank empty.

2 Circled tones indicate places where the bass changes under a chord that remains unchanged. You need not add figures at these points.

3 For guidance in m. 8, beat 1 and m. 13, beat 3, consult Note 10 following Example 4–6.

Your result will be much more heavily figured than Handel's original, which was very sparsely figured.

EXAMPLE 4-7 G. F. Handel: "For unto us a Child Is Born" (from *Messiah*) 🔊))

The figured bass, like lead-sheet notation and all aspects of music, evolved throughout its period of use, with variations and inconsistencies aplenty. Composers often omitted all but the most essential figures from the bass line, even forgoing *all* figures where the harmony could be easily deduced from the other parts. This left much to the interpretative powers of the performers, who, steeped in the style, were accustomed to its anomalies.

CONCEPT CHECK

Following is the Bach-Gounod "Ave Maria" from Chapter 3. Here it is presented in the key of D in the form of a lead sheet. From the chord symbols, construct a figured bass on the bass-clef staff beneath the melody. The process has been started for you. At what points do inversions render the bass line more stepwise than it otherwise would be?

EXAMPLE 4-8 J. S. Bach and C. Gounod: "Ave Maria"

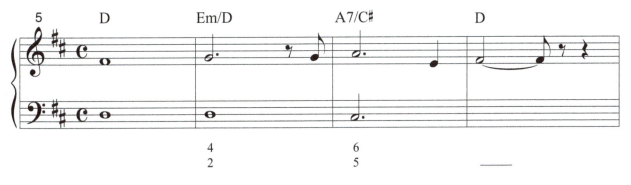

continued

EXAMPLE 4-8 *continued*

Although an elegant system, figured bass remains forever tethered to Baroque music, and it is still a prized skill used by musicians specializing in the performance of that music. However, the figures themselves:

6	6	7	6	4	4
	4		5	3	2

BACK TO BASICS 4.4

Inversion and Figured Bass

eventually found a wider use. In tandem with Roman numerals, they form the composite chord symbols that have become standard in harmonic analysis. (The more recent "Nashville system" of chord labeling supplants Roman numerals with Arabic numerals.) We'll learn about Roman numeral symbols in Chapter 5.

➤ *For assignments on figured bass notation, turn to Workbook Chapter 4, assignments 2A–2F.*

⊕ CODA

In the time of Bach and Handel—and Haydn and Mozart—the ability to improvise was considered to be an indispensable skill of the accomplished musician. Today, regrettably, this is not the case. Musicians tend to gravitate early in their studies toward Classical performance and composition or to jazz and popular styles, improvisation largely the domain of the latter. This is the price of specialization, and even a musician such as Wynton Marsalis, who for much of his career straddled both the Classical and jazz worlds, has since found it necessary to abandon Classical performance because to excel in both is—in his own words—"just too hard." Still, in today's fiercely competitive environment, the more versatile a musician you are, the more likely it is that your musical services will be in demand.

DO YOU KNOW THESE TERMS?

- continuo
- figured bass
- lead sheet
- nonchord tone
- passing tone
- realization

CHAPTER FIVE

Harmonies of the Major and Minor Scales

KEY CONCEPTS IN THIS CHAPTER

- Triads in Major and Minor Keys

- Roman Numeral Chord Symbols

- Seventh Chords in Major and Minor Keys

- Functional Harmony

- The Ground Bass

THE DIATONIC CHORDS

Do you recall the four triad types described in Chapter 3? How about the five seventh chords? If not, review Examples 3-3 and 3-14 now.

These are the only triad and seventh chord types that are **diatonic**—that is, in agreement with the key signature—in major and minor keys. They also comprise the harmonic lexicon for a great many songs and other short musical works.

Diatonic Triads in Major Keys

Example 5-1 shows the seven diatonic triads of G major. Each triad bears a name that reflects the position of its root within the scale. We use the same names to designate the scale degrees, which are indicated through placement of a caret above the degree number.

EXAMPLE 5-1a

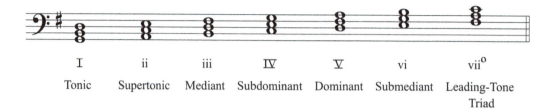

I	ii	iii	IV	V	vi	vii°
Tonic	Supertonic	Mediant	Subdominant	Dominant	Submediant	Leading-Tone Triad

Example 5-1b positions the scale degrees visually above and below the tonic to help you understand the meaning behind their names.

EXAMPLE 5-1b

$\hat{5}$ Dominant: a fifth above the tonic and a point of instability requiring eventual resolution to the tonic

$\hat{3}$ Mediant: the midpoint between tonic and dominant

$\hat{2}$ Supertonic: "above" the tonic

$\hat{1}$ Tonic: **The chord of maximum stability**

$\hat{7}$ Leading tone: "leading" to the tonic by half step

$\hat{6}$ Submediant: the midpoint between tonic and subdominant

$\hat{4}$ Subdominant: a fifth below the tonic

Roman Numeral Symbols

The Roman numerals in Example 5-1 designate the scale degrees of the chord roots *and* the quality of the chords. Uppercase numerals denote major triads, and lower cases denote minor triads. A "+" following an uppercase numeral denotes an augmented triad (not diatonic in major) and a "o" following a lowercase numeral denotes a diminished triad.

In a major scale:

• The three major triads are symbolized I, IV, V

• The three minor triads are symbolized ii, iii, vi

• The diminished triad is symbolized vii°

The "Primary Triads"

I, IV, and V are sometimes called the **primary triads**. Collectively, they contain all of the pitches present in the scale. Because of this, many folk songs, hymns, and other traditional melodies can be harmonized in their entirety with only these three chords.

In Example 5-2a, the folk hymn "Amazing Grace" is harmonized using only the primary triads (some in inversion).

EXAMPLE 5-2a "Amazing Grace" (folk hymn) 🔊

CONCEPT CHECK

Place I, IV, or V under each of the primary triads in Example 5-2a.

"Oh! Susanna" is a melody supported by only primary triads. (Play or sing it.) Based on the melody notes, decide which primary triad (G, D, or C) belongs above each measure and place the lead-sheet symbol in the appropriate blank.

EXAMPLE 5-2b Stephen Foster: "Oh! Susanna"

Although many songs *can* be harmonized using only the primary triads, most songs benefit from greater harmonic variety. In Example 5-3, all seven triads of the key are used, along with two seventh chords. Clear examples of each chord appear on the added staff at the points where they occur. Some of the chords are inverted and some contain nonchord tones for added dissonance and variety.

EXAMPLE 5-3 "Amazing Grace" (folk hymn)

Em	Cmaj7	G	F#°	G	C	G

blind but_____ now I see._____

Diatonic Triads in Minor Keys

⟳ BACK TO BASICS 5.1

Diatonic Triads in Major— Harmonic Function

In the minor mode, the variable sixth and seventh scale degrees ($\hat{6}$ and $\hat{7}$) create a larger pool of potential harmonies (see Appendix A). Example 5-4a shows the most common triads. They use the pitches of the harmonic minor form *except for the mediant*, which is almost always a major triad (III)—*not augmented* (III+). However, $\hat{6}$ and $\hat{7}$—raised ascending and lowered descending—create a second possibility *for every triad but the tonic* (Example 5-4b).

EXAMPLE 5-4a

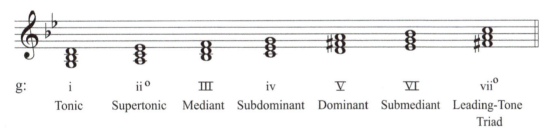

g:	i	ii°	III	iv	V	VI	vii°
	Tonic	Supertonic	Mediant	Subdominant	Dominant	Submediant	Leading-Tone Triad

EXAMPLE 5-4b

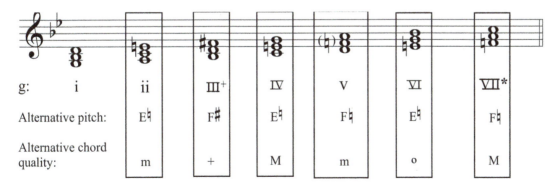

g:	i	ii	III+	IV	V	VI	VII*
Alternative pitch:		E♮	F♯	E♮	F♮	E♮	F♮
Alternative chord quality:		m	+	M	m	o	M

* The VII is named **subtonic**, since it is a whole step (rather than a half step) beneath the tonic

In a minor scale:

- Two triads are normally minor: i, iv

- Three triads are normally major: III, V, VI

- Two triads are normally diminished: ii°, vii°

- V normally has the same quality in major and minor, as does vii°.

- The III+ is the rarest of minor-key harmonies.

➤ *Assignments 1A and 1B on Workbook p. 42 can be completed now.*

BACK TO BASICS 5.2

Diatonic Triads in Minor— Harmonic Function

Showing Inversion

The figured bass symbols you learned in Chapter 4—6 (short for $\frac{6}{3}$), and $\frac{6}{4}$—are used with Roman numerals to show inversion. Recall that the absence of a superscript signifies root position.

EXAMPLE 5-5

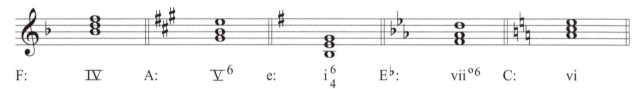

BACK TO BASICS 5.3

Diatonic Triads in Major and Minor Keys

CONCEPT CHECK

Add lead-sheet symbols (with superscripts) above the chords in Example 5-5.

The Diatonic Seventh Chords

Example 5-6 shows the Roman numeral symbols for the diatonic seventh chords.

EXAMPLE 5-6a Major

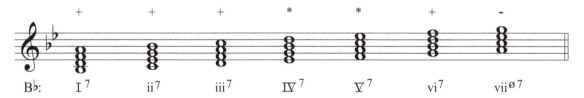

EXAMPLE 5-6b Minor

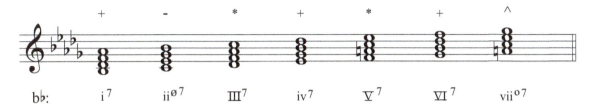

$$b\flat: \quad i^7 \quad ii^{\o 7} \quad III^7 \quad iv^7 \quad V^7 \quad VI^7 \quad vii^{o7}$$

*   Major triad with diatonic seventh: I^7, IV^7, V^7, III^7, VI^7

+   Minor triad with diatonic seventh: ii^7, iii^7, vi^7, i^7, iv^7

~   Diminished triad with diatonic seventh: $ii^{\o 7}$, $vii^{\o 7}$

^   Diminished triad with diatonic seventh: vii^{o7}

In diatonic seventh chords:

- The basic triad is symbolized as before.

- A superscript 7 indicates a diatonic seventh above the chord root—that is, a pitch unaltered from its natural appearance in the key.

- The sole exception is the $vii^{\o 7}$ in major. The ø distinguishes this chord, called a **half-diminished seventh chord**, from the **fully diminished seventh chord** (see diminished seventh chord) that appears on the leading tone in minor keys.

- The chords shown for minor keys are the most common ones. As with triads, they are those of the harmonic minor scale, except that the III^7 is based on a major rather than an augmented triad.

- As with triads, inversions are shown by adding figured bass superscripts: $\frac{6}{5}$ (first inversion), $\frac{4}{3}$ (second inversion), or $\frac{4}{2}$ (third inversion). Each of these figures shows the interval of the seventh formed above the bass by the root and seventh.

↺ **BACK TO BASICS 5.7**

Diatonic Seventh Chords— Harmonic Function

EXAMPLE 5-7

$$F: \quad IV^4_2 \qquad A: \quad V^6_5 \qquad e: \quad i^4_3 \qquad E\flat: \quad V^4_3 \qquad C: \quad vi^7$$

▶ *For assignments on diatonic chords, turn to Workbook p. 42.*

FUNCTIONAL TONALITY

Chord Function

Roman numerals are more useful in harmonic analysis than letter name chord symbols because beyond identifying the chord root and quality, they provide insight into the chord's place in the scale *and* its function in the key. This chord

is represented by the lead-sheet symbol "Am" (or A– or A^mi). However, in the key of C it's vi, while in the key of G it's ii, and in the key of F it's iii. And although it's the same chord, it *has a different purpose and different aural effect* in each of these keys.

If you doubt this, play Example 5-8 a and b, and compare the effect of the G major triad in each song.

EXAMPLE 5-8a Stephen Sondheim and Leonard Bernstein: "One Hand, One Heart" (from *West Side Story*)

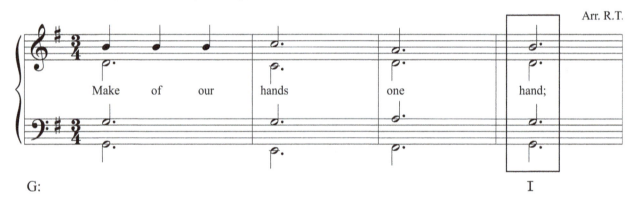

EXAMPLE 5-8b Franz Gruber: "Stille Nacht" ("Silent Night")

Although the boxed chord is voiced identically in both examples, in the key of G it sounds like an ending chord, whereas in the key of C it creates the expectation that something (probably the tonic) will follow. If you like word play, you can think of it this way:

A key is a chord's context, and its context is key.

Functional tonality *is not a democracy.* In it, not all chords are created equal. They vary in status, behavior, and stability. The chord built on the tonic is the chord of maximum stability, the ultimate chord of repose. The vii°, built on the leading tone, is the least stable sounding. Between these extremes roam the other chords, whose behavior depends on the number of tones they share with the tonic, their inversion, and melodic factors, all to be discussed in due course.

The Circle of Fifths

The chords of a key are its citizens, and like the citizens of a country, they are subject to laws and customs. One of these is the **circle of fifths** (see Appendix A if you've forgotten this concept). Play Example 5-9 several times, and listen to the forward momentum created by chords whose roots are related by descending fifth.

EXAMPLE 5-9a

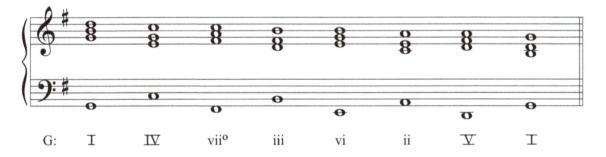

EXAMPLE 5-9b

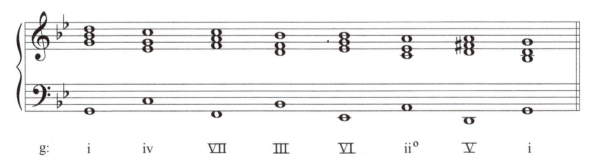

Notes:

1. The root movement in both the major and minor modes is downward by fifth (upward by fourth is the same thing).

2. One of the chords in Example 5-9b uses F♯ while the others use F♮. The reason has to do with the variable seventh degree in the minor scale, to be discussed later.

Example 5-10 shows works separated by time and style that largely travel the same harmonic byway—the circle of fifths.

EXAMPLE 5-10a J. S. Bach: French Suit in D Minor (Menuett II) 🔊

EXAMPLE 5-10b W. A. Mozart: Rondo, K. 494

Note:

The fifth (blackened) has been omitted from each seventh chord, a common practice then and now.

EXAMPLE 5-10c Joseph Kosma and Johnney Mercer: "Autumn Leaves"

Circle of fifths patterns are subject to modification. The IV and ii share common tones and a functional relationship in that they tend most strongly toward the dominant and are thus termed **pre-dominants**. In the same way, vii and V tend toward the tonic. Reconciling the circle of fifths with common tone relatedness yields the following paradigm that governs much functional harmonic motion.

EXAMPLE 5-11

Notice that IV can approach I from either side, as *pre*-dominant because of the common tones it shares with ii, or as *sub*dominant because of its fifth relationship to I. In the former role, it functions as a tonic approach and in the latter role, it often functions as a tonic expansion or elaboration. (More on this later.)

Progression, Retrogression, and Repetition

Any two chords that move toward the tonic in the manner of Example 5-11 are said to "progress," and the chord succession is termed a **progression**. Motion in the opposite direction has been termed **retrogression** and repeated chords or functions (as IV–ii or V–vii) **repetitions**. All three types of motion are found in most of the music we'll study.

The chords of a key might be envisioned as a tonal planetary system with the tonic at its center.

EXAMPLE 5-12

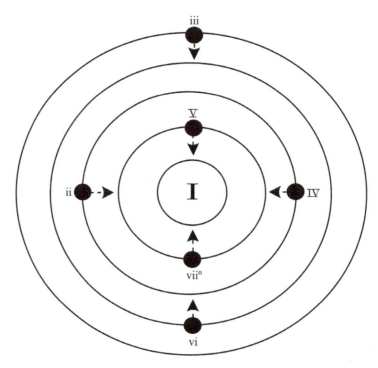

The farther a chord is from the tonic (the musical center of gravity), the weaker the pull of the tonic on it.

One of the songs from the Broadway musical *Grease* was about the fact that much early Rock-era music was based almost obsessively on the circular pattern shown in Example 5-11. The lyrics tell of falling in love to "those magic changes," referring to the chord "changes" that progress from I to vi to IV (or ii) to V and then ride around that harmonic cul-de-sac in song after song recorded during that period.

EXAMPLE 5-13 Jim Jacobs and Warren Casey: "Those Magic Changes" (from *Grease*)

Note:

Circled tones are nonchord tones.

Because the harmonic pull of the tonic is weaker in the outer "orbits" shown in Example 5-12, IV, ii, vi, and iii are generally freer to respond to melodic forces and other factors than V and vii°, which want very much to move to the tonic. This admits more variability in chord succession than is suggested by the diagram. Some theorists consider IV, ii, vi and iii *all* to be pre-dominant *functions*, and in a general way this is true because the goal of most musical phrases is to arrive at either the tonic or dominant (more on this in Part Three).

➤ *Assignments 2A through 2E on Workbook pp. 48 and 49 can be completed now.*

Repeating Harmonic Plans

The preceding example (Example 5-13) is a modern-day adaptation of a **ground bass**, a bass line that repeats over and over throughout a composition. The ground bass was popular in the Baroque era. In that style period, it often took one of three basic forms.

EXAMPLE 5-14

a Diatonic major

b Diatonic minor

c Chromatic

Note:

The minor pattern outlines the descending melodic minor scale form (identical with the natural minor form).

These bass lines support a variety of harmonic patterns that are often at odds with the functional paradigm. Common for the major form are the following, each of which might be continued in several ways:

EXAMPLE 5-15

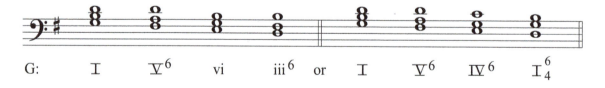

G: I   V⁶   vi   iii⁶   or   I   V⁶   IV⁶   I⁶₄

This plan and numerous variants have been used time and again in every musical style period, as common in popular music today as they were in the music of the Baroque era. Consider two examples widely separated in time.

EXAMPLE 5-16a Hal Davis, Barry Gordy, Willie Hutch, and Bob West: "I'll Be There"

EXAMPLE 5-16b J. S. Bach: French Suite, no. 5, BWV 816 (Gavotte)

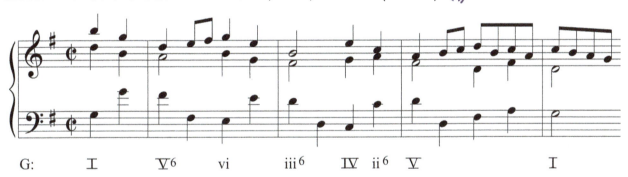

The Baroque composer Handel made extensive use of the scalar bass. While you'll probably feel that Example 5-17 sounds like neither one of the foregoing, the harmonic pattern is almost identical.

EXAMPLE 5-17 G. F. Handel: Concerto Grosso, op. 6, no. 12 (second movement) 🔊

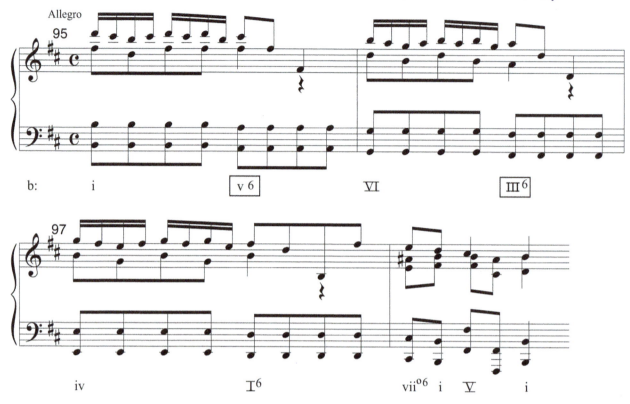

Note:

The descending scale (B–A–G–F♯–E–D–C♯–B) described by the bass and echoed by the melody in embellished form (starting at m. 96) generates the v⁶—an alternative minor-key harmony (See Example 5-3b).

Although the melody and rhythm are much different from the passages in Example 5-16, a more pronounced difference is mode—Example 5-17 is minor while Examples 5-16a and b are major.

Play through the following versions of the same pattern to hear how dramatically the mode affects the sound.

EXAMPLE 5-18a Major

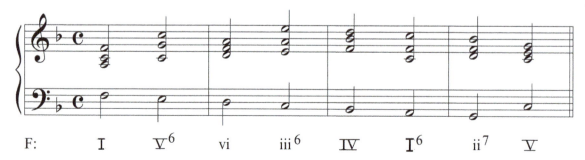

EXAMPLE 5-18b Minor

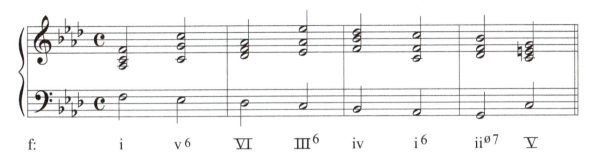

f: i   v⁶   VI   III⁶   iv   i⁶   iiø⁷   V

A compelling melodic pattern, whether in the bass or another voice, can add logic to a retrogressive harmonic pattern. Example 5-19 contains two excerpts worlds apart, musically and chronologically, that demonstrate this. Example a is curious additionally in that it first states a functional pattern (mm. 1–5) and then completely reverses it (mm. 5–9).

EXAMPLE 5-19a J. S. Bach: "Wachet auf" (from *Cantata* 140) 🔊

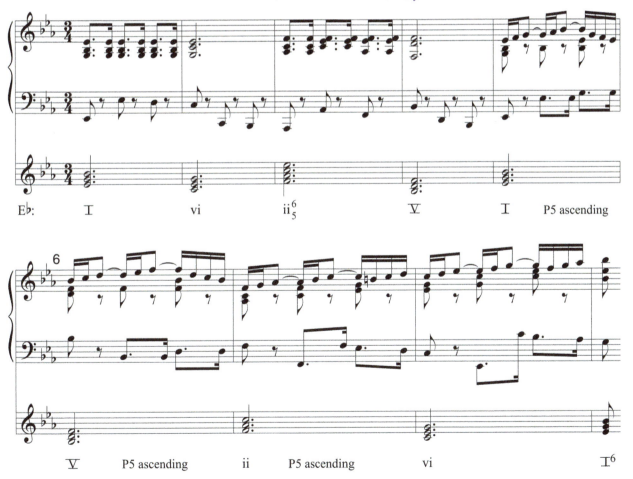

E♭:   I   vi   ii⁶₅   V   I   P5 ascending

V   P5 ascending   ii   P5 ascending   vi   I⁶

EXAMPLE 5-19b Billy Roberts: "Hey, Joe" (from The Jimi Hendrix Experience: *Are You Experienced?* Reprise Records, Div. of Warner Bros., Rs 6261)

Note:

This harmonic pattern is repeated relentlessly.

CONCEPT CHECK

1   What similarities exist between the harmonic patterns of Examples 5-19a and b? What features of the melodies in each add logic to the passages?

2   What harmonic similarities exist between Example 5-19a and Example 5-13?

Rock groups routinely employ other nonfunctional harmonic plans in the relentless manner of a ground bass. The song "Sugar" by Maroon 5 is an example, unfolding over an unusual recurring IV–vi–ii–I pattern.

EXAMPLE 5-20 Mike Posner, Adam Levine, Dr. Luke, and Jacob Kasher Hindlin: "Sugar" (as recorded by Maroon 5)

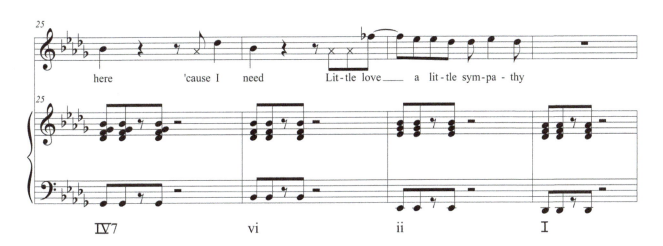

➤ *For assignments on functional tonality, turn to Workbook p. 48.*

⊕ CODA

The Common Practice Period

Functional tonality is the harmonic language of the common practice period—the music composed roughly between 1650 and 1900 (and beyond in some popular and concert music styles) when composers used a more or less standard harmonic vocabulary and syntax. In functional tonality, the diatonic harmonies of a key exist in a hierarchical relationship. At the top of the harmonic food chain stands the tonic. The other chords differ in the ways they approach it, but they often do so via a "chain of command" called the circle of fifths. While nobody can say for sure why descending fifths have remained so remarkably durable, occurring time and again in traditional music, popular music, and jazz, theorists have speculated for centuries. The most compelling part of that pattern is its conclusion—the movement from pre-dominant (IV or ii) to dominant (V or vii°) to tonic. Most musical passages end in this way regardless of chord successions prior to that point. We'll study these end-points, called cadences, next.

DO YOU KNOW THESE TERMS?

- chromatic alteration
- circle of fifths
- common practice period
- diatonic
- dominant
- fully diminished

- seventh chord
- functional tonality
- ground bass
- half-diminished seventh chord
- leading-tone triad
- mediant

- pre-dominant
- progression
- retrogression
- subdominant
- submediant
- subtonic
- tonic

CHAPTER SIX

Cadences/ Harmonic Rhythm

KEY CONCEPTS IN THIS CHAPTER

- The Four Standard Cadences

- Conclusive and Inconclusive Cadences

- Harmonic Rhythm and Meter

CADENCES

A **cadence** is a point of relative repose. Music is filled with such moments, which vary in length, strength, and import. Cadences may entail a breathing point in the melodic line, an ebbing of the harmonic flow, a respite from the rhythmic action, or all of these. They fulfill a function similar to the artfully timed caesuras in an effective orator's delivery—they group, separate, emphasize, and dramatize ideas.

The feeling of musical repose created by a cadence is often rhythmic—a longer note value, or a brief silence.

EXAMPLE 6-1 Mozart: Piano Sonata, K. 332 (first movement)

Perhaps as often, a cadence is harmonic—a two chord succession that conveys one of two messages:

1. "This is the end of something" (a conclusive cadence).

2. "This pause is only momentary" (an inconclusive cadence).

These messages appear repeatedly in the course of a musical work.

EXAMPLE 6-2 Mozart: Piano Sonata, K. 332 (first movement) 🔊

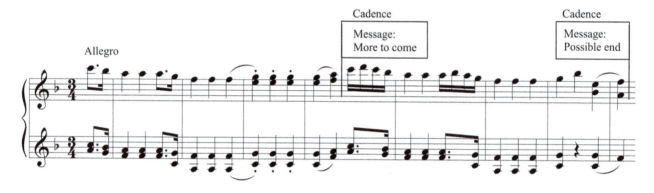

Standard Cadences

In the common practice period, cadences became more or less standardized; the cadence-ending chords were usually I or V. Four types were employed.

The **authentic cadence** (AC) is the most common and conclusive. Signature features are melodic movement from leading tone to tonic, often with bass motion from 5 to 1, as in these progressions: in major, V–I, V⁷–I, or vii°–I; in minor, V–i, V⁷–i, or vii°–i.

EXAMPLE 6-3 Schubert: "Ständchen"

d: $\underline{V}^7$ - i

Some authentic cadences sound more conclusive than others. When the melody (usually the highest voice in the texture) ends on the tonic, and the bass leaps from dominant to tonic, the most conclusive of all effects is produced. This is called a **perfect authentic cadence** (PAC).

EXAMPLE 6-4 Perfect Authentic Cadence

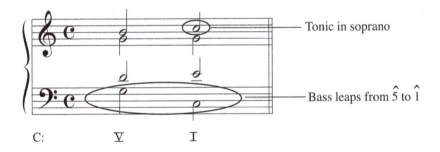

— Tonic in soprano

— Bass leaps from $\hat{5}$ to $\hat{1}$

C: $\underline{V}$ $\underline{I}$

Any authentic cadence lacking *either* the $\hat{5}$–$\hat{1}$ motion at the bottom or the tonic ending on the top is called, logically, an **imperfect authentic cadence** (IAC).

EXAMPLE 6-5 Imperfect Authentic Cadences

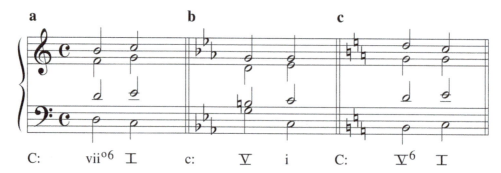

Notes:

1. a and c are imperfect because the bass motion does not move from $\hat{5}$ to $\hat{1}$.

2. b, shown in C minor, is imperfect because the soprano does not end on $\hat{1}$.

CONCEPT CHECK

Is the cadence in Example 6-3 a perfect authentic cadence or imperfect authentic cadence?

We'll not be further concerned with the perfect–imperfect distinction until we discuss phrases.

Also conclusive sounding is the **plagal cadence** (PC) heard in the familiar "Amen" intoned at the end of hymns. The harmonic pattern is IV–I (major) or iv–i (minor). Perhaps because the bass motion is from $\hat{4}$ to $\hat{1}$ (involving an *ascending* rather than *descending* fifth), and because no leading tone is present, the plagal cadence occurs less often in the standard repertory than the authentic cadence. It is considerably more common in rock and other Gospel- and blues-based music, where IV rivals V in importance at cadences and the leading tone is often non-existent.

EXAMPLE 6-6a Palestrina: "Sanctus" from *Missa Aeterna Christi Munera*

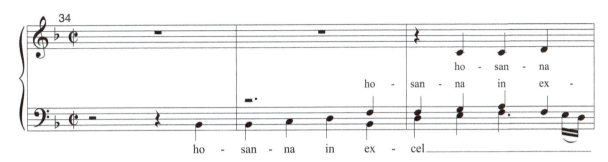

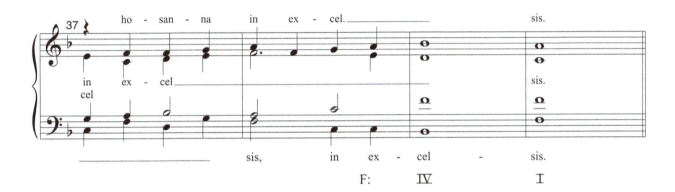

EXAMPLE 6-6b "Michael, Row the Boat Ashore" (spiritual)

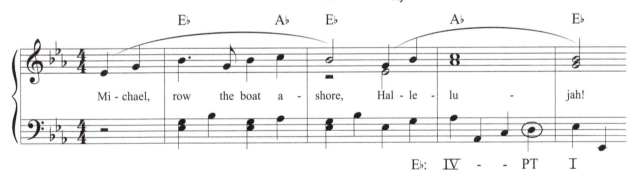

The **half cadence** sends a different message, promising continuation rather than finality. Because of this, it almost never ends a piece. The half cadence embraces a wider variety of harmonic patterns than the authentic or plagal. In theory, it can end on any chord but I. In practice, this final chord is usually V, but a chromatic chord or almost any diatonic harmony might precede it (?–V). One particular pattern that appears in minor keys only, iv6–V, has acquired a special name, the **Phrygian half cadence**. The cadence is named for the descending half step in the bass, a distinctive feature of the Phrygian mode (see Example 1–4). The following examples show a few possible half cadences.

EXAMPLE 6-7a Beethoven: Piano Sonata, op. 26 (first movement)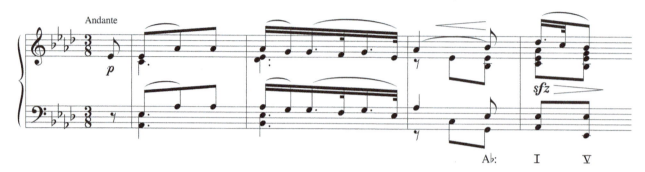

EXAMPLE 6-7b Mendelssohn: *Kinderstück*, op. 72, no. 1

EXAMPLE 6-7c Francesco Maria Veracini: Sonata No. 3 for Violin and Continuo

A **deceptive cadence** is one in which V resolves (deceptively) to anything but the anticipated tonic (V–?). Less conclusive sounding than the authentic and plagal cadences, more conclusive than the half cadence, the most common deceptive cadence—V–vi (V–VI in minor keys)—gives an impression of intermediate finality.

EXAMPLE 6-8a Beethoven: Piano Sonata, op. 7 (third movement)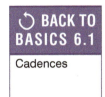

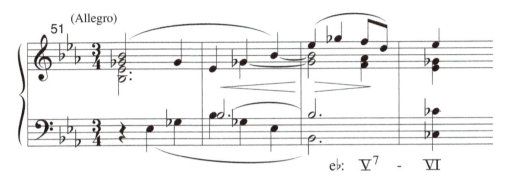

EXAMPLE 6-8b Taylor Swift: "We Are Never Getting Back Together"

Transcribed: R.T.

CONCEPT CHECK

Name the cadences in these examples in Workbook Chapter 5: Assignment 2B, 2C, and 2F

↻ **BACK TO BASICS 6.1**

Cadences

▶ *Assignment 1A in Workbook Chapter 6, p. 54 can be completed at this time.*

Summary of Standard Cadences

(Minor shown in parentheses)

Authentic (AC):	V–I (V–i) can be perfect (PAC) or imperfect (IAC) vii°⁶–I (vii°⁶–i) imperfect (IAC)
Plagal (PC):	IV–I (iv–i)
Half (HC):	IV–V (iv⁶–V); ii⁶–V (ii°⁶–V); I–V (i–V); vi–V (VI–V)
Deceptive (DC):	V–vi (V–VI)

EXAMPLE 6-9a Major

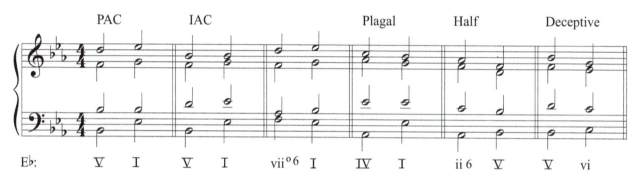

EXAMPLE 6-9b Minor

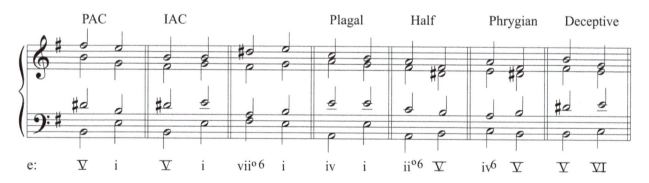

In the standard cadences:

- The final chord is a *root-position triad*.

- The final chord is either a major triad (I, V, or VI) or a minor triad (i or vi).

- The half cadence *always* ends with a major triad (V).

Non-standard Cadences

Traditional thinking holds that a pause on other than I, V, or vi is not truly a cadence. Still, a pause is a pause is a pause (to misquote Gertrude Stein), and it needs a name. Some music theorists use the term "contrapuntal cadence" to describe such musical moments. Be that as it may, melodies can and do pause over other harmonic patterns, as the next examples illustrate.

EXAMPLE 6-10a "Scarborough Fair" (English folk song) 🔊))

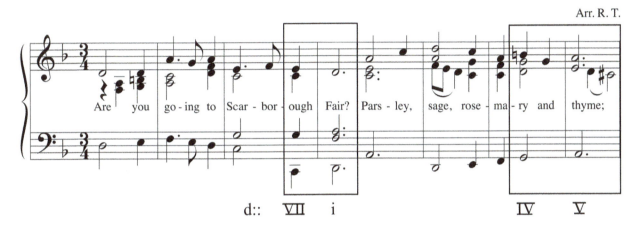

Note:

"Scarborough Fair" has a modal touch, as does much English music. This is chiefly due to the lowered seventh scale degree (subtonic). Refer to Example 1–4 concerning modes.

EXAMPLE 6-10b Jon Hendricks and Bobby Timmons: "Moanin'" 🔊))

Note:

This cadence also has a modal quality, owing to the raised sixth scale degree, C-sharp. Again, refer to Example 1–4 regarding modes.

REVIEW AND REINFORCEMENT

1   Identify the modes implied by the cadences of Examples 6–10a and 6–10b.

2   Example 6-11 contains an unusual cadence. Does it sound conclusive or inconclusive? Which standard cadence does it most closely resemble? What Roman numerals would symbolize it?

EXAMPLE 6-11 Trevor Nunn (after T. S. Eliot) and Andrew Lloyd Webber: "Memory" (from *Cats*)

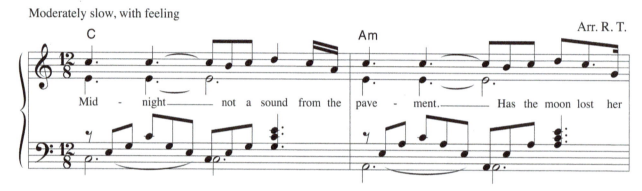

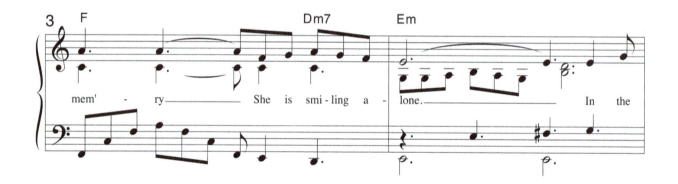

Steeped in both Classical music and jazz, Leonard Bernstein combined elements of both in his music. One of his most enduring scores, *West Side Story*, is filled with distinctive harmonic nuances that give the work a unique stamp. Among these are its unusual cadences.

EXAMPLE 6-12 Stephen Sondheim and Leonard Bernstein: "Maria" (from *West Side Story*)

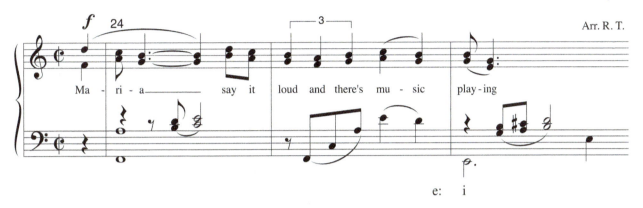

Arr. R. T.

CONCEPT CHECK

What mode is implied in the cadence in Example 6-12?

➤ *For assignments on cadences, turn to Workbook p. 54.*

HARMONIC RHYTHM

Harmonic rhythm refers to: (1) the *rate* at which the chords accompanying a melody change; and (2) the rhythmic *patterns* formed by those chord changes. A new harmony can occur as often as every beat or with every melody note (Example 3–8 on p. 39) or as infrequently as every couple measures or longer (Example 3–1 on p. 34), depending on tempo, meter, melodic complexity, and style. Tempo and harmonic rhythm often display an inverse relationship: "When the tempo runs, the harmonic rhythm walks" (and vice versa). *Often*, but not *always*. In Example 6–13, both harmonic rhythm and tempo amble along at a leisurely gait. In compensation, a moderately florid melody holds center stage.

EXAMPLE 6-13 Beethoven: Piano Sonata, op. 22 (second movement)

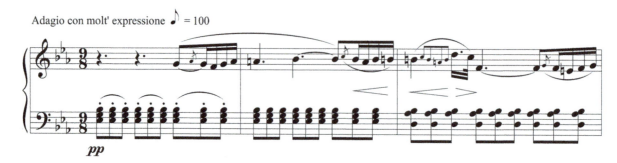

Variables notwithstanding, generalizations can be made:

• Harmonies change more often on strong beats than on weak beats, and more often on *down*beats than on *up*beats.

• The final chord of a cadence is usually metrically stronger than the chord that precedes it.

• The tonic tends to occupy stronger metric positions than the dominant (the half cadence I–V a notable exception).

• The rate of chord change often changes with the approach to a cadence.

Example 6–14 illustrates these four points to a greater or lesser degree.

EXAMPLE 6-14 Schumann: "Volksliedchen" (No. 9 from *Album for the Young*, op. 68)

Common Patterns

Patterns of harmonic change define—in fact, in many cases *create*—meter. Following are typical harmonic rhythms in two common meters. Short works may employ a single pattern whereas longer and more complex music will likely contain more variety.

EXAMPLE 6-15

CONCEPT CHECK

In Example 6-16, the harmonic rhythm is plotted for the first two measures. Continue to do so for the rest of the passage. Which of the common patterns shown in Example 6-15 are present? Which of the generalizations just cited apply? Asterisks indicate nonchord tones.

EXAMPLE 6-16 J. S. Bach: "Herz und Mund und Tat und Leben" (Chorale from *Cantata* 147) 🔊))

Let's try an experiment. Play the following melody. You may not recognize it because the rhythms have been "smoothed out" to avoid clues to the meter.

EXAMPLE 6-17

Now, apply what you already know about accent and meter by placing a bar line *before* each note that has a tonal accent (a pitch emphasized by its registral placement). Play the melody again, and add a *dynamic* accent on the first beat of each of the measures you've created. Notice that it sounds perfectly fine this way—until the cadence, which seems to be misplaced. It begins on beat 4 of m. 3 and ends on beat 2 of m. 4.

Next, play the melody with its harmonies added, as shown in Example 6–18. Do you hear the metric structure to be that indicated by the bar lines shown *above* or *below* the music?

EXAMPLE 6-18 Jack Segal and Evelyn Danzig: "Scarlet Ribbons for Her Hair"

Barred as shown *above* the music, the harmonies change consistently on weak beats—2 and 4—and the cadence ends on beat 2. The harmonic rhythm is relentlessly syncopated:

EXAMPLE 6-19

The barring *beneath* the music shows the song's true metric stripe. It begins on beat 1; the harmonies change on beats 1 and 3, which is *why* we perceive them to be strong beats *even though the tonal accents of the melody suggest otherwise*; and a plagal cadence concludes on beat 3 of m. 4. In sculpting the meter, the harmonic rhythm—not the melody—wields the hammer and chisel.

REVIEW AND REINFORCEMENT

Show both the figured bass symbols and the lead-sheet symbols that describe the harmonies of Example 6-18.

The meter of most music results from the synergy of melodic and harmonic forces. An occasional shift in the harmonic rhythm and/or melodic accentuation adds interest. The excerpt that follows is very much like Example 6–18 in that it employs a melody comprising quarter notes exclusively. However, the harmonic setting is almost the antithesis of Example 6–18. Notice the syncopated subdominant chord in m. 1 and the weak metric position of all the tonic chords except the first, including a weak-beat authentic cadence.

EXAMPLE 6-20 Chopin: Nocturne, op. 37, no. 1 🔊

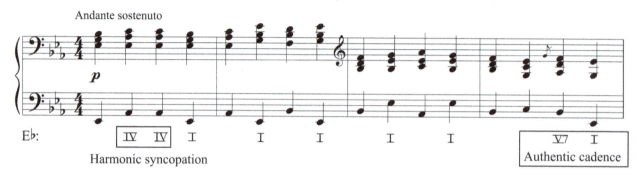

In Example 6–21, the agogic accents (accents by duration) in the melody (>) reinforce harmonic changes on the second beat of each measure to "turn the beat around" at the outset. The common term for this is **metric shift**.

EXAMPLE 6-21 Chopin: Etude, op. 10, no. 3 🔊

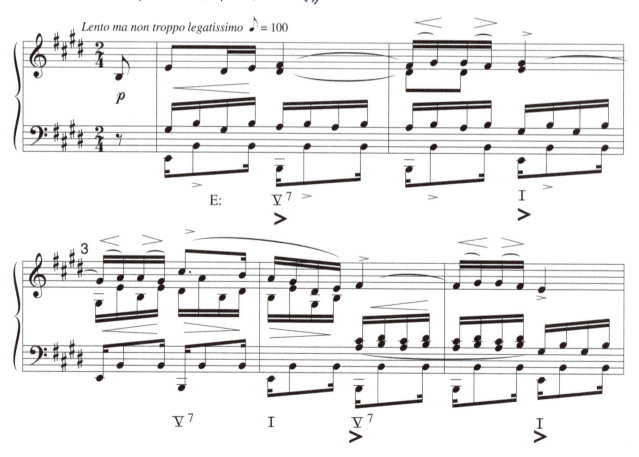

▶ *For assignments on harmonic rhythm, turn to Workbook p. 59.*

⊕ CODA

This chapter has been about the harmonic-rhythmic connection:

Harmony and rhythm in combination create the cadences that separate musical ideas.

The rate and patterns of chord change in a piece comprise its harmonic rhythm.

Meter is an aspect of rhythm, accent creates meter, and harmonic patterns create accents. Conversely, a metric shift can occur when harmonies consistently change on the measures' weak beats.

Later, you'll have the opportunity to apply what you've learned about cadences and harmonic rhythm in a creative and satisfying way—through melody harmonization and composition. Before that can happen, though, we need to explore the harmonic-*melodic* connection. This and other aspects of melody are the focus of Part Three.

DO YOU KNOW THESE TERMS?

- authentic cadence
- cadence
- deceptive cadence
- half cadence
- harmonic rhythm
- imperfect authentic cadence
- metric shift
- perfect authentic cadence
- Phrygian half cadence
- plagal cadence

Melody

PART THREE

Melody is, in the most general sense, a succession of pitches in rhythm. Is music without a melody possible? If you're a flautist or vocalist, you might say no. Percussionists might beg to differ. This is because the way we think about music is conditioned by the way we make music.

The fact is that melody is but one musical element; four other prominent ones are rhythm, harmony, texture, and timbre. Any one of them might be the primary material from which a composer fashions a composition. In certain cultures, melody plays a role secondary to rhythm. And throughout the twentieth century, some American and European composers wrote music that focused either on texture, rhythm, timbre, or a combination of these, with melody excluded or reduced to a secondary role. In rap music, melody is subordinate to rhythm and rhyme and is often absent altogether. Still, it's hard to dispute the historical primacy of melody. It might not be the egg in every musical omelet, but in most, it's the ingredient that we notice first and savor longest.

Part Three comprises three chapters on melody. Chapter 7 deals with some of its more general aspects including pitch and rhythmic structure, repetition in its various guises, the ways a melody defines its tonality, and larger-scale tonal relationships. Chapter 8 takes a melodic look at nonchord tones. Because these appear not only in the principal melodic line but in the bass and inner voices, we'll consider these other parts of the texture as well. Chapter 9 examines melodic form.

Melodic Pitch and Rhythm

RANGE, INTERVAL STRUCTURE, AND GESTURE

A debate that surfaces from time to time concerns a proposal to change the national anthem from "The Star-Spangled Banner" to "America" (known variously as "God save the Queen," "God Save the King," and "My Country, 'tis of Thee"). Proponents of the change argue that the former had less-than-noble origins (as an eighteenth-century English drinking song), that it has too wide a range for the average person to sing comfortably and invites grandstanding by those who perform it, and that its lyrics ill-fit the melody and glorify a battle rather than the country itself.

A study of the two songs will show that, whatever the merits of the argument, the melodies have little in common beyond their patriotic theme and triple meter.

EXAMPLE 7-1a Francis Scott Key and John Stafford Smith: "The Star-Spangled Banner"

Moderately, with spirit

EXAMPLE 7-1b "America" (Old English Air) 🔊

Range

Range is the distance from the highest to the lowest pitch in a melody. Many folk, popular, and traditional songs span less than an octave. Only in **art song**—music composed for trained solo singers and intended for the concert repertory—is the octave routinely exceeded by more than a few pitches.

The range of "The Star-Spangled Banner" approaches that of an art song, whereas "America" has a range more typical of a folk tune.

EXAMPLE 7-1c

"The Star-Spangled Banner"

"America"

Interval Structure

As important as range to a melody's "singability" is its intervallic motion. Although **conjunct motion** (movement from pitch to pitch by step) and **disjunct motion** (anything not conjunct) are balanced in most melodies, the more conjunct are generally less challenging to the singer.

Only 3 of the 41 pitches in "America" move to the following pitch by leap. In *The Star-Spangled Banner*, 32 pitches—nearly a third of the total—do so. Moreover, several of those leaps are wide—two are sixths, and one is a tenth. In this sense, at least, it should be clear that "America" is more a song for the masses, whereas "The Star-Spangled Banner" provides a better showcase for singers with some training.

Gesture

Most melodies unfold in a variety of pitch-rhythm patterns that might be called **gestures**. The gestures in "The Star-Spangled Banner" have dramatic and sweeping pitch contours, perhaps accounting for its inspirational, heroic character.

EXAMPLE 7-2

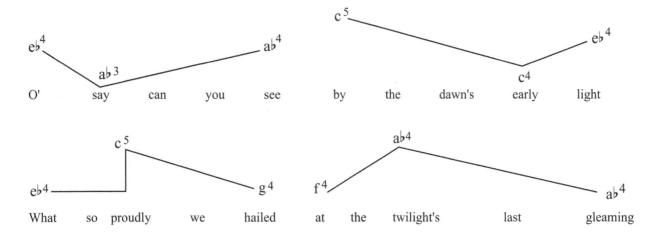

The last two gestures have contours that can be described roughly as arch-like, whereas the first two might be called inverted arches.

The contours in "America" are gentler. They compare to those of "The Star-Spangled Banner" the way the Blue Ridge Mountains compare to the Tetons. The first six measures form a gentle, symmetric arch that spans no more than a diminished fifth (F♯4–C5).

Melodic gestures have the following basic contours:

EXAMPLE 7-3

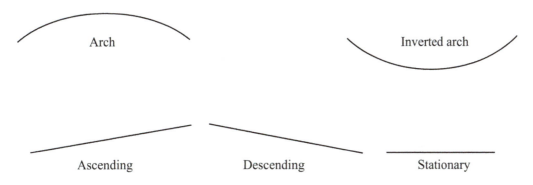

Note:

Of these shapes, the arch and inverted arch can be symmetric or asymmetric (where the rise and fall are of different lengths).

CONCEPT CHECK

Describe the following melodic fragments from the standpoint of range, intervallic motion, and gesture.

EXAMPLE 7-4a Mozart: Piano Sonata, K. 331 (third movement: "Alla Turca")

Range: _____

Interval Structure: _____

Gesture: _____

EXAMPLE 7-4b Schumann: *Kinderszenen*, op. 15, no. 6 ("Wichtige Begebenheit")

Range: _____

Interval Structure: _____

Gesture: _____

EXAMPLE 7-4c Carole King: "You've Got a Friend"

Range: _____

Interval Structure: _____

Gesture: _____

Range, intervallic motion, and gesture are among a melody's most easily recognizable features. They are a logical first step in any description or analysis.

➤ *For assignments on range, interval structure, and gesture, turn to Workbook Chapter 7, p. 64.*

REPETITION

Repeat an idea. *Vary* it. *Create* a new one. These are the options—the *only* options— available to a composer at any point. This is not to diminish the composer's art but rather to provide a helpful perspective from which to view it.

In melodies, repetition can be exact or varied, and it can apply to the largest and smallest units.

EXAMPLE 7-5 Marilyn and Alan Bergman, and Michel Legrand: Theme from *Summer of '42*

Motive

Few melodies make such relentless use of repetition as this one. The first eight measures comprise seven statements of this four-note rhythm:

Short figures such as this are called **motives**, or **motifs**. Architects and interior designers create living spaces around motifs to impart unity and cohesion. Composers are likewise concerned with unity in their compositions.

Although the rhythmic pattern shown above is repeated exactly in Example 7-5, the pitch pattern contains variations. In Example 7-5, only the statements labeled "a" and the two labeled "f" constitute exact repetition.

Sequence

Statements d and e together are a transposition of a and b. A pattern repeated at a different pitch level is called a **sequence**.

Sequences are described by their level of transposition. Although in this song the initial pattern and its repetition are separated by two measures, sequential repetition more commonly occurs immediately.

CONCEPT CHECK

Study each statement of the motive in Example 7-5 and observe how it relates to the original statement in m. 1. Which of the contours shown in Example 7-3 are present?

The following music, written in an earlier time (1825–1849), is equally saturated with repetition:

EXAMPLE 7-6 Chopin: Mazurka, op. 68, no. 3

Notice that b is not an *exact* transposition of a. An exact interval-for-interval transposition would require accidentals. However, this would take the music out of its current tonality of F and place it in D.

EXAMPLE 7-7

Types of Sequences

Although intervallically exact transpositions—called **real sequences**—occur often enough, **tonal sequences**—sequences whose intervals are altered, as in Example 7-6—are more common. The alterations avoid a conflict with the harmony or preserve the current tonality, thus the name "tonal." Some sequences deviate from the rhythm of the original gesture; yet others may alter the contour. These are called **near sequences**, or **modified sequences**.

Question: When is a sequence no longer a sequence?

Answer: When it no longer sounds like one.

Music is tinted with infinite shades of gray. Enough modification (in pitch, rhythm, or contour) will turn a sequence into something no longer classifiable as such. The tipping point is not always absolutely clear.

REVIEW AND REINFORCEMENT

Sequences appear in every example shown thus far in this chapter. Take some time to locate and identify them. Then study Example 7-8. Which type of sequence—real, tonal, or near—does it contain?

↻ **BACK TO BASICS 7.1**

Real and Tonal Sequences

EXAMPLE 7-8 "Amen"

▶ *Assignment 2c and 2d in Workbook Chapter 7 can be completed now.*

Repetition promotes unity—a good thing. But can too much of a good thing be a bad thing? Excessive repetition leads to predictability. Predictability can leach interest from a composition. Composers of concert music appear to have been concerned with this more than have composers of popular music. In fact, the former seem often to have obeyed an unwritten "rule of three," limiting precisely sequential statements of a gesture to that number. The Chopin Mazurka (Example 7-6) illustrates this point. The third complete sequential statement of the two-measure motive (c) is followed by a shortened repetition (d), which is then repeated in modified sequence (e).

EXAMPLE 7-9a

The passage in Example 7-9b comes close to a fourth precisely sequential statement, changing only at the last moment.

EXAMPLE 7-9b Todd Rundgren: "Can We Still Be Friends?"

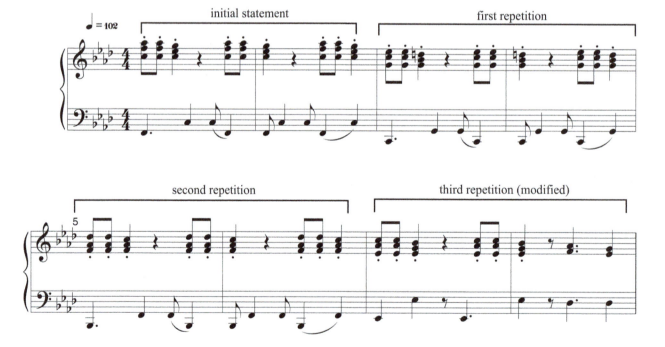

The sequences shown to this point have been short. Example 7-10a is a longer sequence. Some theorists speak of "transposed repetition" to describe longer passages such as this, especially if the pattern is transposed only once, reserving the term "sequence" for shorter patterns such as those in Example 7-9b.

EXAMPLE 7-10a Beethoven: Piano Sonata, op. 10, no. 1 (first movement)

EXAMPLE 7-10b Rodgers and Hammerstein: "Do-Re-Mi" (From *The Sound of Music*)

(In spirited tempo)

Arr. R. T.

Classify the sequences of Example 7-10a and b as real of tonal. Locate the sequence present in Example 7-11 and describe it.

EXAMPLE 7-11 Beethoven: "Für Elise" (From *Albumblatt*)

▶ *For assignments on repetition, turn to Workbook Chapter 7, p. 69.*

MELODIC TONALITY

Scales and Arpeggios

Why do exercises involving scales and arpeggios occupy such an important part of your music lessons? It's because melodies are full of them. Learn to play them, and you're indirectly learning to play your repertoire. A melody is in one sense the surface of a harmonic river that flows beneath it. Scales and—especially—arpeggios reflect that underlying chord stream.

Example 7-12 makes extensive use of arpeggiation.

EXAMPLE 7-12 Billy Joel: "The Longest Time"

REVIEW AND REINFORCEMENT

Identify and describe the sequences present in the melody of Example 7-12.

On the other hand, Example 7-13 is almost entirely scalar. Leaps occur only three times—in mm. 1, 2, and 5. They connect an unbroken C major scale that rises and falls, climbing to a peak in m. 7.

EXAMPLE 7-13 Wagner: *Die Meistersinger von Nürnberg* (Prelude) 🔊

These examples were chosen because they represent extremes. Most melodies balance scales and arpeggiation more equally.

CONCEPT CHECK

Revisit Examples 7-1 and 7-4. In which melodies are scale and arpeggiation more or less balanced?

Tonic-Dominant Axis

Composers often infuse a melody with a sense of tonality by emphasizing the tonic and dominant. These tones often form the pitch boundaries of a melody and are prominent for the following reasons:

- Their sheer number of appearances.

- Their duration.

- Their position as beginning and ending pitches or as metrically accented pitches.

Example 7-14 possesses a particularly strong **tonic-dominant axis**.

EXAMPLE 7-14 Handel: "Alla Hornpipe" (From *Water Music*) 🔊))

T = Tonic;   D = Dominant

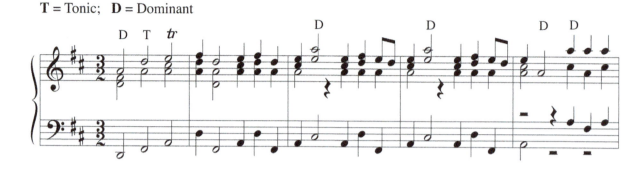

MELODIC STRUCTURE

Large-Scale Events

Example 7-15 illustrates another way that composers use scales. Notice how the three statements of the tonal sequence in mm. 7–10 each begin a step lower.

EXAMPLE 7-15 Wagner: *Die Meistersinger von Nürnberg* (Prelude)

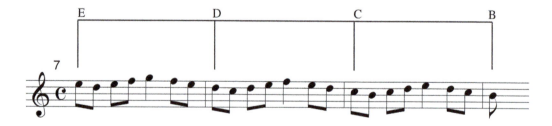

Note:

A scale is formed by the important pitches of this pattern (important because each occurs on the downbeat of the measure and initiates a new repetition of the sequence pattern).

Composer-theorist Paul Hindemith termed the stepwise motion between important melodic pitches as in Example 7-15 **step progressions**. They help to impart a sense of "goal directedness" to a melodic line. So do broken chords that appear not as adjacent notes but over a longer time span—termed **large-scale arpeggiations**. Consider again the Chopin Mazurka, op. 68 no. 3. Notice how the beginning pitches of the sequential statements together form an arpeggiation of the tonic.

EXAMPLE 7-16 Chopin: Mazurka, op. 68, no. 3

CONCEPT CHECK

Can you hear the step progression in the melody that follows?

EXAMPLE 7-17 "We Wish You a Merry Christmas" (English)

Recognizing Important Pitches

In a sentence, the noun and verb carry the basic message, while adjectives, adverbs, and the like add nuance. In a melody, certain pitches create the basic structure while others provide the nuance. How does one recognize the important pitches—the **structural pitches**—in a melody? Your ear will usually recognize them, as it no doubt did in Example 7-17. They stand out for *one or more* of these reasons:

- They're longer than the surrounding pitches.
- They're metrically stronger than the surrounding pitches.
- They're repeated.
- They're the initial notes in sequence patterns.
- They're either part of the underlying harmony *or* they're imbued with an expressive quality because they "stand out" *against* the harmony.

Consider the following musical example.

EXAMPLE 7-18 Haydn: String Quartet, op. 3, no. 5 (third movement)

The melody hovers around the dominant (F), which is stressed in one way or another in four of the first six measures. We might say it's "prolonged." Following this **prolongation** of F is a stepwise descent to the tonic Bb. This is shown in a **melodic reduction**.

EXAMPLE 7-19

In this reduction, the structural dominant (the "verb") and tonic (the "noun") are shown as half-notes and the less important tones connecting them are shown as stemless noteheads (the very least important in parentheses).

Heinrich Schenker

The Austrian theorist Heinrich Schenker developed an elaborate system of melodic reduction to show the relative importance of the pitches in a melody. While Schenkerian graphs are well beyond the scope of this text, we might adapt some of Schenker's elements to better understand the pitch hierarchy in tonal melodies.

EXAMPLE 7-20

♩ =   **Structural tones**--the most important pitches (the "noun" and "verb") of the melody

• =   **Embellishing tones**--tones of the shortest duration, (usually in weaker metric positions), and dissonant with the underlying harmonies

♩ =   **Supporting tones**--tones that rank between structural and embellishing tones in importance

♩ ♩ =   A single tone dominates a time span even though other pitches intervene (prolongation)

These elements are employed in the following two examples.

EXAMPLE 7-21

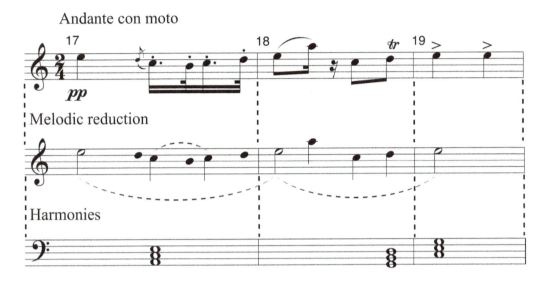

- m. 17: The E is structural. Not only is it the first pitch of the melody, it is the longest and metrically strongest of the measure. The Cs are members of the underlying harmony and are longer and stronger than the embellishing tones. They are therefore designated as supporting tones.

- m. 18: Even though A is prominent as the highest pitch, it supports the E, which is prolonged over the three measures. The final D is a supporting tone—not an embellishing tone—because it is supported by its own harmony.

- m. 19: The E is structural. Immediate pitch repetitions are not shown in a reduction.

EXAMPLE 7-22

Can you explain the graph of this example in the same manner as the explanation of Example 7-21?

> ## CONCEPT CHECK
>
> Create a melodic reduction of the following example that shows the structural, supporting and embellishing tones and prolongations, as shown above.

EXAMPLE 7-23 Rachmaninov: Symphony No. 2 (second movement) 🔊

Incidental Note: Singer/songwriter Eric Carmen (whose aunt was a violinist with The Cleveland Orchestra) based his hit song, "Never Going to Fall in Love Again," on this melody.

The last part of this chapter has focused on three large-scale melodic features: step progressions, large-scale arpeggiations, and melodic prolongations. In addition, it describes a three-element pitch hierarchy: structural tones, supporting tones, and embellishing tones. These concepts have been developed by theorists to help us understand what composers have been doing for centuries. When these features are singled out for individual study, as in this chapter, melody writing might appear to be hopelessly complicated. To the contrary, for those with a melodic gift, the process is largely intuitive. For those without that gift, awareness of a melody's component features can enhance appreciation and provide guidelines for composing satisfying tunes.

➤ *For assignments on melodic tonality, turn to Workbook Chapter 7, p. 73.*

⊕ CODA

The nuts, bolts, chains, gears, pedals, and other parts of a bicycle must be put together correctly or the result will not worK.For the new bicycle owner, assembly instructions are provided. For a beginning melodist, there is no such thing. Fortunately, the components of a melody can fit together in many ways that work (some better than others). Even more fortunately, most of us have in our memories a store of "pre-assembled melodic parts." These we've accumulated since childhood, and they are ready to use, if we just learn how. Think of this chapter and the next two not as your "assembly instructions" but as assembly *guidelines*. Experiment with them. Use them creatively.

DO YOU KNOW THESE TERMS?

- conjunct
- disjunct
- gesture
- interval structure
- large-scale arpeggiation

- melodic tonality
- motive
- range
- real and tonal sequences
- sequence

- step progression
- tonic-dominant axis

CHAPTER EIGHT

Embellishing Tones

Perhaps the only person who could love the following song is a drill sergeant. The melody comprises a mere three pitches (the tonic triad), one of them duplicated at the octave. This is because it's an emulation of a bugle call. (Taps, reveille, and other calls are traditionally blown on valveless trumpets that can play only the overtones of their fundamental.)

KEY CONCEPTS IN THIS CHAPTER

- Standard Voices
- Step-Step Combinations
- Step-Leap Combinations
- Step-"Rep" Combinations
- Embellishing Chord Tones

EXAMPLE 8-1 "You're in the Army Now" (Traditional Army Song)

Although the song does manage some variety, pieces so limited are rare. Even where the harmonic palette is more varied, melodies that do nothing but arpeggiate are uncommon.

Example 8-2 is more complex and interesting.

EXAMPLE 8-2 Julia Ware Howe and William Steffe: "Battle Hymn of the Republic"

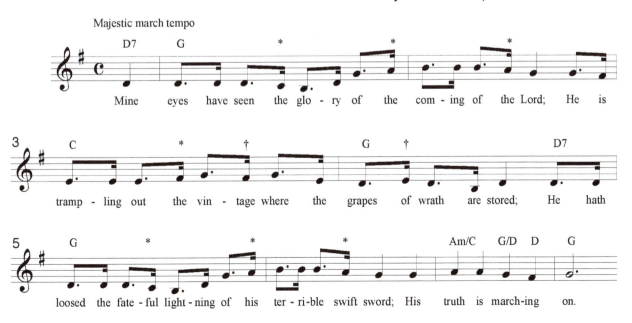

This melody, too, hovers around the tonic triad. Although still no harmonic cornucopia, it includes another chord—a measure-long IV. The stepwise connections between the notes outlining the chords are forged by **embellishing tones**—pitches that decorate or connect more important, consonant, or stable pitches. Although it's possible to view them entirely in a melodic context, most embellishing tones exist within a harmonic environment against which they are either consonant or (more frequently) dissonant. When dissonant against the harmony, they are called **nonchord tones**.

THE STANDARD VOICES

Embellishing tones occur not only in the melody but in all the lines that compose a piece of music. The four standard musical lines—which we call **voices**—are **soprano** (highest), **alto** (next highest), **tenor** (third highest), and **bass** (lowest). We'll examine embellishing tones in all these voices.

Embellishing tones are distinguished by the way they are approached and left: (1) step-step combinations, (2) step-leap combinations, and (3) step-repetition (step-rep) combinations. We'll consider them in this order.

STEP-STEP COMBINATIONS

Passing Tones

The root, third, fifth, and seventh of any chord can be connected by **passing tones** (PT), which "pass" stepwise between the adjacent chord members. Similarly, two pitches a whole step apart can be connected by a "chromatic passing tone."

EXAMPLE 8-3

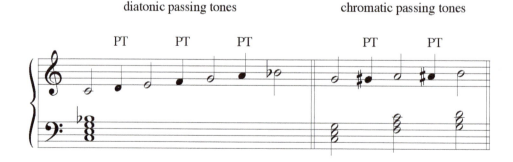

Look again at Example 8-2. Asterisks appear above the passing tones. Some move upward and some move downward. *Passing tones are usually unaccented relative to the following note*. However, they can occur *accented relative to the following note* as well, as in the next example.

EXAMPLE 8-4 Rossini: *Petite Messe Solonelle* ("Kyrie")

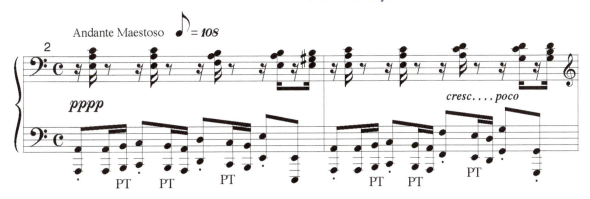

Note:

Six of the nine passing tones in mm. 2–4 are accented.

Neighbor Tones

Look yet again at Example 8-2. The two daggers indicate **neighbor tones** (NT)—pitches that lie a step (or half step) above or below a consonant tone *and its repetition*. Like passing tones, they can be accented or unaccented. Those that lie above the consonant tone are called upper neighbors, and those that lie below it are called lower neighbors.

All the neighbor tones in Example 8-5 are unaccented.

EXAMPLE 8-5

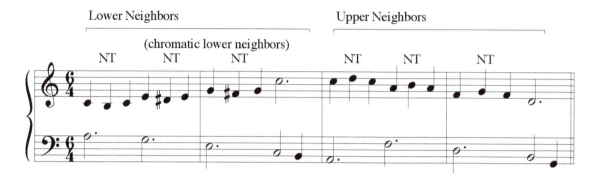

CONCEPT CHECK

Identify the embellishing tones in Example 8-6. The melody begins in the tenor "voice" and moves to the alto. Also identify and describe the sequence.

EXAMPLE 8-6 Mendelssohn: Overture to *The Hebrides*, op. 26 🔊

BACK TO BASICS 8.1

Passing Tones and Neighbor Tones

By inserting steps between chord members, passing tones and neighbor tones create many of the scalar passages in melodies. This is not to suggest that melodies should be viewed merely as filled-in arpeggiations. Although it's often possible to do just that, melody and harmony obey separate laws while influencing and complementing each other. A melody may be, in one sense, "the surface of the harmonic river" beneath it. But it glides over the surface of that river in a way that's both dependent and independent of its flow.

▶ *For assignments on step-step combinations, turn to Workbook Chapter 8, p. 78.*

STEP-LEAP COMBINATIONS

Appoggiatura

This group of embellishing tones includes the appoggiatura and escape tone. The more common of the two is the **appoggiatura** (APP), which is approached by leap and resolved by step. In a true appoggiatura, the dissonance is stronger metrically than its resolution. Unaccented appoggiaturas are called **incomplete neighbors** (IN).

Escape Tone

The **escape tone** (ET) is the opposite of the appoggiatura in that it is approached by step and left by leap (normally in the opposite direction) and is normally unaccented.

EXAMPLE 8-7a Mozart: Piano Sonata, K. 279 (first movement) 🔊

EXAMPLE 8-7b Mozart: Piano Sonata, K. 283 (first movement) 🔊

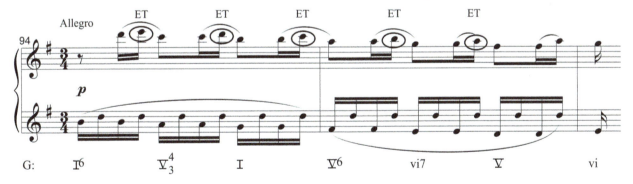

Double Neighbor

Measure 5 of Example 8-7a contains this pitch pattern: C–D–<u>C</u>–B–C. If the underlined C in the middle of the pattern were removed, a step-leap figure called the **double neighbor** (DN) would result: C–D–B–C. This is, essentially, the upper *and* lower neighbor (or vice versa) of a repeated pitch. The repeated pitch most often occurs at the beginning and end of the figure, as in Example 8-8 (G–F♯–A–G), creating the precise interval motion of step-leap-step. Notice that the leap must change direction in order to return to the original pitch by step.

EXAMPLE 8-8 Rodgers and Hammerstein: "Some Enchanted Evening" (From *South Pacific*, act. 1, no. 9) 🔊

(Slowly with expression)

Some en-chant-ed eve-ning   You will see a strang-er

CONCEPT CHECK

Example 8-9 contains double neighbor tones (m. 5) as well as neighbor tones, an incomplete neighbor and an escape tone. Can you locate them?

EXAMPLE 8-9 Chopin: Valse, op. 69, no. 2 🔊

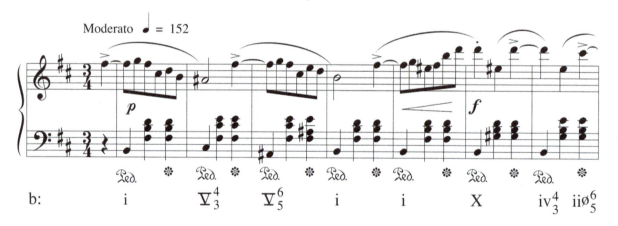

Moderato ♩ = 152

b: i V_3^4 V_5^6 i   i   X iv_3^4 $\text{ii}ø_5^6$

⟳ **BACK TO BASICS 8.2**

Appoggiatura, Escape Tone, and Double Neighbor

▶ *For assignments on step-leap combinations, turn to Workbook Chapter 8, p. 84.*

STEP-REPETITION COMBINATIONS

Anticipation

In this final category are the anticipation, suspension, and retardation. These embellishing tones differ from the others in that they are temporal displacements of *existing* tones rather than *extra* tones added for decoration. In the **anticipation** (ANT), one voice moves by step to its next tone before the other voices move. You might say it "jumps the gun." It gets to the next chord early, usually doing so by step. It forms a dissonance against one or more of the existing voices until they, too, move. At that point, the pitch is repeated but is no longer dissonant.

Example 8-10 shows the most common context for the anticipation—an authentic cadence in which the melody arrives at the final tonic prematurely, ahead of the other voices.

EXAMPLE 8-10 John Francis Wade and J. Reading: "Adeste Fidelis"

Suspension and Retardation

The **suspension** and **retardation** result when a pitch is repeated or sustained prior to its stepwise resolution to a more stable tone. In a suspension, that resolution is downward; in a retardation, it's upward. Suspensions (SUS) and retardations (RET) are opposites of the anticipation in that:

- Their pattern is *rep-step* rather than *step-rep*.

- Their arrival at the next chord tone is *late* rather than early.

- The suspended dissonance is metrically stronger than its resolution.

Example 8-11 illustrates the four common suspensions: 9–8, 7–6, 4–3, and 2–3.

EXAMPLE 8-11 Common Suspensions

Notes:

1. The numbers 9–8, 7–6, and 4–3 show the dissonant interval formed *against the bass* by the suspended tone (either a 9, 7, or 4) and its stepwise resolution to a consonance (8, 6, or 3). These designations are used no matter how many octaves separate the suspended voice and bass.

2. The numbers 2–3 (as in m. 2) show the intervals formed by a suspension *in the bass voice* when the suspended tone resolves stepwise downward, dropping away from the upper voice with which it is initially dissonant (in this case, the tenor). The bass suspension is the only one in which the second number is larger than the first (2–3) because its downward resolution *increases* the distance between it and the upper voice.

3. The characteristic pattern (rep-step) of the suspension is marked. In the first two cases (mm. 1–2 and mm. 2–3), the pitch repetition appears as tied notes. In the last (m. 7), the pitch repetition is present within the half note E♭. The absence of a tie renders this suspension less visually conspicuous. Ties are also absent in **rearticulated suspensions**, as in m. 5, where the repeated E♭ in the alto is sounded again at the point of suspension (beat 2).

Suspensions and retardations comprise three notes: (1) a consonant pitch; (2) its repetition, usually dissonant against a voice that has changed pitch; and (3) its stepwise resolution (downward in a suspension, upward in a retardation) to a pitch once again consonant. These elements are called the **preparation**, **dissonance***, and **resolution**.

EXAMPLE 8-12

p = preparation (as consonance);   **d** = dissonance;   **r** = resolution

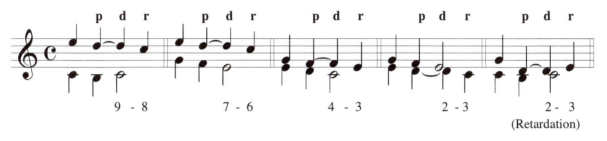

*In certain suspension-like figures such as 6–5, the suspended tone is technically not dissonant.

CONCEPT CHECK

Return to Example 8-11 and label the preparation in each suspension.

Example 8-13 contains 9–8 and 7–6 suspensions and an anticipation.

EXAMPLE 8-13 Beethoven: Piano Sonata, op. 27, no. 2 (second movement)

Other Ways to Designate Suspensions

Certain situations would seem to require a change in the way suspensions are designated. For example, a suspension may occur over a bass and/or harmony *that changes at the point of resolution.*

EXAMPLE 8-14

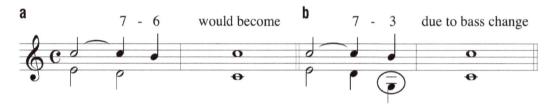

In order to avoid the complication arising from myriad suspension figures such 7–3, 9–6, and so on, it is common to measure both the suspended tone and its resolution against *the point of initial impact.* By this method, the suspension in Example 8-14b remains a 7–6 suspension despite the changing bass.

Another departure would appear to be warranted when the suspension appears *above* a melodic line as in the following arrangement.

EXAMPLE 8-15 Barry deVorzon and Perry Botkin, Jr.: "Nadia's Theme" (From *The Young and the Restless*) 🔊

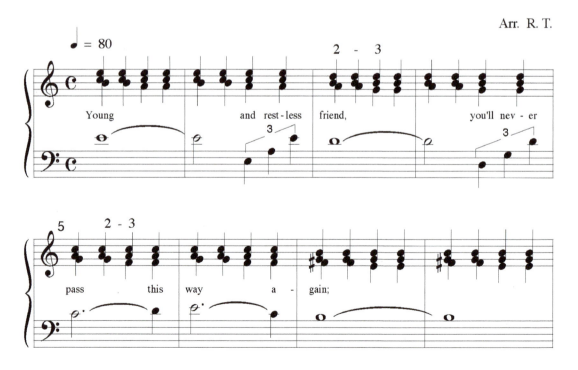

Notes:

1. *Measured against the melodic line beneath them,* these would be called 5–4 suspensions, a designation that ignores the *dissonance melting into consonance* that defines a suspension. Measuring against the accompaniment above them, however, reveals the suspensions to be the familiar 2–3 "bass suspensions" (though not in the bass).

2. When the resolution of one suspension becomes the preparation for the next, as here, the term chain suspension is used. The technique is quite common.

➤ *For assignments on step-repetition combinations, turn to Workbook Chapter 8, p. 87.*

↻ **BACK TO BASICS 8.3**

Anticipation, Suspension, and Retardation

EMBELLISHING TONES AND STYLE

Look again at Example 8-15. The relentless pattern of the accompaniment—dissonance resolving to consonance only to become dissonant again—is an apt metaphor for the television series that featured this song as its theme; it is a restless, endless quest for the resolution of conflict. A distinctive feature of Wagner's music—one that creates the same sense of restlessness in much of it—is the prominence of embellishing dissonance, much of which is longer and stronger than its resolution. In Example 8-16, the first passing tone is three times longer and metrically stronger than its resolution.

EXAMPLE 8-16 Wagner: *Tristan und Isolde* act. 2, scene. 2 🔊

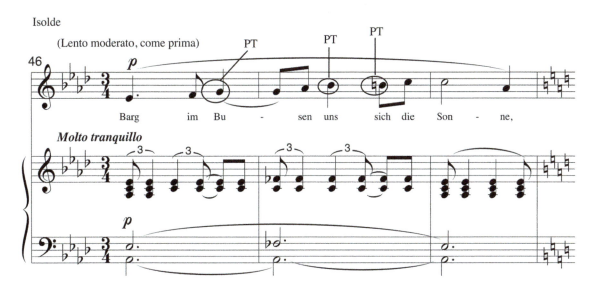

Multiple Embellishing Tones

The second passing tone in Example 8-16 is followed not by its resolution but by *another* passing tone. These are called **consecutive passing tones**.

When simultaneous embellishing tones *of the same type* move *in the same direction in the same rhythm,* they are termed **double passing tones**, **double neighbor tones** (not to be confused with the double neighbor described and shown in Example 8-8), **double suspensions**, and so on. A double retardation at cadences is particularly common in music of the Classical period.

EXAMPLE 8-17 Mozart: Piano Sonata, K. 331 (first movement) 🔊

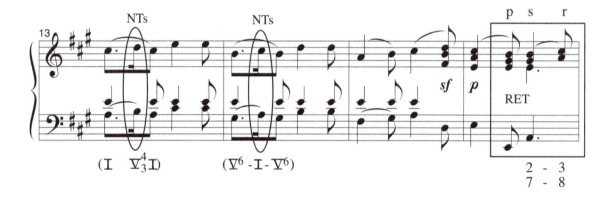

Note:

The double neighbor tones in m. 13 and m. 14 are embellishing tones but not *nonchord tones,* because they actually change the harmony—to a V^7 in m. 13 and to a I in m. 14.

CONCEPT CHECK

Identify the double passing tones and double neighbor tones—upper and lower, accented and unaccented—in Example 8-18.

EXAMPLE 8-18 Tchaikovsky: "Arabian Dance" (From *The Nutcracker*) 🔊

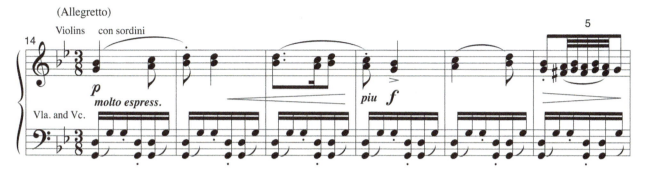

Note:

Some notes have been omitted to simplify performance at the piano.

Western music has witnessed the freedom march of dissonance. By the late Baroque era, all the standard embellishing tones were in place. Moreover, they were "kept in their place," so to speak. In Bach's harmonic garden, embellishing tones form tiny splashes of dissonant color, unaccented and nestled comfortably amid chord tones. In Wagner's (see Example 8-16) they are more prominent—larger blooms planted on downbeats where they command greater attention.

EXAMPLE 8-19 J. S. Bach: "Herz und Mund und Tat und Leben" (Chorale from *Cantata* 147) 🔊

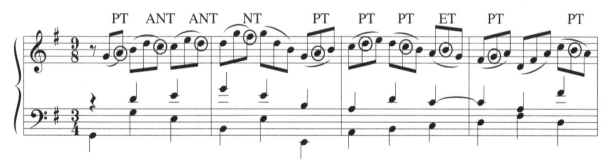

Note:

A line has been omitted to simplify performance at the piano.

Embellishing Tones in Jazz

Embellishing tones are just as common in today's popular and jazz styles as in concert music of the past. The passing tone remains the most common, while retardations and escape tones are perhaps used more liberally. The suspension occurs more often as an inner-voice embellishment.

The bigger, more complex harmonies of jazz blur the distinction between true nonchord tones and chord members, as Example 8-20a illustrates. Even so, the embellishing tones retain their characteristic shapes and rhythmic patterns.

EXAMPLE 8-20a Bill Evans: "Turn Out the Stars" (Transcribed from *Bill Evans at Town Hall* Verve 6-8683)

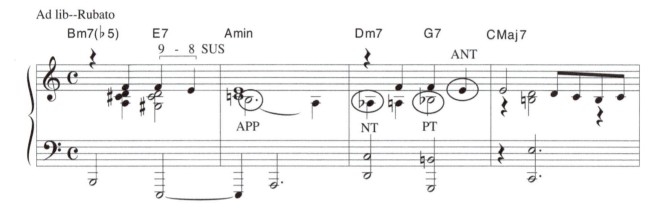

How many embellishing tones in Example 8-20b do you recognize by their shape alone?

EXAMPLE 8-20b Leslie Bricusse and Anthony Newly: "Pure Imagination" (from *Willie Wonka and the Chocolate Factory*)

Note:

In Example 8-20a, only the basic lead-sheet symbols—those likely to appear in fake books (now more accurately called "real books")—are given. The A♭ in m. 3 can be viewed either as a chromatic neighbor tone or as a member of a D∅7 chord. The B♭ that follows it is a chromatic passing tone. The passing tone and neighbor tone in m. 4 are members of the extended chord but still act as embellishing tones to C (the chord root).

Embellishing Tones as Motives

Often a composition, be it Classical, popular, or jazz, will use a nonchord tone in a motivic way. For instance, Example 8-20b is infused with the upper-neighbor figure first seen in m. 17. (Again, the figure can sometimes be viewed as part of the extended chord.)

In the music of Brahms, looking for motivic relationships is like fishing a well-stocked stream. Example 8-21 shows the neighbor-tone motive that dominates the entire movement.

EXAMPLE 8-21 Brahms: Symphony, no. 2, op. 73 (first movement) 🔊

Notes:

1. Double passing tones (mm. 14 and 15), double neighbor tones (m. 12), and double appoggiaturas abound in Brahms' music, in part because of his fondness for doubling melodic lines in sixths or thirds.

2. The large bracket over mm. 7–9 shows Brahms using the neighbor-note motive on a larger scale (D–E–D).

Example 8-21 also illustrates the **pedal point**, a pitch that's sustained while its harmonic environment changes. The pedal point is at times a member of the changing harmonies and at other times dissonant with them. Although introduced with embellishing tones, the pedal point often is arguably the most important pitch in the texture, usually sustaining either a tonic or dominant harmony underneath chords formed by moving voices that are the true embellishments.

In Example 8-21, pedal points occur in the lowest register in mm. 2–4 (A), 6–8 (D), 10–12 (E), and 14–17 (A).

The pedal point derives its name from the sustained pedal pitches played by Baroque organists in toccatas, preludes, and the like. The name notwithstanding, pedal points do occasionally appear in the middle and even upper reaches of the musical texture.

Example 8-22 illustrates a pedal point in a more recent composition:

EXAMPLE 8-22 Eddie Van Halen: "Jump"

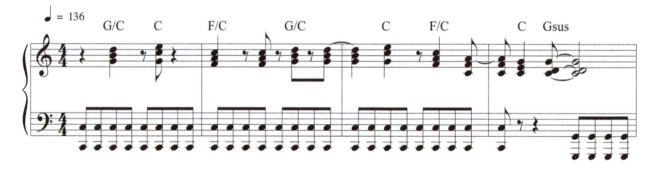

The Embellishing Chord Tone

Although embellishing tones have been presented here in a harmonic context, they should not be regarded solely as nonchord tones that must resolve to a chord tone. In what might seem a harmonic paradox, a chord tone can embellish a nonchord tone.

EXAMPLE 8-23

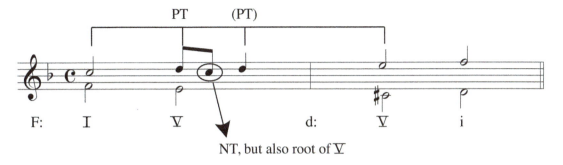

Note:

The passing tone D is itself embellished by its consonant "lower neighbor," C. Although C is the chord root, it's rhythmically subordinate to the passing D.

In the 7–6 suspensions of Example 8-23, the dissonances on the first beat of mm. 2, 3, and 4 are embellished by consonant lower neighbors that are members of the harmony.

EXAMPLE 8-24 Debussy: "Clair de Lune" (from *Suite Bergamasque*) 🔊

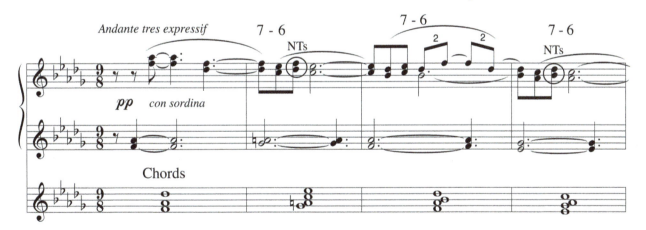

⊕ CODA

> Embellishing tones go a long way toward dressing up a melodic line. They also account for differences in musical styles. We'll have much more to do with them—when part writing and when composing melodies.

SUMMARY OF EMBELLISHING TONES

		Approach	Resolution	Direction
Step-Step Combinations:				
Passing tone	(PT)	S	S	Same
Neighbor tone	(NT)	S	S	Reverses
Step-Leap Combinations:				
Changing tone	(CT)	S L	S	Reverses
Appoggiatura	(APP)	$\overset{>}{L}$	S	Reverses
Escape tone	(ET)	S	$\overset{>}{L}$	Reverses
Step-Rep Combinations:				
Anticipation	(ANT)	S	R	↑ or ↓
Suspension	(SUS)	R	S	Resolves ↓
Retardation	(RET)	R	S	Resolves ↑

S = step; L = leap; R = repetition; > = metric accent

▶ *For assignments on embellishing tones and style, turn to Workbook Chapter 8, p. 92.*

DO YOU KNOW THESE TERMS?

- alto
- anticipation
- appoggiatura
- bass
- double neighbor

- embellishing tone
- escape tone
- neighbor tone
- nonchord tone
- passing tone

- pedal point
- retardation
- soprano
- suspension
- tenor

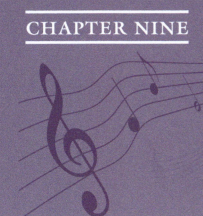

CHAPTER NINE

Melodic Form

KEY CONCEPTS IN THIS CHAPTER

- Phrases and Phrase Relationships

- Periods and Phrase Groups

- Cadential Elision

- Phrase Extension

THE PHRASE

You probably know one when you hear it. You've no doubt played or sung enough of them. How many phrases do you hear in Example 9-1, and where do they begin and end? How do you know?

EXAMPLE 9-1 Beethoven: Symphony, no. 9, op. 125 (fourth movement)

What Is a Phrase?

You probably identified the two four-bar phrases with little effort. However, a minor irony in music and life is that the most fundamental concepts can be surprisingly difficult to define. What is existence? What is a phrase? Many philosophers have weighed in on the first question. Many composers and theorists have weighed in on the second. Compare your definition of a phrase to theirs. A **phrase**:

"... is the portion of music that must be performed, so to speak, without letting go or, figuratively, in a single breath."[1]

"... is the smallest structural unit that terminates with a cadence ..."[2]

"... may be compared to the clause, which, whether or not it is complete enough to warrant a period at its close, contains at least a subject and predicate."[3]

"... is the shortest *passage of music* which, having reached a point of *relative repose*, has expressed a *more or less complete* musical thought."[4]

The last of these definitions is the one we'll adopt. However, did the hazy terminology (italicized) bother you? How long is a "more or less complete musical thought?" And just what is "a point of relative repose?"

Despite their differences, all these definitions suggest that a phrase is longer than a motive and that it reaches a cadence. Many theorists would contend that a phrase also involves harmonic motion. But this last stipulation would eliminate, for example, the bugle call that begins Chapter 8 (Example 8-1), since it's nothing but an arpeggiation of an F major triad. Yet if not some number of phrases, then what is it?

---

1 Sessions, *The Musical Experience of Composer, Performer, and Listener* (Princeton: Princeton University Press, 1950), p. 13.

2 Spencer and Temko, *A Practical Approach to the Study of Form in Music* (Englewood Cliffs, New Jersey: Prentice Hall, 1988), p. 34.

3 Berry, *Form in Music* (Englewood Cliffs, New Jersey: Prentice Hall, 1986), p. 11.

4 Green, *Form in Tonal Music* (New York: Holt, Rinehart and Winston, 1979), p. 7.

The final movement of Brahms' first symphony features a melody with phrase structure identical to that in the final movement of Beethoven's last symphony. Compare Example 9-2 with Example 9-1.

EXAMPLE 9-2 Brahms: Symphony no. 1 (fourth movement)

Notes:

1. Each four-measure phrase states a more or less complete musical idea.

2. The first phrase ends with a half cadence (m. 4), the second with an authentic cadence (m. 8).

3. Harmonic activity occurs within each phrase.

Phrase Length

The repertory is brimming with phrases structured identically to these. However, not all are as clear about their length. In this regard, both meter and tempo must be considered. The next two passages comprise 16 beats of music. However, Mozart's unfolds in a scant ten seconds, whereas Chopin's can take 25 or so. Moreover, both passages contain multiple pauses that might be heard as cadences. Can each be regarded as a single phrase?

EXAMPLE 9-3a Mozart: *Eine kleine Nachtmusik*, K. 525 (first movement)

EXAMPLE 9-3b Chopin: Prelude, op. 28, no. 20

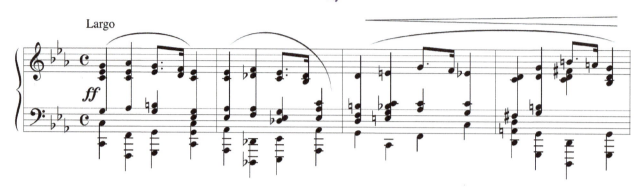

In fact, musicians will occasionally disagree on phrase lengths, and often, multiple views are supportable. Example 9-3b might be heard either as two-measure phrases or as a four-measure phrase.

Phrases and Cadences

The second matter—"relative repose"—can be problematic as well. The strongest cadences are melodic, harmonic, and rhythmic. In Example 9-2, the second phrase (mm. 4–8) ends melodically on the tonic, it is supported by a tonic harmony, and the rhythmic motion ceases. This creates a clear sense of repose.

Not all phrases end so definitively. In Example 9-4, the first phrase careens nonstop right through the dominant in m. 4 to begin anew in m. 5.

EXAMPLE 9-4 J. S. Bach: "Herz und Mund und Tat und Leben" (Chorale from *Cantata* 147)

The four-measure phrase length is very common. But other lengths are by no means rare. And how do we distinguish two four-bar phrases from a single eight-bar phrase (as we must in Example 9-4)?

Example 9-5, like Example 9-4, moves from I to vi and then to a pre-dominant *en route* to a V^7. The melody barges headlong through this dominant (m. 8) to begin a partial restatement. Consider, too, the role played by the text. Measure 8 is mid-sentence ("I've hungered for your . . .")—it's not even the end of a grammatical unit. The music mirrors the rhythmic structure of the text, pausing briefly after each of its commas and coming to a more prolonged repose only at the sentence's end. This passage is best analyzed as a single phrase.

EXAMPLE 9-5 Hy Zaret and Alex North: "Unchained Melody"

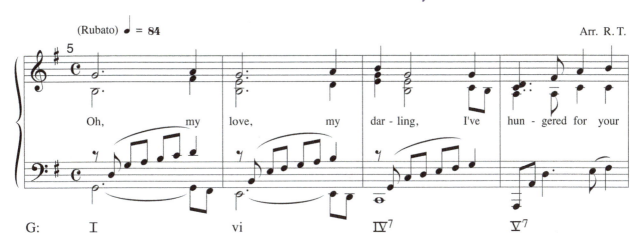

Is Example 9-6 a single 8-measure phrase or two 4-meausre phrases?

EXAMPLE 9-6 Mozart: Piano Sonata, K. 283 (first movement) 🔊

The Musical Sentence

Either analysis is reasonable. Both 4-measure units adhere to the definition of a phrase. The question arises often with structures such as this, called **musical sentences**. A musical sentence is a type of phrase or larger unit common in the Classical period that is structured in proportions of 1 + 1 + 2 (or 2 + 2 + 4), in which the first element is repeated, then followed by an expansion of the idea leading to a cadence. We'll later find that this same structure can characterize passages longer than a phrase as well.

Phrase Relationships

Recall that the composer is confronted at any moment with only three choices—to repeat, vary, or create anew. Because these choices pertain to melody as well as every other musical element, two phrases can be related in one of these three ways only, the relationships symbolized thus:

Repetition: **a a** Octave transposition qualifies as exact repetition, but other changes, no matter how slight, do not.

Varied repetition: **a a′** The second phrase is a repetition of the first with but minor modifications. Rhythmic changes, melodic ornamentation (i.e., the addition of passing tones, suspensions, and so on), sequential repetition, and even some changes in harmony qualify as minor changes.

Different phrases: **a b** The phrases are essentially different, melodically, harmonically, and rhythmically.

In Example 9-4, Bach chose to repeat mm. 1 and 2 of the first phrase but change the last two bars, *including the cadence.* The second phrase is similar enough to the first to be considered a variation of it, and the two would be symbolized a a′.

Consider these two sentences:

- "Standing under the incandescent sun and electric blue sky, Amy felt her mood lighten."

- "Standing under the incandescent sun and electric blue sky, Amy felt her spirit soar."

The second sentence is a variation of the first, beginning the same way but ending more affirmatively—a a′—like Bach's melody.

CONCEPT CHECK

Are the phrases of Example 9-7 two measures or four measures long? Is either analysis reasonable or is one to be preferred over the other? Why? Symbolize the phrase relationships.

EXAMPLE 9-7 Augustus M. Toplady and Thomas Hastings: "Rock of Ages"

continued

EXAMPLE 9-7 *continued*

thee;   Let   the   wa - ter and the   blood,   From thy   wound - ed side that

flowed, Be   of   sin, the   per - fect   cure;   Save me,   Lord,   and make me   pure.

➤ *For assignments on phrases, turn to Workbook Chapter 9, assignments 1A–1C.*

↻ **BACK TO BASICS 9.1**

Phrase and Period Relationships

COMBINING AND EXTENDING PHRASES

The Period

When the second of two phrases ends more conclusively than the first, the phrases usually form a **period**. Like a question followed by an answer, the phrases of a period depend on each other for their complete meaning. The terms **antecedent** and **consequent** refer to the component phrases. Think of the inconclusive cadence that punctuates the **antecedent** as a question mark or a comma.

EXAMPLE 9-8 Beethoven: Symphony, no. 9 (fourth movement)

ends on $\hat{2}$

ends on $\hat{1}$

Periods are described as parallel (a a′) or contrasting (a b). A period can never be expressed as "a–a" because this symbology is reserved for phrases that are identical. In such cases, the second phrase cannot end more conclusively than the first, so the period's defining feature is absent.

Parallel Period

Example 9-8 is a **parallel period** (a a′)—a period because the consequent ends more conclusively than the antecedent, and parallel because the two phrases begin the same way (they "parallel" each other in their construction). Example 9-4 would be termed a parallel period (a a′) for the same reasons, as would the next melody.

EXAMPLE 9-9 Mozart: Piano Sonata, K. 311 (second movement) 🔊

Contrasting Period

In a **contrasting period**, the two phrases may share some motivic material but still differ enough to be designated a b.

EXAMPLE 9-10a Kuhlah: Sonatina, op. 55, no. 4 (Andante) 🔊

EXAMPLE 9-10b Nikolai Rimsky-Korsakov: *Scheherazade* (third movement) 🔊

REVIEW AND REINFORCEMENT

Is either passage in Example 9-10 a musical sentence?

Phrase Group

If we judge the phrases of Example 9-7 to be four-measures long (the likely analysis), then its three phrases form neither a period nor a repeated phrase but a **phrase group** (a b a). In a phrase group, two or more phrases that clearly belong together end *with equally conclusive cadences* and so do not display the antecedent-consequent relationship that defines a period.

Example 9-11 is a phrase group. Neither phrase ends conclusively. The lack of a conclusive cadence enhances the music's floating, ethereal effect.

EXAMPLE 9-11 Debussy: "Clair de Lune" (From *Suite Bergamasque*) 🔊

CONCEPT CHECK

Symbolize the phrase relationships in Example 9-11. If the cadence structure doesn't bind these phrases together, what does?

Although two-phrase periods are the most common, three-phrase periods exist. Example 9-12 is a contrasting period (contrasting because at least one of the phrases differs, and a period because the final phrase completes the harmonic motion begun by the preceding two) whose phrases are symbolized a a′ b:

EXAMPLE 9-12 Zaret and North: "Unchained Melody"

Example 9-13 shows another three-phrase period. The third phrase is much like the second, but with a more conclusive cadence—b′.

EXAMPLE 9-13 Chopin: Mazurka, op. 7, no. 1

The phrase relationships just described are illustrated in Example 9-14. Note that *both* phrases in a, b, and c end on the tonic and for this reason do not form periods.

EXAMPLE 9-14a Repeated Phrase (a a)

EXAMPLE 9-14b Varied Repetition (a a′)

EXAMPLE 9-14c Similar or Contrasting Phrases (a b)

EXAMPLE 9-14d Parallel Period (a a′)

EXAMPLE 9-14e Parallel Period (a a′)

EXAMPLE 9-14f Contrasting Period (a b)

Note:

Both d and e are symbolized a a′ because of their "parallel" construction. The second phrase of d begins as a *repetition* of the first phrase, and the second phrase of e begins as a *sequence* of the first phrase. (Recall that sequences are a form of varied repetition).

Double Period

A still larger melodic unit is the **double period**. A double period comprises *two pairs of phrases*, an antecedent pair and a consequent pair. The consequent pair contains the more conclusive cadence, making the double period a *single unit*:

As shown, the two phrase pairs often share the same first phrase. This is then called a **parallel double period**.

Double periods are shown in Example 9-15.

EXAMPLE 9-15a Beethoven: Piano Sonata, op. 26 (first movement) 🔊)))

EXAMPLE 9-15b Chopin: Fantaisie-Impromptu, op. 66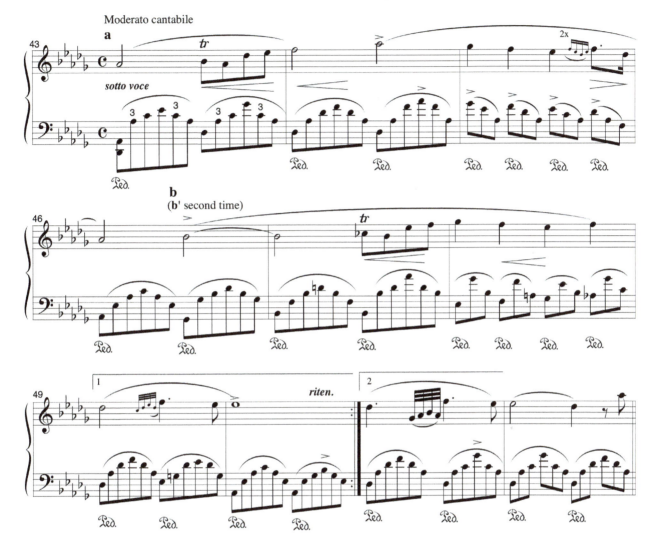

Notes:

1. Beethoven's, op. 26 theme is a parallel double period. Although the four-measure phrases within each pair contrast with each other, the two *pairs* are parallel in construction.

2. Chopin's, op. 66 is also a parallel double period.

3. In both examples, the final phrase ends more conclusively than all the others. Because it is a varied repetition of the second phrase (b), it is symbolized b′.

The Beethoven (a b a′ b′) and Chopin (a b a b′) are symbolized in a way that reflects the parallel beginnings of the phrase pairs.

In Example 9-16, the consequent phrase pair begins *unlike* the antecedent pair (a a′ b c), and therefore does not parallel it. Phrases b and c are separated by a melodic cadence weakly supported by a IV^7 (almost a "non-cadence"). These eight measures might alternatively be viewed as a single phrase. In any event, they provide the "answer" to the first eight measures, completing the harmonic motion to the tonic, and the unit is therefore a period. The term contrasting double period might be applied. Melodic units of this type are rather uncommon.

EXAMPLE 9-16 Gerry Goffin and Carole King: "Will You Love Me Tomorrow?"

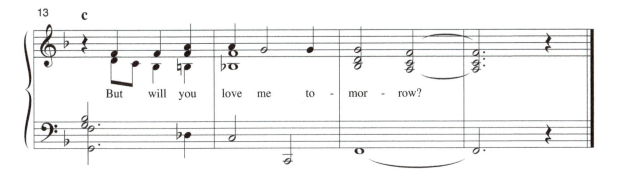

But will you love me to - mor - row?

Notes:

1. Although the second phrase ends differently than the first, both cadences are the same type (half cadences). The second phrase is a variation of the first, symbolized a′.

2. Example 9-16i exhibits the structure of a musical sentence on a larger scale: a (= 4mm.) + a′ (= 4mm.) + bc (= 8mm.)

Combining phrases into periods enhances musical flow. A song written entirely in isolated, independent phrases would be choppy. It would be unsatisfying. It would be like a novella written entirely in simple declarative sentences. *It would be like this paragraph.*

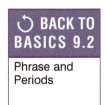

↻ **BACK TO BASICS 9.2**
Phrase and Periods

Cadential Elision

Another technique for creating musical flow is **cadential elision**—overlapping the end of one phrase with the beginning of the next. The technique also mitigates the overly regular effect of an unbroken string of four-measure phrases.

Try this: In Example 9-17, insert this measure between m. 17 and m. 18, and observe the effect.

EXAMPLE 9-17 Mozart: Piano Sonata, K. 309 (first movement) 🔊))

The cadence you inserted completes the four-measure antecedent phrase. But it gives the passage a "blockier," repetitive sound and has a braking effect on the music. By eliding the cadence at m. 18 and directly launching a repetition of the phrase, Mozart gains momentum, mitigates the effect of the repetition, and enhances the musical flow. Film-editing techniques achieve a similar result when one image fades into the next or when the dialogue of the coming scene is heard before the scene itself appears.

Cadential Extension

Composers of concert music are careful to vary phrase lengths. One way is through extension. Although a phrase can be extended at any point in its course, the most common method is the **cadential extension**. This might be nothing more than a repeated cadence, or it might be something more.

EXAMPLE 9-18a Mozart: "Durch Zärlichkeit und Schmeicheln" (no. 8 from *Die Entfürhrung aus dem Serail*)

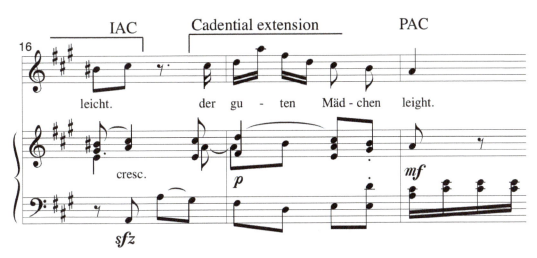

EXAMPLE 9-18b Haydn: Piano Sonata, H. XVI: 34 (first movement) 🔊

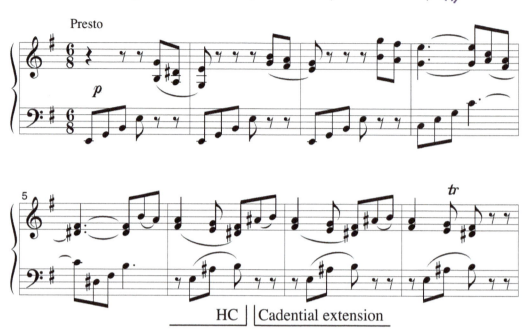

HC | Cadential extension

Notes:

1. a extends an authentic cadence. Notice that the cadence at m. 16 is imperfect—the melody ends not on the tonic but on 3 (C♯). The extension ends on the more conclusive perfect authentic cadence.

2. b extends a half cadence.

Examples 9-18 a and b are **postcadential** extensions—that is, they *follow* the cadence. Extensions can be **precadential** as well, prolonging the *approach* to the cadence chord. They extend the cadence by *delaying* its arrival rather than *prolonging* it. Precadential passages are less obvious than postcadential. They often involve a motive that is repeated—either exactly or sequentially—just prior to the cadence. Example 9-19 contains both types of phrase extension. Here's the difference:

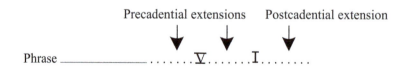

EXAMPLE 9-19 Alan and Marilyn Bergman and Dave Grusin: "It Might Be You" (Theme Song from *Tootsie*)

Popular music tends to be less varied than concert music in its phrasing. This is partly because popular songs are relatively short and strongly tied to dance, which fosters regular phrase lengths. Yet, there are exceptions. Leonard Bernstein's music treads the line between popular and concert music with particular skill and balance. Consider Example 9-20.

EXAMPLE 9-20 Stephen Sondheim and Leonard Bernstein: "Maria" (From *West Side Story*)

REVIEW AND REINFORCEMENT_____

Symbolize the phrases in Example 9-20. What is the prevailing phrase length?

▶ *For assignments on combining and extending phrases, turn to Workbook Chapter 9, assignments 2A–2G.*

⊕ CODA

Just how long is "a more or less complete musical thought?" How much similarity between two phrases warrants the analysis a a' *versus* a b? Can one perfect authentic cadence be more conclusive than another? Phrase analysis is tinted with shades of gray.

Yet, phrasing accounts for important similarities and differences among composers. Chopin wrote some of the most balanced, symmetrical phrasing in the repertoire. Haydn, on the other hand, wrote some highly irregular-length phrases. Both Bach and Wagner, for all their style differences, wrote long, winding phrases whose cadences overlap to form almost nonstop melodies. Schubert's songs are full of short postcadential extensions (sometimes called "cadential echoes"). At the other extreme, Mozart's piano concertos are full of phrases that, like the cab of an eighteen-wheeler, trailer an extension two or three times their length. Rock and blues-based songs contain phrases whose hypermetrical structure is quite different from those in art song.

The study of phrasing can reveal many truths about a composer or a style. This alone justifies the time spent on the study.

DO YOU KNOW THESE TERMS?

- antecedent
- cadential elision
- cadential extension
- consequent
- contrasting period
- double period
- musical sentence
- parallel period
- period
- phrase
- phrase group
- postcadential
- precadential

Voice
Leading

PART FOUR

When interesting melodies combine to form attractively voiced harmonies that flow creatively and logically, we say the result is "musical." The technique that makes it happen is called **voice leading**, because each voice in the texture is led from one pitch to the next in a way that forms a pleasing melodic line while producing in consort with the other voices a pleasing succession of harmonies. Since around 1650, composers have observed principles of voice leading that seek to balance two forces, one horizontal (the melodic force) and the other vertical (the harmonic force). These forces, music's yin and yang, make opposing demands, and balancing those demands has never been easy. But voice-leading principles endure for a simple reason: They produce "musical" results. In this respect, they are as vital and relevant to the study of music today as they were 200 years ago. Chapter 10 addresses the melodic and harmonic concerns involved in composing one voice against another (two-part textures). Chapter 11 is an overview of voice-leading principles in four-voice textures. Chapters 12 through 14 then isolate specific aspects and examine their application in various styles. In the process a corpus of four-part music by J. S. Bach is introduced. The timelessness and relevance of this repertoire is underscored by comparison with examples of present-day practice.

CHAPTER TEN

Melodic Principles of Part Writing

The Outer-Voice Framework

Counterpoint and its more general synonym **polyphony** describe the simultaneous sounding of two or more melodic lines displaying independent rhythms and contours. The lines must complement one another in such a way that they form a *coherent combination*. (Two *different* compositions heard simultaneously constitute counterpoint only in the most liberal sense.) A convincing counterpoint between melody and bass provides a musically sound framework that facilitates writing inner voices. Since the eighteenth century, counterpoint has been fashioned in such a way that it clearly reflects the functional harmonies that undergird it.

MELODIC PRINCIPLES

Counterpoint is only as strong as the individual melodic lines that compose it. The principles that follow apply to every voice in the texture. Adhering to them produces melodic lines that are likely to be musical and singable.

1. Range: *Keep each voice in its proper range.*

EXAMPLE 10-1

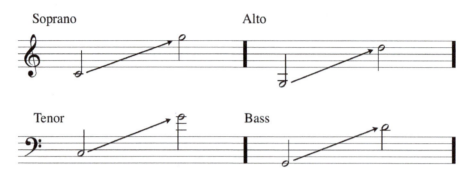

Note:

The ranges shown are approximate. The pitch ranges of the tenor and bass replicate the ranges of the soprano and alto an octave lower.

---

2. Motion: *Move each voice primarily by stepwise motion.*

3. Chromatic Intervals: *Avoid writing the augmented second formed by $\hat{6}$ and $\hat{7}$ of the harmonic minor scale in melodic passages.*

4. Leaps: *Use leaps larger than a fifth sparingly. Follow all leaps with stepwise motion—in the opposite direction when possible (as in an apoggiatura)—or a pitch repetition.* Avoid successive leaps in the same direction except when those pitches arpeggiate the underlying harmony. (The bass has more latitude here because it functions both as a melodic voice and a harmonic foundation.)

5. Sensitive Tones: *Resolve **sensitive tones**.* Also called "tendency tones," these tones are inclined to behave in a certain manner. They include the leading tone—resolve it upward by half step; chord sevenths—resolve them stepwise downward; $\hat{6}$ and $\hat{7}$ in minor keys, which form a sensitive duo—raise them to move upward to the tonic and lower them to move downward to the dominant; and altered tones—resolve them by half step *in the direction of the chromatic inflection* (raised pitches go up, lowered pitches go down).

EXAMPLE 10-2 F Minor

Notes:

a = leading tone (resolves upward)

b = chromatically raised pitch (resolves upward)

c = $\hat{6}$ and $\hat{7}$ (raised in ascent, lowered in descent)

6. Counterpoint: *Create strong counterpoint between the outer voices.* This can be accomplished by using contrary and oblique motion between voices where possible. Too much parallel motion—particularly intervals of the same type (thirds in succession, for example)—tends to undermine counterpoint by creating the impression of a single harmonized line.

EXAMPLE 10-3 Types of Motion Between Voices

a = **similar motion**: voices move in the same direction but by different intervals

b = **parallel motion**: voices move in the same direction by the *same* interval (avoid too much of this)

c = **contrary motion**: voices move in opposite directions (favor this)

d = **oblique motion**: one voice remains stationary while the other voice moves toward or away from it

Note:

In parallel motion, the numerical value of the interval between the two voices is maintained, although its *quality* may change. That is, a major third A/F moving to a minor third Bb/G is considered parallel motion.

CONCEPT CHECK

Identify additional examples of parallel, similar, contrary, and oblique motion in Example 10-3.

CREATING AN OUTER-VOICE FRAMEWORK

1:1 Counterpoint

The simplest way to create a soprano-bass counterpoint is to start with a single note in one voice against a single note in the other. This is called **note-against-note counterpoint**, or 1:1 species. The soprano's traditional role is the melody, and the bass performs the dual role of secondary melody and functional harmonic support. We'll begin with an existing melody and its harmonic underpinning.

EXAMPLE 10-4 Jean Paul Égide Martini: "Plaisir d'Amour" (adapted)

If the melody sounds familiar, it may be because this eighteenth-century French love song served as the basis for the popular song, "Can't Help Falling in Love with You." We'll first convert the Roman numeral symbols into a bass line.

EXAMPLE 10-5 Connecting Arrows Show Contrary Motion

Connection arrows show contrary motion

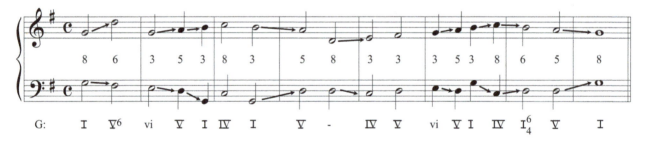

Notes:

1. Every note of the melody is supported by a single note in the bass.

2. The bass, a realization of the given chord symbols, supplies the root of each harmony in all but two cases (m. 1 and m. 7).

3. Together, the two voices sound *only consonances* (shown between the staves). This is typical in 1:1 counterpoint.

4. Despite the bass's confinement mostly to chord roots, it has been disposed in a way that maximizes contrary motion against the melody (shown by the arrows).

Example 10-5 is **contrapuntal** in that the soprano and bass display independent contours. But if you play or sing only the bass, you'll be struck by its *melodic* shortcomings—too many leaps, too many Ds, too repetitive sounding, and it combines with the melody to produce a large number of hollow-sounding perfect consonances. These problems are alleviated in Example 10-6 by the circled changes in the bass.

EXAMPLE 10-6

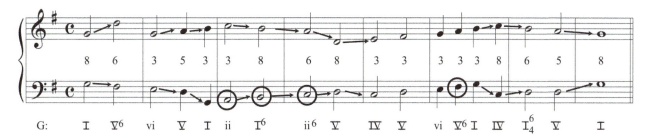

Notes:

1. Changes have been made in mm. 3, 4, and 6. The use of inversions and the minor changes in harmony result in a more stepwise bass.

2. The number of perfect consonances has been reduced from 9 to 7, and the number of imperfect consonances has been correspondingly increased, resulting in a fuller-sounding counterpoint.

3. Contrary motion still outnumbers any other single motion (9 occurrences).

Despite the solution of previous contrapuntal problems, there's still room for improvement. The string of successive thirds in mm. 5 and 6 robs the top line of its melodic independence. Let's make one more attempt to enhance the counterpoint.

EXAMPLE 10-7

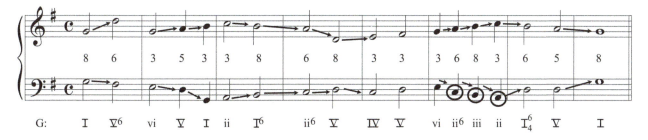

Note:

The changes in m. 6 (circled) reduce the number of consecutive thirds to three, a generally practiced limit for thirds or sixths in succession. A further benefit is the additional contrary motion, especially desirable in approaching the cadence.

REVIEW AND REINFORCEMENT

Tabulate the number of oblique, similar, and parallel motions in Example 10-7.

Although you'll observe parallel motion in the foregoing and following examples—even successive parallels such as the thirds in m. 5–6 of Example 10-7—notice the absence of *perfect consonances of the same type* in succession. **Consecutive (also called parallel) perfect octaves, perfect fifths, perfect fourths, and perfect unisons** have long been avoided in counterpoint for reasons to be discussed in due course. You should start to develop the habit of avoiding them now.

EXAMPLE 10-8

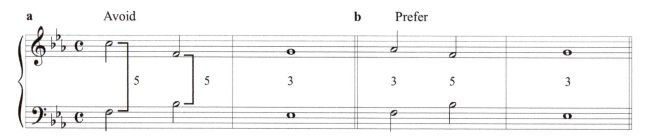

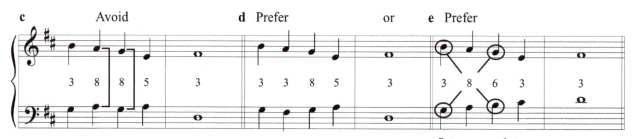

Octave occurs between
voice exchange.

Note:

Eliminating the consecutive octaves in c has produced consecutive thirds instead (d). Consecutive *imperfect* consonances do not carry the restriction of perfect consonances. Another solution is offered (e) by creating a stepwise ascent from G to the tonic D, resulting in a "voice exchange" between the upper and lower voices.

CONCEPT CHECK

Complete the exercises that follow. Use only consonances. Strive for as much contrary motion between the voices as possible. When adding the bass, use inversion to create more stepwise motion. When adding the soprano, try to adhere to the melodic principles presented earlier in this chapter. Try to avoid consecutive fifths, octaves, or unisons.

a

1. Supply the bass using all chord roots, and add Roman numeral symbols.

EXAMPLE 10-9a

2. Now identify with a check mark which of the following problems are present in this bass line of chord roots:

    a. ___   contains successive leaps in the same direction

    b. ___   is too disjunct

    c. ___   contains an unresolved leading tone

    d. ___   produces with the soprano more perfect than imperfect consonances

    e. ___   produces with the soprano parallel fifths or octaves

    f. ___   moves in similar and parallel motion more often than in contrary and oblique motion

    g. ___   forms dissonances as well as consonances against the soprano.

3. On this system, rewrite the bass, using inversions to create an entirely stepwise line.

EXAMPLE 10-9b

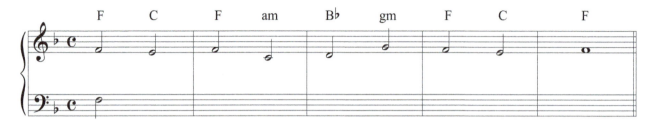

4.   Which of the problems you identified have now been resolved?

b

Add a soprano that (1) moves in contrary or oblique motion against the bass as often as possible while (2) achieving a balance of conjunct and disjunct motion. Take care to avoid consecutive perfect consonances, and write no more than three parallel thirds or sixths in succession.

EXAMPLE 10-9c

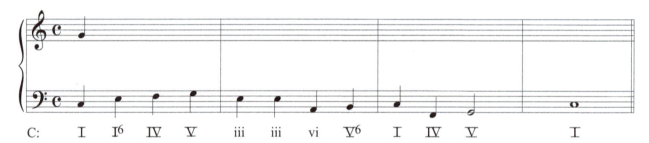

c

Compose a soprano and bass over the given harmonic framework. Use as much contrary and oblique motion as possible, balance conjunct and disjunct motion, and use as many imperfect consonances as possible for a full sound. Again, take care to avoid consecutive perfect consonances.

EXAMPLE 10-9d

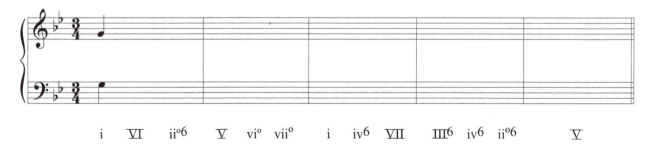

2:1 Counterpoint

1:1 species counterpoint lacks rhythmic independence. This is not necessarily a bad thing. In fact, hymns, anthems, folk music, and the like involve mostly this species, as we'll see later. However, counterpoint *for only two voices* demands the rhythmic independence achieved through 2:1 and 3:1 relationships, as we'll also see later. The simplest way to convert 1:1 counterpoint to 2:1 (two note against one) or 3:1 counterpoint is to add passing tones and neighbor tones to one or both voices.

To create a 2:1 relationship, a passing tone can be inserted between two notes a third apart and a neighbor tone can be inserted between a pitch and its repetition:

EXAMPLE 10-10

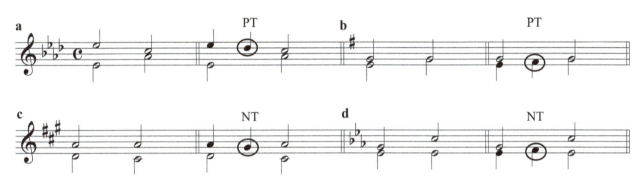

Passing tones and neighbor tones inject another element of interest—dissonance—into the counterpoint. Dissonance and its resolution create a sense of musical "respiration," or tension and relaxation, absent in the note-against-note species. However, it's possible to convert 1:1 to 2:1 counterpoint *without* adding dissonance simply by changing a single chord tone into two chord tones in one voice.

EXAMPLE 10-11

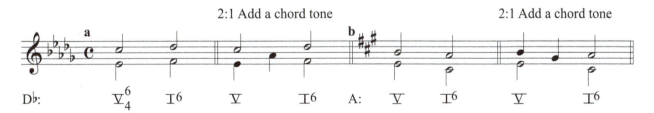

In the following example, the two-voice version of "Plaisir d'amour" from Example 10-7 has been enlivened using just these techniques along with a few modest harmonicchanges.

EXAMPLE 10-12

CONCEPT CHECK

1   Compare Example 10-12 with Example 10-7 and explain each change to the left-
    hand line. Name the chord tones that have been added to create 2:1 relation-
    ships.

2   Convert the following 1:1 counterpoint to 2:1 adding to the soprano or bass as
    needed.

Create 2:1 counterpoint.

EXAMPLE 10-13a

Eb: I   V6   I   I6   IV   V   vi   V   I

Create 2:1 counterpoint.

EXAMPLE 10-13b

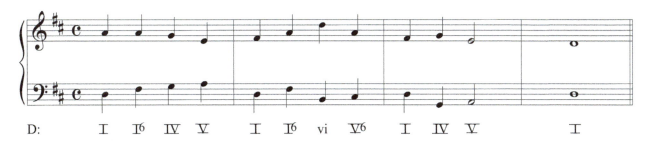

Create 2:1 counterpoint.

EXAMPLE 10-13c

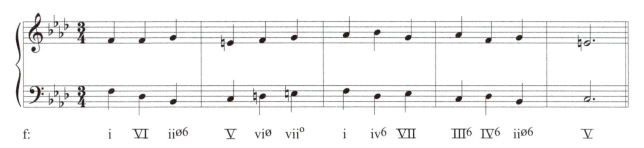

Passing tones, neighbor tones, and chord tones are not the only means of embellishing 1:1 counterpoint. Any and all of the embellishing tones presented in Chapter 8 can be used. In Example 10-14, Bach used escape tones in addition to passing tones and a neighbor tone to create a consistently 2:1 counterpoint.

EXAMPLE 10-14 J. S. Bach: French Suite, no. 2 (Menuett) 🔊

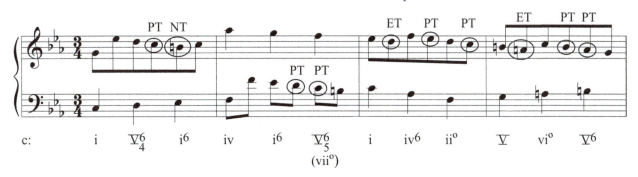

➤ *For drill and assignments, turn to Workbook Chapter 10.*

⊕ CODA

This brief chapter is the spiritual offspring of a method for teaching counterpoint developed in the eighteenth century by Johann Joseph Fux. Fux's time-honored species counterpoint approach has been greatly pared here and modified to conform to eighteenth-century harmonic practice and to provide an introduction targeting more directly the skills required of today's musician. Although only the bass has been subject to embellishment in the chapter's musical examples, the same techniques can be applied to the soprano. The final examples in the chapter involve more elaborate counterpoint than is typical of the outer voices of the four-voice music we'll study next. We'll revisit two-voice counterpoint in greater detail in Chapter 18.

DO YOU KNOW THESE TERMS?

- 2:1 counterpoint
- consecutive fifths
- consecutive octaves
- contrary motion
- counterpoint

- note-against-note
- oblique motion
- outer-voice framework
- parallel motion
- polyphony

- sensitive tones
- similar motion
- voice ranges

CHAPTER ELEVEN

The Melodic Factor in Four-Voice Part Writing

Voicing and Connecting Chords

KEY CONCEPTS IN THIS CHAPTER

- Melodic Principles in Four-Part Writing

- Motion between Voices

- Chord Voicing (Spacing and Doubling)

- Chord Connection Principles

PERSPECTIVE: WHY FOUR PARTS?

The four-voice texture has been around so long that it's considered standard. The bulk of the choral repertory is written for soprano, alto, tenor, and bass (SATB). Over the years, vocal groups in popular styles have favored four-part harmony; examples are the barbershop quartets of the twenties and thirties, the "doo-wop" groups of the fifties and early sixties, high school and college glee clubs, and ensembles such as The Four Seasons, The Beach Boys, and Boyz 2 Men. The legendary Woody Herman saxophone section, The Four Brothers, and vocal groups such as The Four Freshmen and Take Six have applied the four-part tradition in the jazz idiom. The string section of the Classical orchestra was basically a four-part ensemble. And the string quartet arguably has been the most successful of all chamber groups.

Why four parts? It's not hard to explain. Four voices are necessary for the complete sounding of a seventh chord. And simple triads sound best when their roots are reinforced (doubled). The four-voice texture provides fullness without turbidity, permit-ting the melodic motion of the individual voices to be heard clearly. Finally, the soprano, alto, tenor, and bass format conforms to the ranges of the basic male and female voice types.

In much music, the number of musical lines, or "voices," varies. Composers may reinforce a line at the octave, add notes to thicken a chord's texture, and so on. However, we'll start with music for four *fixed* lines, and we'll focus at first on vocal music for these reasons:

- Voice ranges are narrower and thus more manageable than instrumental ranges.

- Timbral contrast is less pronounced.

- Problems of instrumental transposition do not exist.

- Although most musicians tend to imagine a pitch before playing it, singers must then produce that pitch unaided by keys or valves. This requires that extra care be taken with voice leading in vocal music.

REVIEW OF MELODIC PRINCIPLES

The melodic principles cited in Chapter 10 apply equally to all voices in the texture. They are summarized here:

1. Keep each voice in its proper range.

2. Move each voice primarily by stepwise motion.

3. Avoid writing dissonant (augmented or diminished) melodic intervals such as the augmented second formed by $\hat{6}$ and $\hat{7}$ of the harmonic minor scale in melodic passages.

4. Use leaps larger than a fifth sparingly, and follow them when possible with stepwise motion or a pitch repetition.

5. Resolve the sensitive tones.

6. Create good counterpoint between the outer voices.

Most of these principles can be observed in the example that follows.

EXAMPLE 11-1 Stephen Sondheim and Leonard Berstein: "Somewhere" (from *West Side Story*)

Notes:

1. All voices are within their respective ranges. The inner voices, sandwiched between the soprano and bass, necessarily display a more restricted range.

2. Stepwise motion prevails. The largest leaps aside from those in the melody occur in the bass. The leap of a sixth in m. 124 is followed by stepwise motion, as are all the other leaps in the bass.

3. Seventh chords appear in mm. 123–128. In each case, the seventh is resolved stepwise downward.

4. Next to the melody itself, the bass is the voice with the greatest melodic interest. Its balance of conjunct and disjunct motion is achieved through passing tones and inversion.

5. Nearly 80 percent of the motion between the melody and the bass line is contrary or oblique.

➤ *For assignments on melodic principles, turn to Workbook Chapter 10.*

VOICING CHORDS

As important to effective part writing as the melodic principles just presented is the voicing of harmonies. Voicing involves spacing, doubling, and chord position.

Spacing

The better the blend, the better. This aphorism has held for centuries, and it translates into a guideline:

> Use **homogeneous** (more or less equidistant) spacing between the upper voices by keeping adjacent pairs (soprano and alto, alto and tenor) within an octave of one another.

Greater distance is acceptable—in fact, often desirable—between the tenor and bass. One reason is that the bass needs the freedom to move about to fulfill its harmonic role in the most melodic way. Another is that a wider interval between the bass and tenor generally produces less conflict among the overtones of those voices than do smaller intervals.

EXAMPLE 11-2

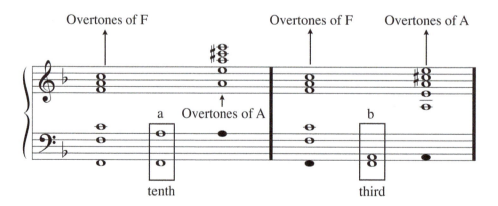

Notes:

1. Interval a: The overtones of A produce no conflicts with the first six overtones of F.

2. Interval b: The second and fourth overtones of A are dissonant against the third and fifth overtones of F.

Chords spaced with a wider interval on the bottom tend to sound "cleaner"—more transparent—than those with a smaller interval on the bottom. The lower the pitches involved, the more pronounced the "muddiness" becomes. Thus, a *very conservative* (and poetic) corollary to the spacing guideline might be:

When the bass is below C³, place the tenor above E³.

EXAMPLE 11-3

a recommended

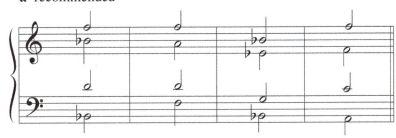

b not recommended

Notes:

1. In a, spacing is more or less equal among the upper three voices.

2. In b, the spacing is less uniform. In the first three chords, the distance between the alto and tenor is greater than an octave. In the first chord, moreover, the small interval between the tenor and bass produces a thick sound. In the fourth chord, the distance between the alto and soprano is greater than an octave.

▶ *Assignment 1B in Workbook Chapter 11 can be completed at this time.*

Doubling

When a three-note chord is distributed among four voices, a note must be doubled. Composers' preferences have been remarkably consistent and can be stated as guidelines, starting with an emphatic negative:

1. DO NOT double the sensitive (tendency) tones (the leading tone, altered tones, and sevenths).

2. For major and minor triads, you can usually double the bass. In root position and second inversion, it's the preferred doubling. In first inversion, it's an option, although a doubled soprano is slightly favored.

3. For diminished (and augmented) triads, place them in first inversion and double the bass (the third of the chord and the only tone not a part of the dissonant interval in these harmonies).

A moment's thought about these guidelines will lead you to realize that they can be further distilled into this "short rule of doubling":

The Short Rule of Doubling

The bass of a triad can usually be doubled unless it's a sensitive tone.

Example 11-4 is a four-voice arrangement of "Plaisir d'amour" (from Chapter 10), here presented in its adapted American form by numerous popular artists.

EXAMPLE 11-4 George Weiss, Hugo Peretti, and Luigi Creatore: "Can't Help Falling in Love"

Notes:

1. Eleven triads are in root position. The bass (root) is doubled in eight of these.

2. Three triads are in first inversion. In the first (m. 1), the soprano is doubled. In the second (m. 5), a diminished triad, the bass is doubled. In the last (m. 6), the bass is doubled.

3. Two triads are in second inversion (in m. 2 and m. 7). The bass is doubled in both.

4. Spacing among the upper three voices is fairly uniform throughout, varying with the melodic contours but never exceeding an octave between any two voices.

5. When the bass drops to C3 or lower, the interval formed by it and the tenor is never smaller than a fifth.

6. A complete dominant seventh chord appears at m. 5, beat 4. The seventh (C), a sensitive tone, is resolved stepwise downward.

Alternative Doubling

Not one of the foregoing principles is sacrosanct. Melodic considerations might demand different doubling. When doing so, it's usually better to double scale degrees 1, 4, and 5 than degrees 2, 3, and 6. ($\hat{7}$ is too unstable to be doubled in most situations.) At other times it might be desirable to omit a chord member from a triad. The tone most often omitted is the fifth.

Question: In m. 6 of Example 11-4, the E minor triad contains a doubled third instead of a doubled bass (the root). Why?

EXAMPLE 11-5 mm. 5–6 from Example 11-4

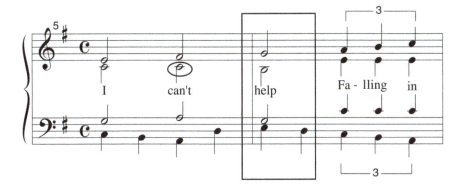

Answer: The alto C in m. 5 (circled) is the chord seventh, a sensitive tone that wants a stepwise downward resolution. The tenor—the only other voice available to double the bass note E in m. 6—would need to leap downward to do it. This would then be followed by another leap. Doubling the third, G, produces a more singable tenor line.

↻ BACK TO BASICS 11.1

Voicing
Triads

In m. 8 of Example 11-4, the triad is incomplete, containing a tripled root and a third. Again, this is a child of the melodic force. The tenor leading tone in m. 7 invites a resolution to the tonic. Because the bass and melody both move to the root, the alto is the only voice that can add another chord member. Play the chord giving the alto the fifth (D) instead of B. As you'll hear, the third (B) is the better note to include because a root and a fifth alone produce a hollow, unsatisfying sound.

➤ *For assignments on voicing chords, turn to Workbook p. 120.*

CONNECTING CHORDS

The central mission in part writing today is to guide the voices through a harmonic succession by leading them down separate melodic corridors. The corridors tend to be narrow, and they normally neither merge nor cross. Within these confines, each line should be musical and singable and faithful to the melodic tendencies of the pitches while producing harmonies that are spaced and doubled well. Visualize it this way:

EXAMPLE 11-6

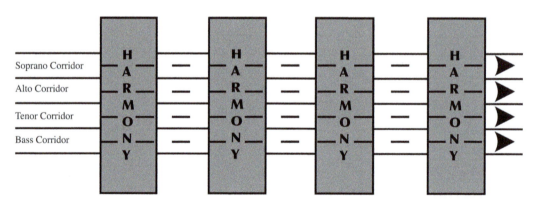

In addition, certain principles govern the *combined* movement of the individual voices.

Consecutive Perfect Fifths and Octaves

When two voices forming a perfect fifth or a perfect octave (or a perfect unison) move to pitches that form an identical interval, the result—termed **consecutive fifths** or **consecutive octaves**. (Some theorists prefer to use the terms "parallel fifths" and "parallel octaves.") This practice was avoided from the fifteenth century onward

EXAMPLE 11-7

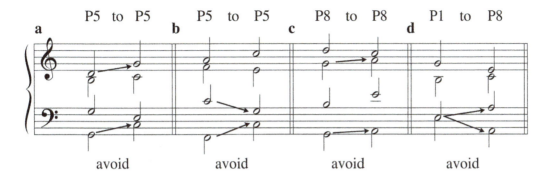

P5 to P5   P5 to P5   P8 to P8   P1 to P8

a   b   c   d

avoid   avoid   avoid   avoid

Although Bach characterized consecutive fifths, octaves, and unisons as the most egregious part writing error, attitudes vary with time and style, as the following more recent examples show.

EXAMPLE 11-8a Aaron Copland: *Fanfare for the Common Man* 🔊))

EXAMPLE 11-8b Alicia Keys: "If I Ain't Got You" (Introduction)

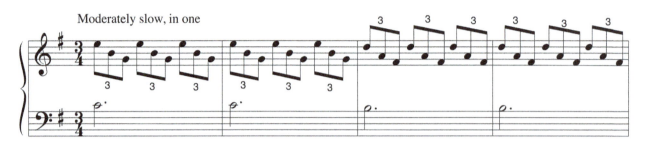

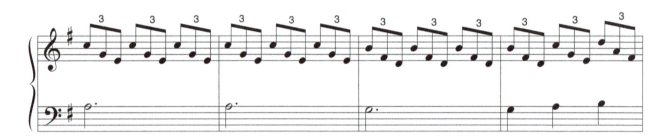

Notes:

1. In 11–8a, the "parallel" perfect fifths (enclosed in boxes) produce a spacious, elemental sound that has been used and imitated at athletic events and festivals.

2. In 11–8b, consecutive fifths occur between the lowest pitch of the chord on the upper staff and the bass as the chords move downward by step.

Today, even in more traditional settings, we are likely to view the effects of parallels as less adverse than poor doubling, poor spacing, or a poorly contoured line. When part writing in the Baroque manner, then, you should follow Bach's lead and avoid consecutive octaves, fifths and unisons, but in more contemporary styles, we'll observe the principle less stringently.

Voice Crossing and Overlap

Voice crossing—a soprano pitch placed lower than the alto pitch, a bass pitch placed higher than the tenor pitch, and so on—and **voice overlap**—the soprano dipping *below* an immediately preceding alto pitch, the bass rising *above* the preceding tenor pitch, and so on—are practices that tend to obscure the melodic action of the individual lines.

EXAMPLE 11-9

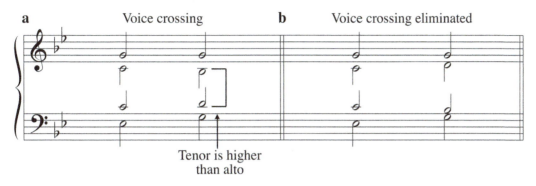

Tenor is higher
than alto

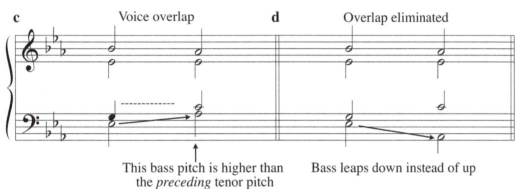

This bass pitch is higher than   Bass leaps down instead of up
the *preceding* tenor pitch

Be sure to check the alto and tenor carefully for voice crossing and overlap. Because their range of motion is restricted at times by the soprano and bass, they are most prone to the problem. Furthermore, crossing and overlap are less visible in these voices because in closed-score notation alto and tenor occupy separate staves.

REVIEW AND REINFORCEMENT

Return to Example 11-4. Earlier you were asked for a possible reason for the nonstandard doubling on beat 1 of m. 6. Can you now suggest another reason?

Voice crossing and overlap are not so much errors as they are exceptional practices that can be justified for melodic or other reasons. When they occur, their duration should be brief. Also, the less extreme the crossing or overlap, the less problematic it is.

EXAMPLE 11-10 J. S. Bach: "In Dulci Jubilo"

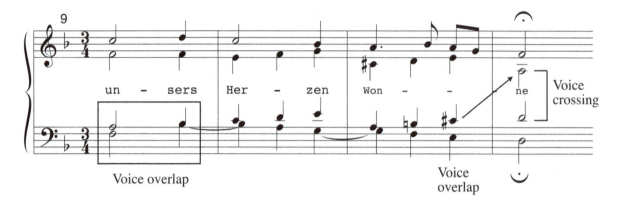

Notes:

1. The voice overlap between the tenor and bass in m. 9 could have been avoided by moving the bass *down* to the lower-octave Bb. But this would have given Bach the unfortunate choice of continuing the ensuing scalar descent into the bass's extreme low register or breaking up the scale by transposing part of it up an octave. Possibly reluctant to do either, he opted for a brief and minimal overlap.

2. The voice overlap and voice crossing in mm. 11–12 permit the tenor to resolve the sensitive tone C♯, and they avoid the "offensive" consecutive octaves that would result if both the alto and bass moved from E in m. 11 to D in m. 12.

Common Tones

Where common tones are present between two adjacent chords, retaining them in the same voices provides the smoothest voice leading.

EXAMPLE 11-11

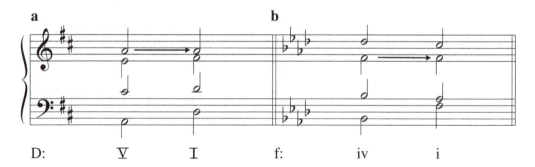

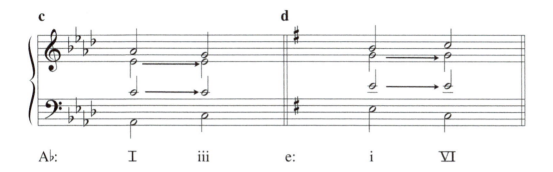

$A\flat$:   I   iii   e: i   VI

When No Common Tones Are Present

When no common tones are present between chords, moving the upper voices in contrary motion to the bass minimizes the chances of writing consecutive perfect fifths or octaves.

EXAMPLE 11-12

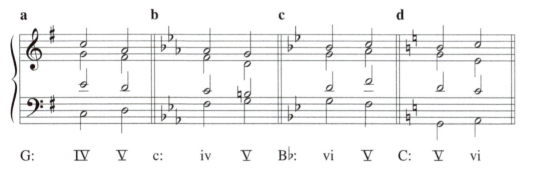

G: IV   V   c: iv   V $B\flat$:   vi   V   C: V   vi

Move upper voices contrary to bass

Notes:

1. In a, b, and c, the three upper voices move in contrary motion to the bass.

2. In d, the soprano moves *parallel* to the bass because the melodic force requires that the leading tone resolve to the tonic, producing alternative doubling.

Arrows indicate where common tones have been retained in Example 11-13.

EXAMPLE 11-13 John Fawcett and Hans George Naegeli: "Blest Be the Tie"

Note:

Where a common tone is present, it has been retained in the same voice in all but one case (m. 11–12), where the composer opted for consecutive unisons between the soprano and alto (m. 12, beats 1–2).

↻ **BACK TO BASICS 11.2**

The Fiendish Five

▶ *For assignments on connecting chords, turn to Workbook Chapter 11, assignments 2A–2E.*

⊕ CODA

With emphasis on harmonic matters—spacing, doubling, inversion, and Roman numeral analysis—it's far too easy to think of part writing as the act of arranging a given chord succession for some number of voices. In fact, our music evolved in *just the opposite way*: harmony was the end product of melodic lines in combination. It's possible to approach part writing from either direction, so long as both the melodic force and harmonic force are respected.

All the principles important to effective part writing have been presented in this chapter. With part writing, though, you must consider many things at once:

- voice ranges

- treatment of sensitive tones

- spacing

- doubling

- chord connection procedures.

Chapters 12 and 13 reinforce these various aspects of voice leading and provide further detail.

DO YOU KNOW THESE TERMS?

- consecutive perfect consonances
- contrary motion
- counterpoint
- homogeneous spacing
- oblique motion
- parallel motion
- power chords
- sensitive tones
- similar motion
- voice crossing
- voice leading
- voice overlap
- voicing

CHAPTER TWELVE

The Chorale
Part Writing with Root-Position Triads

PART WRITING AND GOLF

Golf lessons usually begin with the seven iron, the club most pros consider a good tool for learning the basic swing. After that, the lessons become situational—chipping, putting, driving, difficult lies, all facilitated by that good basic swing. Chapter 11 was our seven-iron lesson—structuring individual lines, voicing chords, and connecting chords. Chapters 12, 13, and 14 are the situational lessons. In these chapters, we'll apply the principles of Chapter 11 to specific situations.

THE CHORALE

Part writing is most easily observed and practiced through music of limited melodic range that is rhythmically uncomplicated, harmonically compact, and **syllabic**—that is, each syllable of text accorded a pitch of its own—in a word, music that's hymnlike.

One of the legacies of J. S. Bach and his contemporaries is a large corpus of harmonized chorales. A **chorale** is a Lutheran hymn. Chorale melodies were drawn from a number of sources and used for congregational singing in the Protestant worship service during the sixteenth century. Bach and others made four-part arrangements as part of larger sacred compositions called cantatas and Passions.

In their harmonic imagination and in their balance of melodic and harmonic forces, Bach's harmonizations surpass those of his contemporaries. Not only do they provide a compendium of eighteenth-century harmonic practice, they have remained models of voice leading for succeeding generations of musicians.

Melodic Features

An aspect of chorale melodies that make them particularly useful for the study of voice leading is their prevailingly stepwise nature. This and their limited range (not much beyond an octave) facilitate keeping the spacing between the upper voices more or less uniform without requiring excessive leaps.

One factor we'll omit for now is the text. Although obviously an important consideration in all vocal music, a discussion of text setting would encumber our study of the voice leading. Accordingly, the chorale excerpts in this unit will be shown without the words.

PART WRITING WITH ROOT-POSITION TRIADS

To restate the guideline given on p. 192: *Where common tones are present between two chords, keeping them in the same voices promotes the smoothest voice leading.*

Fifth Relationship/Part Writing the Authentic Cadence, Plagal Cadence, and Half Cadence

Triads whose roots lie a fifth or fourth apart, as in authentic, plagal, and some half cadences, contain one common tone. Note how it is retained in the same voice.

EXAMPLE 12-1

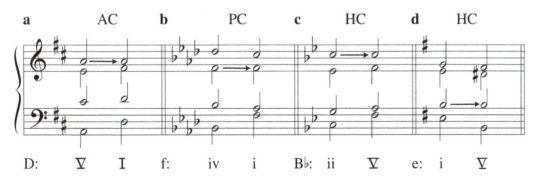

Note:
Each root-position chord contains a doubled bass (root).

For melodic or other reasons, you may choose *not* to retain the common tone in the same voice. In most cases, preferred doubling and spacing can then be obtained by moving the three upper voices contrary to the bass. But when doing this, be especially watchful for consecutive fifths and octaves and voice overlap.

EXAMPLE 12-2 J. S. Bach: "Herr Christ, der ein'ge Gottes-Sohn"

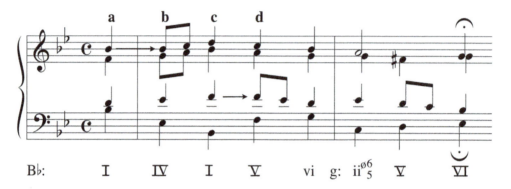

Notes:

1. From a to b and from c to d, the common tone between the chords has been retained.

2. From b to c, the common tone has not been retained. (Bach would have had to change the melody to do so.) The upper voices ascend while the bass descends.

▶ *Assignment 1A in Workbook Chapter 12 can be completed at this time.*

Third Relationship

Chords whose roots are related by the interval of a third or a sixth have two common tones. *Retaining both produces the smoothest voice leading.*

EXAMPLE 12-3 Common Tones Retained (Minimal Feeling of Harmonic Motion)

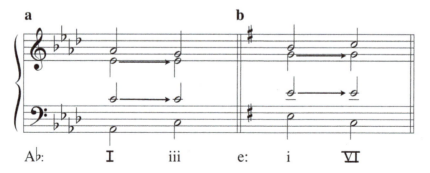

If you choose to retain *neither* common tone, proper doubling dictates that *all four voices move to a new pitch.* To safeguard against parallels, move the soprano contrary to the bass.

EXAMPLE 12-4 No Common Tones Retained (For Greater Feeling of Harmonic Motion)

Bb: I   iii   f#:   i   VI

Note:

Moving all the voices produces leaps in more than one voice at the same time and so should not be overused since it undermines smooth voice leading.

➤ *Assignment 1C in Workbook Chapter 12 can be completed now.*

Second Relationship

Chords with roots a step (or half step) apart, as in the half cadences IV–V or vi–V, have no common tones. When no common tones exist, *move the three upper voices contrary to the bass.*

EXAMPLE 12-5

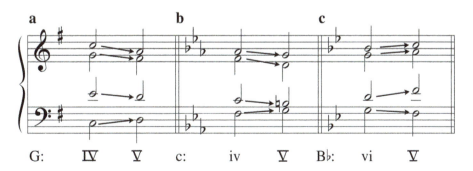

G: IV   V   c: iv   V   Bb: vi   V

Warning! Part Writing Hazard!

Occasionally, the melody and the bass will move through a second relationship in parallel motion. Because this situation is especially prone to producing consecutive fifths and/or octaves, you should be diligent about moving the inner voices *contrary to the bass*.

EXAMPLE 12-6 J. S. Bach: "Jesu Leiden, Pein und Tod"

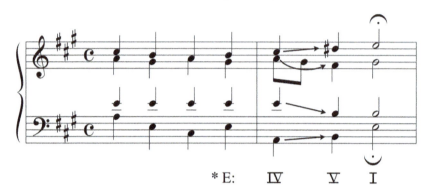

*E: IV   V   I

*As you'll often see, even in short works, the key of the moment may not be the home key reflected in the key signature.

REVIEW AND REINFORCEMENT

Rewrite Example 12-6 moving the alto and tenor in parallel with the soprano and bass. What is the result?

The parallelism between soprano and bass may have been one reason why J. S. Bach more often followed IV with vii°6 than with V.

Part Writing the Deceptive Cadence

Root movement by second occurs in the deceptive cadence. You already know that the leading tone in the soprano sounds best when resolved upward to the tonic. Doing so in a deceptive cadence creates parallel motion between the soprano and bass. Once again: Send the inner voices hurrying in the opposite direction

EXAMPLE 12-7

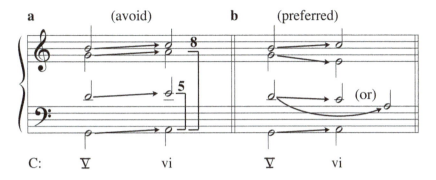

Notes:

1. In a, the alto and tenor produce consecutive octaves and fifths against the bass. The consecutive fourths between the alto and tenor are, in themselves, permissible. (Recall that, in two-voice counterpoint, they were considered objectionable.)

2. In b, the tenor has the option of doubling the bass note A (normal doubling) or—as here—doubling the tonic, which is the chord third. This is an acceptable alternative doubling that produces smoother voice leading.

In minor-key deceptive cadences, the leading tone should resolve to the tonic *even in an inner voice*. This is because the leading tone has only two possible ways to go—*up to the tonic* (preferred) or down *to the submediant* by way of an augmented second (not a good idea).

EXAMPLE 12-8

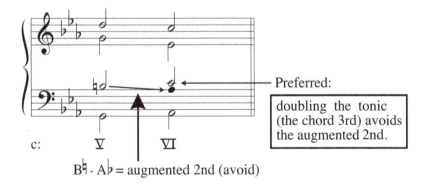

Note:

Recall that the augmented second was considered to be an awkward melodic interval. Here, the tenor should ascend to double C—the *third* of VI. This alternative doubling is preferred over the augmented second.

CONCEPT CHECK

Discuss Bach's part writing of the minor-key deceptive cadences in Examples 12-2 and 12-9. In Example 12-9, identify the embellishing tones present in m. 9. Disregard the enclosed chords.

EXAMPLE 12-9 J. S. Bach: "Christ lag in Todesbanden"

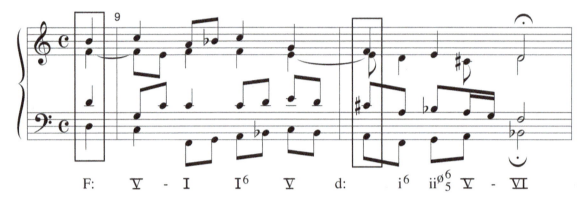

➤ *Assignment 1E in Workbook Chapter 12 can be completed now.*

A summary of procedures for connecting root-position triads follows.

GUIDELINES FOR CONNECTING ROOT-POSITION TRIADS

1. **In fifth relationship**: Retain the common tone in the same voice; if not retaining the common tone, move the three upper voices contrary to the bass.

2. **In third relationship**: Retain *both* common tones, or retain *neither while moving the soprano contrary to the bass*, taking care to avoid large leaps or voice overlap.

3. **In second relationship**: Move the soprano and, if possible, the other voices contrary to the bass. *But in the deceptive cadence:* resolve the leading tone when it appears in the soprano, and in minor keys, resolve the leading tone in *all* cases.

Perhaps you see a theme here—that the soprano and bass should move in contrary or oblique motion as often as possible. In fact, a concise guideline for connecting chords begins with that recommendation:

The Short Rule of Chord Connection

Move the soprano and bass in contrary or oblique motion, favor steps over leaps, avoid awkward melodic intervals, and retain common tones between chords where possible.

In Example 12-10, numbers on the music correspond to the numbered procedures listed in the foregoing summary.

EXAMPLE 12-10 J. S. Bach: "Ermuntre dich, mein schwacher Geist" 🔊))

G: I   vi   V̲   I   ii⁷   I⁶   I   ii⁷   X*   V̲   I

IV   I   V̲   vi   V̲   I

* This harmony will be studied in Chapter 7

Notes:

1. A 4–3 suspension occurs in the soprano in m. 3. It will be discussed in the ensuing section.

2. A triad with tripled root and omitted fifth appears in m. 4. Here Bach yielded to the melodic force rather than the harmonic by resolving the alto's leading tone upward to the tonic G instead of moving it downward to the chord fifth D to obtain a complete triad.

REVIEW AND REINFORCEMENT

In Example 12-10 there are 14 root-position triads. In how many is the bass doubled? Review the melodic principles on p. 170 of Chapter 10. Which ones do you observe?

Example 12-11 affords the opportunity to study all three root movements—by fifth, third, and second.

EXAMPLE 12-11 George Elvey and Henry Alford: "Come, Ye Thankful People Come" 🔊⟩⟩

↻ BACK TO BASICS 12.1

Root-Position
Triads

CONCEPT CHECK

1. Numbers 1 and 2 identify root-position triads in third relationship. Numbers 3–10 locate root-position triads in fifth relationship. Number 11 marks a root-position triad in second relationship. Describe the voice leading and doubling in all cases. (Disregard the circled passing tone.)

2. Which type of motion between the soprano and bass is most common—contrary, oblique, similar, or parallel?

3. Triads in inversion appear in mm. 4, 7, and 8. Identify the inversions. Which of these conform to the doubling principles presented on p. 186?

➤ *For assignments on part writing with root-position triads, turn to Workbook Chapter 12, assignments 1A–1I.*

PART WRITING SUSPENSIONS

Note:

You might wish to review the discussion of suspensions in Chapter 8 (pp. 129–133) at this point.

Measure 3 from Example 12-10 is reprinted next. A 4–3 suspension appears in the soprano. The only note that changes from beat 2 to 3 is the suspended tone, which resolves stepwise downward. (The octave leap in the bass doesn't count as a change.) In b the suspension has been removed.

EXAMPLE 12-12

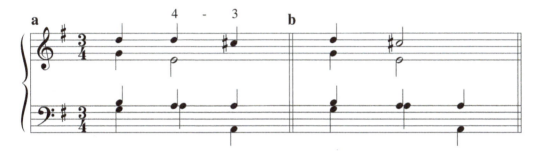

Notes:

1. The two chords are in second relationship. Accordingly, the upper voices move contrary to the bass.

2. Both triads are in root position with the bass doubled.

Doubling in Suspensions

The doubling in a chord containing a suspension should be the same as it would be in the absence of the suspension.

Because both the 4–3 and 9–8 suspensions occur over root-position triads, the bass (root) should be doubled. In the 4–3 suspension, the resolution note is the chord third. This means one of the remaining two voices must double the bass, and the other must supply the chord fifth, as in Example 12-12. In the 9–8 suspension, the resolution tone doubles the bass. The remaining voices must supply the third and fifth of the chord.

Example 12-13 shows 9–8 suspensions added to authentic and deceptive cadences.

EXAMPLE 12-13

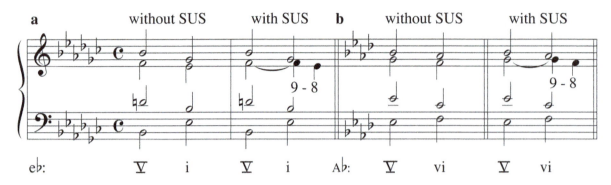

Note:

The suspensions are reflected in the chord symbols themselves. The doubling in the resolution chord, a root-position triad, is the same with or without the suspension.

Most of Bach's chorale harmonizations contain suspensions—one to four on average. Although they can be found in all voices, the alto is by far the preferred voice, followed by the tenor.

EXAMPLE 12-14a J. S. Bach: "Jesu, Jesu, du bist mein"

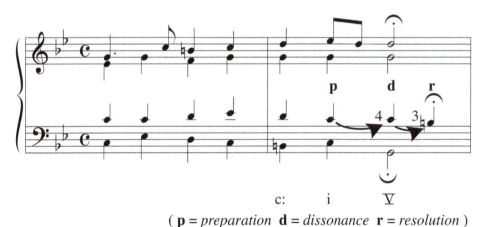

(**p** = *preparation* **d** = *dissonance* **r** = *resolution*)

EXAMPLE 12-14b J. S. Bach: "Du grosser Schmerzensmann"

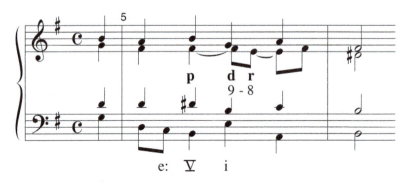

Notes:

1. a contains an anticipation in the soprano (m. 2) in addition to the 4–3 suspension in the tenor.

2. In both a and b, doubling is normal (a doubled bass) at the points where the suspensions resolve.

3. When a 4–3 or 9–8 suspension occurs over two triads whose roots are fifth-related, the common tone can usually be retained in the same voice, as shown in a, where the alto retains its G on beat 3.

Both 4–3 and 9–8 suspensions are possible between root-position triads a fifth or a second apart. The most common harmonic settings are:

4–3 suspension		*9–8 suspension*	
p	**d–r**	**p**	**d–r**
I	V	V	I
IV	I	I	IV
V	vi	V	vi
IV	V	IV	V

p = preparation d = suspension dissonance r = resolution

The 9–8 and 4–3 are the most common suspensions. They're also the only ones that resolve over root-position triads. You can think of the relatively rare 2–3 retardation as an upward-resolving suspension:

EXAMPLE 12-15

Note:

The voice leading must change in b in order to preserve a doubled bass when the suspended tone resolves *upward to the chord third instead of downward to the chord root.*

Because the 7–6 suspension and the 2–3 *suspension* (not 2–3 retardation) resolve over first inversion triads, we'll consider them in Chapter 13.

➤ *For assignments on part writing suspensions, turn to Workbook Chapter 12, assignments 2A–2G.*

⊕ CODA

Root-position triads are the foot soldiers of four-part harmony. Central to most cadences, they shoulder the harmonic weight in phrase interiors as well, outnumbering both first inversion and second inversion triads. They support 9–8 and 4–3 suspensions.

Because bass leaps are common among root-position triads, more conjunct motion in the other voices is desirable. The smoothest route is through common tones, retained in the same voices. Otherwise, it's best to move the soprano, and other voices if possible, in contrary or oblique motion to the bass. Although exceptions occur, the best tone to double is the root.

Much about the treatment of root-position triads applies to triads in inversion as well. This makes the handling of root-position triads arguably the most important part writing skill you'll acquire.

DO YOU KNOW THESE TERMS?

- chorale
- fifth relationship
- part writing
- second relationship
- syllabic
- third relationship

Part Writing with Triads in Inversion

PERSPECTIVE

Inverted inverted triads initially occurred as the byproducts of melodic lines in combination (counterpoint), and the idea that a root-position triad and its inversions might be considered *one and the same harmony* was foreign to composers prior to Bach's time.

Today, composers use inversion for many reasons. One is simply to vary the sound of the harmonies. Another is to reduce the finality and weight that root position lends a chord. Perhaps the most important reason is to smooth out the bass line.

To reiterate a truism, music's second most important melody is often the bass. Against the true melody, this line forms a counterpoint that is to some degree melodic and independent. A wonderful melody with the most imaginative harmonies can be undermined by a bass that does nothing but hop from one chord root to the next. In this chapter, we'll see how inversion provides an antidote for the "lunging bass line."

FIRST INVERSION

Inversion and Bass Line

Composers constantly make choices that obey either the melodic force or the harmonic, and perhaps nowhere do the opposing forces do more frequent battle than in the bass. To use the jargon of corporate America, the bass is voice leading's "multi-tasker."

Let's consider the melodic function of the bass. Play or listen to Example 13-1 a and b. The melody is the same; the bass line differs. Which version do you prefer? Why?

EXAMPLE 13-1a J. S. Bach: "Schmücke dich, o liebe Seele"

EXAMPLE 13-1b With Bach's Bass

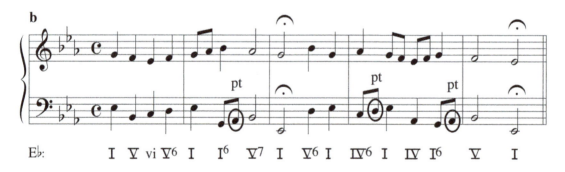

You've probably decided that version a should remain hypothetical. Confined only to chord roots, the bass hops—like a disoriented jackrabbit—to the tonic first from one side and then from the other. In b, the bass is more tuneful. With a better balance between steps and leaps, it sounds less erratic and more directed. Moreover, it's independent of the soprano, with its own rhythms and contour.

Wherein lies the improvement? The passing tones in mm. 2 and 4 help, of course. As we learned in Chapter 8, any leap of a third can be smoothed out by inserting a passing tone.

Equally useful, though, is first inversion. In fact, a most important function of first inversion is to *make the bass more melodic.*

Recall from Chapter 11 (p. 186) that the bass is the preferred doubling in root position and second inversion and also is an option in first inversion. Because doubling in first inversion triads is governed more by melodic factors than by concern for sonority, composers' preferences can be restated this way:

Doubling in First Inversion

1. Any doubling option except sensitive tones (the leading tone, altered tones, and raised $\hat{6}$ and $\hat{7}$ in minor) may be employed to improve voice leading. (In major and minor triads, this will more often than not be a doubled soprano or bass.)

2. In diminished and augmented (rare) triads, double the third—which, in first inversion, is the bass.

Let's study the complete harmonization of the preceding chorale phrases.

EXAMPLE 13-2 J. S. Bach: "Schmücke dich, o liebe Seele" 🔊

Note:

First inversion triads appear at points a through e. At a and c, the soprano is doubled by an inner voice. At b and d, the bass is doubled by an inner voice. At e, the soprano *is* the bass (soprano and bass double each other).

Why Not the *Other* Tone?

Inquiring minds might ask: "Why not double the *other tone,* the one that is *neither* the soprano nor the bass?" While not faulty *per se,* this procedure can restrict subsequent melodic movement or create spacing problems. At a, the inner voice B♭ could be doubled only at the unison, in which case the alto and tenor are close to overlapping or crossing each other. At c, the inner voice F could be doubled only at the octave, in which case the alto and tenor are almost too widely spaced. The clearest voice leading results when each voice remains for the most part within its rather narrowly defined corridor. Doubling "the other voice" tends to expand the corridors, creating either heterogeneous (as opposed to homogeneous) spacing or making voice crossing and overlap unavoidable.

Play and compare three versions of "One Hand, One Heart."

EXAMPLE 13-3a Bernstein: "One Hand, One Heart" (from *West Side Story*)

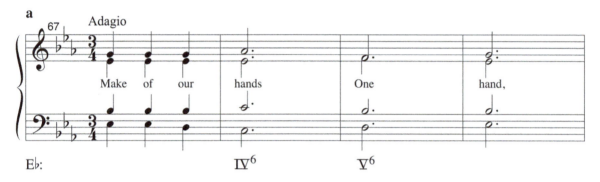

EXAMPLE 13-3b

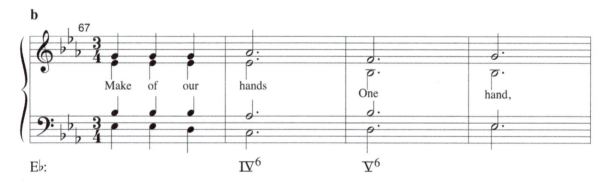

EXAMPLE 13-3c

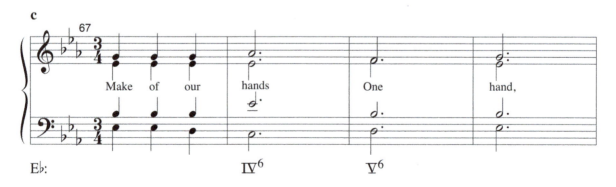

Notes:

1. All three versions sound fine and are acceptable. They differ mainly in the doubling of the first inversion chords.

2. Doubling the bass in the V⁶ is not an option (it *never* is) because it's the leading tone.

3. With the harmonic aspect more or less equal, version a is perhaps the most satisfactory since it contains the most conjunct voice leading.

▶ *Assignments 1A and 1B in Workbook Chapter 13 can be completed now.*

Chord Connection

Little is really new in part writing first inversion triads beyond the general guidelines given in Chapter 11 (see "Review of Melodic Principles" on p. 182 and "Connecting Chords" on p. 188). Those guidelines may be summarized thus:

1. If common tones are present, retain them in the same voices and move the remaining voices in the most conjunct manner possible. If no common tones, move the soprano and—if possible—the other voices contrary to the bass.

2. Avoid large leaps, voice crossing and voice overlap.

3. Avoid consecutive perfect fifths, octaves, or unisons.

    Two more guidelines specific to first inversion are:

4. Step to and/or away from the bass if possible.

5. Leave *doubled tones* in contrary or oblique motion where possible.

Numbers corresponding to these guidelines show where they've been observed in Example 13-4.

EXAMPLE 13-4 J. S. Bach: "Wo soll ich fliehen hin" 🔊

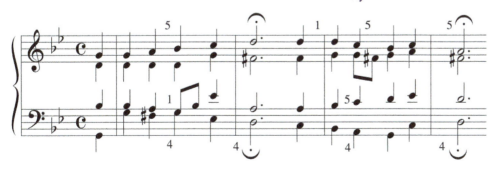

▶ *Assignment 1C on Workbook p. 143 can be completed now.*

Inversion and Harmonic Weight

A second reason for using first inversion is to give less weight and finality to triads in phrase interiors. Play Example 13-1 again. In a, each bass note and its implied harmony has about the same "weight." This creates a blockiness absent in b, where "lighter" notes seem to push toward the "heavier" ones. The bass in b acquires a dimension beyond the melodic and harmonic in that it reflects the relative importance of the melodic tones above it. For example, m. 1, beat 4 contains a weak-beat "passing" F. A V^6 lends less harmonic weight to this note than would a root-position V.

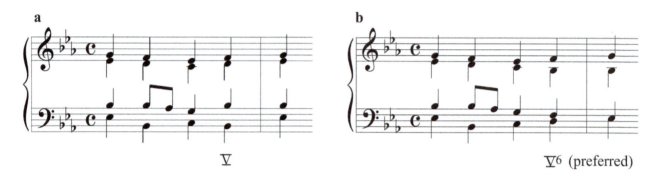

In Example 13-5, a smoother bass line and improved musical flow result from the large number of first inversion triads.

EXAMPLE 13-5 Bernstein: "One Hand, One Heart" (from *West Side Story*)

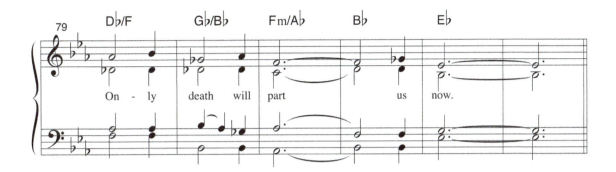

CONCEPT CHECK

1   In how many first inversion triads is the soprano pitch doubled? The bass pitch? The "other" tone? A sensitive tone?

2   How many first inversion triads are either approached or left by a stepwise bass? In how many is the doubled tone left in contrary or oblique motion?

Suspensions and First Inversion

Play Example 13-6 and compare it to Example 13-5.

EXAMPLE 13-6 Bernstein: "One Hand, One Heart" (from *West Side Story*)

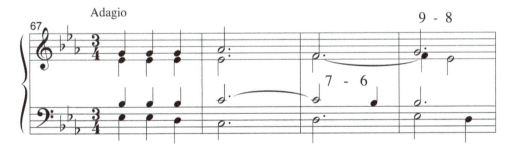

Here the music has been embellished with suspensions. The 9–8 should be familiar from Chapter 12 (see p. 207). In m. 69, a 7–6 suspension occurs. The "6" indicates that the resolution occurs over a first inversion triad. Although first inversion is full of doubling options, you should *avoid doubling the resolution of a 7–6 suspension*. Why? Because much of the "suspense" in a suspension is siphoned off when its resolution is heard prematurely in another voice. This can happen when the suspension occurs in the soprano. (Double the soprano—normally a preferred doubling in first inversion—and you double the suspension resolution.)

In Example 13-7, the soprano and tenor voices from Example 13-6 have been exchanged.

EXAMPLE 13-7

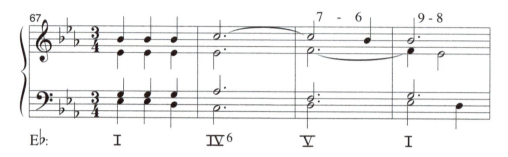

Now the V^6 in m. 69 contains a doubled inner voice (F). Normally the least preferred doubling, it's now the *only* choice because the soprano's B♭ is the suspension resolution and the bass D is the leading tone.

Bach and others used the 7–6 suspension most often over a vii^{o6}. When doing so, they usually doubled the *fifth* of the diminished triad, probably for voice-leading reasons. (Recall that, in first inversion, almost any doubling option can be used to improve the voice leading.)

EXAMPLE 13-8 J. S. Bach: "Als Jesus Christus in der Nacht"

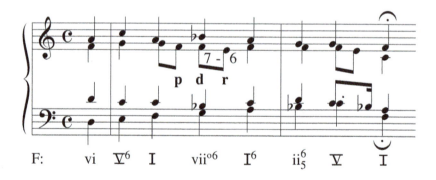

> **CONCEPT CHECK**
>
> What part writing problem would doubling the bass in the diminished triad create? Identify the other two suspensions in Example 13-8.

One other suspension resolves over a first inversion triad—the 2–3, or more properly, 2–6/3. (Again, the "6" is an indication that the resolution chord is in first inversion.) This bass suspension occurs almost exclusively over one progression: $I–V^6$.

EXAMPLE 13-9

C: I $\underline{V}_2$ - $\overset{6}{3}$

Again, the preferred doubling is the soprano. Doubling the inner voice G is also possible, although it would push the tenor to its extreme high register. Doubling the bass is not recommended, for two very good reasons: it's the suspension resolution and it's the leading tone.

○ **BACK TO BASICS 13.1**

First Inversion Triads

Example 13-10 shows Bach's treatment of the 2–3 suspension.

EXAMPLE 13-10 J. S. Bach: "Schaut, ihr Sünder" ◀))

g: i $\underline{V}_2$ - $\overset{6}{3}$

Bb: I $\underline{V}_2$ - $\overset{6}{3}$

▶ *For assignments on part writing triads in first inversion, turn to Workbook p. 141.*

SECOND INVERSION

For reasons that might be difficult to understand given today's wide-ranging practices, the second inversion triad was historically considered a dissonant sound. Because of this, it appears much less frequently in our concert repertoire than do root position and first inversion. In this section, we'll examine common past practices and compare them to those of the present day. In all cases, the bass is the preferred doubling.

Play Example 13-11 and listen to the effect of the two endings, a and b. Which ending do you prefer? Why?

EXAMPLE 13-11 Beethoven: Seven Variations on "God Save the King" (theme)

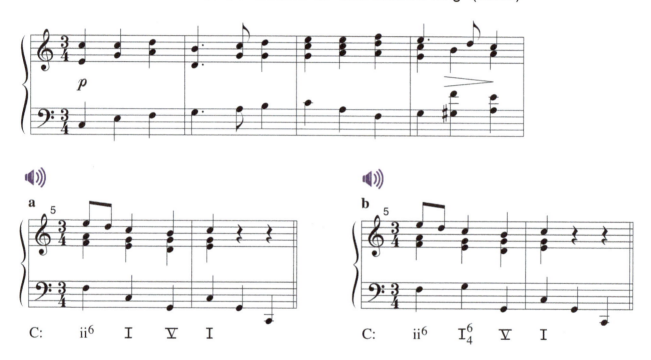

The two endings are practically identical. However, if you prefer b, there are good reasons. In a, the root-position I in m. 5 follows a ii—a rather uncommon progression. Furthermore, this chord has about the same "weight" as the final tonic in m. 6, diluting the effect of that chord's arrival. The I in b, however, is in second (six-four) inversion, and the difference is dramatic. Because second inversion is less stable and "lighter" than root position, the chord no longer robs the final tonic of its impact.

And now, a riddle for you:

When is a I chord not a tonic?

Answer: When it's a cadential six-four chord.

The Cadential Six-Four Chord

You're likely to hear the I chord in b as a V with two nonchord tones (C and E) *that give it the appearance* of a I until they resolve. Herein lies the harmonic truth about the cadential six-four chord: *It looks like I but sounds and acts like V.* You might even think of it as V disguised as I.

EXAMPLE 13-12 The Cadential Six-Four Chord

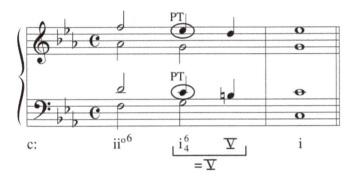

Notes:

1. The two passing tones (circled) mask the V by creating a chord that *looks* momentarily like a tonic (the i$_4^6$). Upon their resolution, however, the mask comes off, clearly revealing the V.

2. The bass and the tone doubling it remain stationary through the resolution to become the doubled bass in the root-position V.

The cadential six-four chord is the most common second inversion. These are its defining features:

- It usually (not always) occurs at cadences (hence the name).

- It spells like I but sounds like V with nonchord tones a sixth and fourth above the bass.

- It is metrically stronger than its resolution.

- The bass and the voice doubling it remain stationary while the two other voices step down.

Play and study Example 13-13 keeping these characteristics in mind.

EXAMPLE 13-13 Beethoven: Symphony, no. 9 (fourth movement) 🔊

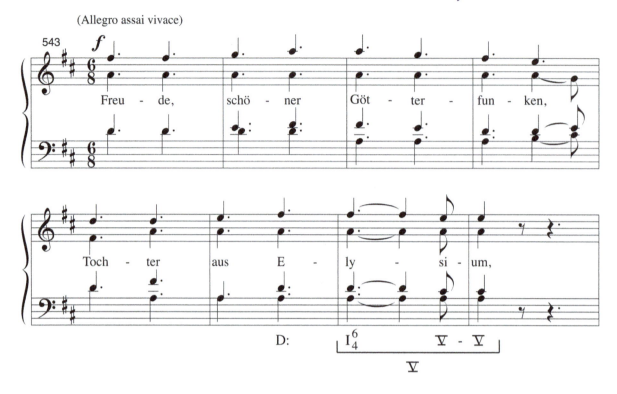

The Passing Six-Four Chord

The passing six-four chord is usually a V connecting a I and its inversion (I–V$_4^6$–I^6 or I^6–V$_4^6$–I); occasionally, a passing I connects a IV and its inversion or a ii$_5^6$. It is usually metrically weak. The bass and the voice doubling it resemble passing tones (circled in the following example), giving the chord its name.

EXAMPLE 13-14 Frederick W. Faber, Henry F. Henry, and J. G. Walton: "Faith of Our Fathers" 🔊

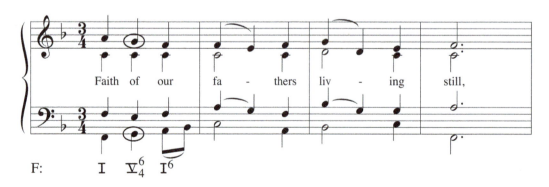

CONCEPT CHECK

What other six-four chord occurs in Example 13-14?

Bach's chorale harmonizations, a vast repertoire for the study of so many things, do not contain many passing six-four chords. One of them, an I$^6_4$, is shown in Example 13-15.

EXAMPLE 13-15 J. S. Bach: "Valet will dir geben" 🔊

B♭:   IV^6 I$^6_4$ ii$^6_5$ V

Note:

The doubled tones (bass and tenor) resemble passing tones. The chord is metrically weak.

Bach's voice-leading and harmonic practice were extraordinarily consistent. Compare the second phrase of Example 13-15 with the fourth phrase of Example 13-10 on p. 217.

Three of the four voices in the passing six-four chord typically move in the following manner:

EXAMPLE 13-15a The Passing Six-Four Voice-Leading Template

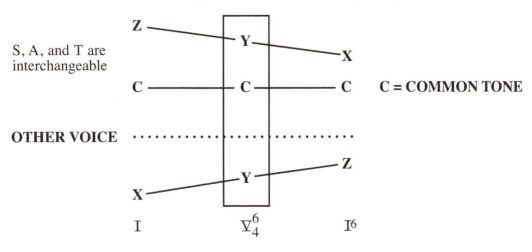

S, A, and T are interchangeable

C = COMMON TONE

OTHER VOICE

I   V$^6_4$ I^6

The bass and one upper voice—in this diagram the soprano—are retrogrades of each other, exchanging pitches by passing through the same tone "y"—the doubled pitch in the passing V. One of the other voices remains stationary on the common tone "c" between the chords. (The harmonic pattern can appear in reverse as well.)

REVIEW AND REINFORCEMENT_____

In Example 13-16:

1   Identify the just-described voice-leading template in the two passing six-four chords.

2   Identify the other six-four chord in the example.

3   Complete the lead-sheet symbols.

4   Identify all nonchord tones.

EXAMPLE 13-16 George Elvey: "Come, Ye Thankful People Come" 🔊

* Secondary Dominants will be discussed in Chapter 15

The Pedal Six-Four Chord

Occasionally, a second inversion triad appears over a repeated or sustained bass. In Example 13-17, upper neighbors create, if only fleetingly, a six-four chord.

EXAMPLE 13-17 Franz Grüber: "Stille Nacht" ("Silent Night")

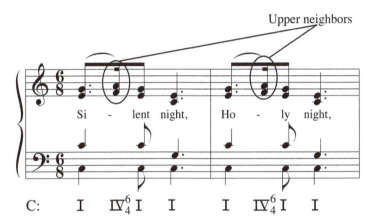

Since the bass and (usually) the doubling tone resemble pedal points, this is called the pedal six-four chord. Typically IV or I, it is usually metrically weak. Because the non-doubling tones (circled) resemble upper neighbors, the chord is also called a "neighboring six-four."

The Arpeggiated Six-Four Chord

The last standard type is the arpeggiated six-four chord, which results from a bass arpeggiation, usually of the tonic or dominant. It is more often metrically weak than strong.

EXAMPLE 13-18 Sabine Baring-Gould and Arthur Sullivan: "Onward, Christian Soldiers"

CONCEPT CHECK

Example 13-19 contains all four types of six-four chord. Identify each and explain its characteristics.

EXAMPLE 13-19 "Michael, Row the Boat Ashore" (spiritual) 🔊

Six-Four Chord Variants

Variations on these practices are common enough. Example 13-20 shows two.

EXAMPLE 13-20a Beethoven: Piano Sonata, op. 26 (first movement) 🔊

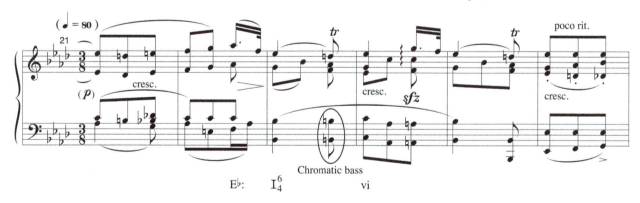

EXAMPLE 13-20b Elton John and Tim Rice: "Can You Feel the Love Tonight?" (from *The Lion King*)

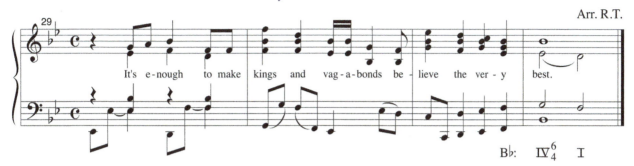

Arr. R.T.

Notes:

1. **a** involves a chromatic resolution. The six-four chord moves deceptively to vi (m. 24) by way of a chromatic bass in m. 23. The chord resulting from this chromaticism is discussed in Chapter 15. In m. 25 the cadential six-four chord returns to resolve without the chromatic interruption.

2. **b** is a popular variation often found in Gospel music. It shares characteristics of the pedal and cadential six-four chords. The IV lends a plagal ("Amen") sound to the cadence, and it looks like the final part of a pedal six-four chord. However, it is metrically strong like the cadential six-four, and its true identity as a I is revealed when the non-doubling tones step downward, as in the cadential six-four chord.

> ↺ **BACK TO BASICS 13.2**
> Second Inversion Triads

⊕ CODA

> Voice leading involves spacing, doubling, and chord connection. The summary that follows subsumes and distills the guidelines presented earlier and will serve you well in most part-writing situations.
> For triads in all positions:
>
> 1. **Spacing**: Keep each voice within its range and in its corridor, maintaining homogenous spacing among the upper voices. Avoid voice crossing and overlap. (See Ch. 10, p. 4 and Ch. 11, p. 6 and p. 14.)
>
> 2. **Doubling**: Normally double the bass (in second inversion always double the bass) unless it's a sensitive tone. Double a different chord member (but never a sensitive tone) to improve a melodic line or to satisfy the preceding spacing guideline. (See Ch. 11, p. 7.)
>
> 3. **Chord Connection**:
>   a. Move the soprano and bass in contrary or oblique motion as often as possible. (See Ch. 10, pp. 5–7.)
>   b. Favor conjunct motion, avoid awkward melodic intervals, and resolve sensitive tones. (See Ch. 10, p. 4.)
>   c. Where common tones between chords exist, retain them in the same voices. (See Ch. 11, p. 16.)
>   d. Avoid consecutive octaves, fifths or unisons between any two voices. (See Ch. 11, p. 11.)

Additional guidelines for triads in second inversion:

1. In the cadential and pedal six-four chords, the bass and the tone doubling it remain stationary.

2. In the passing six-four chord, the bass and the tone doubling it resemble passing tones moving in opposite directions.

3. In the arpeggiated six-four, the bass leaps to the fifth from another member of the same chord.

Each of the standard six-four chords is defined by: 1) its function in the key; 2) its metric position; 3) its bass motion.

Type	Chord	Metric Position	Bass Motion	Example in C
Cadential	I	Strong	S - R	
Passing	V (or I)	Weak	S - S	
Pedal	IV (or I)	Usually weak	R -R	
Arpeggiated	I (or V)	Usually weak	L - L	
S = Step;		L = Leap;	R = Repeated	

▶ *For assignments on second inversion, turn to Workbook Chapter 13, p. 150.*

DO YOU KNOW THESE TERMS?

- arpeggiated six-four chord
- cadential six-four chord
- passing six-four chord
- pedal six-four chord

CHAPTER FOURTEEN

Part Writing Seventh Chords

PERSPECTIVE

In Part Two you learned about seventh chords—their structure, classification, inversions, figured bass, and chord symbols. Regarding voice leading, just four words suffice concerning the chord seventh:

The Short Rule of the Seventh

Don't double; do resolve.

The resolution should be stepwise downward.

Though not without exception, this principle governs almost everything about the classical behavior of seventh chords, and it covers most part writing situations. It also applies in a general way to jazz and popular music, although the seventh has more autonomy in these styles.

The remaining voices in seventh chords follow a time-worn path: They move to the nearest chord tone consistent with normal doubling.

SEVENTH CHORDS OF DOMINANT FUNCTION

The Dominant Seventh Chord

The dominant seventh (V^7) and leading-tone seventh chords (vii^{ø7} or vii^{o7}) possess a more urgent need to resolve than do all others because they contain *both* $\hat{7}$ and $\hat{4}$. The tritone formed by these highly charged pitches cries out for resolution, and the only chords that can provide it are I (i) and vi (VI). In Example 14-1, broken lines show the resolution of the tritone.

EXAMPLE 14-1

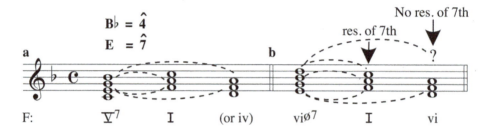

Note:

$\hat{7}$ and $\hat{4}$ can resolve into *either* the I or the vi. However, the vi provides no stepwise resolution for the seventh of the leading-tone seventh chord (see **b**). Perhaps because of this, leading-tone seventh chords do not often progress to vi (VI in minor).

The V^7

The V^7 has the same structure—a Mm7—in both major and minor keys. Despite its occurrence on only one scale degree (hence its name "dominant seventh"), it is the most commonly occurring seventh chord. It is used freely in all inversions. Example 14-2 shows the usual voice leading *regardless of inversion*.

EXAMPLE 14-2

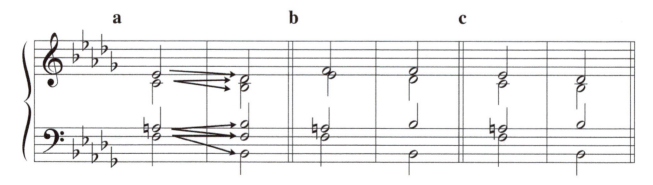

Notes:

1. The seventh always steps down. The other chord members have options (shown by the lines in **a**), depending on inversion, voicing, and whether the composer or arranger elects to obey the melodic or harmonic force. For example, the leading tone (A in the example) almost always resolves to the tonic when in an outer voice. When in the alto or tenor, as in **a**, it may move to the fifth of the tonic to form a complete chord.

2. With both chords in root position, resolving $\hat{7}$ and $\hat{4}$ necessitates omitting the fifth in *either* the V⁷, as in **b**, or the I, as in **c**. In both cases, the chord root replaces the fifth.

The seventh can resemble any nonchord tone *that resolves stepwise downward*, the passing tone and suspensions the most common.

Chord Member or Not?

Whether to analyze a seventh as a chord member or as one of these nonchord tones depends in part on its length. A generally reliable guideline is:

> *A seventh as long as the chord*
>
> *Usually belongs to the chord.*

Compare the voice leading in Example 14-2 with that in the following phrases.

EXAMPLE 14-3a J. S. Bach: "Für deinen Thron tret' ich hiermit" (Root-Position V⁷) 🔊

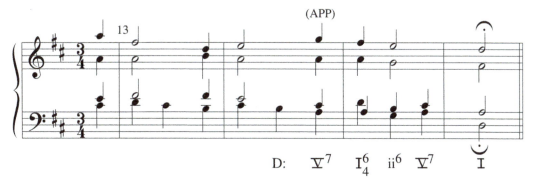

Notes:

1. The fifth in the first V⁷ is replaced by a doubled root. The second V⁷ is complete. To resolve it to a complete I, Bach chose to leave the tenor's leading tone C♯ (m. 15) unresolved.

2. The seventh of the V⁷ in m. 14 resembles an appoggiatura. Another example of the seventh as an appoggiatura figure occurs in Bernstein's "Somewhere" (see Example 11-4).

3. To understand the voice crossing in m. 15, let's try to step into Bach's mind. Placing the bass D an octave lower would eliminate the voice crossing but change the I $^6_4$ into a root-position chord, duplicating the bass's cadence pitch and thereby sapping its weight and sense of finality. On the other hand, interchanging the bass and tenor pitches (tenor = D, bass = A) would create consecutive octaves (A–G) between the alto and bass while destroying the scalar tenor line A–B–C♯ in m. 15.

EXAMPLE 14-3b J. S. Bach: "Christ lag in Todesbanden" (First-Inversion V⁷) 🔊

Notes:

1. The V $^6_5$, with less harmonic weight than the V⁷, is consistent with the auxiliary nature of the upper-neighbor melody note E.

2. In resolving the root-position V⁷ in m. 2, Bach again chose not to resolve the inner-voice leading tone in order to obtain a complete I.

3. In Baroque music, it was common to end a minor-key composition, and sometimes phrases within that work, with a major tonic triad. The raised third has been dubbed the "Picardy third," probably derived from the Old French *picart*, which means "sharp" or "pointed."

EXAMPLE 14-3c J. S. Bach: "Gott lebet noch" (Second-Inversion V⁷) 🔊

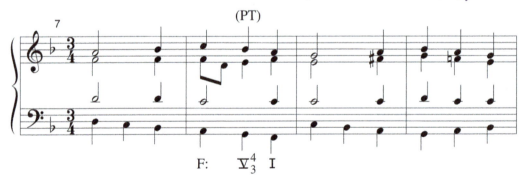

Note:

The V $^4_3$ in m. 8 is similar to the passing V $^6_4$ in that both harmonize a melodic passing tone.

EXAMPLE 14-3d J. S. Bach: "Wach' auf, mein Herz" (Third-Inversion V⁷)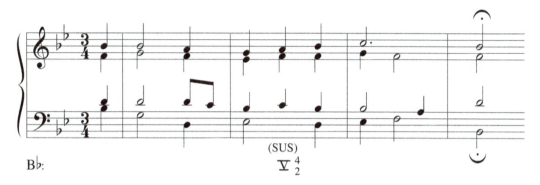

CONCEPT CHECK

In Example 14-3b and c, dominant seventh chords can be found in third inversion. Locate them and compare their resolutions.

▶ *Assignments 1A–1F in Workbook Chapter 14 can be completed now.*

The Unresolved Leading Tone

As we've seen, an inner-voice leading tone is sometimes denied resolution to obtain normal doubling in the chord that follows. Example 14-4 shows this in a deceptive cadence. Both resolutions are acceptable, a favoring the melodic force, b the harmonic.

EXAMPLE 14-4

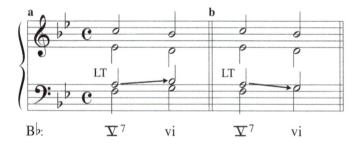

Note:

In a, resolving the leading tone to the tonic creates a doubled third in the vi. In b, the leading tone instead descends to double the bass (G).

The Unresolved Seventh

In the melodic pattern $\hat{3}$–$\hat{4}$–$\hat{5}$, scale degree 4 is often harmonized with a V_3^4. This is one of the few situations where the seventh routinely moves upward.

EXAMPLE 14-5 "Prayer of Thanksgiving" (Traditional Dutch Air) 🔊))

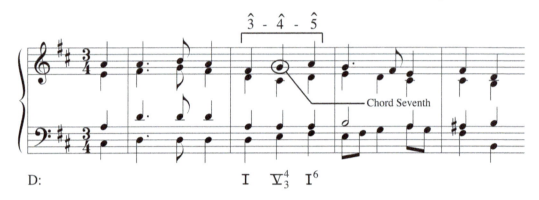

Delayed Resolution

The resolution of the seventh is sometimes delayed or omitted entirely.

EXAMPLE 14-6 Beethoven: Piano Sonata, op. 10, no. 1 (third movement) 🔊))

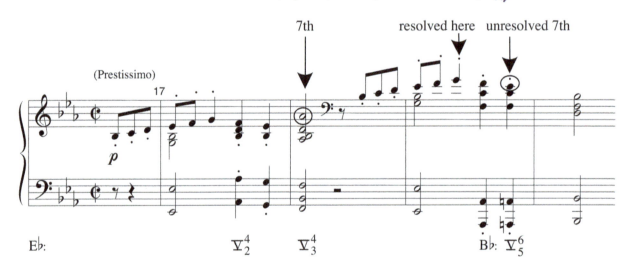

The Leading-Tone Seventh Chord

Like the dominant seventh chord, the leading-tone seventh chord appears in all inversions. As in the dominant seventh chord, the leading tone resolves up, the seventh resolves down, and the other voices move stepwise. This might or might not produce normal doubling in the tonic.

But where the dominant seventh chord has only one structure, the leading-tone seventh chord takes two forms—half-diminished in major (vii^{ø7}) and fully diminished in minor (vii^{o7}). (You'll find the vii^{o7} in major keys as well. This is discussed in Chapter 20.)

EXAMPLE 14-7 Arrows Show Resolution of Leading Tone and Seventh

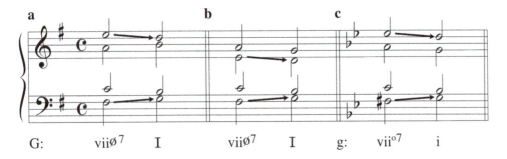

Notes:

1. In a the alto A moves upward to double the third of the tonic—B—rather than downward to double the bass, in order to avoid consecutive perfect fifths with the soprano.

2. In b the soprano and alto have been interchanged so that the interval between them is a perfect *fourth*. Because consecutive fourths do not carry the same historical restriction as fifths (except in two-voice counterpoint), the A (in the soprano) resolves downward to double the bass.

3. Although the voicing of the vii^{o7} in c is identical to a, the alto is free to move downward to double the bass in the tonic, because the fifth formed by it and the soprano is diminished rather than perfect. Even so, it may still move upward.

Notice that the vii^{o7} contains not one but *two* tritones. A common procedure is to resolve them both so that all voices move stepwise.

CONCEPT CHECK

Discuss the resolution of the vii°7 in the following example. Explain the alteration to the final chord.

EXAMPLE 14-8 J. S. Bach: "Das neugeborne Kindelein"

d: iv⁶   vii°7

➤ *For assignments on dominant-functioning seventh chords, turn to Workbook Chapter 14, assignments 1A–1J.*

NONDOMINANT SEVENTH CHORDS

Features and Functions

Every nondominant seventh chord has a major-key and minor-key form. (Refer to Example 5-6 on p. 64.) The "short rule of the seventh" given at the beginning of this chapter applies to them all. Additional points:

1. *Function:* With few exceptions, seventh chords function identically to their triadic counterparts.

2. *Resolution:* The seventh may resemble any downward-resolving nonchord tone (passing tones are the most common).

3. *Frequency:* The further removed a seventh chord is from the tonic (*via* the circle of fifths), the less often it appears.

4. *Inversion:* The ii⁷ (ii°7) is the only nondominant seventh chord to appear more often in inversion than in root position.

5. *Third inversion:* The seventh in the bass is often part of a descending scale.

6   *Incomplete seventh chords:* Most inverted seventh chords are complete. For voice-leading reasons, the fifth of a root-position seventh chord is often omitted and the root or third doubled.

7   *Altered forms:* Applying the melodic minor principle (Appendix A, p. 663) sometimes alters a seventh chord's quality.

These points are illustrated in the examples that follow.

EXAMPLE 14-9 Martin Corrigan: "Cockles and Mussels"

Note:

Every one of the seventh chords plays a role in creating the completely stepwise bass line. The I $\frac{4}{2}$ and vi $\frac{4}{2}$ are merely byproducts of descending passing tones in the bass.

EXAMPLE 14-10 J. S. Bach: "O Ewigkeit, du Donnerwort" 🔊

F: IV⁽⁷⁾   ii⁷   vi⁷

ii⁷   ii⁶₅

Note:

In m. 2, the passing tone A in the alto (beat 1) creates a fleeting IV⁷. Because the seventh is short and unaccented, it might be regarded as a passing tone rather than a full-fledged member of the chord.

Incomplete seventh chords appear in mm. 3 and 4 of Example 14-10. In each case, the chord fifth has been omitted and the third has been doubled. Let's see what happens if we add the fifth to each chord, making all three complete.

EXAMPLE 14-11

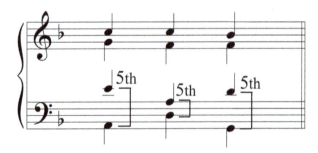

As Example 14-11 shows, the price to be paid for complete seventh chords in succession is consecutive fifths, a cost considered to be too high by Bach, and by Henry Purcell as well. Notice how Purcell consistently omitted the fifth in the harpsichord art in the following chain of seventh chords.

EXAMPLE 14-12 Henry Purcell: *Ode for St. Cecilia's Day*

CONCEPT CHECK

The arrangement that follows contains what might appear to be dominant and nondominant seventh chords in succession. (Original harmonies are indicated by the lead-sheet symbols.) Can you cite two reasons why the chords on beat 1 of m. 18 and m. 20 should not be analyzed as seventh chords? Complete the harmonic analysis.

EXAMPLE 14-13 Rodgers and Hammerstein: "Climb Ev'ry Mountain" (*The Sound of Music*, act. 1, no. 28)

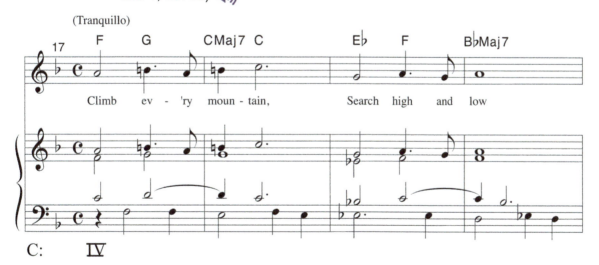

Seventh Chords and Chain Suspensions

Seventh chords can succeed each other in chain suspensions. This is especially common in circular-fifth patterns. The chords are often incomplete, with the usual suspects missing (the chord fifths). Example 14-14 shows the essential voice leading.

EXAMPLE 14-14

Variations on this pattern appear in diverse times and styles.

EXAMPLE 14-15a Kenny "Babyface" Edmonds: "I Said I Love You"

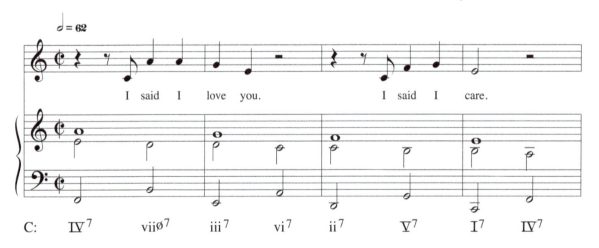

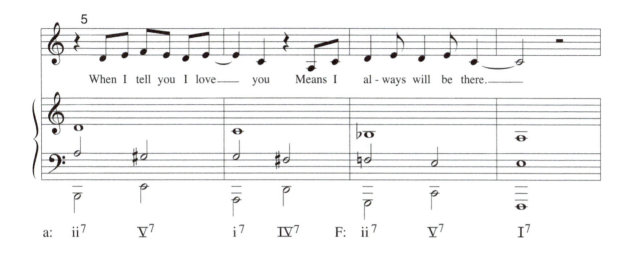

EXAMPLE 14-15b Mozart: Rondo, K. 494

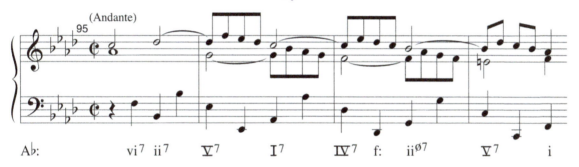

CONCEPT CHECK

The popular song that follows (Example 14-16) is arranged in a way that accentuates its similarities with Mozart's Rondo. Study the seventh chords in both examples and compare the voice leading.

EXAMPLE 14-16 Vicki Wickham, Simon Napier-Bell, Pino Donaggio, Vito Pallavicini:
"You Don't Have to Say You Love Me"

The I⁷

The final measures of Examples 14-15a and b illustrate a distinction between Classical music and jazz and popular music. Even though the rising stature of the seventh prompted composers of Mozart's time to adorn their harmonies with it ever more liberally, the one chord likely to remain dissonance-free was the tonic. In jazz and popular circles, however, the well-dressed tonic is every bit as likely to be wearing an unresolved seventh as is any other chord.

In Examples 14-17a and b, the seventh in the tonic chord appears as a prominent melody note, clearly showing its complete acceptance as a chord tone not requiring resolution.

EXAMPLE 14-17a Eddie Delange, Irving Mills, and Duke Ellington: "Solitude" 🔊

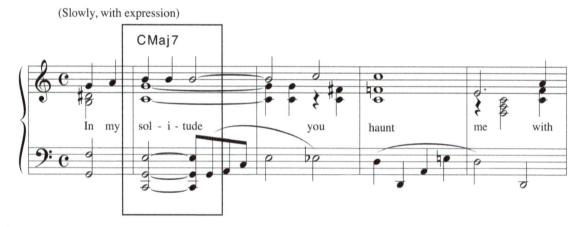

EXAMPLE 14-17b Miles Davis: "Four"

Note:

In a, the seventh moves upward to C. In b, it moves downward to D♭. In both examples, it lasts longer than a measure and is the most important melodic pitch for the duration of the tonic harmony.

The I⁷ (with unresolved seventh) appears prominently in sequential statements of the ii⁷–V⁷–I⁷ progression. Example 14-18 shows this as well as another feature of the jazz style—a seventh on every chord (with or without resolution).

EXAMPLE 14-18 Miles Davis: "Tune Up" 🔊

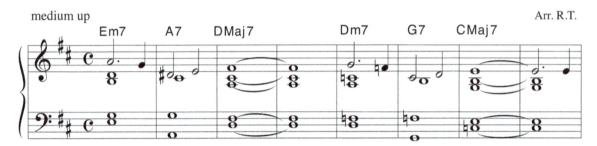

Note:

The chords of m. 3 and m. 7 are heard as I7 in D and C respectively.

▶ *For assignments on nondominant seventh chords, turn to Workbook p. 163.*

The Voice-Leading Summary from Chapter 13 is reprinted below with additions that address the practices presented in this chapter.

Voice-Leading Summary

For triads in all positions:

1. *Spacing: Keep each voice within its range and in its corridor, maintaining homogenous spacing among the upper voices. Avoid voice crossing and overlap. (See Chapter 10, p. 170 and Chapter 11, p. 190 and p. 191.)*

2. *Doubling: Normally double the bass (in second inversion always double the bass) unless it's a sensitive tone. Double a different chord member (but never a sensitive tone) to improve a melodic line or to satisfy the preceding spacing guideline. (See Chapter 11, p. 186.)*

3. *Chord Connection:*

   a. *Move the soprano and bass in contrary or oblique motion as often as possible. (See Chapter 10, p. 172.)*

   b. *Favor conjunct motion, avoid awkward melodic intervals, and resolve sensitive tones. (See Chapter 10, p. 170.)*

   c. *Where common tones between chords exist, retain them in the same voices. (See Chapter 11, p. 192.)*

    d. *Avoid consecutive octaves, fifths or unisons between any two voices. (See Chapter 11, p. 188.)*

For triads in second inversion:

1. *In the cadential and pedal six-four chords, the bass and the tone doubling it remain stationary.*

2. *In the passing six-four chord, the bass and the tone doubling it resemble passing tones moving in opposite directions.*

3. *In the arpeggiated six-four, the bass leaps to the fifth from another member of the same chord.*

Seventh chords and suspensions:

1. *Don't double the seventh but do resolve it stepwise downward.*

2. *Omit the chord fifth when a part writing situation requires an incomplete seventh chord.*

3. *Don't double a suspension dissonance. Because a suspension merely delays the resolution of a chord member, doubling in a suspension resolution should be the same as it would be in the absence of the suspension. Except for the 9–8 suspension, the note of resolution should not be present in the preceding chord.*

⊕ CODA

Effective part writing requires effective melody writing for each voice. However, effective melody writing requires a sensitivity to the tendencies of the individual pitches. But the tendencies of the individual pitches depend on their harmonic context. And the harmonic context is the result of the individual lines.

The circle is complete. The chicken lays the egg that hatches the chicken that lays the egg . . .

In Chapter 5, you learned that a key is a chord's context. Similarly, *a chord is a pitch's context.* In the key of E♭, for example, "D" drips with tendency as the third of the V^7. Its tendency evaporates a bit as the fifth of the iii^7. Likewise, A♭ has less stability as the seventh in the V^7 than as the root of the IV.

In any harmony containing *both* $\hat{7}$ and $\hat{4}$, it is rarely wrong to resolve this tritone; and with seventh chords, you can rarely go astray by resolving the seventh stepwise downward.

Still, a melodic tendency can be denied for the sake of obtaining a complete harmony; and an incomplete triad or seventh chord can be the acceptable result of satisfying a melodic tendency. The melodic and harmonic forces should constantly be weighed, and the balance changes with each piece.

DO YOU KNOW THESE TERMS?

- chain suspension
- delayed resolution
- nondominant seventh chord
- Picardy third

Basic Chromatic Harmony

PART FIVE

Most of the harmonies discussed to this point have been diatonic—that is, they occur naturally within the key. Few works, however—especially works of appreciable length—consist solely of diatonic chords. This unit examines two ways of extending the harmonic gamut.

Chapters 15 and 16 focus on **altered chords**—chords that contain accidentals. Known also as **chromatic chords**, these harmonies are spawned by various processes. The earliest was **tonicization**—briefly endowing a chord *other than the tonic* with the aura and weight of a tonic by preceding it with a chord that functions as its V, V^7, vii°, or vii°⁷ (vii^{ø7}).

Modulation—changing tonal centers by establishing a new tonic—is the subject of Chapter 17. As you'll learn, tonicization and modulation are siblings. Both were born during the Renaissance and reached maturity by the time of Bach and Handel. They persist as fundamental elements of the harmonic system used in jazz and popular music, from barbershop quartets and ragtime to John Coltrane and Steely Dan.

CHAPTER FIFTEEN

Secondary Function I

KEY CONCEPTS IN THIS CHAPTER

- Tonicization by the Dominant and Dominant Seventh Chord

- Secondary Leading Tones and Tonicizing Tritones

- Melodic Chromaticism and Harmonic Sequence

- Tonicization by Leading-Tone Triads and Seventh Chords

SECONDARY DOMINANTS

Example 15-1 is in A♭ major. However, the B♭ major triad in m. 2 is not diatonic. It *could* be symbolized II, the upper case indicating its quality—major. It and the chord that follows *could* be analyzed V–I if the key were E♭ major. But the key is A♭, and the two chords form a dominant-tonic relationship that is secondary to that key. For this reason, the B♭ major triad is called a **secondary dominant**, and its symbol V/V (which we read "V *of* V") reflects this (Analysis 3).

The V/x

EXAMPLE 15-1 Sir Harold Bolton: "All Through the Night" 🔊))

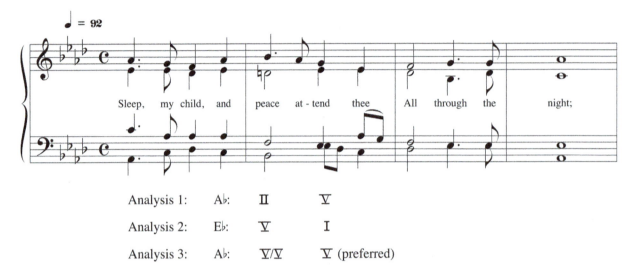

Analysis 1:   Ab: II   V

Analysis 2:   Eb: V   I

Analysis 3:   Ab: V/V   V (preferred)

Tonicization

The Bb major triad can be said to **tonicize** the Eb major triad that follows it because it causes it to sound—*for a fleeting moment*—like the tonic. In the symbol V/V, the Roman numeral left of the slash shows the function of the chord being analyzed *in relation to its chord of resolution*, which is shown to the right of the slash.

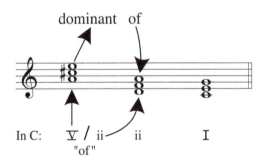

Consider the next song, in the key of F. The A major triad in m. 41 *could* be symbolized III (upper case because it's major). But it and the following chord (A–Dm) sound like V–I in D minor, a tonicization of vi, and the best way to express this is with the symbol V/vi.

EXAMPLE 15-2 Sara Bareillis: "She Used To Be Mine"

Compare the analysis of the A major triad (V/vi) with that in Example 15-1a (V/ii). The chord is the same but its symbol is different because the key (and thus its function within that key) is different.

Any major or minor triad in a key can be tonicized by preceding it with a *major triad whose root lies a perfect fifth above*. The third of this secondary dominant acts as a **secondary leading tone**. However, not all possible tonicizations occur with equal frequency. In Example 15-3, asterisks mark the most common ones. Play the example and listen to the tonicizing effect of each secondary dominant on the following chord.

EXAMPLE 15-3a The Second Chord of Each Measure Is a Dominant of the Following Chord—Major

a Major

EXAMPLE 15-3b Minor

b Minor

Notes:

1. A secondary dominant is always *a major triad* whose root is a *perfect fifth above* that of the chord it tonicizes. All secondary dominants except V/IV in major, and the V/III and V/VI in minor contain a chromatic pitch. They become major through a chromatically raised third, the secondary leading tone.

2. Diminished triads such as vii° or the ii° cannot be tonicized unless altered to become major or minor triads.

3. In a, it would be technically possible to call the I in m. 3 a V/IV; in b, it would be technically possible to call the VII in m. 2 a V/III and the III in m. 5 a V/VI; however, a chord really requires a chromatic note to be heard as a secondary dominant.

4. Three secondary dominants in minor (V/ii, V/iv, and V/v) are identical to their counterparts in major. The other three (V/III, V/VI, and V/♭VII) are different because they tonicize chords whose roots are a half step lower than in major.

5. Although the V/v in minor is rare, the V/V (tonicizing the *major* dominant) is quite common.

REVIEW AND REINFORCEMENT_____

1   Identify and symbolize the secondary dominant in Example 15-4.

2   Construct a melodic reduction similar to those of Examples 7-21 and 7-22
    (see p. 119) that show structural, supporting, and embellishing tones and melodic
    prolongations.

EXAMPLE 15-4 Elvey and Alford: "Come, Ye Thankful People Come" 🔊

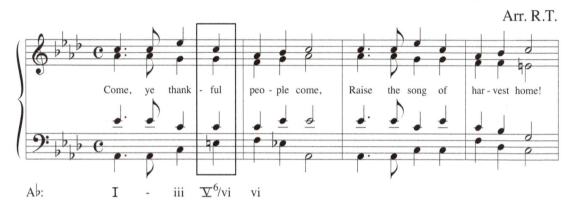

Arr. R.T.

Ab: I - iii   V⁶/vi   vi

➤ *Assignment 1A in Workbook Chapter 15 can be completed now.*

The Tonicizing Tritone

Let's try an experiment. Play a major triad. What tonal center does it suggest? Your first
inclination might be to name the chord root. But think again. The chord *could* be I. But
it could also be V or IV, or III or VI in a minor key. How would you know? The truth
is, a major or minor triad alone offers no clue to the tonality.

Now play a Mm7 chord. What tonal center does it suggest? This time the answer's different.
Because the Mm7 chord appears on only one scale degree, it strongly suggests a tonic—
the note a perfect fifth lower. That's what conditioning can do. It's the way the chord
has been used for centuries. The reason it has been so used lies with scale degrees 4 ("fa")
and 7 ("ti"). Sounded together, this "tonicizing tritone" tends toward the root and third
of a tonic triad.

When any seventh chord is altered to become a Mm7, Western ears hear "dominant seventh chord," and the triad a *perfect fifth* lower sounds fleetingly like its tonic.

The V⁷/x

When a Mm7 chord appears on a scale degree *other than* $\hat{5}$, it can be analyzed as a secondary dominant seventh chord. The chords in Example 15-5a could be symbolized V^7/G, $V^7/B\flat$, $V^7/A\flat$, and so on (read V^7 *of* G, V^7 *of* B♭, and V^7 *of* A♭).

EXAMPLE 15-5a

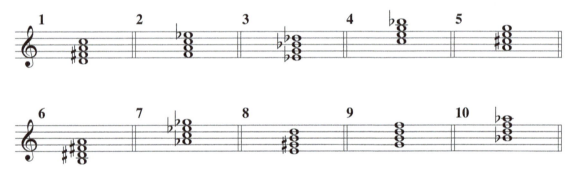

The D7 in Example 15-5a can never be a V^7 of anything but G. If this D7 chord appeared in C major, it would be symbolized V^7/V (G being V in C). If instead the key were D minor, it would be symbolized V^7/iv (g being iv in that key). In E♭ it would be symbolized V^7/iii (g being iii in that key). And so on.

Examples 15-6 a and b both tonicize IV.

EXAMPLE 15-6a John Lennon and Paul McCartney: "The Long and Winding Road"

EXAMPLE 15-6b Beethoven: Symphony, no. 1, op. 21 (first movement)

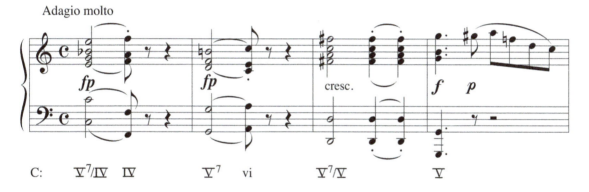

Note:

In b, tonicizations of IV (m. 1) and V (m. 3) occur before the tonic itself (C) is heard. Even without hearing the tonic, we know by m. 4 what it is and anticipate hearing it. That's functional tonality at work.

CONCEPT CHECK

Identify the tonicizing tritone in each of the chords of Example 15-6b. How do these pitches resolve?

Since the Mm7 chord more forcefully suggests a tonic than a major triad ever can, V^7/x is more common than V/x. Any of the secondary dominants in Example 15-3 can become a V^7/x simply by adding a minor seventh above the chord root.

EXAMPLE 15-7a Brackets Show Resolution of Secondary Leading Tone. Arrows Connect Chord Sevenths With Their Resolutions (Blackened Notes)

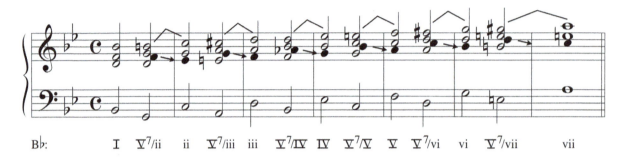

B♭:   I   V⁷/ii   ii   V⁷/iii   iii   V⁷/IV   IV   V⁷/V   V   V⁷/vi   vi   V⁷/vii   vii

EXAMPLE 15-7b Jesse Harris: "Don't Know Why" 🔊

B♭:

Notes:

1. A secondary dominant seventh chord is always the *major–minor seventh chord* whose root is a *perfect fifth above* (or perfect fourth below) the chord it tonicizes. Its tonicizing effect is stronger than a simple triad's.

2. When a minor seventh (a chromatic pitch) is added above the root of I, the chord's tonicizing effect is magnified. In a I–IV harmonic motion, the I *could* be analyzed as V/IV, but why do so? Adding the minor seventh above the root, however, clearly creates the tonicization, V⁷/IV.

▶ *Assignment 1C in Workbook Chapter 15 can be completed now.*

In Chapter 5, an analogy was drawn to show the way the chords of a key function (see Example 5-12). The addition of secondary dominants to the chord vocabulary greatly expands the "tonal planetary system."

EXAMPLE 15-8 The Expanding "Tonal Planetary System"

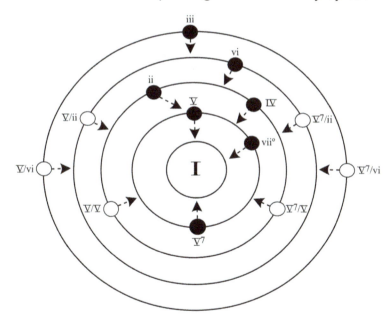

The added harmonies create many more options for harmonic progressions. Even more are created by adding secondary leading-tone chords, which we'll consider next.

▶ *For assignments on secondary dominants, turn to Workbook Chapter 15, assignments 1A–1G.*

SECONDARY LEADING-TONE CHORDS

Example 15-9 begins with a tonicization of ii (V^7/ii) in m. 10 followed by a harmonic and melodic sequence a step lower. In m. 12, a diminished triad that is not diatonic in D appears. This chord is a secondary leading-tone triad, functioning momentarily as a vii° in the key of the cadence chord, A. It is symbolized vii°/V because A (the tonicized chord) is V in the home key. (Notice also that the V is preceded by a cadential six-four chord.)

EXAMPLE 15-9 Mozart: Piano Sonata, K. 284 (third movement) 🔊

The passage in Example 15-10 is in A major. Three chords are not diatonic. The B major triad of m. 2 is a V/V. The other two chords are secondary leading-tone chords that function momentarily as vii°7 with respect to the chords they tonicize (iii and vi).

EXAMPLE 15-10 Schumann: *Kinderszenen*, no. 6 ("An Important Event") 🔊

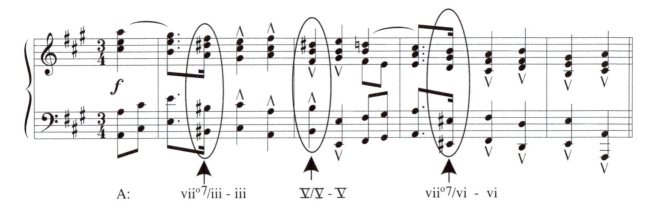

viiº/x, viiº⁷/x, vii⍉⁷/x

The leading-tone triad and leading-tone seventh chords contain the tonicizing tritone, just as does the V^7. And like the V^7/x, secondary leading-tone chords (viiº/x, viiº⁷/x, and vii⍉⁷/x) can be used to tonicize any major or minor triad. The root is always *a minor second below* the chord tonicized. (As the temporary leading tone to the tonicized chord, it *must* be.) Examples are shown in C major.

EXAMPLE 15-11 Arrows Show Resolution of Tonicizing Tritone

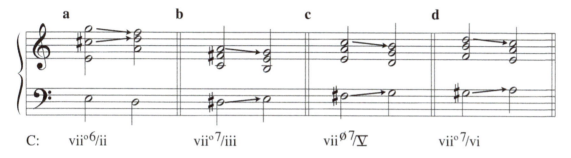

Notes:

1. The chord *must* take one of three forms: a diminished triad viiº/x, shown in a, a diminished seventh chord viiº⁷/x, shown in b and d, or a half-diminished seventh chord vii⍉⁷/x, shown in c.

2. The viiº/x (a) is in first inversion. Secondary diminished triads, like their diatonic counterparts, are commonly in this inversion.

The fully diminished seventh chord is the most common type of secondary leading-tone chord. With its seventh only a half step from its resolution, the chord has a stronger tendency than the half-diminished seventh chord (vii⍉⁷/x). *Always* the best choice when tonicizing a minor triad, it's frequently used to tonicize a major triad as well.

a Half-diminished:
(less common)

b Fully diminished:
(more common)

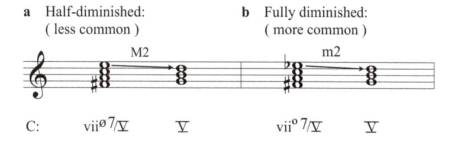

CONCEPT CHECK

Play Example 15-12. What pitch change in mm. 37 and 39 would turn the diminished seventh chords into half-diminished sevenths? Make those changes, and play the passage again. As you'll hear, either chord (°7 or ⌀7) works. Which do you prefer? Why? What other secondary functions are present in the passage? What chord most likely follows m. 40? Why?

EXAMPLE 15-12 Beethoven: String Quartet, op. 18, no. 1 (third movement) 🔊

Notes:

↺ BACK TO BASICS 15.1

Secondary (Applied) Chords

1. Double suspensions are present in the first and second violin parts at the resolution of both secondary diminished seventh chords (in m. 38 and in m. 40).

2. In mm. 39–40, the vii°7/vi resolves to a chord that is itself altered—the suspension resolution F♯ turns vi major (VI).

▶ *Assignments 2A and 2B on Workbook p. 176 can be completed now.*

VOICE LEADING

Doubling and Resolution

If you remember all previous voice-leading guidelines, then you need bear only two things in mind regarding secondary function:

- The same voice-leading practices that relate to the V, V⁷, vii°, vii°7, and vii⌀7 apply to their secondary counterparts, regardless of style or medium.

- Secondary functions behave as though they are in the key of the tonicized chord.

What these two statements mean is this:

1. Don't double the secondary leading tone, but *do* resolve it when it's in an outer voice. In an inner voice this tone can remain unresolved for the sake of obtaining a complete chord of resolution (although Bach rarely met a secondary leading tone he didn't resolve).

2. Resolve sevenths, if present, stepwise downward.

3. Avoid doubling the other altered tones, and if possible, resolve them *in the direction of their inflection (up when raised, down when lowered)*.

4. If it's impossible to resolve *all* tendency tones (the chord seventh, the secondary leading tone, and other altered tones) without creating doubling or voice-leading problems, then follow this guideline: *Part write as though the music were in the key of the tonicized chord*.

Example 15-13 shows these practices applied to common secondary functions in a variety of keys.

EXAMPLE 15-13a J. S. Bach: "Ach wie nichtig, ach wie flüchtig"

a: VI   iv   V   i   V⁶₅/V   V   i   I

Note:

In m. 10, the seventh of the chord (A) resolves downward to the leading-tone G♯. This creates an apparent problem. The other altered tone, F♯, cannot resolve *upward* (as chromatically raised pitches normally do) without doubling the leading tone. But remember: *Secondary functions behave as if they are in the key of the tonicized chord*. In that key (E), F♯ is not an altered tone at all and so does not need to resolve upward. The problem is only an "apparent" one.

EXAMPLE 15-13b J. S. Bach: "Nun lob', mein' Seel', den Herren"

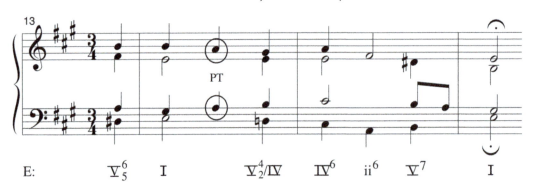

E: V^6_5 I V^4_2/IV IV^6 ii^6 V^7 I

Note:

In m. 13, the secondary leading tone (G♯) is resolved upward and the chord seventh (D) is resolved downward. (Remember that, in the V^7/IV, the secondary leading tone is not a chromatically altered pitch.)

EXAMPLE 15-13c J. S. Bach: "Was frag' ich nach der Welt"

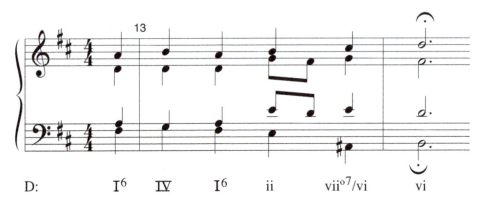

D: I^6 IV I^6 ii $\text{vii}^{\circ 7}/\text{vi}$ vi

Note:

The secondary leading tone (A♯) resolves upward, and the chord seventh (G) resolves downward. *Both* tritones in the secondary $\text{vii}^{\circ 7}$ are resolved, just as they often are in the primary $\text{vii}^{\circ 7}$. (See Note no. 3 following Example 14-7 on p. 233).

EXAMPLE 15-13d J. S. Bach: "Herr Christ, der ein'ge Gottes-Sohn"

F: V^6 I   vii°^{7}/ii   ii   vii°/iii   V/vi   V^7/vi   IV

Deceptive resolution

Notes:

1. In both the vii°^{7}/ii and vii°^{7}/iii, the secondary leading tone resolves upward (even though it necessitates voice crossing in m. 8). In both chords, the seventh resolves downward.

2. The v^7/vi in m. 8 resolves deceptively to IV. If the key were D minor, Roman numeral analysis would show this to be a typical deceptive cadence: V^7-VI.

Secondary Function and Chromatic Lines

Secondary functions create signature linear patterns. One is a chromatic rising line formed in the bass or other voice by the secondary leading tone and the following chord's root.

EXAMPLE 15-14 Schubert: Impromptu, op. 142, no. 3

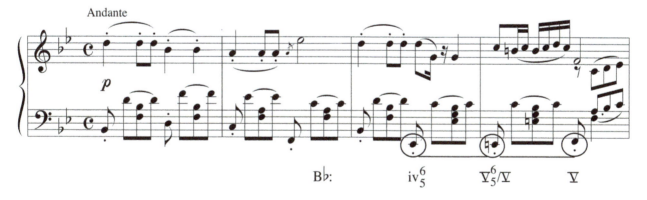

B♭:   iv$^6_5$ V$^6_5$/V   V

Note:

The E natural in m. 4 (circled) is a secondary leading tone that enhances the push toward V.

Extended chromatic lines can be created by stringing together a series of secondary functions. Ascending lines are more common than descending, probably because they are generated by the normal upward resolution of the secondary leading tone, as in Example 15-15a.

EXAMPLE 15-15a Ascending Chromatic Bass Line

The descending chromatic lines in b result from elided resolution of the secondary leading tones, one of the few situations in which sensitive tones in an outer voice are denied their normal resolution (see the note that follows the example).

EXAMPLE 15-15b Descending Chromatic Soprano and Bass Lines

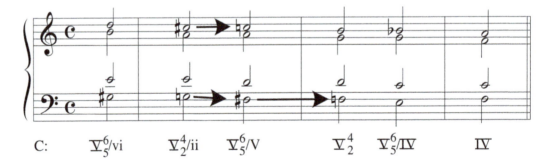

Notes:

1. The secondary leading tone in each secondary V[7] (except the last) omits (elides) its normal upward resolution, instead moving chromatically *downward* (shown by arrows) to become the seventh of the next chord.

2. Each seventh resolves *downward* (its normal resolution).

3. Each tonicized chord is inverted and altered to become a *new* secondary V[7], so that a chain of secondary dominant seventh chords tracing the circle of fifths results.

Pianist Bill Evans used the process in Example 15-15b (although with some voice-leading license). Observe the chromatic descent in the bass, the succession of nondominant seventh chords, and the secondary dominants in succession.

EXAMPLE 15-16 Bill Evans: "Waltz for Debby" (as played at the Bach Dancing and Dynamite Society, Half Moon Bay, CA, 1973) 🔊

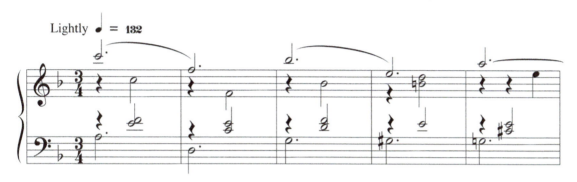

REVIEW AND REINFORCEMENT

Add Roman numerals beneath the chords in Example 15-16. Above the chords, show the corresponding lead-sheet symbols.

Harmonic Sequence and Secondary Function

Secondary dominants play prominent roles in harmonic sequences—chord patterns that are repeated at different pitch levels.

EXAMPLE 15-17 Kuhlau: Sonatina, op. 55, no. 5 (first movement)

Note:

The harmonic sequence a step lower in mm. 18–19 results in a descending scalar bass line.

When secondary dominants are involved in harmonic sequences, chromatic lines are often the result. In Example 15-18a, a chromatic step progression (B–C–C♯–D) results in the highest voice. In b, the chromatic line is in the bass.

EXAMPLE 15-18a J. S. Bach: Prelude No. 11 from *WTC*, Book I

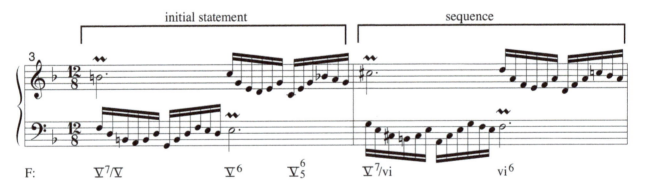

EXAMPLE 15-18b Handel: Concerto Grosso, op. 6, no. 1 (Allegro)* 🔊

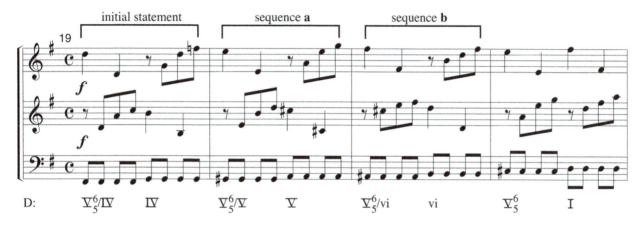

Note:

Some rhythmic elements have been omitted from this reduction to render it more easily playable. All melodic and harmonic elements are present.

REVIEW AND REINFORCEMENT

Can you find the chord pattern of example 15–18b in either of the patterns given in Example 15-15? Compare Roman numerals, not the chords themselves, as Handel's passage is in a different key.

Harmonic sequences abound in jazz, and tonicization is almost always involved. (See Example 14-18 on p. 242.) We'll consider this in greater detail in Chapter 16.

▶ *For assignments on secondary leading-tone chords, turn to Workbook p. 176.*

✛ CODA

Certain types of music (some non-Western music, for example) contain severely limited harmonic resources. Other aspects of that music are richer and more complex in compensation. However, the Western repertory (the music nurtured in Europe and transported to America) is harmonic to the bone, and for that reason, we expect a certain amount of harmonic variety. The oldest and most common way to achieve it is secondary function.

Three key points to remember:

- A secondary dominant or dominant seventh chord is always situated a perfect fifth above (or perfect fourth below) the chord it tonicizes and is always a major triad or Mm seventh chord. If both conditions are not present, the chord is not a secondary function.

- A secondary leading-tone chord always has its root a minor second below the chord it tonicizes and is either a diminished triad or a diminished (or half-diminished) seventh chord. If both conditions are not present, the chord is not a secondary function.

- Four of the five secondary functions—V^7/x, vii°/x, viiø⁷/x, and vii°⁷/x—contain a "tonicizing tritone," $\hat{4}$ and $\hat{7}$ in the key of the tonicized chord. *All* contain $\hat{7}$, which is chromatically raised as the secondary leading tone. $\hat{4}$, if altered, will be chromatically lowered. These tones are "sensitive," and they demand resolution. Proper treatment of the tonicizing tritone practically guarantees proper treatment of the chord containing them.

DO YOU KNOW THESE TERMS?

- altered chords
- chromatic chords
- elided resolution
- harmonic sequence
- secondary dominants
- secondary leading
- tone
- tonicization
- tonicizing tritone

CHAPTER SIXTEEN

Secondary Function II

KEY CONCEPTS IN THIS CHAPTER

- Tonicization in Jazz and Popular Styles

- Expanding Tonicization (The Tonicizing Chord Group)

- Harmonization with Secondary Function

PRELIMINARY NOTE

Some of the musical examples in this chapter contain chords with added tones and chromatic alterations not yet discussed. Where a chord symbol contains an unfamiliar element, you'll be asked to disregard that element for time being.

"Add-ons" such as ninths and elevenths do not dramatically affect the quality of the basic seventh chord types, which you already know to be these:

EXAMPLE 16-1a The Five Basic Seventh Chords

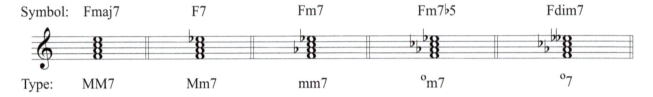

Symbol:	Fmaj7	F7	Fm7	Fm7♭5	Fdim7
Type:	MM7	Mm7	mm7	°m7	°7

For example: $D^{-9}/7$ derives from and sounds similar to D7; DMAJ9 derives from and sounds similar to DMAJ7; Dm11 derives from and sounds similar to Dm7.

Where a melody note appears not to be a member of the basic seventh chord whose symbol has been given, it probably represents an upward extension of the chord. In chapters that follow, you'll be introduced to expanded chord symbols that account for upward extensions, added tones and altered tones.

JAZZ AND POPULAR STYLES

V⁷/x

Secondary function has a long history in vernacular styles. Lavish use of secondary dominant seventh chords was a hallmark of so-called barbershop quartets. The turn-of-the-century all-male **a capella** group—tenor, lead, baritone, and bass—was unusual in that the *second* highest voice (logically called the "lead") carried the melody. The following tune, written in 1861, has been given several lyric settings. As "Aura Lee" it was popular with college glee clubs and barbershop quartets in the 1880s.

EXAMPLE 16-1 W. W. Fosdick and George R. Poulton: "Aura Lee"

Notes:

1. The intensely chromatic tenor line is typical of the style. It reflects the presence in that voice of either the secondary leading tone or the seventh of the many secondary dominant seventh chords, followed by their half step resolutions.

2. In mm. 13–14, the secondary leading tone G♯ moves *downward* to become the seventh in the next chord. In mm. 14–15, the secondary leading-tone C♯ does the same thing. Refer back to Example 15-15b for the voice-leading prototype.

Also around the turn of the twentieth century, a piano style called ragtime became popular. The term derives from an African-American word for clog-dancing. To "rag" a tune meant to perform it in a highly syncopated (rhythmically "ragged") manner. The relentless syncopation and chains of secondary dominants tumbling down the circle of fifths give the music of ragtime composers such as Scott Joplin and Ferdinand ("Jelly Roll") Morton its unique stamp.

EXAMPLE 16-2a Scott Joplin: "The Sycamore (A Concert Rag)" 🔊

C:　vii°$^4_2$/iii　　iii$^6_4$　　vii°$^4_2$/ii　　ii$^6_4$　　vii°$^6_5$/iii　I$^6_4$　　V̲^{7}/V̲　V̲^{7}　I̲

Note:

The melody note E in the final measure is an add-on (a ninth) to the basic seventh chord (V^7/V).

Gospel music, too, is richly infused with secondary function. Oscar Peterson's "Hymn to Freedom" displays a strong Gospel influence.

EXAMPLE 16-2b Oscar Peterson: "Hymn to Freedom" 🔊

REVIEW AND REINFORCEMENT

1 Identify all secondary functions in Example 16-2b by Roman numeral.

2 In Example 16-2b, add lead-sheet symbols that show both the chord and the bass note, as begun in mm. 1 and 2.

3 Locate and discuss the six-four chords in the passage. Each can be viewed as a variation of a standard six-four chord.

Expanding (Prolonging) a Tonicization

A secondary V or vii° can be preceded by its associated predominant, expanding a tonicization into a two chord affair that prolongs and enhances the tonicizing effect. In Example 16-3, the F♯7 in m. 9 (V⁷/V in E) is preceded by a C♯m7 (the "ii⁷/V" in E), creating a *secondary* ii–V motion.

EXAMPLE 16-3 Peter Cetera: "If You Leave Me Now"

continued

EXAMPLE 16-3 *continued*

The tonicizing chord group (specifically the "two-five" as it's called) has been a recipe for countless harmonizations in jazz and popular music. It can be expressed several ways:

EXAMPLE 16-4a

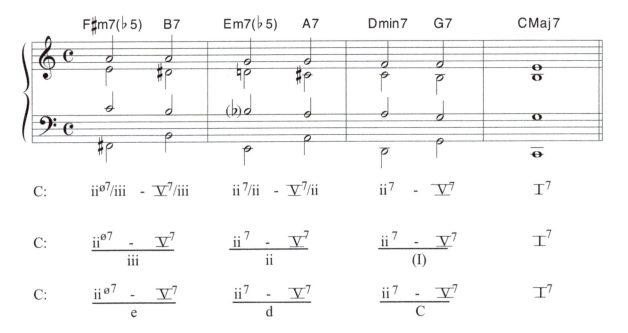

1. The first method symbolizes both the secondary dominant (V) and the secondary predominant (ii) individually.

2. The second method more clearly shows that the ii and V form a *pair* of chords that tonicize the chord shown beneath the line.

3. The third method replaces the Roman numeral of the tonicized chord beneath the line with the letter name of that chord.

4. The secondary supertonic seventh can be either a mm7 (Em7)or a om7 (Em7♭5). Sometimes the decision depends on whether the chord being tonicized is major or minor.

5. Even more chords can be included in a tonicizing chord group. But the longer a tonicization lasts, the more likely it is to be viewed instead as a modulation (more on this in Chapter 17).

EXAMPLE 16-4b William "Boz" Scaggs: "We're All Alone"

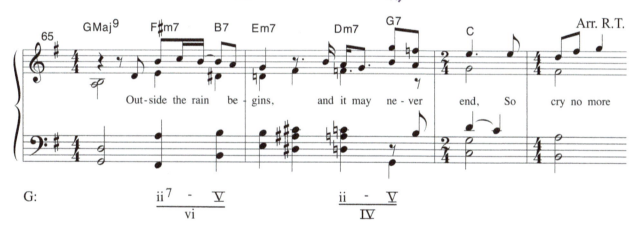

Note:

Example 16-4b lends itself immediately to two tonicizing chord groups, the first tonicizing vi and the second tonicizing IV.

The **tonicizing chord group** plays a significant role in the two works shown in Example 16-5. As mentioned at the beginning of this chapter, some of the chords contain notes or alterations not indicated by the basic chord symbol (the first melody note in both a and b, for example). Overlook this for now. The extra notes do not affect the quality of the basic chord shown by the symbol.

EXAMPLE 16-5a Miles Davis: "Tune Up" 🔊

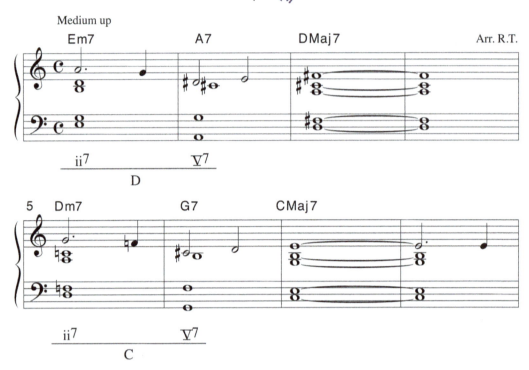

EXAMPLE 16-5b Victor Young: "Stella by Starlight" 🔊

Just as the dominant does not always resolve directly to the tonic (recall the deceptive cadence), secondary dominants do not *always* resolve directly to the tonic of the moment. And the same is true of tonicizing chord groups. "Stella" (Example 16-5b), in F major, first tonicizes D (mm. 1–2) then B♭ (mm. 3–4), then E♭ (mm. 5–6), and finally D♭ (mm. 7–8) *while never sounding the tonicized chord*. More than a single V^7, the ii^7–V^7 combination powerfully suggests a tonic, even without resolving to it.

The other predominant—IV—is less often found in tonicizing chord groups. This may be because the IV is present as the upper three chord members of the ii^7 and also because the circular-fifth motion of the II–V is so powerful.

vii°⁷/x

While not nearly as common as the secondary dominant seventh chord, secondary leading-tone chords can also be found in jazz and popular styles. The most common *form* is the fully diminished seventh chord, and the most common *chords* are:

EXAMPLE 16-6 Leading tone (root) resolves up, seventh resolves down

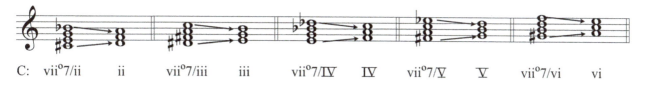

C: vii°7/ii   ii   vii°7/iii   iii   vii°7/IV   IV   vii°7/V   V   vii°7/vi   vi

Note:

The ø7 is *rarely, if ever,* used to tonicize a minor triad.

Example 16-7 illustrates the use of secondary leading-tone seventh chords. In b, vii°⁷/V, vii°⁷/vi, and vii°⁷/ii help to create a chromatically ascending bass line.

EXAMPLE 16-7a Leslie Bricusse and Anthony Newley: "Pure Imagination" (from *Willie Wonka and the Chocolate Factory*) 🔊

EXAMPLE 16-7b Michael MacDonald and Lester Abrams: "Minute by Minute" (from *The Doobie Brothers: Minute by Minute*, Warner Bros. Reva. Inc–3192-3) 🔊

In Example 16-7b, the vii°7/V (*) moves to a I 6/4. We know the I 6/4 to be a V with nonchord tones that mask its true identity. Here, though, when the "mask comes off" at the end of the measure, the V is itself transformed (by the G♯) into a secondary leading-tone chord—vii°7/vi.

EXAMPLE 16-8 a is elaborated to become **b**

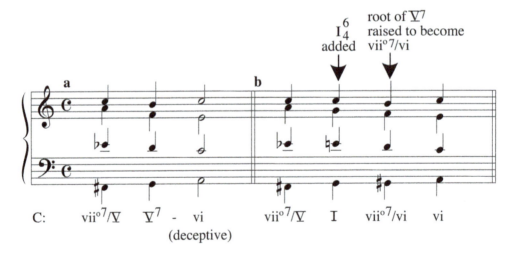

The Tonicizing IV?

Until now, we've recognized only two chords capable of tonicizing—the V and the vii°.
Can any other chord perform a tonicizing function? A sound that's become fashionable
in popular styles and in music for film and television is I–♭VII–IV.

EXAMPLE 16-9a Gary Portnoy and Judy Hart Angelo: "Where Everybody Knows Your
Name" (theme song from *Cheers*)

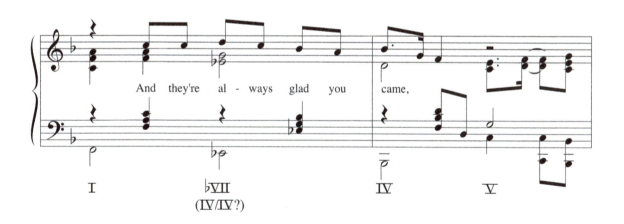

EXAMPLE 16-9b Tim Rice and Andrew Lloyd Webber: "I Don't Know How to Love Him"
(from *Jesus Christ Superstar*)

The approach to IV *from its* IV parallels the approach to V *from its* V. Whether the ♭VII in this context might be symbolized IV/IV (read "IV of IV") is a matter for debate. Also called a "double-plagal-motion," it's perhaps a product of the same tendency in rock music to use retrogressive chord successions, as in "Hey, Joe" (see p. 76), and Mixolydian chord combinations (note that ♭VII–IV–I comprise the pitch material of the Mixolydian mode). In any case, ♭VII –IV provides a sense of arrival on IV similar to that created by V⁷/IV, perhaps due to the prominence of the secondary "fa" (♭7) in both chord successions.

▶ *For assignments on jazz and popular styles, turn to Workbook Chapter 16, assignments 1A–1F.*

MELODY HARMONIZATION

In harmonizing a melodic line, a secondary dominant-tonic relationship can be established between any two chords whose roots descend by perfect fifth (ascending a perfect fourth is the same), so long as the second chord is a major or minor triad. Consider this well-known song of celebration.

EXAMPLE 16-10 Scottish Air: "Auld Lang Syne" (Words by Robert Burns) 🔊

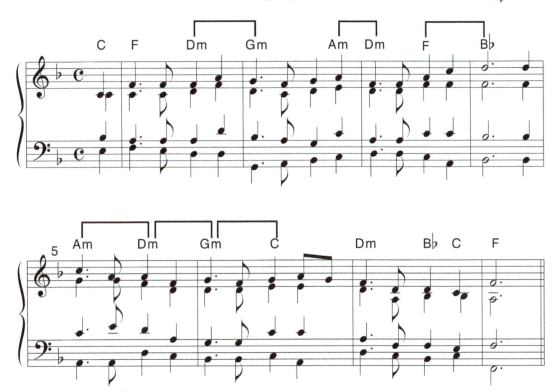

Over countless New Year's Eve celebrations, this tune has been dressed up many ways. The harmonization in Example 16-10 affords several opportunities to add secondary dominants. The possibilities—where chord roots descend by perfect fifth—are bracketed. The second chord in each pair can be tonicized by chromatically altering the first, as at points 1–5 in Example 16-11.

EXAMPLE 16-11

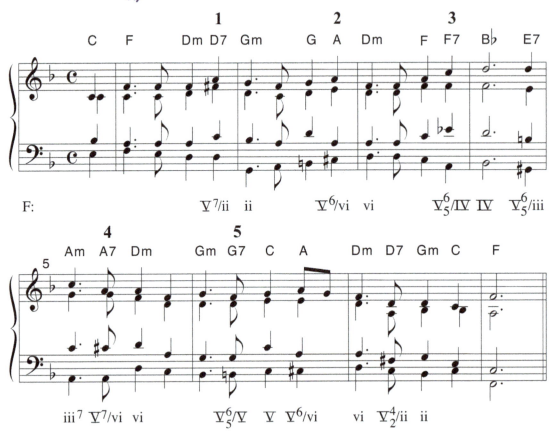

Notes:

1. Concerning 1: The chord on beat 3 can't become a V/ii because the melody note F would have to be changed to F♯. When the melody note changes on beat 4, however, tonicization becomes possible.

2. Concerning 2: Altering the bass note to become a secondary leading tone (C♯) transforms the chord into a secondary dominant. However, this change creates an augmented second (B♭–C♯). The solution is to raise the B♭ (beat 3). If you think of the three beats as temporarily in D minor, you'll see that this is the melodic minor principle at work.

Purely as an academic exercise, every diatonic triad has been tonicized in Example 16-11—ii, iii, IV, V, and vi—and at almost every opportunity. (Remember, the vii° can't be tonicized without first altering it.) The result sounds a bit overloaded. Just because a chord *can* be tonicized, this doesn't mean it *should* be. The cloying sound of many school songs is due to just this sort of excess. Check your own *alma mater*, and see how many secondary dominants are used in its harmonization.

Secondary leading-tone chords can usually be created where chord roots ascend by second.

F: V   -   vi   can become   vii°⁷/vi - vi

It is also often possible to replace a V⁷/x with a vii°⁷/x. Example 16-12 shows the first four measures of "Auld Lang Syne" reharmonized.

EXAMPLE 16-12 🔊

F: vii°⁷/ii   vii°⁷/IV   vii°⁷/iii

Note:

If you compare the indicated chords with those at the corresponding points in Example 16-11, you'll see that, in each case, a secondary leading-tone seventh chord has replaced a secondary dominant seventh chord. The first substitution resulted in a change of the bass line.

CONCEPT CHECK

Return to Ex. 16–10 and locate one additional point where reharmonization with a vii°⁷/x is possible.

▶ *For assignments on voice leading and harmonization, turn to Workbook Chapter 16, assignments 2A–2C.*

⊕ CODA

Jazz styles make extensive use of the tonicizing chord group ii–V/x. In theory, these tonicizations could be expanded to include additional chords (vi–ii–V/x for example). However, the longer a tonicization, the more likely it is to be heard as a modulation instead. Modulation is the topic of Chapter 17.

DO YOU KNOW THESE TERMS?

- a capella
- expanded tonicization
- ragtime
- tonicizing chord group two-fives

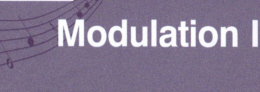

Modulation I

A PRELIMINARY QUIZ

By this point in your music studies, you've probably heard—possibly used—the term modulation. So let's find out what you know of the topic going into it.

True or False?

1. A modulation is a new tonal center.

    T___   F___

2. A modulation must last at least three full measures.

    T___   F___

3. Modulations can always be recognized by the change in key signature.

    T___   F___

4. A change from C major to C minor is an example of a modulation.

    T___   F___

5. A change from C major to A minor is an example of a modulation.

    T___   F___

Answers

1. False: A new tonal center is the *consequence* of a modulation. Modulation is the actual *process* by which the change occurs.

2. False: The question itself is bogus. How long are the measures? How slow is the tempo? How many harmonies transpire in process? Does the music reach a cadence in the new key? All of these affect whether or not a new tonal center is established, the usual test of a modulation.

3. False: Most modulations are too brief to be reflected by a change in key *signature*. A more common sign of a modulation is the *consistent appearance of accidentals*.

4. False: Although the key signatures for C major and C minor are different, their *tonal center* is the same. A change between parallel major and minor keys is not a modulation but a **change of mode**.

5. True: Although the key signatures for C major and A minor are the same, their tonal centers are different. A change between relative major and minor keys is a modulation.

While seven diatonic chords might seem like sufficient variety, the Western ear doesn't "see" it that way. It's true that many folk songs, hymns, and traditional songs contain no modulations—see, for example: "Amazing Grace" (Example 5-3); "The Star-Spangled Banner" (Example 7-1a); "America" (Example 7-1b); "Rock of Ages" (Example 9-7); "Michael, Row the Boat Ashore" (Example 13-19)—but even short pieces often modulate. And those that don't may be transposed on repetition. It has become almost formulaic in popular music, for example, to end a song by repeating the refrain, modulating upward each time. The catch phrase "Cue the strings" refers to these emotionally charged endings, where the violins enter the background in tandem with a rising tonal plateau.

All modulations, however simple or complex, are reducible to two categories: those that contain a common chord and those that don't. We'll discuss both.

MODULATION BY COMMON CHORD

A **common chord modulation** (also called a **pivot chord modulation**) turns on a chord diatonic in both keys. If we think of modulation as the door to a new tonality, the common chord is the "hinge." Usually, it *directly precedes the first chord no longer diatonic in the old key*.

EXAMPLE 17-1a J. S. Bach: "Wach auf, mein Herz" 🔊

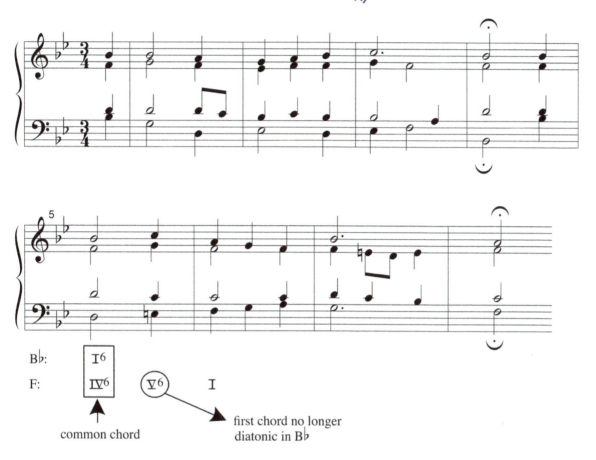

Bb:

F:

common chord

first chord no longer
diatonic in Bb

EXAMPLE 17-1b Kenneth Follese and Michael Delaney: "The Way You Love Me" 🔊

continued

EXAMPLE 17-1b *continued*

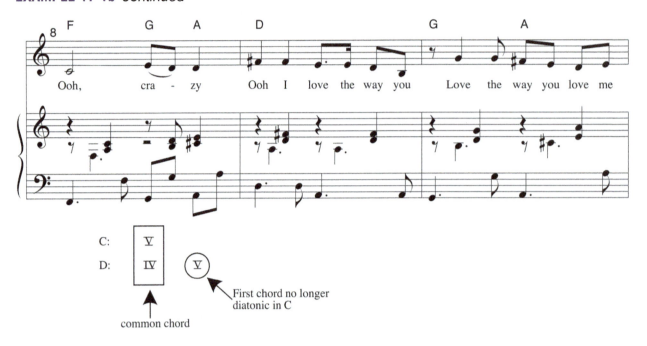

EXAMPLE 17-1c Richard Dehr, Terry Gilkyson, and Frank Miller: "Greenfields"

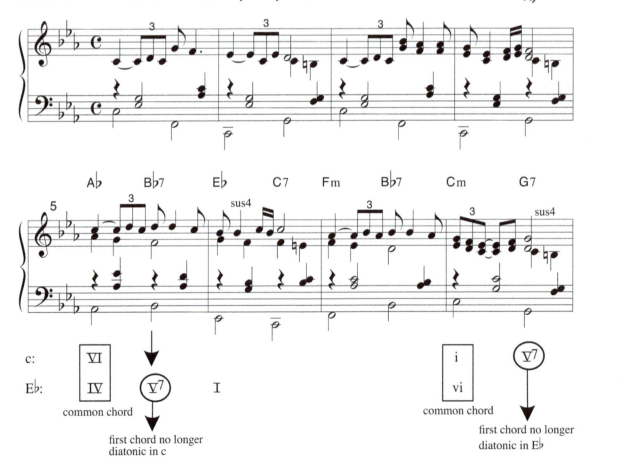

Notes:

1. In each case, the common chord precedes the new dominant, which is the first chord *not diatonic* in the old key.

2. In a and b, the common chord functions as a predominant in the new key.

REVIEW AND REINFORCEMENT

1   What two Roman numeral analyses are possible for the B♭ major triads in b? (Refer back to Chapter 15 if you've forgotten.)

2   Based on the lead-sheet symbols, what embellishing tones can you identify in c?

3   Identify a tonicization that occurs in c.

Crossing the "Tonal Border"

Many pieces travel across the "tonal border" into the new key *via* a pre-dominant. Predominants are the most "fuel-efficient" vehicles for carrying music to a new key because they take the most direct route, a mere three chord span: predominant–dominant–tonic. However, IV and ii are not the only rides in the garage.

EXAMPLE 17-2 Mozart: Symphony, no. 40 in G minor, K. 550 (third movement) 🔊

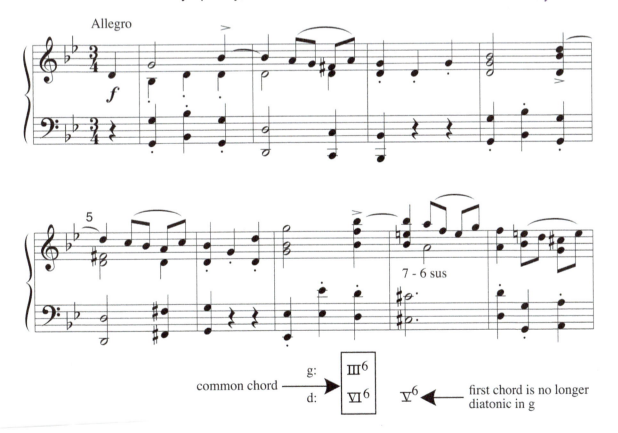

REVIEW AND REINFORCEMENT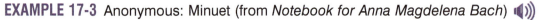

What large-scale melodic event described in Chapter 7 is prominent in Example 17-2?

Multiple Common Chords

In Example 17-2, the common chord is easy to identify because neither the chord preceding it (E♭) nor the chord following it (C♯°7) are diatonic in *both keys*. However, two keys may be separated by more than one chord diatonic to both.

EXAMPLE 17-3 Anonymous: Minuet (from *Notebook for Anna Magdelena Bach*) 🔊

Question: Which is the common chord?

Answer: Any chord from m. 16 through m. 19 might be so analyzed.

While musicians may differ on the precise point of modulation, multiple common chords tend to produce smoother-sounding modulations than does a solitary common chord.

What Is Closely Related about Closely Related Keys

Common chord modulations occur most often between **closely related keys**—those that differ by no more than one flat or one sharp. For a given tonality, the closely related keys consist of the relative major or minor, the dominant plus *its* relative, and the subdominant plus *its* relative.

EXAMPLE 17-4

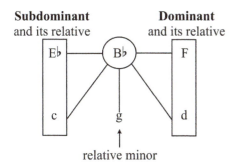

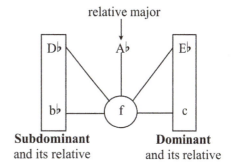

While modulation to *any* of the closely related keys is commonplace, perhaps *the most common* are modulations to the dominant and the relative major or minor key. Example 17-5 shows why this is so.

EXAMPLE 17-5 Lines connect common chords between the keys

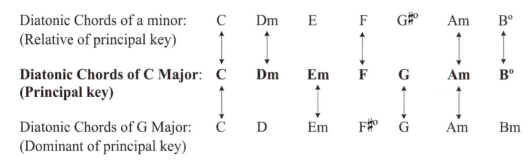

You can see why relative major and minor keys are so called. They are "relatives" by virtue of the number of chords they have in common (five). The dominant is the next most closely related key, with four chords in common. The sheer number of common chords available makes modulation to the dominant or relative both effortless and smooth sounding.

Equally significant is the fact that the relative and dominant keys are the only closely related keys in which *both pre-dominants* exist as common chords (diatonic in the home key).

EXAMPLE 17-6a

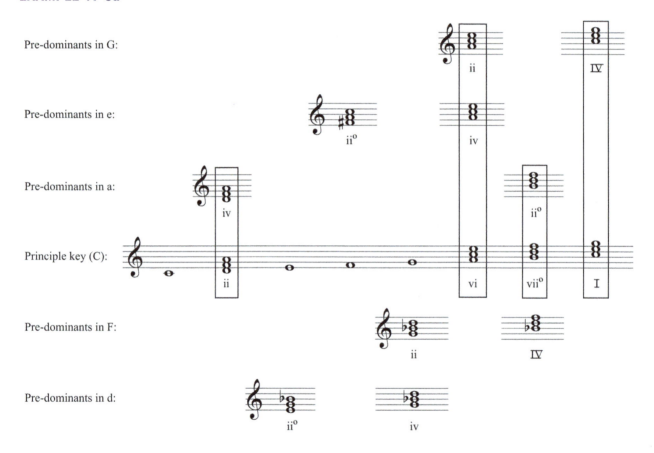

EXAMPLE 17-6b

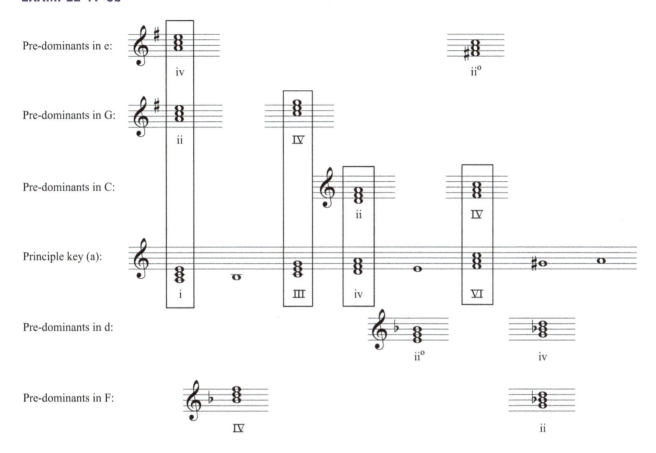

Note:

Again, pre-dominants (ii and IV) are the prime vehicles of modulation because they lead directly to the dominant. The keys that contain both of these chords—i.e., the relative and the dominant—have been, logically, the most frequent modulatory destinations.

▶ *For assignments on modulation by common chord, turn to Workbook Chapter 17, assignments 1A–1E.*

REVIEW AND REINFORCEMENT

Which of the examples of common chord modulations given thus far in the chapter *do not* involve closely related keys?

CHROMATIC MODULATION

A **chromatic modulation** is one that does not involve a common chord. It can often be recognized by the presence of a pitch followed by its chromatically altered form in one or more parts at the tonal border. Generally, *but not always*.

The Rule of Chromatics

- A chromatically raised pitch is the new "ti" (the new leading tone).

- A chromatically lowered pitch is the new "fa" (the new $\hat{4}$).

"The Rule of Chromatics" is illustrated in the examples that follow.

EXAMPLE 17-7 J. S. Bach: "Du großer Schmerzensmann"

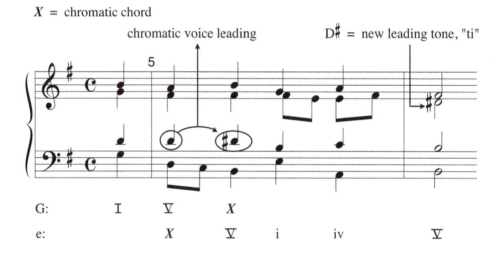

Notes:

1. The V in G (the old key) progresses directly to the V in e (the new key). Neither of these chords is diatonic in the other key, thus no common chord exists. The chromatically raised pitch is the new leading tone.

2. The V in G (beat 1) is also the subtonic (VII) in e. Theorists express mixed feelings about the subtonic. When is it diatonic and when is it chromatic? The authors consider it diatonic when progressing through a minor-key circular-fifth pattern and chromatic when tonicizing III or when accompanied by chromatic voice leading as here.

EXAMPLE 17-8 Chopin: Mazurka, op. 56, no. 1 🔊

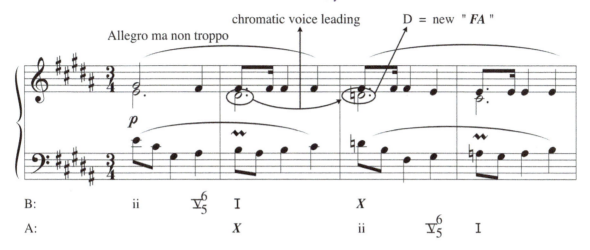

Note:

The I in B (the old key) is followed directly by ii in A (the new key). Neither of these chords is diatonic in the other key, thus no common chord exists. The chromatically lowered pitch is the new "fa."

Lacking the lubrication of a common chord, chromatic modulations often sound more abrupt and perhaps for this reason are less prevalent than common chord modulations. Just as common chord modulations occasionally involve keys not closely related (as Example 17-1b), chromatic modulations *can* involve closely related keys (as Example 17-7). However, they more often lead to tonalities more distant. In most, a chord diatonic *only in the old key* is followed by a chord diatonic *only in the new key* (as in Examples 17-7 and 17-8). But sometimes a chord diatonic *in neither key* straddles the modulation. Both types are shown in Example 17-9.

EXAMPLE 17-9a Schubert: "Kennst du das Land" 🔊

continued

EXAMPLE 17-9a *continued*

EXAMPLE 17-9b Bernstein: "Tonight" (from *West Side Story,* act 1, no. 7)

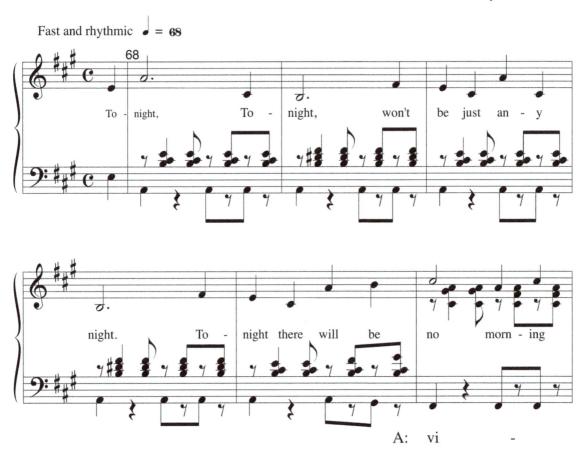

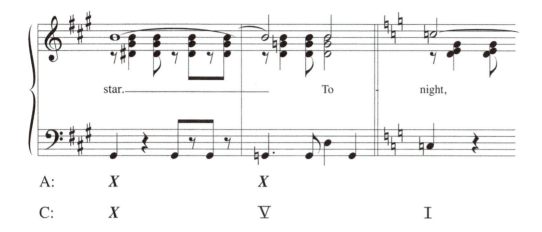

A: X   X

C: X   V   I

Notes:

1. In a, the *last chord diatonic in the old key* is followed directly by the *first chord diatonic in the new key* (m. 6). This is the simplest and most common type of chromatic modulation. Chromatic voice leading appears in the piano part.

2. In b, the last chord diatonic in the old key (m. 73) and the first chord diatonic in the new key (m. 75) are separated by a chord diatonic in *neither* key (m. 74).

REVIEW AND REINFORCEMENT

What mode is suggested in mm. 68–71 of Example 17-9b?

In more complex chromatic modulations, *several* chords diatonic in neither key may intervene. These and other variants of common chord and chromatic modulations will be discussed in Chapter 23.

Multiple Accidentals

The more distant the modulation, the more likely that it will be signaled by multiple accidentals. To "The Rule of Chromatics" on p. 292 we can add:

When a modulation is signaled by the consistent appearance of more than one accidental, the one most remote from the original key often functions as the new "ti" (if raised) or the new "fa" (if lowered).

Thus, if B♭ and E♭ appear consistently in the key of C, the E♭ (two accidentals removed from C) likely functions as "fa" and the key is probably B♭. If F♯, C♯, and G♯ appear consistently in the key of C, the G♯ likely functions as "ti," and the key is probably A.

EXAMPLE 17-10 Brahms: "Erinnerung", op. 63, no. 2

Note:

The appearance of F natural, B♭, E♭, and A♭—all chromatically lowered pitches—signal a modulation away from G. A♭, the accidental most remote from G major, functions as the new "fa," here the seventh of the V^7 in E♭ (m. 26).

CONCEPT CHECK

Look again at Example 17-9, and explain how the guideline concerning multiple accidentals can aid in the determination of the new key. In b, remember that the guideline applies only to *consistent* accidentals. Which accidental should be disregarded when attempting to identify the new key?

Modulation or Tonicization?

Modulations are usually not reflected by a change of key *signature* unless the new key remains in effect for a protracted length of time. How, then, to distinguish a modulation from a tonicization? In general:

1. A single secondary function does not establish a new tonal center.

2. Persistence of the same accidental(s) over several measures *may* signal a modulation.

3. A cadence in the new tonality tends to strengthen the feeling that a modulation has occurred.

4. Modulations are made more convincing by tonicizing the dominant in the new key (*e.g.,* V/V–V or vii°⁶/V–V).

Sometimes it's not the persistent *appearance* of an accidental but the persistent *lack* of an accidental that signals a modulation. Example 17-11 illustrates this point along with those just made. Mozart takes a tortuous route to C major from the home key of A minor.

EXAMPLE 17-11 Mozart: Piano Sonata, K. 310 (first movement) 🔊

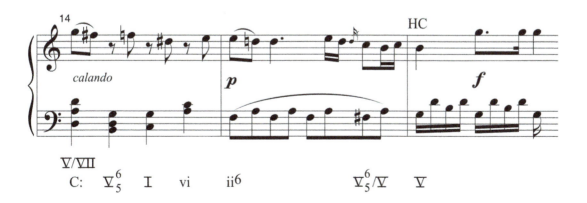

Notes:

Addressing each of the foregoing points in order:

1. Each tonicization is brief.

2. The persistent lack of G♯ (and the presence of G naturals) in mm. 11, 12, and 13 signal a modulation away from A minor.

3. A half cadence in the new key appears in m. 16.

4. The cadence chord (V) is tonicized in m. 15, solidifying the new tonic.

A final word: Tonicizations can be viewed as merely momentary modulations, and modulations can be seen as extended tonicizations—the difference is one of degree, not kind.

In Example 17-12, a contains a two-measure modulation while b contains a three-measure tonicization. a is analyzed as a modulation because it comes to a cadence in the new key, whereas b returns to the old key for its cadence.

EXAMPLE 17-12a Brahms: *Variations on a Theme of Robert Schumann*, op. 9

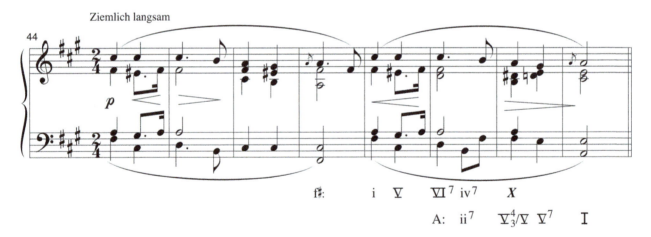

EXAMPLE 17-12b Schubert: Symphony, no. 8 (first movement) 🔊))

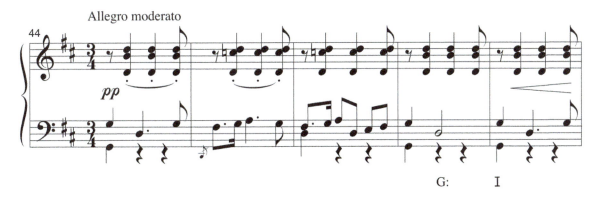

REVIEW AND REINFORCEMENT

Example 17-12b could be described as a prolonged tonic G with (large-scale) lower and upper neighbors (F♯ and A). On separate manuscript, show a melodic reduction similar to that on p. 118 that supports this analysis. Then show a more detailed reduction that accounts for additional supporting and embellishing tones.

CONCEPT CHECK

Example 17-13 contains two tonicizations. Identify them. The chromatic chord of m. 1 appears again in m. 2 and the music appears to come to a cadence on beat 3. What is it that weakens this "cadence" and prevents us from calling this a modulation? Do you see the melodic minor principle at work in this passage?

EXAMPLE 17-13 J. S. Bach: "Helft mir Gott's Güte preisen"

➤ *For assignments on chromatic modulation, turn to Workbook Chapter 17, assignments 2A–2H.*

✆ CODA

> All modulations have what might be called a tonal border. When the music drives across, it enters a new tonality. Sometimes, the tonal border is clear—a single chord that is a signpost announcing the new key. Sometimes, the tonal border is obscured by additional chromatic harmonies that belong to *neither* tonality. The keys to understanding a modulation are (1) to correctly identify the new key from the *consistent* accidentals that signal it, and (2) to discover exactly where the tonal border is. In all but the more complex cases, the harmonies before and after the tonal border will be easily analyzable in either the old or the new tonality.

DO YOU KNOW THESE TERMS?

- change of mode
- chromatic modulation
- closely related keys
- common chord
- common chord modulation
- modulation
- tonicization

Counterpoint

PART SIX

Western music sprouted from the soil of counterpoint, the study of which has long been an essential aspect of composers' training. One of the earliest textbooks on the subject was Johann Josef Fux's *Gradus ad Parnassum* ("Steps to Parnassus"), written in 1725. Fux taught five "species," beginning with note-against-note counterpoint and progressing to two, three, and then more notes against one. In the tradition of the day, the lessons took the form of a dialogue—between the all-knowing (and somewhat condescending) "Revered Master" Aloysius and the fawning and deferential student Josephus, who sounds today like an apple-polishing sycophant of the first order. Fux's method was painstaking, but it was the only show playing. It was studied by the Classical masters as well as such nineteenth-century composers as Schumann and Brahms.

This unit comprises two chapters. Chapter 18 focuses on two-voice counterpoint and builds upon the foundation laid in Chapter 10. The basics of that modified species approach are followed by a look at those principles as applied in jazz and popular styles and in the Bach Two-Part Inventions. Chapter 19 targets fugues from the Baroque era, the "golden age" of counterpoint. While there is a tendency to associate counterpoint with that musical period in general and with J. S. Bach in particular, contrapuntal writing informs most of the music you hear and play to one degree or another.

CHAPTER EIGHTEEN

The Art of Countermelody

THE BASICS OF TWO-VOICE COUNTERPOINT

Motion between Voices Redux

You already know that, between two voices, only four types of motion are possible: parallel, similar, oblique, and contrary. Of these, contrary and oblique provide the greatest melodic independence. In Example 18-1, parallel motion occurs only in m. 2. Similar motion does not appear at all. The remaining motion between the voices is contrary or oblique.

EXAMPLE 18-1 "America" (Old English Air)

Note-Against-Note Counterpoint

The counterpoint in Example 18-1 is composed almost exclusively of consonant intervals (thirds and sixths predominating). Recall from Chapter 10 that these features are typical of the note-against-note (1:1) style.

Converting 1:1 to 2:1

Rhythmic uniformity may be desirable in a marching band or chorus line, but in counterpoint—not so much. More effective are *rhythmically* independent lines and a *mix of consonance and dissonance*. These goals, we learned, can be achieved by filling in leaps with passing tones and by embellishing repeated or sustained pitches with neighbor tones. Of course, *more* notes mean *faster* notes. In Example 18-2, the resulting eighth note bass motion against prevailing quarters in the soprano transforms 1:1 counterpoint into 2:1 counterpoint.

EXAMPLE 18-2 "America" (Old English Air)

Note:

All bass notes a third apart have been connected by diatonic passing tones. Some notes a whole step apart have been connected by chromatic passing tones (the C♯ in m. 1, for example). The sustained D in m. 2 and the repeated D in m. 5 have been embellished by neighbor tones. The bass is now rhythmically independent of the melody.

CONCEPT CHECK

Count the number of times each type of motion occurs in Example 18-2. Which type now predominates? Count the number of dissonant intervals now present.

2:1 counterpoint involves oblique motion because—by definition—oblique motion pits a moving voice against a stationary one.

▶ *Assignment 1A in Workbook Chapter 18 can be completed now.*

Essentials of Counterpoint

Although musical styles have changed, the essentials of counterpoint have not. In tonal styles from the Baroque era to the present day, we find the following characteristics:

1. Counterpoint is harmonically conditioned. Lines sculpted to be melodically independent of each other (oblique and contrary motion predominating) combine to imply the harmonic foundation.

2. Each musical line occupies its own corridor, with minimal intrusion into the other line's pathway.

3. Consonant intervals appear in accented metric positions more often than do dissonant intervals.

4. **Imperfect consonances**—thirds and sixths (or their compounds)—are more abundant than **perfect consonances**—unisons, octaves, fourths, and fifths. They are normally the only intervals that move in parallel motion.

5. **Dissonance** emerges from or resolves into consonance. It is followed and/or preceded by stepwise motion, forming the nonchord tones we've already studied; the most common is the passing tone, followed by the neighbor tone and suspensions.

6. The 2:1 relationship is the basis for most counterpoint in simple meters, 3:1 for compound meters.

7. Rhythmic activity in one voice is often pitted against repose in the other. Moreover, active and passive moments are usually distributed between the voices.

8. Leaps in one voice are often balanced by steps in the other voice.

CONCEPT CHECK

In Example 18-2, identify the intervals that appear on the downbeats as either perfect or imperfect consonances. Which are more numerous?

The following two passages are composed mostly of 2:1 counterpoint. They differ from Example 18-2 in that they involve little more than arpeggiation of the underlying harmonies, suggesting that dissonance (nonchord tones) is not an essential feature of counterpoint. Still, one sounds more contrapuntal than the other. Which one? Can you explain why?

EXAMPLE 18-3a J. S. Bach: French Suite, no. 3 (Minuet) 🔊

EXAMPLE 18-3b J. S. Bach: Two-Part Invention, no. 13, BWV 784 🔊

Do you feel that b sounds more truly contrapuntal than a? This is because the rhythmic activity is more equally divided between the two parts. In a, the less active lower voice sounds supportive and thus subordinate. It fulfills its melodic role in a harmonic way, sounding a chord root at least once in each measure.

➤ *Assignment 1C in Workbook Chapter 18 can be completed now.*

Converting 2:1 to 4:1

Although 2:1 and 3:1 are the most common rhythmic relationships, much counterpoint contains more variety than this. 2:1 counterpoint can be converted to 4:1 counterpoint (four notes to one) in some of the ways shown in Example 18-4.

EXAMPLE 18-4

This 2:1 counterpoint

can be converted to 4:1 counterpoint in these or other ways:

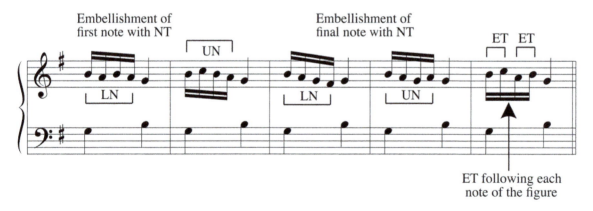

Other decorations of the figure:

CONCEPT CHECK

Following is a variation of the original figure in Example 18-4. Convert it to 4:1 counterpoint by similar methods.

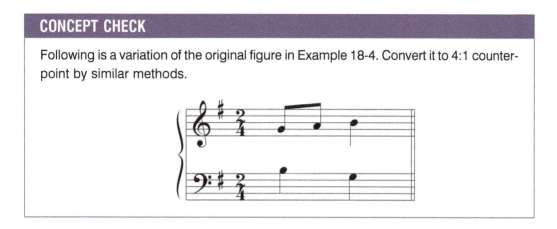

The first bars of "America" might be converted completely (if inelegantly) to 4:1 counterpoint using these techniques.

EXAMPLE 18-5 "America" (Old English Air)

CONCEPT CHECK

Circle the notes of the original bass line (reproduced here) still present in Example 18-5. Which of the embellishing techniques just demonstrated are used?

While the essentials of counterpoint are present in this all-too-busy bass, it lacks rhythmic variety. A more interesting result can be obtained through a better balance of 2:1 and 4:1 counterpoint. Circled notes in Example 18-6 show original bass notes still present.

EXAMPLE 18-6 "America" (Old English Air) 2:1 and 4:1 counterpoint

Examples 18-5 and 18-6 are a bit extreme and are simply provided to give you ideas for contrapuntal elaboration.

▶ *Assignment 1E2 in Workbook Chapter 18 can be completed now.*

Counterpoint in Film, Jazz, and Popular Styles

Film composers routinely employ the compositional techniques of the Classical masters, and counterpoint is no exception. John Williams' scores are awash in it. In the movie *Jaws*, Williams' vigorous two-voice counterpoint initiates and lends intensity to the contest between hunters and hunted in the famous "One Barrel Chase" scene.

EXAMPLE 18-7 John Williams: "Barrel Chase Scene" from *Jaws*

Effective arrangements of popular music contain at least a modicum of contrapuntal interest, and jazz is drenched in it. Even if the main business of the bass in these styles is to lay down chord roots and reinforce the beat, the bass usually contains melodic interest. At the very least, it will be similar to the lower voice in Example 18-3a. More contrapuntal are the musical dialogs in piano trios such as McCoy Tyner's, or in a Bob Brookmeyer composition, or the examples that follow.

EXAMPLE 18-8 Marilyn and Alan Bergman and Michel Legrand: "How Do You Keep The Music Playing?" (from *Best Friends*)

Notes:

1. In most measures, the bass sounds the chord root. The connection of chord tones with passing tones in mm. 3–6 gives the bass a scalar character.

2. Although slower moving than the melody, the bass has its own contour and a degree of rhythmic independence. Notice how it tends to be active during the melody's passive moments (m. 2 and m. 4).

EXAMPLE 18-9 Richard Rodgers and Lorenz Hart: "My Romance" (as performed by The Jack Schantz Quartet, Interplay Recordings, 1993)

Note:

The bassist knows where the pauses are in the melody (mm. 1, 3, 4, 5, and 8) and makes it his business to fill those moments with motion, enhancing the melodic independence of the two parts.

The bass line notwithstanding, counterpoint in jazz and popular styles more often resides in middle- or high-register lines called countermelodies. In orchestral arrangements, that role is often given to the strings. In a jazz or studio ensemble, any of the sections— trumpets, trombones, horns, or saxophones—can carry a countermelody.

Following is the melody of Example 18-8 with a countermelody placed above it in the strings.

EXAMPLE 18-10 Bergman and Legrand: "How Do You Keep The Music Playing?"

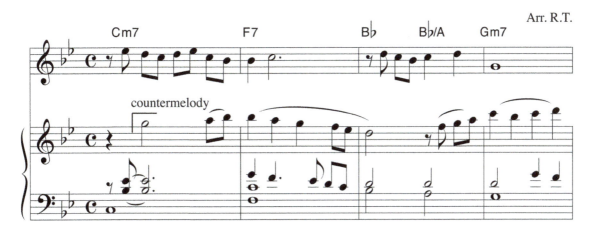

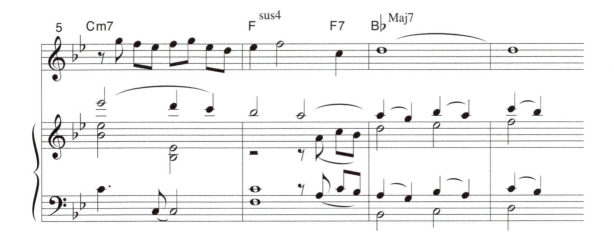

Notes:

1. This countermelody is a bit more complex than what is typical in popular "charts." Many string "countermelodies" are only borderline melodic, consisting mostly of sustained tones. (Violinists refer to the hordes of whole notes as "footballs.") Simplicity and "clean lines" (unburdened by too many simultaneous nonchord tones) appear to be a part of the style.

2. Active and passive moments alternate between the melody and countermelody.

3. Dissonance, measured against the underlying harmonies, is present in both melody and countermelody. The longer note values are usually harmonic, and the moving part contains the dissonances. For example, the countermelody in m. 1 has a chord tone G while the melody has passing tone Ds. In m. 4, the melody note G is harmonic while the countermelody contains Cs that are nonharmonic.

Example 18-11 shows the "bridge" (more on this term later) in Stan Kenton's recording of "What's New?".

EXAMPLE 18-11 Johnny Burke and Bob Haggart: "What's New?" Arr. Bill Holman

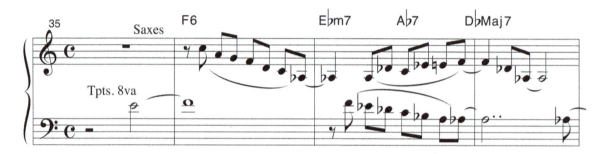

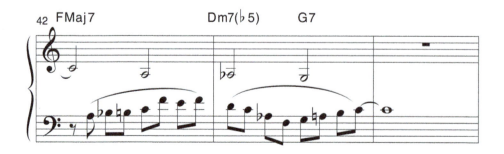

Notes:

1. Except for m. 37, activity is continually plotted against repose, providing rhythmic independence.

2. Seventh chords and other harmonic extensions afford a wider selection of consonances than is available in Baroque counterpoint.

3. Consecutive dissonances do not occur.

4. Rhythmic relationships of 1:1, 2:1, 3:1 and 4:1 are used.

5. Oblique motion prevails, followed by contrary motion.

6. Consecutive unisons appear in m. 43 (Ab-G on beats 2–3). Although not entirely forbidden in popular and jazz styles, they appear infrequently since, even today, they can undermine the independence of the lines.

JOHANN SEBASTIAN BACH'S CHORALE HARMONIZATIONS

Polyphonic or Homophonic?

Are Bach's chorale harmonizations homophonic—a melody supported by three subordinate and dependent voices—or polyphonic—four equal and independent voices?

Many things exist in one of only two states—your Smart Phone is either ON or OFF, you're either ON the bus or OFF the bus, and so on—but melodic independence is not one of them. Any of Bach's chorale harmonizations—any piece of multiple-part music, in fact—can be described as polyphonic or homophonic to varying degrees. Compare these two passages.

EXAMPLE 18-12a Johann Crüger: "Nun danket alle Gott". Harmonization by Crüger 🔊))

EXAMPLE 18-12b Harmonization by J. S. Bach 🔊

Notes:

1. Example a is clearly more homophonic than b. Its voices lack rhythmic independence, and the inner voices also lack strongly individual contours. The soprano and bass display slightly greater melodic independence, as you would expect.

2. Example b is clearly more polyphonic than a. Its voices are rhythmically independent, and the tenor and bass display highly individual contours.

Although the harmonizations are practically identical, Bach's has the added interest of more independent and interesting lines.

REVIEW AND REINFORCEMENT

Provide harmonic analysis of Examples 18-12a and b.

Example 18-13 shows Bach's soprano-bass counterpoint. The notes of Crüger's bass line (Example 18-12a) have been circled. Note the similarity. Bach's bass line is primarily an elaboration of Crüger's through the addition of passing tones and extra chord tones.

EXAMPLE 18-13 J. S. Bach: "Nun danket alle Gott" (soprano-bass framework)

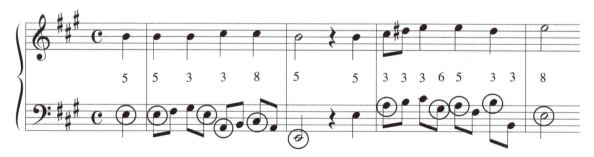

Notes:

1. It's unlikely that Bach started with 1:1 counterpoint and embellished it. Although that method is an effective learning technique, composers generally don't work that way.

2. Bach's finished version is basically 2:1 counterpoint. The intervals formed on downbeats are thirds, fifths, and octaves. The embellishing tones add dissonance and rhythmic independence and sand down the line's rough edges. Three of the four thirds in the 1:1 counterpoint have been filled in with a passing tone.

3. The F♯ in m. 7 (bass) is an added chord tone, the root of a ii^7 (the key is E).

Do not interpret this discussion to mean the more polyphonic, the better. Most hymnlike melodies benefit from some counterpoint because of their simplicity. (They were, after all, created with congregational singing in mind.) More complex melodies can actually suffer from too much contrapuntal competition from the lower voices. It's another judgment call composers and arrangers must make.

➤ *For assignments on the art of countermelody, turn to Workbook Chapter 18, assignments 1A–2B.*

BACH'S TWO-PART INVENTIONS

It was stated at the beginning of Part Six that contrapuntal lines must complement one another so as to form a cohesive tandem. One way to accomplish this is through **imitation**—the restatement of melodic material from one voice in another voice. Do you recall the three choices available to a composer at any point in a composition—to repeat, vary, or create? Imitation can be a form of either repetition or variation. Examples 18-3b and 18-11 both contain imitation. Review them now, and see if you can spot it. This chapter deals with a type of composition that is heavily infused with imitative counterpoint.

Bach: The "Mother of Inventions"

In 1723, Bach (1685–1750) composed two sets of short keyboard studies, one for two voices, the other for three voices. These are known today as the Two-Part and Three-Part Inventions. Just as his chorale harmonizations provide concise and uncomplicated material for studying eighteenth-century harmonic practice, his inventions provide a valuable microcosm of eighteenth-century contrapuntal technique.

A well-known anecdote concerns a theory instructor who, when asked why Bach's Invention no. 1 in C major had become such a favorite for analysis, replied, "Because it's the only one that's typical." Although there's no such thing as a *typical* Bach invention, the following generalizations apply:

Motive and Countermotive

1. A motive is stated and then developed.

2. Typically, the motive appears in one voice and is then imitated in the other voice an octave lower.

3. A distinctive counterpoint called a countermotive sometimes accompanies the motive, appearing more or less consistently above or beneath it.

4. Various contrapuntal devices (to be described in the discussion that follows) may be employed.

5. Often, a modulation to the dominant (or relative major) is followed by a cadence. Other keys may then be tonicized before the tonic returns.

6. Although weak internal cadences may occur, inventions lack strong sectioning or sectional contrast.

Example 18-14 contains the first seven measures of J. S. Bach's "typical" Invention no. 1 in C major.

EXAMPLE 18-14 J. S. Bach: Two-Part Invention, no. 1, BWV 772 🔊

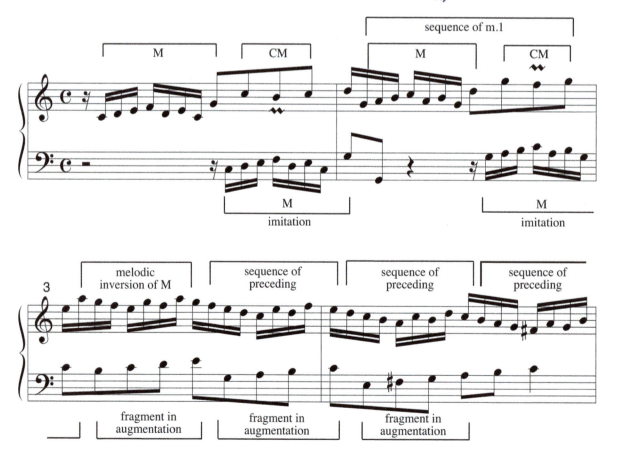

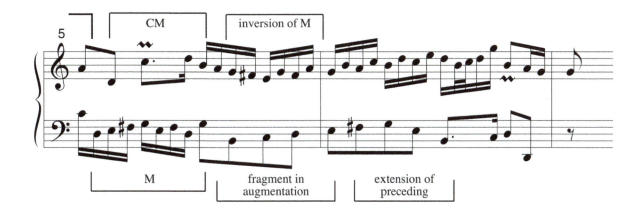

The Devices of Counterpoint

The motive and countermotive are developed through:

- **Sequence** (present in almost every measure).

- **Imitation**: In mm. 1 and 2, the left hand imitates the right an octave lower.

- **Fragmentation**: In mm. 3 and 4, the left hand states the first four notes (a fragment) of the motive, which it then repeats in sequence, on G and then on E.

- **Augmentation**: The fragment stated in the left hand in mm. 3–4 is in longer note values than the original motive. The opposite process—diminution (repeating an idea in shorter note values)—is not used in this work.

- **Melodic inversion**: In m. 3 (right hand) and elsewhere, the motive is stated in contrary motion, a mirror image of its original form, with upward intervals replacing downward intervals and *vice versa*.

➤ *Assignments 3A and 3B in Workbook Chapter 18 can be completed now.*

BACH: INVENTION NO. 6

Analytical markings in Example 18-15 are explained in the discussion that follows the music.

EXAMPLE 18-15 J. S. Bach: Invention, no. 6 in E major, BWV 777

Fragment of mm.1-4 R.H.

Fragment of mm.1-4 L. H

continued

EXAMPLE 18-15 *continued*

Invertible Counterpoint

Invention no. 6 relies heavily on **invertible counterpoint**, a type of *mutual imitation* where each voice states what the other just did, like this:

Higher voice: Gesture a ⟍   ⟋ Gesture b

Lower voice: Gesture b ⟋   ⟍ Gesture a

Sometimes called **voice exchange**, this cross-corridor sharing of musical material addresses two compositional concerns—unity (through repetition) and variety (through registral exchange). In invertible counterpoint, the gestures themselves are not *melodically* inverted—they're simply restated in the other voice, in *its* register. In mm. 5–8, for example, the right hand imitates the left hand of mm. 1–4 an octave higher while the left hand imitates the right an octave lower. We say that *the counterpoint* has been inverted at the octave.

CONCEPT CHECK

Clear examples of inverted counterpoint are present at two other locations. Can you find them?

Less obvious perhaps are mm. 51–62, which are a *transposed inverted counterpoint* of mm. 9–20 (with a few minor pitch changes).

Sequence

After invertible counterpoint, the most prevalent device used in this invention (and in counterpoint in general) is sequence. For example, mm. 11–12 are a tonal sequence, in both hands, of mm. 9–10 a step lower.

REVIEW AND REINFORCEMENT_____

Identify the sequence that begins at m. 29. In which voice does it appear, and how long does it last? What is the pitch level of the repetition? Measure 38 represents the final measure of another sequence. Where does it begin? In which voice does it appear? What is the pitch level of repetition? Locate and describe one other sequence.

Fragmentation

Augmentation and diminution, least common of the contrapuntal devices, are not used in this invention. On the other hand, fragments of the first four-measure phrase appear throughout. The right-hand part of mm. 29–32 is a sequential repetition of the figure from m. 4. Count the number of times this same figure appears. The right hand of measures 33–34 can likewise be regarded as fragmentation of mm. 1–4. And the left hand of m. 1 appears divorced from the rest of its phrase a total of seven times (in mm. 13, 17, 33, 35, 37, 56, and 59).

Tonality

Pieces written in the Baroque era rarely breach the perimeter established by the closely related keys. You should no more expect any single movement by Bach to stray farther from the tonic than one key in either direction than you'd expect rap to sound like "Rigoletto." It's a style thing! And Bach's style was partly conditioned by the state of tuning and temperament in his day and earlier.

Invention no. 6 modulates to the dominant, then to its relative minor, and then back to the tonic:

m. 1	m. 9	m. 29	m. 43
E	B	g♯	E

REVIEW AND REINFORCEMENT

Identify the common chord in each of the modulations. Within the g♯ tonality (mm. 29–42) two tonicizations occur. Identify them.

Implied Harmony

As with all tonal music, two-voice counterpoint is most effective when the underlying harmonies are entirely clear. But two voices can only *imply* a harmony since two pitches do not constitute a chord. In analyzing the harmonic implications of 1:1 counterpoint:

1. Octaves, unisons, fifths and thirds usually imply root-position triads, so the lower note in these intervals can be regarded as the root.

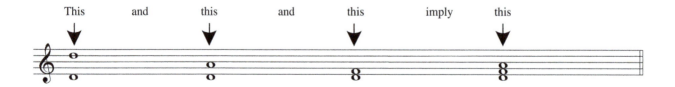

2. Sixths usually imply first inversion triads, so the upper note in these intervals can be regarded as the root. Occasionally, a sixth will imply a six-four chord, in which case, *neither* note is the root. These chords are almost always cadential (I), passing (V), pedal (IV), or arpeggiated (usually I or V).

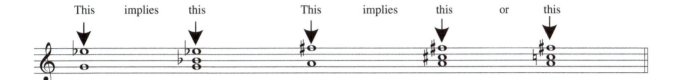

3. Tritones most often comprise scale degrees 4 and 7, which are the third and seventh of V^7 or the root and fifth of vii$^{\circ}$. If one of the pitches is chromatic, this suggests a secondary function (V^7/x or vii$^{\circ}$/x).

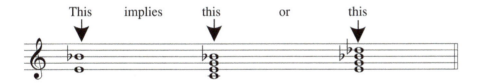

4. When one of the voices arpeggiates a complete triad, that chord is usually the underlying harmony.

5. Scalar passages contain triads filled in with passing tones. The chord tones are usually in an accented metric position relative to the passing tones.

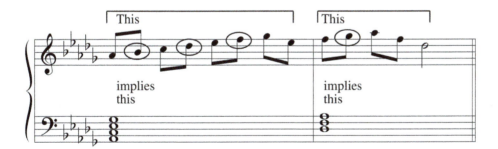

► *Assignment 3D in Workbook Chapter 18 can be completed now.*

Let's apply these guidelines to Bach's Invention no. 6. Because the piece features syncopation in an almost obsessive way, where one hand lags the other by a sixteenth note, we'll need to push and pull the notes into alignment.

EXAMPLE 18-16 (mm. 1-4 realigned)

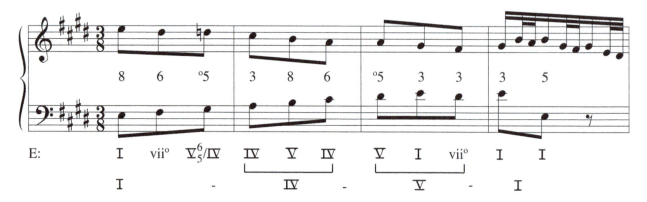

Notes:

1. Strict application of the preceding guidelines produces this harmonic analysis, which makes functional sense and sounds harmonically correct *except for m. 2, where V is pressed between two IV chords.* This chord might be better regarded as a passing I 6/4. Optionally, the octave Bs can be regarded as passing tones within a full-measure IV.

2. In like manner, the pitches that suggest I in m. 3 could be heard as a passing tone and neighbor tones within a measure-long V.

3. The four measures make perfect functional sense on a hypermetric scale. This is shown by second layer of Roman numerals. (Return to Chapter 1 to review hypermeter.)

The clearest harmonic moments in this invention are those where the underlying harmony is given a complete arpeggiation, as at mm. 9–12 (arpeggiation in both hands) and mm. 29–32 (pure arpeggiation in the left hand and embellished arpeggiation in the right hand).

> **CONCEPT CHECK**
>
> Provide harmonic analysis of mm. 9–12, 29–32, mm. 39–42, and mm. 51–55. What similarities do you observe between mm. 9–12 and mm. 51–55?

Passages of two-voice counterpoint that contain successive dissonances can create harmonic ambiguity. Because of this, these moments are usually few and widely separated by passages where the harmonies are utterly clear. Measure 14 is an example.

EXAMPLE 18-17

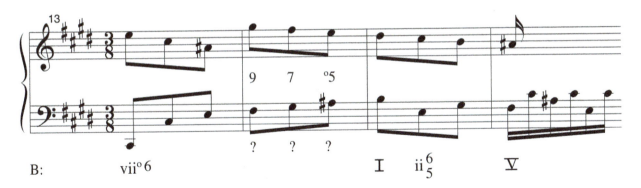

Note:

Although the successive dissonances 9 and 7 in m. 14 are ambiguous, the tritone (°5) that follows them suggests a V^7 or vii°. The F♯ on beat 1 in the bass argues in favor of a V^7 for the entire measure, the G♯ on beat 2 a passing tone. The preceding and following measures are harmonically rather clear. Functionally, the succession—vii°⁶ | V^7 | I–ii 6/5 | V | —makes sense and it sounds right.

Form

Invention no. 6 contains decisive cadences at m. 20 and m. 42, dividing it into three parts. We'll consider how those parts relate to each other in Chapter 25, where we consider musical form.

INVENTION ANALYSIS: A CHECKLIST

1. Identify every appearance of the motive and countermotive.

2. Identify the following contrapuntal devices where present:

   a. Sequence

   b. Imitation

   c. Invertible counterpoint

   d. Fragmentation

   e. Augmentation and/or diminution

   f. Melodic inversion

3. Identify all major cadences.

4. Identify all tonalities.

Optional at this point:

- Do a complete harmonic analysis based on your understanding of the harmonic implications of two-voice counterpoint.

- Identify the divisions created by the important cadences.

⊕ CODA

Bach's inventions and fugues constitute some of the most intensely motivic music ever composed. During the discussion of Invention no.1 and Invention no.6, you may have been tempted to ask, "Did Bach *really* intend all those motivic relationships?" Our answer is, "Does it really matter?" Intended or not, relationships among pitches, rhythms, and musical ideas are the factors that create unity within a composition and therefore are, for those seeking to understand the music, important elements of analysis.

Bach's Inventions afford an excellent introduction to the fugue. The genres share many features. Generally, though, fugues are the longer works, and they're usually for three or four voices. They've been written by a host of composers from the Baroque era through the twentieth century, and they follow a more consistent procedure—at least in the opening measures—than do the inventions. We'll consider the fugue in Chapter 19.

➤ *For assignments on J. S. Bach's two-part inventions, turn to Workbook Chapter 18, assignments 3A–3G.*

DO YOU KNOW THESE TERMS?

- augmentation
- countermelody
- countermotive
- counterpoint
- diminution
- dissonance
- form
- fragmentation
- homophonic
- imitation
- imperfect consonance
- implied harmony
- invention
- invertible counterpoint
- melodic inversion
- motive
- perfect consonance
- polyphony
- sequence

CHAPTER NINETEEN

The Fugue

KEY CONCEPTS IN THIS CHAPTER

- Fugal Process
- Fugue Subjects and Answers
- Contrapuntal Devices Found in Fugue

Bach's inventions afford an excellent introduction to the fugue since these genres share many features. A **fugue** is a composition born of imitative counterpoint, usually containing a fixed number of voices—most often three or four. In it, a theme, called a **subject**, is stated at the outset by a single unaccompanied voice, followed by a restatement or imitation in each of the voices in turn. In the subsequent course of a fugue, the subject returns attired in varied tonal and textural garb. The offspring of processes employed in the Middle Ages and Renaissance, the fugue reached maturity in the Baroque era and remains a viable form of composition in art music.

Like the invention, the fugue rarely contains strong sectional contrast or sharply divisional cadences. It differs mainly in its more structured opening.

THE BASICS OF FUGUE

Fugues may be long or short, fast or slow, solemn or exuberant, vocal or instrumental. Despite this variety, certain procedures are common to all fugues.

Subject and Answer

The first event in a fugue is a statement of the subject. Although subjects average perhaps two to four measures, both longer and shorter subjects exist.

EXAMPLE 19-1a J. S. Bach: *The Well-Tempered Clavier*, Book I, BWV 849 (Fugue no. 4)

EXAMPLE 19-1b J. S. Bach: Fugue for Organ, BWV 578

Real and Tonal Answer

The second event to occur in a fugue is the **answer**—the imitation of the subject, usually at the level of dominant. Even though a dominant answer may be heard *a fourth below* the subject, intervals are calculated ascending, and so the entry is termed "at the fifth." The imitation may be an exact transposition to the level of the dominant, called a "real answer," or it may contain one or more pitch modifications, called a "tonal answer." (The "real" and "tonal" distinction is similar to that for sequences.) Tonal answers are more common than real answers, and the effect of the tonal alteration is to reinforce the principal tonality.

EXAMPLE 19-2a J. S. Bach: *The Well-Tempered Clavier*, Book I, BWV 846, (Fugue no. 1, C Major)

Subject

Real Answer (transposition of subject up P5)

EXAMPLE 19-2b J. K. F. Fischer: Fuga from *Ariadne Musica* (F Major)

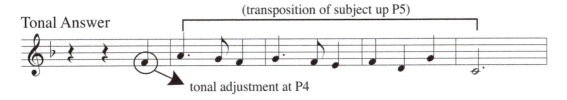

Note:

Bach's answer is an exact transposition of the subject to the dominant; Fischer's contains a pitch modification—its first note answers the subject's first note a *fourth* (rather than *fifth*) higher.

A tonal answer generally occurs for one of these reasons: 1) the subject ends on the tonic at its completion; 2) the 5th scale degree (the dominant) is prominent near the beginning of the subject; 3) the subject modulates to the dominant.

Look again at Example 19-2b. The subject begins on $\hat{5}$. It also ends on $\hat{1}$. The beginning of a fugal answer typically coincides with the end of the subject. A real answer's first pitch (G) would sound atop the subject's last pitch (F), a dissonance. (Play it and see.) Answering $\hat{5}$ (C) with $\hat{1}$ (F) instead of with $\hat{2}$ (G) accomplishes two things: it avoids opening the counterpoint on a dissonance, and it creates a tonic–dominant axis that reinforces the tonality.

When a subject modulates to the dominant, as does Example 19-3a, a tonal answer is in order. Notice that a real answer (b) would take the music immediately to a remote key (the dominant of the dominant). Bach's tonal answer keeps the music in C.

EXAMPLE 19-3a J. S. Bach: Fugue for Organ, BWV 547

EXAMPLE 19-3b

Real answer (modulates to D–not a closely related key)

EXAMPLE 19-3c

Bach's answer (tonal)   ends on tonic

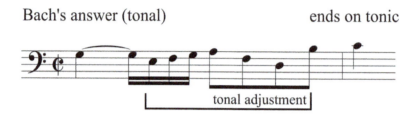

tonal adjustment

Note:

The entire modulating part of the subject is transposed a step lower to return to the tonic.

Bridge and Link

The tonal level at the end of a subject or answer often determines what follows. A **bridge** is a short passage that modulates from the end of an answer to the next subject announcement. A **link** is a short passage that modulates from the end of a subject to an answer. The tonal motion of the two is opposite—from dominant to tonic (bridge) and from tonic to dominant (link).

EXAMPLE 19-4

Subject (no modulation)	LINK (modulation to dominant) free counterpoint	Answer
I		V

Answer (no modulation)	BRIDGE (modulation to tonic) free counterpoint	Subject
V		I

The need for a link or bridge depends on the way a subject or answer ends. Both types of passage are usually composed of free counterpoint. **Free counterpoint** is devoid of motivic material obviously related to the subject, whereas **strict counterpoint** is based on the subject motive. The more common passage is the bridge, shown below:

EXAMPLE 19-5 J. S. Bach: *The Well-Tempered Clavier*, Book II, BWV 885 (Fugue No. 16) 🔊

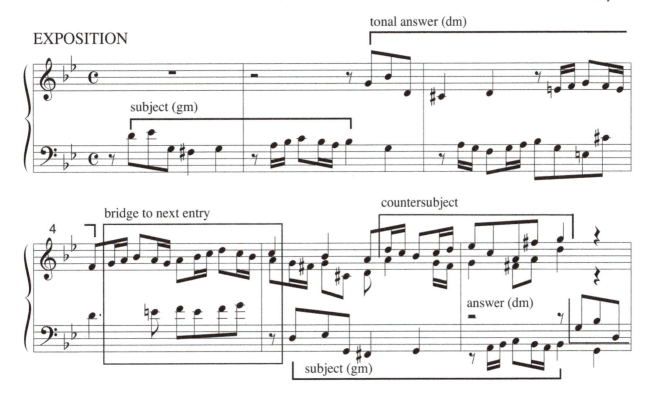

CONCEPT CHECK

Explain the reason for the tonal answer in Example 19-5.

The Exposition

The subject and answer are the first events in a fugue's **exposition**, or opening "section." The exposition comprises the **initial announcements** of the subject (or answer) in each voice in turn, and the number of these defines the number of voices in the fugue. In a three-voice fugue, three voices alternate—subject, answer, and subject; in a four-voice fugue, four voices do so, and so on. In most fugues, the statements appear alternately in the tonic and dominant, like this:

S (in tonic)

A (in dominant)

S (in tonic)

A (in dominant)

Fugues are also defined by the *order* of entries in the exposition, the highest voice numbered "1." In Example 19-6, the highest voice states the subject in measure 9. The order of entries in this exposition is 3, 2, 1, 4.

EXAMPLE 19-6 J. S. Bach: *The Well-Tempered Clavier*, Book II, BWV 885 (Fugue No. 16)

Once the final voice to enter has stated the subject or answer, the exposition is considered to be over, although it might be terminated by a brief episode and cadence.

Notice in Example 19-6 that an identical counterpoint (labeled CS) appears with each subject (S) or answer (A) except the first. If used often against the subject during the course of a fugue, this counterpoint is termed a **countersubject** (meaning "against the subject"). It may be fashioned from motives in the subject or, as here, it may be unrelated. Typically, it makes its debut in the exposition, stated by the opening voice against the answer.

REVIEW AND REINFORCEMENT

Where in Example 19-6 does inverted counterpoint appear?

Subsequent Entries and Episodes

Working out a musical idea is called development, something that occurs in most extended musical works. Any or all of the contrapuntal devices listed in Chapter 18 (see p. 319) may be used to develop a musical idea. "Development" is what takes place in the part of the fugue directly following the exposition. The subject reappears—either in single isolated statements, called single entries, in successive statements in two or more voices, called entry groups (or group entries), and/or in overlapping statements in two or more voices, called **stretto** (meaning "tight"). Reappearances are separated by passages where the subject is absent. These episodes provide digressions from the main thematic material. In addition, they may develop some aspect of the subject, modulate to a new key, or provide a change of texture. *The one defining feature of an episode is the absence of the complete, intact subject.*

Example 19-7 shows the final entry in the exposition of a three-voice fugue and the ensuing episode.

EXAMPLE 19-7 J. S. Bach: *The Well-Tempered Clavier*, Book II, BWV 881 (Fugue No. 12)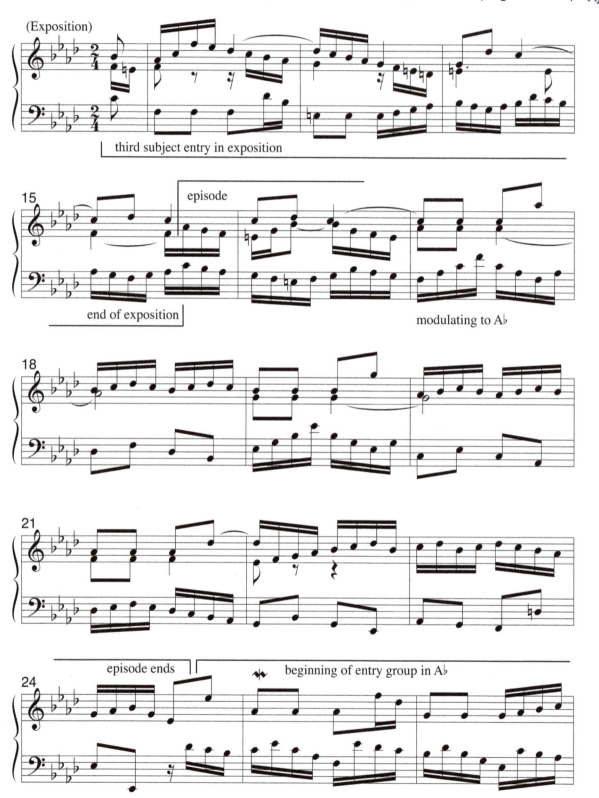

Notes:

1. In m. 15, the third and final voice to enter completes its statement of the subject, bringing the exposition to a close.

2. The episode provides a digression that includes a simplification of the counterpoint and a modulation to the relative major key of A♭ through sequential development of the opening eighth notes of the subject (see mm. 17, 19, and 21).

3. The episode ends with the reappearance of the subject in its entirety. The beginning of this entry group is shown (mm. 24–25).

The episode in Example 19-7 "develops" the subject through fragmentation and sequence. These, you may recall, are the most common contrapuntal devices, along with invertible counterpoint. Less common is melodic inversion. Least common are augmentation, diminution, and retrograde (stating an idea backward).

The Final Statement—Closing Section

As in most compositions, fugues end in the home key, and they may do so with a single entry, an entry group, or less often, with an episode.

Summary

Here, then, are the essentials of the fugue:

1. A subject is stated alone and then imitated (answered) by a second voice in the key of the dominant. The remaining voices follow with statements of either the subject or its answer to complete the exposition.

2. A fugue may also contain a countersubject—a "ready-made" counterpoint that is used against ("counter to") the subject at many of its appearances. If so, its first appearance is in the exposition, against the answer.

3. The remainder of the fugue comprises reappearances of the complete subject (either single or in groups), usually in various keys and textures. These reappearances are separated by episodes, which do *not* contain the intact subject but usually develop its ideas. Often, episodes are modulatory and conclude with cadences that signal the next appearance of the subject.

4. The fugue can end with an entry, an entry group, or an episode. If it ends with an entry group, it is sometimes called a **recapitulation**.

A postcadential extension called a coda may occur at the very end of a fugue.

EXAMPLE 19-8 J. S. Bach: *The Well-Tempered Clavier*, Book I, BWV 847, Fugue No. 2 (Final Entry and Coda)

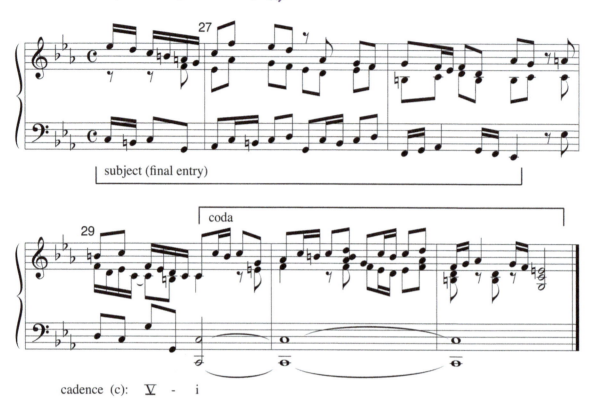

subject (final entry)

coda

cadence (c):   V - i

Notes:

1. Codas often unfold over a tonic pedal point, as in the preceding example.

2. Codas may include a final subject statement, as in the preceding example.

3. Additional voices may be added in the coda to create a stronger ending, as in the preceding example.

ANALYSIS

EXAMPLE 19-9 J. S. Bach: *The Well-Tempered Clavier*, Book I, BWV 861 (Fugue No. 16) 🔊

continued

EXAMPLE 19-9 *continued*

continued

EXAMPLE 19-9 *continued*

About This Fugue

This four-voice fugue contains a countersubject that accompanies the subject at practically every appearance. Following the exposition, entry groups containing five statements, three statements, and then five statements are separated by episodes based on material from both the subject and countersubject. Other observations follow:

1. The countersubject (mm. 3 and 4) is derived from a melodic inversion of the latter half (the "tail") of the subject (m. 2).

2. The answer (m. 2–4) is in the dominant, requiring a link (m. 4) to prepare harmonically for the next subject entry.

3. The exposition ends without a clear cadence (m. 8). This is typical. Fugues usually flow seamlessly from the exposition to episodes and entries.

4. The second half of the subject (m. 2) dominates this fugue in motivic fashion. Scarcely a measure passes where it is not heard in some form.

5. The subject and countersubject exchange registral positions (inverted counterpoint) throughout the fugue (as in mm. 12–16).

6. The entry group beginning in m. 28 features a three-voice *stretto* (each subject statement begins before the preceding statement has been completed).

7. The fugue ends with the "Picardy third."

⊕ CODA

J. S. Bach was the ultimate contrapuntist. Never before and never since has a composer been able to wrestle independent melodies simultaneously and pin them to the harmonic mat so successfully. His fugues are the most intense and compact—and thus the most challenging—of his works. They constantly pull our ears from voice to voice, and attempts to grasp all that's unfolding can be almost futile. The intensity that results from the interacting voices, the fast-paced harmonic rhythm, the overlapping cadences and the relentless rhythmic drive is almost physical. Bach's fugues invite—they *require*—repeated listening. The more you hear them, the more *in them* you hear.

DO YOU KNOW THESE TERMS?

- answer
- bridge or link
- coda
- counterexposition
- countersubject
- development
- entry group
- episode
- exposition
- fugue
- recapitulation
- stretto
- subject

Advanced Chromatic Harmony

Musical style evolves because composers' practices change. The flow of time erodes the affective power of any technique, be it melodic, harmonic, or contrapuntal. Composers, quick to intuit this, respond by seeking new ways to do the same old things. The process is gradual, and one style period yields to the next reluctantly. During the transitional years, elements of the old and new usually co-exist.

For example, at the dawn of the seventeenth century, the dominant seventh chord was a striking dissonance used only for moments of deepest feeling. By the century's twilight, seventh chords on every scale degree were commonplace. Likewise, secondary dominants were initially applied sparingly to selected chords, mainly V, IV, and vi. Eventually, they were used liberally to tonicize every diatonic triad.

Perhaps the greatest musical legacy of the nineteenth century was the continuation of this harmonic expansion to encompass more chromaticism and more distant tonal relationships. Part Seven considers the more important elements of this larger harmonic palette.

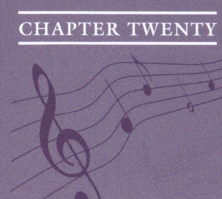

CHAPTER TWENTY

Mixing Modes

KEY CONCEPTS IN THIS CHAPTER

- Change of Mode
- Keys Related through Mode Mixture
- Modal Borrowing
- Voice Leading with Borrowed Harmonies
- Common Chromatic-Third Relationships
- Voice Leading in Chromatic-Third Relationships
- Chromatic-Third Relationship and Mode Mixture

PERSPECTIVE: ADDING TO THE PALETTE

Vocabulary and Syntax

The harmonic vocabulary of Baroque music consisted of all the diatonic triads and seventh chords along with the secondary functions attending each of those harmonies, in the home key and in the keys closely related. (Also included were a few other chromatic chords to be discussed in Chapter 21.) Its syntax—the way this vocabulary was used in musical phrases—involved heavy reliance on circular-fifth root movement and harmonic sequence.

The latter part of the eighteenth century saw the addition of chromatic elements to the Baroque vocabulary. One important source of chromaticism was **mode mixture**—combining the resources of *parallel* major and minor modes. The process provided additional harmonies without entailing a modulation (change of tonal center).

CHANGE OF MODE

Change of mode involves the shift from a major key to the parallel minor, or the reverse. The effect is dramatic, and if a composer seeks variety and contrast, he or she often need do nothing more than change mode. Examples 20-1 and 20-2 illustrate the process in both directions.

EXAMPLE 20-1 Michel Legrand: "The Summer Knows" (from *The Summer of '42*)
            *Minor to Major

* The preceding four measures of this song can be found in Chapter 7, Example 7-5.

Notes:

1. The change from G minor to G major in m. 9 is attended here by a change of key signature. While this *is* a change of key, it is *not* a modulation because the tonal center (G) hasn't changed.

2. Measure 10 contains an altered chord within the new key, actually a "residue" from G minor. We'll discuss this chord in the next section, "Modal Borrowing."

3. In m. 6, the secondary leading-tone Bn moves downward to the seventh of the next chord. Here it is part of a chromatic scalar bass (C–B–Bb–A) that has the tonic (in m. 9) as its ultimate goal. Refer back to Example 15-15 to see the elided resolution of the seventh in chromatically descending lines.

REVIEW AND REINFORCEMENT

Add lead-sheet symbols that correspond to the Roman numeral symbols in Example 20-1.

EXAMPLE 20-2 Mozart: Piano Sonata, K. 332 (second movement) Major to Minor 🔊

Notes:

1. The change of mode in m. 5 effects a change of key (to B♭ minor) *without* a change in key signature.

2. The melody and harmonic pattern of mm. 1–2 are simply repeated in mm. 5–6, but in the parallel minor key.

3. The I⁶ in m. 6 (boxed) is actually an altered chord in the new key. Again a "residue" of the former key, it would more clearly appear altered if the key *signature* had changed to reflect the mode change as in Example 20-1. We'll discuss this chord further in the next section, "Modal Borrowing."

REVIEW AND REINFORCEMENT

To what key does Example 20-2 modulate in the last two measures? What type of modulation—common chord or chromatic—is this? What happens on the last two beats of m. 8?

Mode and Mood

Examples 20-1 and 20-2 show how a change of mode can effect a change in *mood*. In the former, the music seems to brighten with the shift to major. In the latter, the mood seems to darken with the change to minor. The association of major and minor with gaiety and gloom has a history dating back to the first light of the tonal era.

Keys Related through Mode Mixture

In addition to its mood-altering powers, change of mode provides instant access to a new set of closely related keys. If the chords of a key are likened to a tonal planetary system (as they were in Chapter 5) within a galaxy containing five other planetary systems—the closely related keys—then think of change of mode as a wormhole to a parallel galaxy.

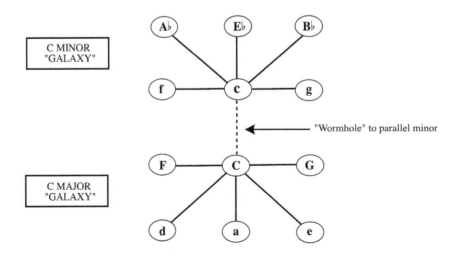

Enharmonic Change of Mode

Occasionally a change of mode is accompanied by enharmonic respelling. The intent usually is to place the music in a key with fewer flats or sharps.

EXAMPLE 20-3 Beethoven: Piano Sonata, op. 26 (second movement) 🔊

Note:

The cadence in m. 8 is in C♭ major. A change of mode at this point would place the ensuing music in the fearsome key of C♭ *minor*. For this reason, the following measures are notated enharmonically in B minor, a much less terrifying key.

REVIEW AND REINFORCEMENT_____

Complete the harmonic analysis of Example 20-3.

MODAL BORROWING

Example 20-4 begins and ends in C minor. Within the passage are two chromatic harmonies —a secondary dominant (V^7/V) and a IV. The IV is "on loan" from the parallel C major.

EXAMPLE 20-4 Adele Adkins: Theme from *Skyfall*

Modal Borrowing versus Change of Mode

While change of mode involves the *consistent and protracted* use of harmonic resources from the parallel key, **modal borrowing** involves the *brief and occasional* use of those resources. These harmonies (for better or worse) have been termed **borrowed harmonies**. You might think of them as temporarily on loan from the parallel key. The process may be viewed as an extremely brief change of mode.

Modal borrowing bears the same relationship to change of mode that tonicization bears to modulation: The former process in each case is more local in effect, the latter more lasting. If you recall ratio-and-proportion from your high school mathematics, we might symbolize the relationship thus:

$$\frac{\text{Modal Borrowing}}{\text{Change of Mode}} = \frac{\text{Tonicization}}{\text{Modulation}}$$

This is read: "Modal borrowing is to change of mode as tonicization is to modulation."

Look again at Example 20-1. In m. 9 the music changes mode to G major. It continues in this new key, although the continuation is not shown. However, in m. 10, the chords in the right-hand part (above the D pedal point) still appear as they would in G minor.

G: ii°6   iv6

borrowed from G minor

These isolated holdovers from the parallel minor are borrowed harmonies.

Look again at Example 20-2. In m. 5 the music changes mode to B♭ minor. However, in m. 6, the chord on beat 3 appears as it would in B♭ major. This, too, is a borrowed harmony.

b♭:   I⁶

borrowed from B♭ major

Common Borrowed Harmonies

As this illustrates, borrowing goes both ways. However—Example 20-4 notwithstanding—modal borrowing occurs most often in the major mode, which can be greatly enriched by loans from the parallel minor. Example 20-5a shows the most common borrowed harmonies, all of them resources from minor's harmonic bank.

EXAMPLE 20-5

a   All use the lowered sixth scale degree   **b** Both use the lowered third scale degree

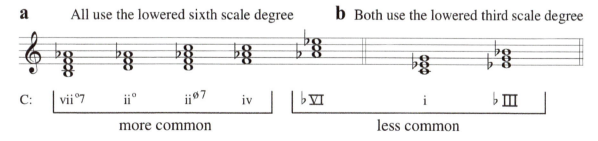

C: vii°7   ii°   ii°⁷   iv   ♭VI   i   ♭III

            more common   less common

Note:

All are "borrowed" from C minor. The most common borrowed harmonies feature the lowered sixth scale degree.

The lowered sixth degree and the harmonies that house it can lend a momentary somber cast to a major-mode work. They became favorites of the Romantic composers, whose music often involved themes of sorrow. Though somewhat melodramatic-sounding today when overused, they remain a way to lend a poignant touch to a passage.

EXAMPLE 20-6a Brahms: "Die Mainacht"

(translation: ". . . and a lonely teardrop falls.")

EXAMPLE 20-6b Tchaikovsky: "Waltz of the Flowers" (from *The Nutcracker*) 🔊

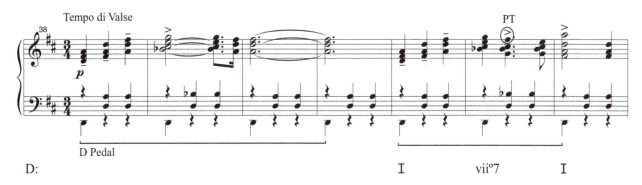

D: I   vii°7   I

EXAMPLE 20-6c Gilbert O'Sullivan: "Alone Again, Naturally" 🔊

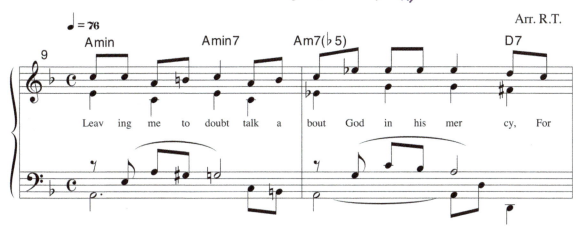

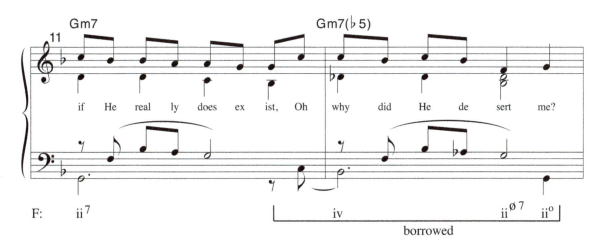

REVIEW AND REINFORCEMENT

Identify a secondary function in Example 20-6a. Then, identify a tonicizing chord group in Example 20-6c, and symbolize it in the manner described in Chapter 16.

Voice Leading

Because the minor sixth scale degree most often resolves stepwise *in the direction of its inflection*, borrowed harmonies containing it are apt to resolve to a chord containing $\hat{5}$ (either V or I). The resolution of the altered tone is the overriding voice-leading consideration. If ♭VI resolves first to a predominant, as in e below, the predominant is often borrowed as well, retaining the altered tone (♭$\hat{6}$) until its eventual resolution to $\hat{5}$.

Vii°⁷

EXAMPLE 20-7

Notes:

1. Borrowed harmonies normally function identically to their diatonic counterparts.

2. The lowered sixth scale degree (the altered tone) typically resolves downward by half step.

Examples 20-8a and b contain the two most common of all borrowed harmonies—vii°⁷ and iv. Observe the resolution of $\hat{6}$ in each.

EXAMPLE 20-8a Carole Bayer Sager and Marvin Hamlisch: "Nobody Does It Better" (from the movie *The Spy Who Loved Me*) 🔊

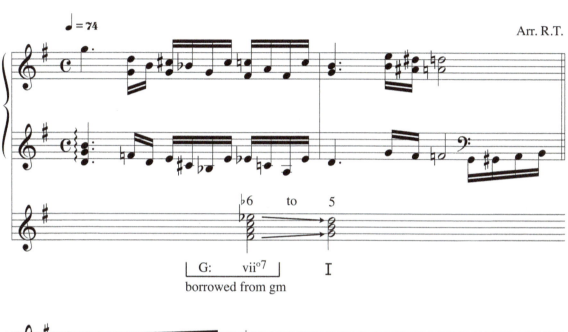

EXAMPLE 20-8b Leslie Bricusse and John Williams: "Can You Read My Mind?" (from the movie *Superman*)

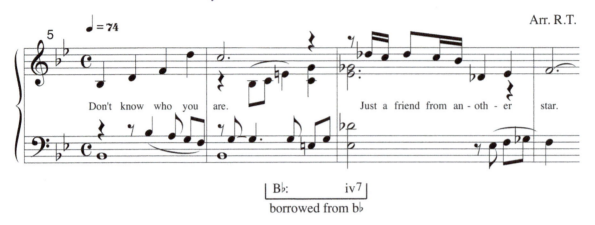

REVIEW AND REINFORCEMENT

1   In a, what recently studied chord is arpeggiated in m. 1, beat 3? Can you trace the resolution of each of the altered tones in this chord? How would you symbolize the chord of m. 4, beat 4? How would you expect it to resolve?

2   In b, how would you symbolize the chord of m. 6? How would you expect it to resolve?

If vii°⁷ and iv are the most common borrowed harmonies, ♭VI is probably the *least* common of those that employ ♭$\hat{6}$. The chord appears in Examples 20-8. Notice that ♭$\hat{6}$ in the bass resolves as expected, in both the bass and the interior voice.

EXAMPLE 20-9 George David Weiss and Bob Thiele: "What a Wonderful World"

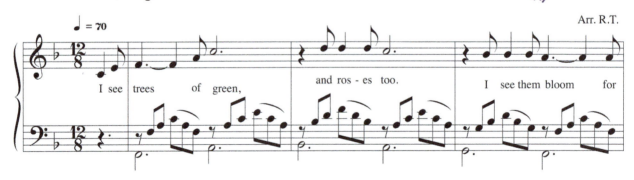

▶ *For assignments on change of mode and modal borrowing, turn to Workbook Chapter 20.*

REVIEW AND REINFORCEMENT

Symbolize the chromatic chord of m. 4.

↻ **BACK TO BASICS 20.1**

Mode Mixture and Change of Mode

CHROMATIC-THIRD RELATIONSHIPS

Chromatic vs. Diatonic-Third Relationship

Two triads whose roots are a third apart share two notes of the same letter name. In a **diatonic-third relationship**, these two notes are common tones. However, in a **chromatic-third relationship**, one common tone or both are chromatically altered.

EXAMPLE 20-10

Diatonic-third relationship   Chromatic-third relationship

E and G are common tones   G becomes G♯, thus no
                                longer a common tone

A chromatic-third relationship exists between any two chords a third apart that do not share two common tones. Examples are A major and C major, D minor and B minor, E♭ minor and G major, and D♭ major and E minor.

Toward the end of the eighteenth century, composers seemed to develop a fascination with the fresh sound of particular chromatic-third relationships. Beethoven—and after him Schubert, Liszt, Brahms, and Wagner—frequently juxtaposed both tonalities and chords so related.

EXAMPLE 20-11 Schubert: "Kennst du das Land" 🔊

The tonal relationship in Example 20-11—A major to C major—is one of the more commonly used chromatic-third relationships of the late eighteenth and early nineteenth centuries.

The Common Chromatic-Third Relationships

While the number of chromatic-third relationships is quite large, we'll consider only the most common four.

EXAMPLE 20-12

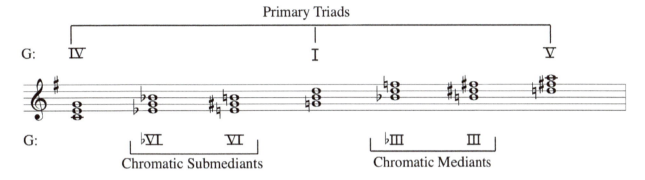

Notes:

1. All the common chromatic-third relationships to the tonic are major triads.

2. Chromatic mediants are so called because they are the midpoint between tonic and dominant. Chromatic submediants are so called because they are the midpoint between tonic and *sub*dominant. Each chromatic mediant or chromatic submediant shares with the tonic one common tone with the second one chromatically altered.

3. Chromatic-third relationships can exist between tonal centers or between individual chords. Between chords, the seventh may be present as well (as in G–B♭^{7}).

4. The flat sign is used to indicate a lowered chord root, whether the actual alteration involves a flat (as here) or a natural (as it would in the key of E).

5. The tonic is usually, but not always, part of a chromatic-third relationship. For example, the chromatic mediants (III and ♭III) form chromatic-third relationships with V, and the chromatic submediants (VI and ♭VI) form chromatic-third relationships with IV.

CONCEPT CHECK

Construct an illustration similar to Example 20-12, showing all common chromatic-third relationships to an A major tonic.

Chromatic Thirds, Mode Mixture, and Tonicization

The four common chromatic-third relationships can result from processes we've already discussed—secondary function or mode mixture. For example, ♭III and ♭VI are borrowed harmonies with respect to a major tonic, while III and VI might be tonicizations (V/vi and V/ii).

EXAMPLE 20-13

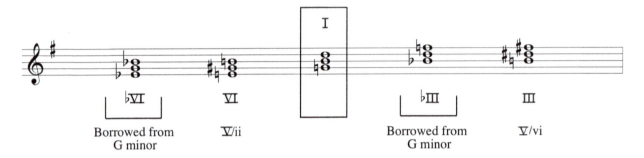

However, the chromatic-third relationship is often exploited for its unusual sound—as a *primary* technique rather than the incidental result of another process.

EXAMPLE 20-14a Beethoven: Piano Sonata, op. 14, no. 1 (third movement) 🔊

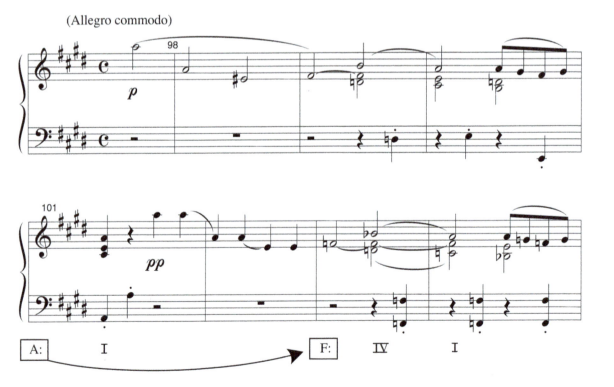

EXAMPLE 20-14b Brahms: Symphony, no. 3, op. 90 (second movement)

EXAMPLE 20-14c John Williams: *Star Wars* (main theme)* 🔊

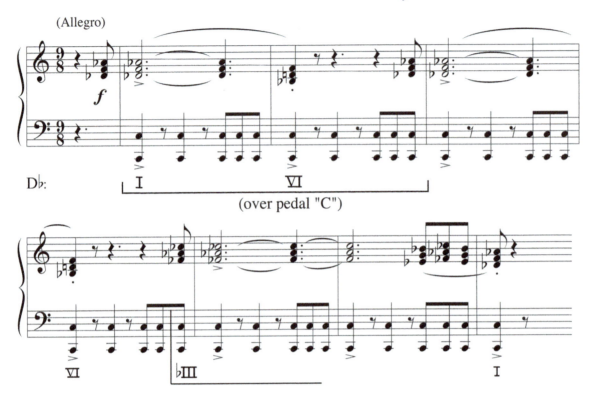

Notes:

1. In a, the tonalities A and F are chromatically-third-related while the chords at the tonal border (mm. 102–103) are not. F, the lowered submediant (♭VI) in A, is the submediant (VI) in A minor, making this chromatic-third relationship a form of mode mixture.

2. In b, the chromatic-third relationship (I–♭VI) exists not between tonalities but between chords. The ♭VI might also be analyzed as a borrowed harmony. The second time it appears, it resolves to a borrowed iv, retaining the lowered sixth scale degree (A♭), which resolves in the direction of its inflection—downward to $\hat{5}$—in m. 133.

3. In c, both the VI (B♭) and the ♭III (F♭) appear. In another context VI might be analyzed as a V/ii. Here, it clearly does not tonicize ii, as ii does not appear. ♭III is likewise employed purely for the sake of its chromatic-third relationship to the tonic D♭ rather than as a borrowed harmony. (The C in the bass is a pedal point that creates a strong dissonance against the music that unfolds above it.)

---

* It would seem that film composers and popular song writers seem to have rediscovered what Haydn, Beethoven, Brahms, and Wagner knew—that the sudden elevation to a new tonal plane through chromatic-third relationship is a refreshing aural change that can make a repeated phrase sound new.

Roman numeral analysis does not always directly reveal a chromatic-third relationship. Example 20-15 is such a case.

EXAMPLE 20-15 Haydn: Piano Sonata, H. XVI: 34 (first movement) 🔊))

a: V   C: I

Note:

The chords at mm. 50–51 (a: V and C: I) are chromatic-third related while the two *keys* (A minor and C major) are in a *diatonic*-third relationship (minor to relative major).

REVIEW AND REINFORCEMENT

1   Identify the type of six-four chord that appears in this passage.

2   What secondary function appears prior to the fermata? (Look for it in an arpeggiation.)

Voice Leading

Chromatic-third relationships were governed by less rigorous part writing practices than were seventh chords and the like. Rather than being generated by linear processes, they were often employed for the "shock value" of their sound. Then, too, they came into frequent use in instrumental music that involved a more homophonic style, with smooth voice leading less an issue than it previously had been. Still, conjunct lines are easily attainable by retaining the common tone in the same voice and moving the other voices as stepwise as possible.

Example 20-16 shows a typical problem when part writing root-to-root chromatic-third relationships and a possible solution.

EXAMPLE 20-16a Doubling the root in the same voice (m. 1 and mm. 2–3) produces consecutive octaves against the bass. Parallel soprano and bass (m. 2) lead to consecutive fifths

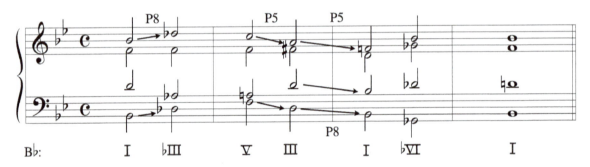

EXAMPLE 20-16b Doubling the root in different voices eliminates consecutive octaves. Contrary and oblique motion predominate in the outer voices. Blackened notes show doubled root. Arrows show common tones retained

As with change of mode, chromatic-third relationships can necessitate enharmonic spellings in certain keys. This can generate unusual-looking melodic intervals. The smaller these intervals are, the better. In Example 20-17, the individual voices move largely by enharmonic half steps and whole steps.

EXAMPLE 20-17 Antonin Dvořák: New World Symphony, op. 95 (Largo) This four-voice passage results when the instruments doubling the lines at the octave are removed.

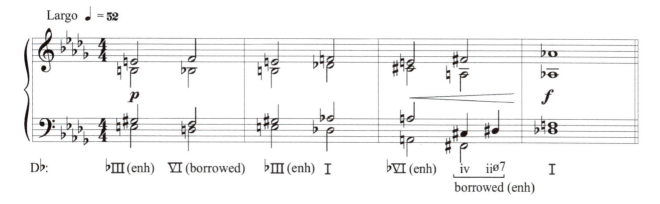

Db: ♭III (enh)   VI (borrowed)   ♭III (enh)   I   ♭VI (enh)   iv   iiø7   I

                                                                  borrowed (enh)

Your instructor will decide how rigorously you should apply voice-leading principles to chromatic-third relationships. Musical style and medium are factors to consider.

> **↻ BACK TO BASICS 20.2**
>
> Types of Mediant Relationships

⊕ CODA

> **Mode mixture** is a general process that combines the resources of the major and minor scales. It includes specific techniques—**change of mode** and **modal borrowing**, which differ mainly in duration—the former is like leasing an apartment, the latter akin to renting a motel room. Modulation, to carry the analogy further, is like moving out of town. When modulating between chromatic-third-related keys, the harmonies at the tonal border are often those of parallel major and minor modes, as in C–E♭ (I–♭III) and thus actually examples of mode mixture.
>
> In musical analysis, a passage might invite description in multiple ways. For example, a chromatic modulation might lead to a chromatic-third-related key, with one chord or the other described as a borrowed harmony. These multiple analytical observations are part of a complete description that addresses all facets of the passage.

➤ *For assignments on chromatic-third relationships, turn to Workbook Chapter 20, assignments 2A–2H.*

DO YOU KNOW THESE TERMS?

- change of mode
- chromatic-third relationship
- diatonic-third relationship
- enharmonic change of mode
- modal borrowing
- mode mixture

CHAPTER TWENTY-ONE

Altered Pre-Dominants

KEY CONCEPTS IN THIS CHAPTER

- Neapolitan Sixth Chord: Construction, Function, and Voice Leading

- Augmented Sixth Chords: Construction, Function, and Voice Leading

PERSPECTIVE

Think back to your coloring-book days. Do you recall the excitement packaged in that new, larger box of markers? The feeling must have been similar for composers of the nineteenth century. Most of their new colors were attractive variants of existing harmonic hues. This chapter introduces two important ones. Though both can be found in Classical and Baroque music, their wider use in the nineteenth century kept pace with the Romantic composers' fascination with mood and color.

By the nineteenth century, the four-part vocal style had lost the primacy it enjoyed in the Renaissance and Baroque eras, and composers applied those voice-leading principles—particularly in matters of spacing and doubling—in a more general way to their larger orchestrations. Still, they continued to respect the two basic needs of the sensitive tones, which are: 1) to be left alone (e.g., not doubled); and 2) to do what they want (resolve).

You'll observe this in the examples.

THE NEAPOLITAN SIXTH CHORD

What's in a Name?

The so-called **Neapolitan chord** made cameo appearances in the seventeenth century and debuted as a more central member of the harmonic cast in a type of opera centered in Naples in the first half of the eighteenth century. As its Roman numeral symbol—♭**II**—suggests, the chord is a major triad built on the lowered second scale degree. At least initially, the chord appeared in first inversion—called the **Neapolitan sixth chord** (or more appropriately, the Neapolitan "Six Chord")—reflecting its linear origin as a chromatically inflected first inversion iio. As the sound became familiar, composers then began to employ it in root position as well.

EXAMPLE 21-1

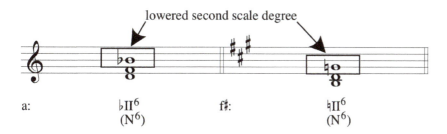

Note:

The designation N^6 remains unchanged whether lowering the second scale degree is achieved by a natural (as it is in sharp keys) or by a flat. For this reason, N^6 is the preferred way to symbolize the chord.

▶ *Assignments 1A and 1B in Workbook Chapter 21 can be completed at this time.*

The Harmonic Nature of the Neapolitan

In first inversion, the Neapolitan behaves like its diatonic siblings, the ii^{o6} and iv. They are all pre-dominants, and in all:

1. The bass is doubled and *steps up to the dominant.*

2. The tone that constitutes the single pitch difference among the three chords moves *down to the leading tone.*

EXAMPLE 21-2

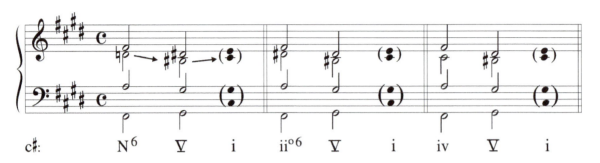

The N⁶ voiced above is present in Example 21-3. Notice that the N⁶ could be replaced by ii°⁶ or iv without altering the functional sense or voice leading of the passage.

EXAMPLE 21-3 Beethoven: Piano Sonata, op. 27, no. 2 (first movement) 🔊))

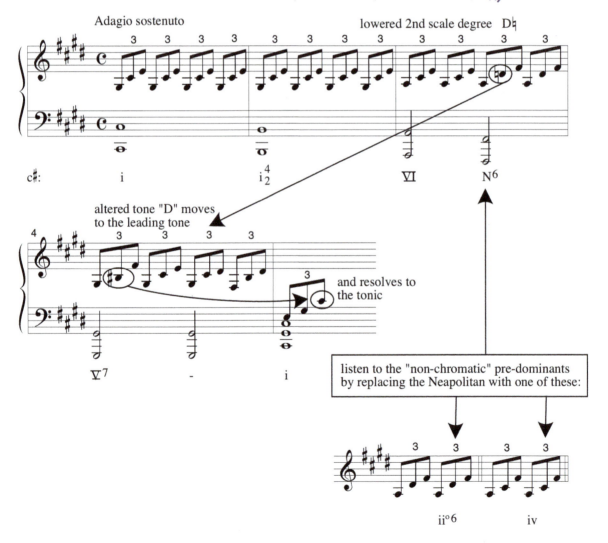

In the Neapolitan, the altered tone goes the way of all chromatic tones—undoubled, it moves *in the direction of its inflection*. It is important to understand, though, that the note's ultimate destination is the tonic, which is thus approached by half step *from above and below*. This motion—♭$\hat{2}$–$\hat{7}$–$\hat{1}$—creates a melodic diminished third that enfolds the tonic:

EXAMPLE 21-4

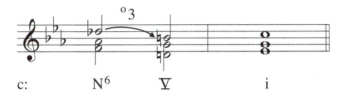

c: N⁶ V i

The o3 that creates this wrap-around motion is one of the few nondiatonic intervals tolerated under the strict part writing canon. In fact, composers seemed to relish the interval's unique sound.

Observe the treatment of the altered tone in the following musical examples.

EXAMPLE 21-5a Chopin: Prelude, op. 28, no. 20

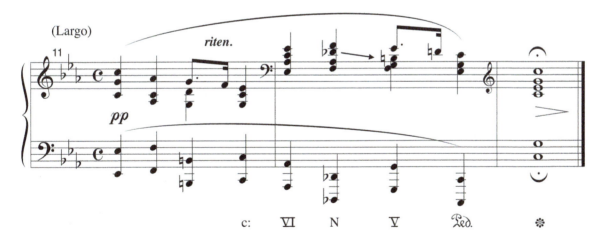

Note:

The root-position Neapolitan typically resolves, as here, to a root-position V. Even though the bass must move from root to root, the ♭$\hat{2}$ in the upper voice moves downward to $\hat{7}$ and then on the tonic C, producing the "wrap-around" effect just described.

EXAMPLE 21-5b Verdi: "Stride la vampa!" from *Il Trovatore* (act 2, scene 1) 🔊

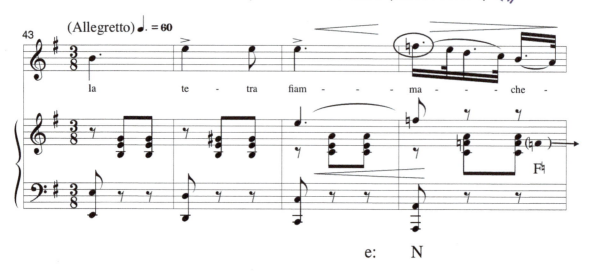

Note:

The altered tone F♮ moves to the leading tone *via the tonic* E in the cadential six-four chord (see the circled tones). The leading tone then resolves to the tonic in the piano part in m. 49. The melodic motion in b is smoother, but the harmonic progression in a is perhaps more poignant.

Insertions before V

The cadential i $^6_4$ sandwiched between the N⁶ and V "planes out" the melodic diminished third. So does the vii°⁷/V, which creates an additional chromatic passing tone in the bass. Notice, however, that the basic voice leading remains the same in all.

EXAMPLE 21-6

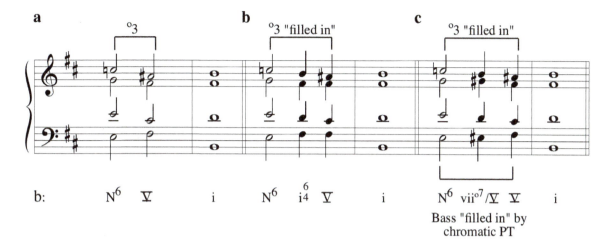

Example 21-7 incorporates both insertions illustrated above. vii°⁷/V is followed by i $\frac{6}{4}$ before moving on V.

EXAMPLE 21-7 Mozart: Piano Sonata, K. 280 (second movement) 🔊))

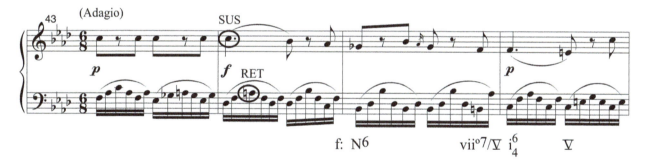

REVIEW AND REINFORCEMENT

Provide harmonic analysis of Example 21-8, and discuss the treatment of $\flat\hat{2}$ in the passage. Then identify the large-scale melodic event that takes place in the passage.

EXAMPLE 21-8 Chopin: Valse, op. 64, no. 2 🔊

The Neapolitan in Popular Culture

The Neapolitan appears occasionally in the music of our popular culture. In Gounod's "Funeral March of a Marionette," it enhances the undertone of playful menace that perhaps induced renowned film director and producer Alfred Hitchcock to use the work as the theme song for a weekly television show in the 1960s.

EXAMPLE 21-9 Gounod: "Marcha Funebre de un Volatin" 🔊

d: N⁶   i⁶₄   V⁷   i

REVIEW AND REINFORCEMENT

1   Locate and symbolize two tonicizations in Example 21-9.

2   Describe the melodic form.

In the score for the 1972 movie *The Godfather*, the Neapolitan enhances the brooding undertone of the theme song.

EXAMPLE 21-10 Larry Kusik and Nina Rota: "Speak Softly Love" (Theme from *The Godfather*) 🔊

More recently, film composer Danny Elfmann exploited the dark sound of the Neapolitan to create the oppressive atmosphere that shrouds the score to the first of the *Batman* movies.

EXAMPLE 21-11 Danny Elfmann: Theme from the movie *Batman*

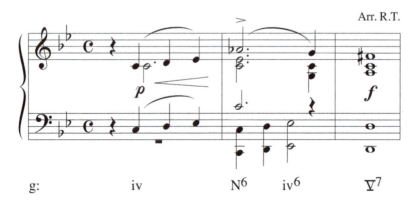

Note:

Here the N⁶ is followed by iv⁶ and by V⁷. Still, ♭$\hat{2}$ moves downward to $\hat{1}$ and onward to $\hat{7}$, much like Example 21-5b.

➤ *For assignments on the neapolitan sixth chord, turn to Workbook Chapter 21, assignments 1A–1H.*

↺ **BACK TO BASICS 21.1**

Neapolitan
Sixth Chord
Construction

AUGMENTED SIXTH CHORDS

The bass in Example 21-12 approaches the dominant G through ♯$\hat{4}$ followed by ♭$\hat{6}$, a °3 that again creates a "wrap-around."

EXAMPLE 21-12 J. S. Bach: *The Well-Tempered Clavier*, Book I, BWV 844 (Prelude No. 1) 🔊

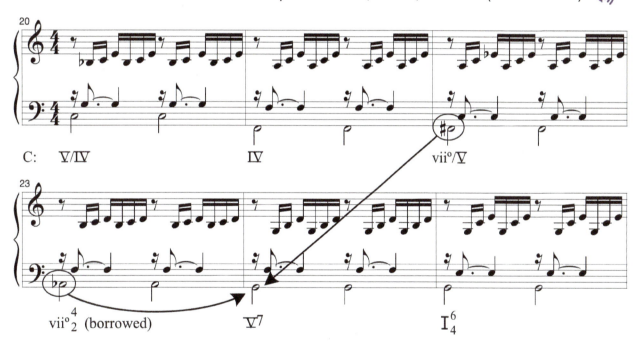

C: V/IV   IV   vii°/V

vii°$^4_2$ (borrowed)   V⁷   I$^6_4$

What would be the effect if these two potent melodic forces (♯$\hat{4}$ and ♭$\hat{6}$) that push so strongly toward the dominant by half step were combined within a single harmony?

Example 21-13 shows us. This is the theme from one of Beethoven's sets of piano variations. The reduction following the music shows the outer voices to be an expanding wedge from the double octave tonic to the triple octave dominant, approached by half step from above and below.

EXAMPLE 21-13 Beethoven: Thirty-Two Variations on an Original Theme in C Minor, WoO.80 🔊

EXAMPLE 21-13a Reduction 🔊

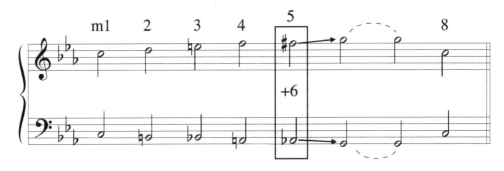

The Augmented Sixth Interval

At m. 5, the push toward the dominant is enhanced through the altered tone F♯. This note and the bass note A♭ are both a half step from the dominant G. The interval they form is an augmented sixth, and the chord they frame (see m. 5 of the reduction) is called, logically, an **augmented sixth chord**. Because of the double tendency tone, the chord has an especially urgent need to resolve to the dominant.

Two ways, both linear, of altering a pre-dominant to create an augmented sixth chord in C minor are shown in Example 21-14.

EXAMPLE 21-14

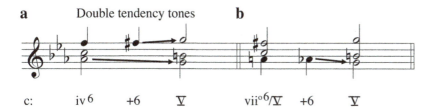

a   Double tendency tones   b

c: iv⁶   +6   Ⅴ   vii°⁶/Ⅴ   +6   Ⅴ

Note:

In a the chord results when a chromatic passing tone is inserted in a Phrygian half cadence. In b the chromatic passing tone is added following a secondary vii°.

The Augmented Sixth Chord in Three Flavors

Example 21-15 shows the three types of augmented sixth chords in A minor; their aural differences are slight and their functions are identical.

EXAMPLE 21-15

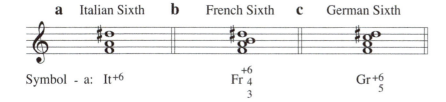

a Italian Sixth   **b** French Sixth   **c** German Sixth

Symbol - a: It+6   Fr $^{+6}_{4\,3}$ Gr$^{+6}_{5}$

Notes:

1. In all three chords, the raised fourth scale degree ($+\hat{4}$) creates a leading tone below the dominant.

2. In all three chords, $\hat{6}$—the half step *above* the dominant—is the lowest tone. This bass note and $+\hat{4}$ create the *double tendency tone* to the dominant—one from above and one from below—that form the augmented sixth interval.

3. All three chords contain the tonic.

4. The French and German sixth chords have an additional tone—the French contains $\hat{2}$, the German $\hat{3}$.

5. Superscripts in the chord symbols are the ones that would appear in a figured bass to show the chord's inversion. In most cases, the designations It+6, Fr+6 and Gr+6 suffice.

Constructing an Augmented Sixth Chord

Remember the foregoing points, and you have a simple method for constructing an augmented sixth chord in any key:

EXAMPLE 21-16a In G minor: Step 1: Place the dominant in the bass and any upper voice

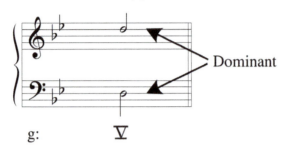

EXAMPLE 21-16b Step 2: Place a m. 2 *above* the dominant in the *bass* and a m. 2 *below* the dominant in the upper voice. This bit of "double-talk" might actually be easier to remember: *"Minor second above below and minor second below above"*

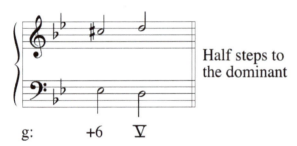

EXAMPLE 21-16c Step 3: Add the tonic in one of the remaining voices. Completion of this step produces an Italian sixth chord

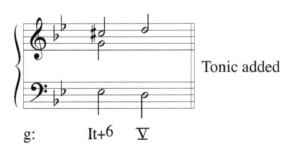

EXAMPLE 21-16d Step 4: Think: "The rest is as easy as one-two-three." For the Italian sixth: Double $\hat{1}$; For the French sixth: Add $\hat{2}$; For the German sixth: Add $\hat{3}$

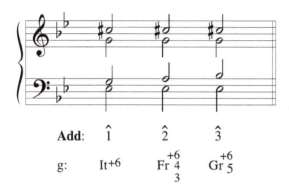

Add: $\hat{1}$ $\hat{2}$ $\hat{3}$

g: It+6   Fr $^{+6}_4{}_3$ Gr $^{+6}_5$

Note:

The minor second *above* the dominant must be in the bass. The other chord members can be distributed in any upper voice.

CONCEPT CHECK

Look again at Example 21-10. Which type of augmented sixth chord appears in passing in m. 11?

Voice Leading

Voice leading in an augmented sixth chord amounts to resolving the augmented sixth interval *outward to the octave dominant* and moving the other pitches by step.

EXAMPLE 21-17

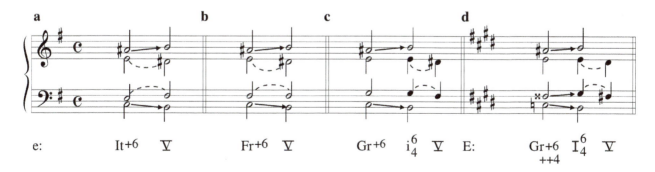

e: It+6   V   Fr+6   V   Gr+6   i$^6_4$ V   E: Gr+6   I$^6_4$ V
                                                               ++4

This voice leading can be studied in the examples that follow.

EXAMPLE 21-18a Schubert: Sonatina for Piano and Violin, op. posth.137, no. 2 🔊

d: It⁺⁶   V

EXAMPLE 21-18b Mozart: String Quartet, K. 421 (third movement) 🔊

d: Gr⁺⁶   i⁶₄   V⁴₂   i⁶

EXAMPLE 21-18c Chopin: Etude, op. 10, no. 3

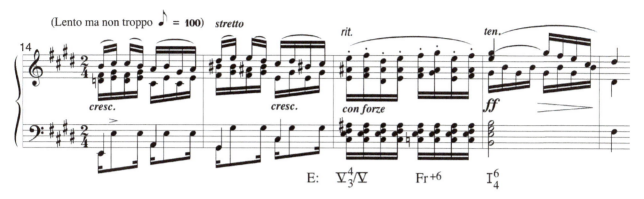

E: V_3^4/V Fr +6 I_4^6

Notes:

1. Examples a and b, both in d minor, facilitate comparison of the Italian sixth (in a) and German sixth (in b). As shown in b, the German sixth often resolves by way of the I 6/4, since a resolution directly to V would cause consecutive perfect fifths (in this case, between the soprano (moving from F to E) and the bass (moving from B♭ to A).

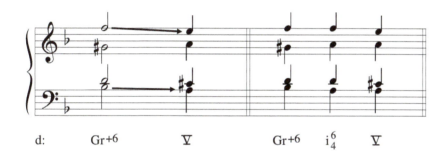

d: Gr+6 V Gr+6 i_4^6 V

2. Examples a and c display two ways of creating an augmented sixth chord, similar to those shown in Example 21-14. In a, the Italian sixth is created by inserting a chromatic passing tone into the Phrygian half cadence (see Example 21-14a). In c, a French sixth is created by the alteration of a secondary dominant (compare to Example 21-14b).

As Example 21-18 also shows, augmented sixth chords appear in major keys as well as minor, although they—like the Neapolitan—originated as minor-key sounds. However, in major keys, they are more highly altered chords. Note in Example 21-19 that the bass note (C natural) in the Fr+6 is a chromatically lowered pitch in E major, whereas it is diatonic in E minor.

EXAMPLE 21-19

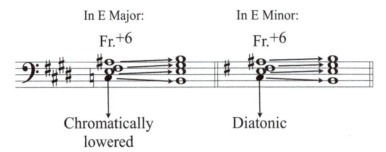

The Gr+6 in a major key is an even more highly altered chord because $\hat{3}$ is also chromatically lowered:

EXAMPLE 21-20

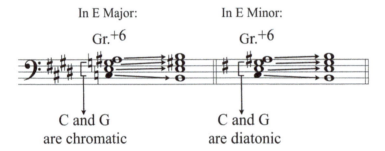

The Enharmonic German Sixth Chord

When the German sixth appears in major keys and resolves to a *major* I $^6_4$, $\flat\hat{3}$ is often written enharmonically as $\sharp\hat{2}$ to reflect its *upward* resolution. (Remember that chromatic pitches resolve in the direction of their inflection.) The chord is often called an enharmonic German sixth (Gr+6$_{enh}$) or a doubly augmented fourth chord (++4).

EXAMPLE 21-21

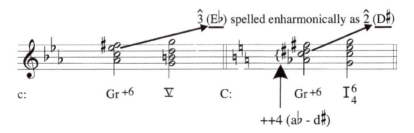

Note:

The ++4 in the chord symbol refers to the interval created above the bass, not to +4 (in this case F$\sharp$).

CONCEPT CHECK

How would you respell the Gr.+6^{enh} in the following example to reflect its resolution more properly?

EXAMPLE 21-22 Scott Joplin: "The Sycamore (A Concert Rag)" 🔊

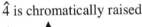

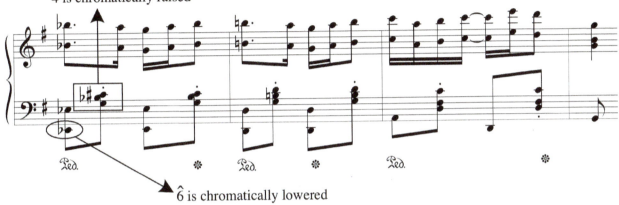

$\hat{3}$ is chromatically lowered

$\hat{4}$ is chromatically raised

$\hat{6}$ is chromatically lowered

For keyboard instruments or guitar, the doubly augmented fourth chord is a mere notational technicality. However, for instruments that can adjust their pitch, enharmonics such as D♯ and E♭ are not played identically; each is nudged in the direction of its inflection.

Jazz harmony is heavily laced with German augmented sixth chords, rarely spelled as such. A common convention is to spell the chord as a dominant seventh chord a half step above the true dominant.

EXAMPLE 21-23 Thelonius Monk: "Round Midnight" 🔊

Note:

The chord in m. 7 begins life as a German sixth (enharmonically spelled as B⁷. It then becomes a French sixth, changing when the melody slips from Gb ($\hat{3}$) to F ($\hat{2}$), and finally turns Italian when F falls to Eb ($\hat{1}$). Many augmented sixth chords occur in this context, under a melody that passes among scale degrees 1, 2, and 3, resulting in a "cosmopolitan" version of the chord that is, by turn, Italian, French, and German.

↺ BACK TO BASICS 21.2

Augmented Sixth Chord Construction

CONCEPT CHECK

1   Respell the chord of Example 21-23, m. 7 as a true German sixth chord.

2   In Example 21-24, what type of augmented sixth chord appears in m. 1 and m. 6? Discuss the resolution of the altered tones in this chord.

EXAMPLE 21-24 Robert Schumann: "Am leuchtenden Sommermorgen" (no. 12 from *Dichterliebe*, op. 48) 🔊

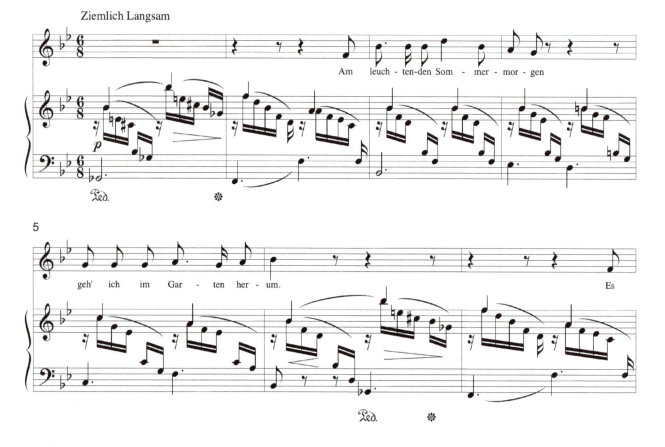

▶ *For assignments on augmented sixth chords, turn to Workbook Chapter 21, assignments 2A–2G.*

⊕ CODA

Did you notice that a +6 is the inversion of a o3? In augmented sixth and Neapolitan sixth chords, these intervals wrap themselves around important scale degrees, one melodically, the other harmonically. In the Neapolitan sixth chord, the o3 *collapses inward to the tonic*. In the augmented sixth chords, the +6 *expands outward to the dominant*. In this sense, the chords share a kinship beyond their harmonic function as pre-dominants. The chords have other things in common:

- They both are linear, in the sense that they spring from chromatic voice leading, and the altered tones enhance the harmonic push toward the chord of resolution.

- They both are distinctive, highly colorful chords that appear much less often than secondary dominants and borrowed harmonies, which remain the staples of chromatic harmony.

DO YOU KNOW THESE TERMS?

- altered pre-dominant
- augmented sixth chord
- doubly augmented fourth chord
- French sixth chord
- German sixth chord
- Italian sixth chord
- Neapolitan chord

CHAPTER TWENTY-TWO

Other Chromatic Harmonies

KEY CONCEPTS IN THIS CHAPTER

- Altered Dominants and Altered Dominant Seventh Chords

- Embellishing Diminished Seventh Chords

ALTERED DOMINANTS

The dominant was the last bulwark of diatonic harmony to buckle under chromaticism's relentless advance. Really, the only alterable member of the chord is the fifth, because modifying either the root or the third (the leading tone) would strip the chord of its two defining features—its root relationship to the tonic and its major quality. **Altered dominants** are therefore a small category of chromatic harmonies that involve either raising or lowering the chord fifth:

1. The altered chord fifth is normally not doubled and usually resolves as all altered tones do—*in the direction of its inflection* (a, b, c, and d).

2. Resolution of three sensitive tones—the altered fifth, the leading tone, and the seventh—results in an incomplete tonic triad—no fifth (b and d).

3. The raised fifth appears more often *without* the seventh (V+) and is found in both the Classic and Romantic periods (a). By contrast, the lowered fifth usually appears *with* the seventh (V$^{7/-5}$) and is more common in the later nineteenth century (d).

EXAMPLE 22-1 (Arrows show the tendency tones and their resolutions)

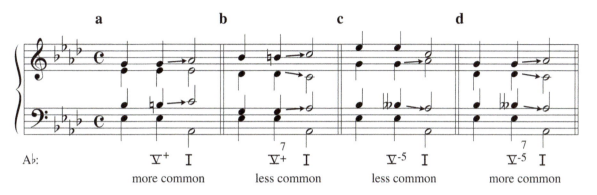

It is common practice to symbolize the four chords as shown in Example 22-1 *regardless of inversion* since showing the inversion can necessitate an unwieldy chord symbol that actually obscures the chords' most salient feature, the altered fifth.

The Raised Fifth

Altered dominants are usually linear, and the altered tone can usually be analyzed as a chromatic passing tone (a, b, c, and d).

EXAMPLE 22-2a Beethoven: Sonata, op. 28 (third movement) 🔊

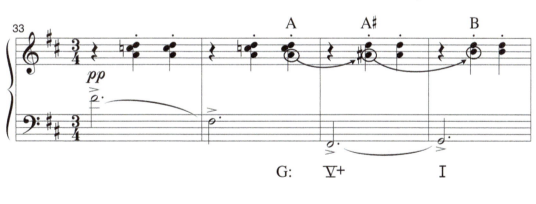

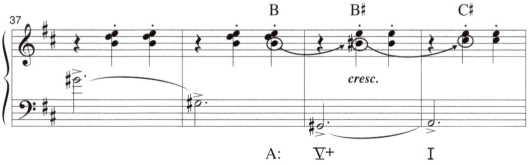

EXAMPLE 22-2b Chopin: Nocturne, op. 27, no. 1

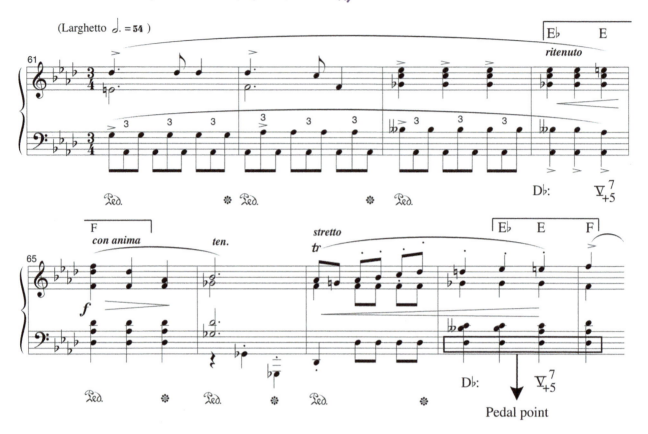

Note:

In both **a** and **b**: The raised fifth resembles an ascending passing tone. The seventh resolves downward, the resolution delayed by a measure in **a**.

The Lowered Fifth

The lowered fifth is less common than the raised fifth. It is usually accompanied by the seventh. The chord is often in second inversion, making it identical—in spelling and resolution, but *not in function*—to a French sixth chord. The two chords are analogous to homonyms (words spelled and sounding alike but have different meanings, such as *note* (a memo) and *note* (a musical symbol)). A French sixth resolves to the dominant whereas an altered dominant resolves to the tonic.

EXAMPLE 22-3 Note the difference in key

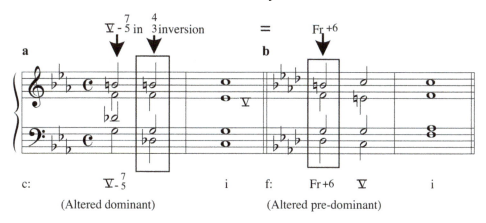

(Altered dominant) (Altered pre-dominant)

Note:

The chords in **a** and **b** are identical. However, in **a**, the chord's resolution is to the tonic; in **b**, it's to the dominant.

CONCEPT CHECK

The altered dominant in Example 22-4 is spelled exactly the same way a French sixth would be spelled. In what key would it be analyzed as a French sixth chord (an altered pre-dominant) rather than an altered dominant?

EXAMPLE 22-4 Dello Joio: Piano Sonata, no. 3 (first movement) 🔊))

CONCEPT CHECK

On the grand staff that follows, construct a French sixth chord for soprano, alto, tenor, and bass in the key of E minor and resolve it. Then, treat it instead as a second inversion V^{7-5}, changing the key accordingly, and resolve it to the tonic.

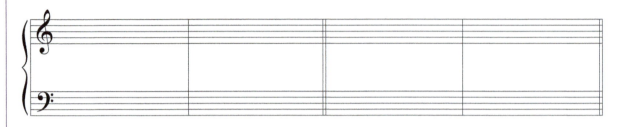

Altered Dominants as Secondary Functions

Like their diatonic counterparts, altered dominants can function at a secondary level (V+/V and so on). Did it occur to you while completing the foregoing CONCEPT CHECKS that a French sixth chord is in fact a second inversion $V^{7/-5}$/V? Either analysis is correct.

EXAMPLE 22-5 Schubert: "Die Liebe hat gelogen" 🔊

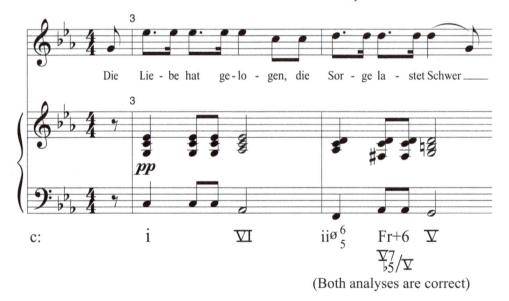

(Both analyses are correct)

The V+/IV is arguably more common than the V+.

EXAMPLE 22-6a Beethoven: Bagatelle, no. 8, op. 119 🔊

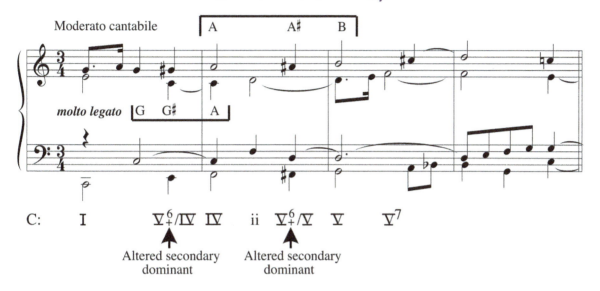

Altered secondary
dominant

Altered secondary
dominant

EXAMPLE 22-6b Wolf: "Gebet" (No. 28 from *Mörike Songs*) 🔊

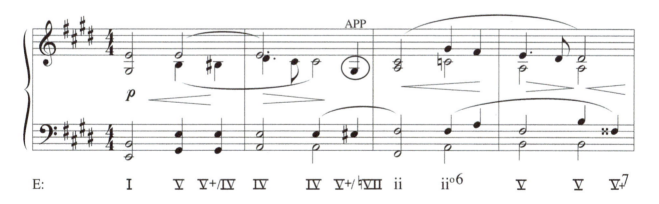

Notes:

1. The raised fifth (B♯) in m. 1 resolves upward to C♯ *by way of* an appoggiatura D♯ (m. 2).

2. The altered secondary dominant of m. 2 resolves deceptively to ii rather than to the chord it tonicizes.

EXAMPLE 22-6c Richard Rodgers: "Some Enchanted Evening" (from *South Pacific*)

EXAMPLE 22-6d Scott Joplin: "Pleasant Moments" (Ragtime Waltz)

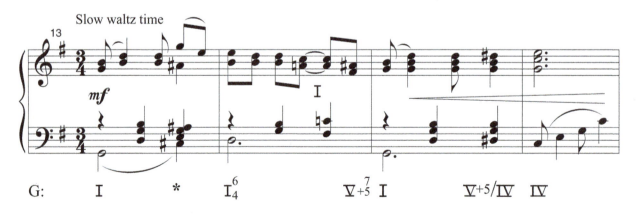

*This harmony will be discussed in the ensuing section.

CONCEPT CHECK

In Example 22-6a, two instances where the raised fifth functions as a chromatic passing tone are bracketed. In which of the other altered dominants (in a, b, c, and d) is this the case? In the blank measure that follows, write the chord that you would expect to follow m. 4, beat 4 of Example 22-6b.

Altered dominants, especially the V^{7-5}, have been used extensively in jazz and popular styles. We'll consider them further in Chapter 32.

➤ *For assignments on altered dominants, turn to Workbook Chapter 22, assignments 1A–1F.*

EMBELLISHING DIMINISHED SEVENTH CHORDS

You might compare hearing a major–minor seventh chord to seeing a guy with a snowboard on a chair lift. You can be reasonably sure which direction he'll be going next. (Down!) When you hear a diminished seventh chord, however, it's like seeing a guy dressed for snowboarding in the lodge. You can *guess* which direction he'll go next, but you can't be sure. This is because the diminished seventh chord—like the rider in the lodge—has options. It might act like a vii°7 and head for its tonic (the anticipated function) or it might instead *embellish* a different chord (behavior of a completely different sort).

The **embellishing diminished seventh chord** (emb°7) is a "maverick" in that:

1. It *embellishes* a chord, typically I or V (less often another chord), rather than *tonicizing* it.

2. Its root is a chromatically raised pitch that sounds not at all like a root. It steps up (in the direction of its inflection), but not to the *root* of the next chord.

3. Its seventh does not resolve downward but usually stays on as the root of the embellished chord. For this reason, some theorists refer to this chord as a **common tone diminished seventh** (CT°7).

4. Roman numeral symbols serve only to emphasize that the chord lacks traditional function. For this reason, the designation "emb°7" will be used in place of Roman numerals.

Example 22-7 shows the two most common embellishing diminished seventh chords—embellishments to I and V.

EXAMPLE 22-7 Example 22-7 R=Root

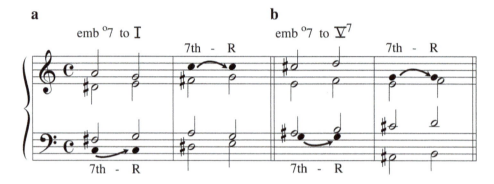

Notes:

1. Arrows connect the common tones relating the chords. The seventh of the "embellish *or*," because it is the root of the "embellish*ee*," can have no downward resolution.

2. The three *non-common tones* slide stepwise into the chord of resolution, much like embellishing tones (hence the chord's name). This can produce nonstandard doubling in the resolution chord (as in a).

3. The harmonic motion—♯iio7–I or ♯vio7–V—is not functional. That is, it does not follow the functional paradigm previously described (see Chapter 5, see p. 70).

Functional versus Embellishing Diminished Seventh Chords

Example 22-8a shows how functional and embellishing diminished seventh chords differ in their approach to the same tonic.

EXAMPLE 22-8a Black notes = roots; sevenths are circled

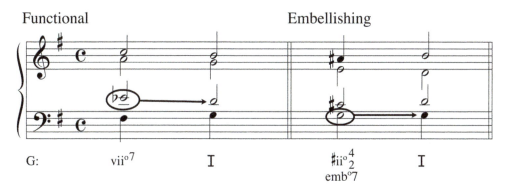

Notes:

In the functional diminished seventh chord:

1. The root movement is up by half step to the tonic (F♯–G).
2. No common tone exists between it and the tonic. (Recall that this is true of any two chords whose roots are related by second.)
3. The seventh resolves stepwise downward (its normal trajectory).

In the embellishing diminished seventh:

The root is an altered tone that acts more like a chromatic embellishment than a chord root. The seventh is a common tone and is therefore unable to resolve downward. In both cases, the remaining tones move stepwise into the tonic.

Example 22-8b shows how *the same* diminished seventh chord acts as both a functional and embellishing chord.

EXAMPLE 22-8b Black notes = roots; sevenths are circled

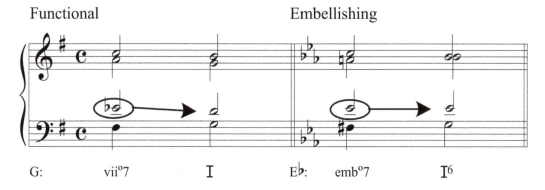

Spelling and Resolving the Embellishing °7

Because the *root of the embellished chord* is typically the *seventh of its embellishing chord*, an embellishing diminished seventh chord can be constructed in a manner somewhat opposite the way we construct functional diminished seventh chords—by stacking minor thirds *downward* from the root of the chord it embellishes.

EXAMPLE 22-9a To spell and resolve the emb°7 to V⁷ in the key of A

a   To spell and resolve the emb°7 to $\underline{V}$7 in the key of A:

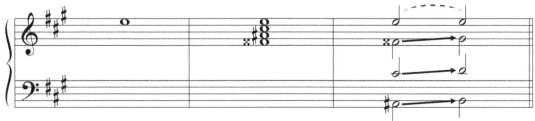

1. Notate the root of $\underline{V}$ 2. Stack m3's downward   3. Voice the chord and resolve. Retain the common tone in the same voice and resolving the others by step

EXAMPLE 22-9b To spell and resolve an emb°7 to I in the key of A

b   To spell and resolve an emb°7 to I in the key of A:

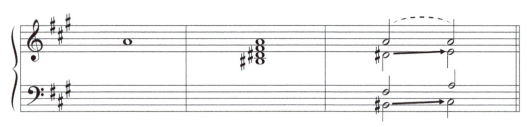

1. Notate the root of I   2. Stack m3's downward   3. Voice the chord and resolve. Retain the common tone in the same voice and resolving the others by step

The following passages use the emb°7 in a typical way.

EXAMPLE 22-10a Haydn, String Quartet, op. 76/4, (first movement) 🔊

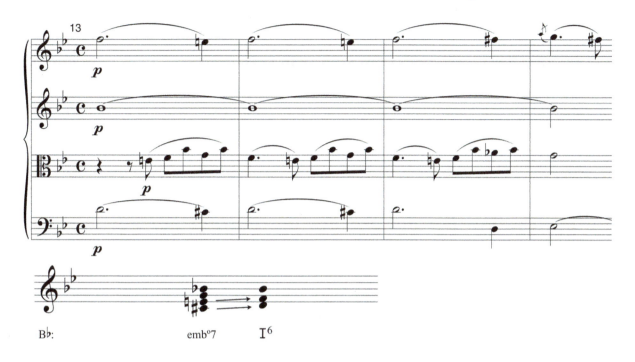

EXAMPLE 22-10b Tchaikovsky: Symphony, no. 6, op. 74 (first movement) 🔊

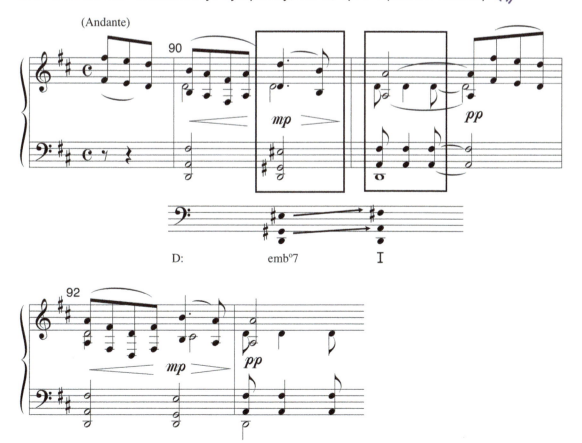

Examples 22-11 and 22-12 contain both functional and embellishing diminished seventh chords.

EXAMPLE 22-11 Schubert: Moment Musicale No. 6 from *Sechs Moments Musicaux, op.* 94 (D. 780) 🔊

EXAMPLE 22-11a Schubert: Moment Musicale No. 6 from *Sechs Moments Musicaux, op.* 94 (D. 780) Reduction

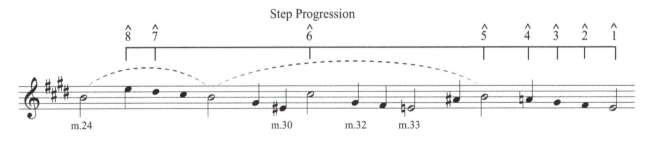

EXAMPLE 22-12a Mahler: "Rheinlegendchen" (from *Des Knaben Wunderhorn*) 🔊

EXAMPLE 22-12b Reduction

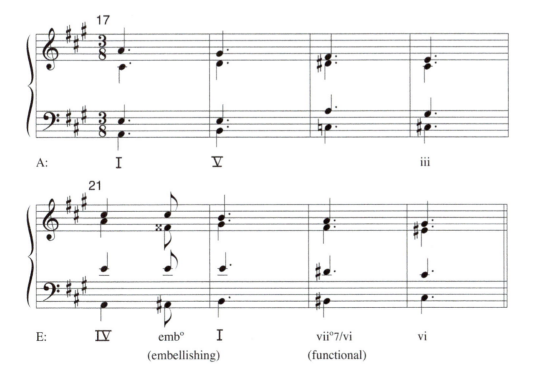

CONCEPT CHECK

Example 22-12a contains *three* diminished seventh chords. The one in m. 19 (see reduction in Example 22-12b) is not spelled in a manner that reflects its resolution. Given its spelling, what would you expect the chord of resolution to be? Respell it enharmonically to better reflect its actual resolution.

➤ *For assignments on embellishing diminished seventh chords, turn to Workbook Chapter 22, assignments 2A–2F.*

⊕ CODA

Some points to remember:

- Of the altered chords considered in this chapter and Chapter 21, two—the Neapolitan and the embellishing diminished seventh chords—were familiar structures (a major triad and a diminished seventh chord). Two others—the augmented sixth chords and altered dominants—were new *sounds*.

- Three of the chords function as *approach* chords—the Neapolitan and augmented sixth chords approach the dominant, and the altered dominants approach the tonic. They function identically to their diatonic (unaltered) counterparts.

- Historically, the Neapolitan and augmented sixth chords were the earlier harmonies. Initially minor-key chords, they crept into major keys in increasing numbers during the nineteenth century. Embellishing diminished seventh began life in major keys and remained primarily major-key sounds. Altered dominants appear in both major and minor contexts.

- Of the chromatic harmonies discussed in this chapter and the last, the altered predominants are the most common. Still, none of these chords are as prevalent as secondary functions and modal borrowings, which constitute the bulk of the harmonic chromaticism in tonal music.

DO YOU KNOW THESE TERMS?

- altered dominant

- embellishing diminished seventh chord

CHAPTER TWENTY-THREE

Modulation II

KEY CONCEPTS IN THIS CHAPTER

- Clue Chords
- Identifying the Tonal Border
- Chromatic Pivot
- Enharmonic Pivot
- Pivot Tone
- The Enharmonic German Sixth Chord
- The Enharmonic Diminished Seventh Chord

PERSPECTIVE: "IN SEARCH OF HARMONIC LOGIC"

The Musical Road Trip and the Tonal Border

Most art music is a "road trip" through several tonal regions. In this metaphor, modulation is the act of crossing a "tonal border," and any of the harmonies discussed in the preceding chapters might be the vehicle that carries the music across it. *Every* modulation can be approached with the same two goals: (1) to identify the "tonal border," and (2) to discover the means of transportation across it.

Each chord at the tonal border is likely to function in the old key or the new in a familiar way—as a dominant seventh or secondary dominant seventh chord, a functional or embellishing diminished seventh chord, a borrowed harmony, a chromatically third-related triad, a Neapolitan or augmented sixth chord, or an altered dominant. These recognizable functions give the modulation harmonic logic.

A simple yet workable approach to modulation is based on the premise, stated in Chapter 17, that *only two basic types of modulation exist*—those with a common chord and those without.

THE THREE CS: RECOGNIZING THE SIGNALS

Think of them as "the three Cs":

1. Chromatics

2. Clue chords

3. Cadences

These are a modulation's "tells."

Chromatic Pitches

Earlier, you learned how the consistent appearance of accidentals signals a tonal change. A quick review:

1. A chromatically raised pitch is probably the new leading tone ("ti"). A chromatically lowered pitch is probably the fourth scale degree ("fa") in the new key, either the seventh of a V^7 or the fifth of a vii°.

2. With multiple accidentals, the one *most remote from the current key* probably functions in one of the ways just described. Accidentals that cannot belong in the same key signature (F♯ and B♭, for example) suggest a minor key.

Clue Chords

But beware! Accidentals can mislead; and in short modulations, the tell-tale tone might appear no more than once. Fortunately, a musical passage usually offers multiple clues to its tonal center. The following chords are signposts on the road to a new tonality:

1. The Mm7 chord is a harmony that functions *almost exclusively* as a dominant (hence the common designation "dominant seventh"). Its consistent appearance suggests a modulation to the key whose tonic lies a perfect fifth below its root.

    If you see this:  think A (a).

2. The o7 (diminished seventh) chord *usually* functions as a leading-tone chord, suggesting a tonic a minor second above its root.

    If you see this:  think E (e).

3. A second inversion triad *often* functions as a cadential six-four chord.

   If you see this:    think D♭.

4. Italian and German augmented sixth chords *almost always* function as pre-dominants, resolving to V or I $^6_4$.

   If you see this:    think a.

   (The French augmented sixth chord is not quite so categorical because, as you learned in Chapter 22, the V^{7-5} in second inversion is structurally identical with the Fr+6.)

These "clue chords" are the foot soldiers in any tonal skirmish, and you should develop the ability to recognize them quickly.

CONCEPT CHECK

What tonalities are suggested by the appearance of the following clue chords?

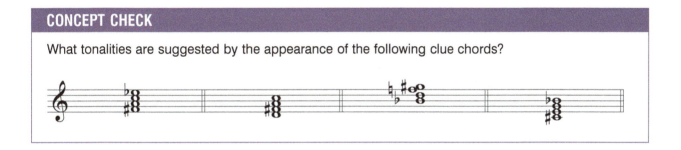

▶ *Assignment 1A on Workbook p. 278 can be completed at this time.*

Cadences

Because most phrases end with an authentic or half cadence, the final chord in most cadences will be I or V. Thus, phrase endings are also important clues to the tonality.

These clues—*chromatic pitches, clue chords, and cadences*—will usually build the case for one tonality or another in a modulating passage.

EXAMPLE 23-1 Brahms: "Wie Melodien zieht es mir", op. 105, no. 1

Thinking Through a Modulation

If at first glance a passage seems a lot to digest, as the foregoing might, try breaking it into bite-sized morsels:

- Mm. 14–16: These measures are entirely diatonic in A, the key implied by the key signature.

- Mm. 17–18: Despite the accidentals in m. 17, the first phrase comes to a cadence in m. 18 over a root-position A major triad. Conclusion: The music is still in A.

REVIEW AND REINFORCEMENT

What chromatic harmony occurs in m. 17, beat 1? What is unusual about its resolution?

- Mm. 19–22: No accidentals appear consistently in these measures. But the phrase comes to a cadence in m. 22 on a D major triad, preceded by its altered dominant. Together, the two chords produce an authentic cadence—V^{7+5}-I. Conclusion: The music has either modulated to D or is tonicizing it.

- Mm. 22–25: No accidentals appear consistently. But the cadence chord is an F♯ minor triad (m. 25). Is it I or V? Because half cadences end on *major* (not minor) triads, this minor chord probably is the tonic. The chord preceding it is a V^7 in f♯, creating an authentic cadence. Conclusion: The music has traveled to the relative minor, f♯, following a brief layover in D.

▶ *For assignments on recognizing signals, turn to Workbook Chapter 23, assignments 1A–1C.*

BACK TO THE TONAL BORDER

The harmonic logic of a modulation lies near the tonal border, where one of three circumstances will likely exist:

Case 1: *The first chord diatonic in the new key is the last chord diatonic in the old key.* This is the familiar **common chord modulation**.

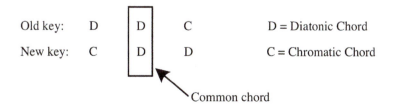

Case 2: *The first chord diatonic in the new key follows the last chord diatonic in the old key.* This is a simple **chromatic modulation**.

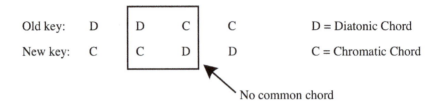

Case 3: *The first chord diatonic in the new key and the last chord diatonic in the old key are separated by one or more chords diatonic in neither key.* This is a more complex **chromatic modulation**. If several chromatic chords intervene, they might be tonicizing a third key.

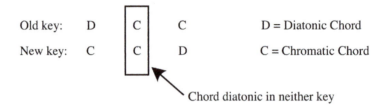

In the following discussion, we'll refer back to these three cases. Look again at the Brahms song. The last four measures begin in D and end in f♯. Example 23-2 shows the ground-level harmonic structure.

EXAMPLE 23-2

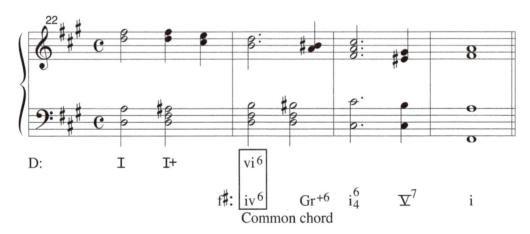

Q: Where does the modulation occur?

A: To find out, home in on the tonal border from points before and after. Working backward from the cadence, the first clear indication of f♯ is the cadential six-four chord at m. 24. The chord before it (m. 23, beat 3) is chromatic in f♯ but recognizable—a Gr+6. Working forward, everything up to this chord analyzes well enough in D. The tonal border, then, lies in m. 23.

Q: How does the music cross the tonal border?

A: The new key (f#) takes root with the appearance of the German sixth chord. The chord preceding it (m. 23, beat 1) is common to *both keys* (b = vi in D and iv in f#) and can therefore be considered a common chord (Case 1).

MODULATIONS CASE-BY-CASE

Case 1

Example 23-3 shows a Case 1 modulation. We've seen this type—a common chord modulation—in Chapter 17, but what's new here is the isolation of a single tone (E♭), which is a member of both the i in C minor and the iii in A♭ major. A modulation in which a single tone, common to two tonalities, serves as the pivot is called a **pivot tone modulation** (or **common tone modulation**).

EXAMPLE 23-3 Beethoven: Sonata, op. 10, no. 1 (first movement)

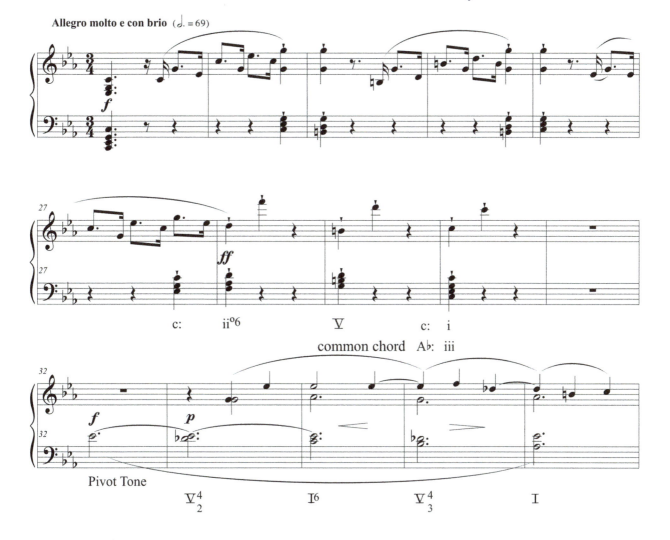

Case 2

A pivot tone need not be a member of a common chord, as shown in the Case 2 modulation that follows. In this passage, the first phrase ends in one key and the second phrase begins in another, separated by a single isolated tone. The modulation occurs *between* rather than *within* phrases. Recall from Chapter 17 that such modulations are sometimes termed "tonal shifts."

EXAMPLE 23-4a Beethoven: Trio, op. 1, no. 3 (fourth movement)

Example 23-4b is another simple Case 2 modulation.

EXAMPLE 23-4b Richard Smith and Felix Bernard: "Walking in a Winter Wonderland" 🔊))

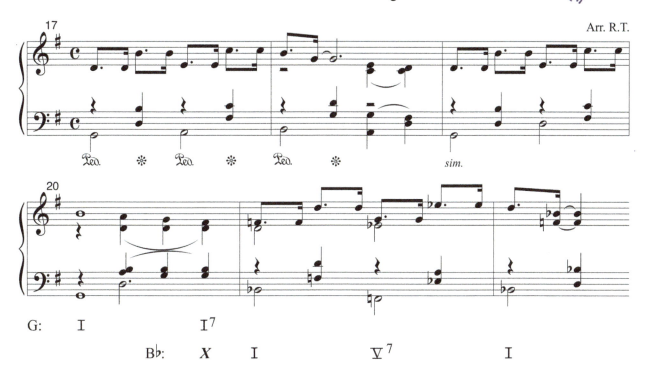

G: I   I⁷

B♭:   X   I   V⁷   I

In Example 23-4c, the striking change from flats to sharps leaves little doubt about *where* the tonal border lies. But *how* does the music cross it?

EXAMPLE 23-4c Beethoven: Sonata for Violin and Piano, op. 24 (second movement) 🔊))

continued

EXAMPLE 23-4c *continued*

Gb: I

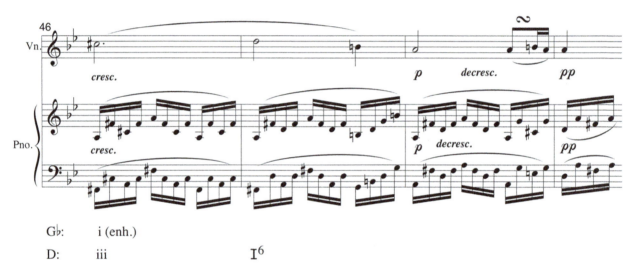

Gb: i (enh.)

D: iii   I⁶

Here the borrowed tonic (i in Gb) functions as iii in D (and is respelled enharmonically in that key—as f♯):

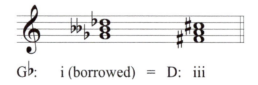

Gb: i (borrowed) = D: iii

The two keys, incidentally—Gb and D—are enharmonically a chromatic third apart (Gb = F♯, and F♯–D = I–bVI). Modulations to bVI are frequent in music of the Romantic era (ca. 1825–1900). Be watchful for them.

Case 3

Example 23-5a and b typify Case 3. In a, a single chord (m. 8, beat 1) *follows* the last chord diatonic in F and *precedes* the first chord diatonic in D. Separating the two tonalities and chromatic in both, it's the pivotal point—the "tonal border"—in this modulation. The chord can be termed a **chromatic pivot**.

EXAMPLE 23-5a Brahms: Quintet, no. 1, op. 88 (first movement) 🔊))

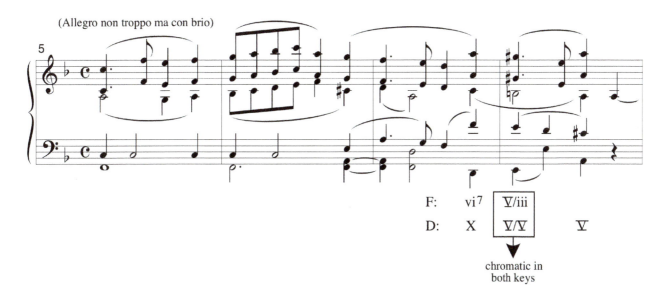

In Example 23-5b, backing up from the authentic cadence in mm. 15 and 16 and moving forward from the beginning of the passage brings us to mm. 12 and 13—the tonal border. Here, the last chord diatonic in E (m. 11) and the first chord diatonic in C (m. 14) stare at each other across a harmonic divide created by two chords diatonic in *neither* key. Even so, both are recognizable chromatic harmonies in E, and the second is a common chromatic harmony in C. This chord again might be called a **chromatic pivot.**

EXAMPLE 23-5b Franz Liszt: Consolation, no. 2 🔊

Putting Things Together

Example 23-6, teeming with accidentals, looks formidable. However, it can be cut down to size by breaking it apart based on its cadences. Listen to the example and/or play it, and see if you can answer the questions posed on the music before reading the paragraphs that follow. If you can, you'll have a head start on the analysis.

EXAMPLE 23-6 Schubert: "Sehnsucht"

1. The song begins in A♭ and the first phrase arrives at a cadence on E♭ in m. 4. *Is the cadence chord I or V?* If I, then the music must have modulated to E♭. But the only hint of that key—the D natural of m. 2—is offset by the returning D♭ in m. 3. Measure 4 is a half cadence—no modulation.

REVIEW AND REINFORCEMENT

What type of chromatic harmony precedes the cadence chord in m. 4?

2. The second phrase also ends with a cadence on E♭ (m. 11). *Is the cadence chord I or V?* The Mm7 chord on beat 4 of m. 9 is a clue chord, almost always to be regarded as V^7. If so, it resolves to a minor tonic. So m. 11 is, like m. 4, a half cadence, and the approach chord of m. 10, beat 3—familiar from Ch. 21, perhaps—is a further clue. Measures 10 and 11 are in A♭ minor (a change of mode with respect to the beginning): i–Gr+6–V.

3. This leaves the middle measures. The key signature of mm. 6–9 suggests either E major or C♯ minor. In C♯ minor, we'd expect B♯ (the leading tone) to appear more often than B natural. This, however, is not the case, so the key is probably E, the enharmonic ♭VI of A♭.

4. On beat 3 of m. 7, a very weak cadence on a first inversion F♯ major triad occurs. *Is this chord I or V?* You might make a case for either or both. The two following measures contain conflicting accidentals—D♮ and A♯—that, when seen together, suggest B minor. And the chord of m. 9 is an A♯o7, whose usual function is vii°7 in B minor. It seems, then, that the music modulates first to E in m. 6, then quickly to B in m. 7, then changes mode to B minor:

	m.6				m.7		m.8
E:	I	vii°$^6_5$/ii	ii6	ii	$\underline{\text{V}}$6		
B:			I6	vii⌀$^4_3$/$\underline{\text{V}}$	$\underline{\text{V}}$6	i	
b:						i	

Notice that none of these chords are unusual or complicated when analyzed in the proper keys.

5. So how does the music swing into E? Consider m. 5. The chord on beat 4 is a Mm7 (= V^7 in A♭). The preceding chord is a *minor* iv. Perhaps the mode has changed to A♭ minor. If so, the V^7 resolves in an understandable way—*if* you think enharmonically: ab: V^7–VI^{enh}. The modulation to E in m. 6 is by enharmonic pivot.

EXAMPLE 23-7a

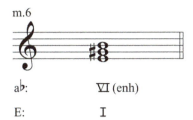

In this last song, the trek across the tonal border might seem tortuous. But analysis of complex passages requires this methodical thinking of this sort. You need to use what you know about chromatics, chord functions, and cadences—the three Cs. If you've trained your ear to recognize these harmonic clues, simply hearing a passage will often provide insights that elude the eye.

➤ *For assignments on crossing the tonal border, turn to Workbook Chapter 23, assignments 2A–2C.*

THE SECRET LIVES OF CHORDS

In the tonal drama, all chords whose functions are disguised by enharmonic spelling might be said to lead a "secret life." Two chords are particularly notorious for this behavior.

The Enharmonic German Sixth Chord

Play the following:

EXAMPLE 23-7b

Though they sound identical, the two chords' spellings reflect their differing functions, a as a V^7 in E♭ and b as a Gr+6 in D minor. A modulation up a half step from d to E♭ (its Neapolitan) or the reverse can be accomplished with maximum efficiency by using this chord.

EXAMPLE 23-8

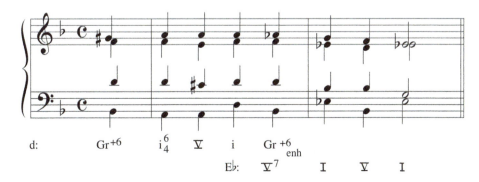

Note:

Resolving the +6 interval enharmonically as a m7 transforms a German sixth chord into a dominant seventh chord, and vice versa.

CONCEPT CHECK

Is Example 23-8a *Case 1, 2,* or *3* modulation? In Example 23-8a, respell the dominant seventh chords as German sixth chords and vice versa. Then resolve the respelled chord.

EXAMPLE 23-8a

The difficulty in recognizing modulations that exploit this enharmonic potential comes when composers spell the chord *in only one key.* (They usually do. Why be redundant?) We then must discover for ourselves the chord's "secret life" (its function in the other key).

EXAMPLE 23-9 Tchaikovsky: Onegin's Aria from *Eugene Onegin*

It's almost as if Tchaikovsky were teaching a lesson on using the German sixth chord enharmonically. He spells the chord in m. 29 in *both* the old and new keys, making clear its dual function as a V⁷/V in B♭ and Gr+6 in e (note the resolution of the augmented sixth interval outward to the octave dominant B). However, he spells the chord of m. 30, beats 3 and 4, *only* in e (as a V⁷). That spelling conceals its secret life—as an enharmonic German sixth chord (a doubly augmented fourth chord, actually) in the ensuing key of E♭.

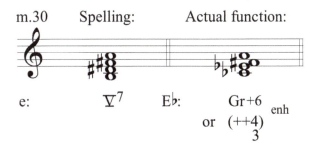

CONCEPT CHECK

Voice the doubly augmented fourth chord above for soprano, alto, tenor, and bass and resolve it.

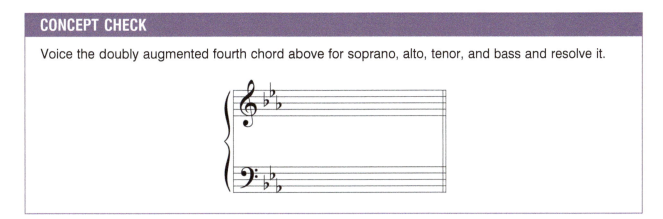

EXAMPLE 23-10 Chopin: Fantasy in F Minor, op. 49 🔊))

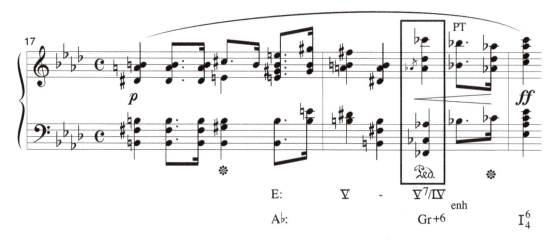

E: V   -   V⁷/IV
                           enh
A♭:   Gr +6   I⁶₄

Note:

The chord of m. 18, beat 3, is spelled as a German sixth chord in A♭ (F♭–A♭–C♭–D) rather than a doubly augmented fourth chord (F♭–A♭–B♮–D) probably because the melody descends (C♭–B♭–A♭). If the C♭ on beat 3 were to rise directly to C, it would be better spelled as B♮, creating the doubly augmented fourth chord.

▶ *Assignment 3D in Workbook Chapter 23 can be completed at this time.*

The Enharmonic Diminished Seventh Chord

The enharmonic capability of the German sixth chord pales beside that of the diminished seventh chord. This is because any one of the four chord members in a o7 can be heard as the root.

EXAMPLE 23-11

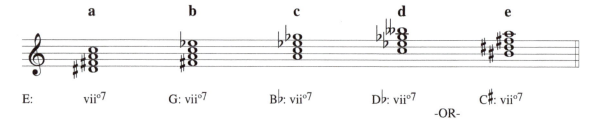

E: vii°⁷   G: vii°⁷   B♭: vii°⁷   D♭: vii°⁷   C♯: vii°⁷
                                              -OR-

Notes:

1. All five chords sound identical but are spelled differently.

2. In each chord, the root functions as the leading tone in the key.

3. Examples d and e are the same leading-tone seventh chord spelled enharmonically.

CONCEPT CHECK

Resolve the following chord correctly. Then, keeping the same voicing, respell the chord members enharmonically so each of the other chord members in turn becomes the root. Resolve these chords, and give the analysis symbol for each.

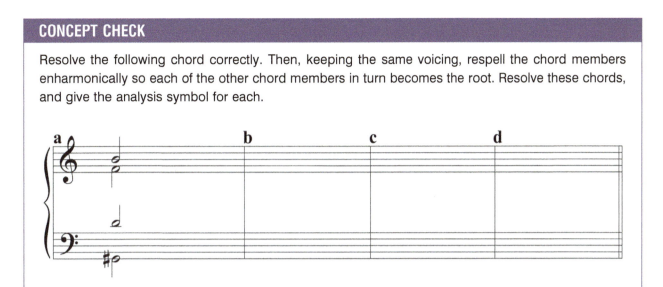

Composers have exploited the enharmonic potential of the diminished seventh chord, though not as often as one might expect given its versatility. Examples follow.

EXAMPLE 23-12 Brahms: Ballade, op. 10, no. 4

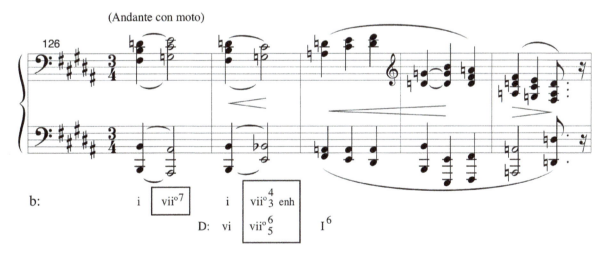

Note:

The diminished seventh chord in m. 126 is spelled according to its function in B minor (A♯–C♯–E–G) and then, in m. 127, according to its function in D major (C♯–E–G–B♭). Aurally, the tonal border is not crossed until m. 128, but all the chords from m. 126 on are diatonic in either the old or new key. The boxed chords are enharmonic common chords, diatonic in both keys through respelling.

In the passage that follows, the enharmonic common chord of m. 135 is spelled first in the old key of g, then in the chromatic-third related key of e.

EXAMPLE 23-13 Beethoven: Piano Sonata, op. 13 (first movement) 🔊

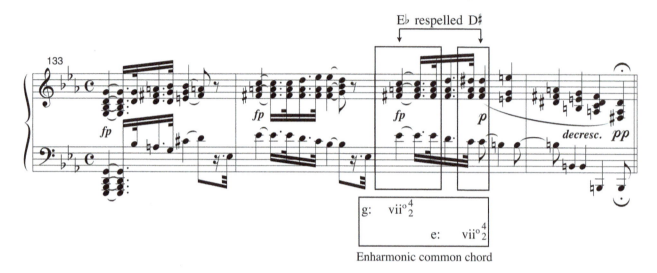

Example 23-14 shows how the chord in m. 135 of the Beethoven piano sonata might be respelled enharmonically to enable modulations to three other keys. To hear the differences, try playing through the four measures in sequence.

EXAMPLE 23-14 🔊

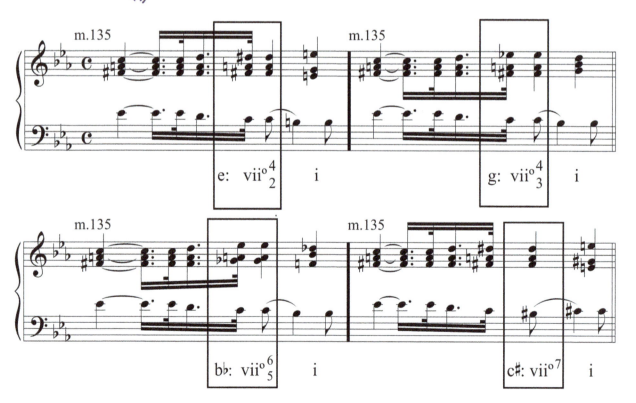

Did you notice in the preceding example that lowering the C on beat 3 to B turns the diminished seventh chord into a dominant seventh chord? The same thing happens regardless of which member of a diminished seventh chord is lowered: a dominant seventh chord results.

EXAMPLE 23-15

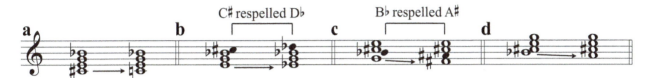

REVIEW AND REINFORCEMENT

Recall from p. 417 that an enharmonic respelling is all that separates a German sixth chord from a dominant seventh chord. With this in mind, respell the dominant seventh chords in Ex. 23–15 as German sixth chords voiced for soprano, alto, tenor, and bass and resolve them.

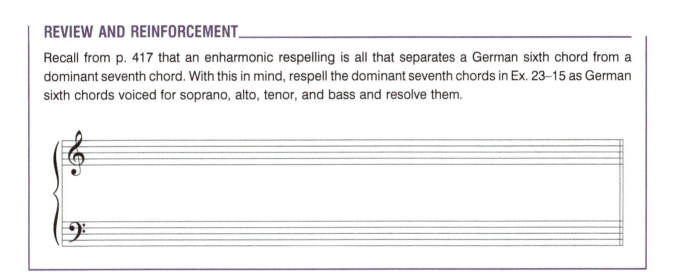

In the following passage, Beethoven consolidated the steps just described, transforming a diminished seventh chord into a German sixth chord to effect a modulation to a chromatic-third related key.

EXAMPLE 23-16 Beethoven: Symphony, no. 5, op. 67 (second movement)

REVIEW AND REINFORCEMENT_____

Based on what you learned in Chapter 21, how might the Gr+6 chord in Example 23-16 be respelled to better reflect its resolution?

EXAMPLE 23-17 Liszt: Consolation, no. 2

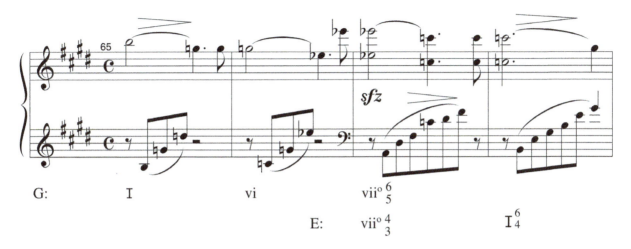

G: I   vi   vii°⁶₅

E: vii°⁴₃   I⁶₄

In Example 23-17:

1. The first thing you might notice about the chord in m. 67 is its unusual spelling—both E♭ and D♯ are present. Here's the chord, spelled both ways:

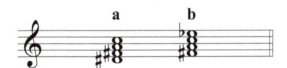

    In the left-hand part, the chord is spelled as a—a leading-tone seventh chord in the new key, E (D♯ = root). However, the chord also functions as b—a leading-tone seventh chord in the old key, G (F♯ = root). Although the E♭ is the seventh of this chord (F♯–A–C–E♭), it doesn't step down as sevenths normally do. In fact, it's probably spelled ♭ rather than D♯ to more clearly reflect the melodic descent by third in mm. 65–68 (B–G–E♭–C).

2. The C♮ in m. 68 appears to be a suspension lacking a resolution. It exemplifies the freedom granted nonchord tones by Romantic composers.

EXAMPLE 23-18 Summary: Enharmonic Juggling with the Diminished Seventh Chord. You can:

1 Respell the chord enharmonically so that each chord member, in turn, functions as the root.

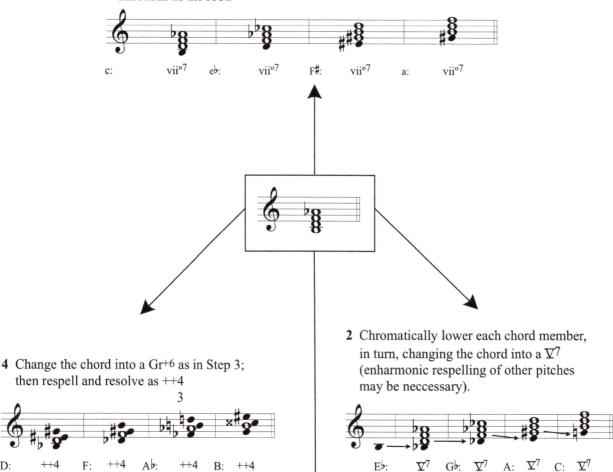

4 Change the chord into a Gr+6 as in Step 3; then respell and resolve as ++4/3

2 Chromatically lower each chord member, in turn, changing the chord into a V⁷ (enharmonic respelling of other pitches may be neccessary).

3 Change the chord into a V⁷ as in Step 2; then respell the m7 above the root enharmonically as an +6, turning the chord into a Gr+6.

Enharmonic Juggling with the Diminished Seventh Chord

CONCEPT CHECK

Part-write and resolve all or some of the transformations of the diminished seventh chords shown above.

⊕ CODA

As music approaches a tonal border, signs will normally appear—in the form of chromatically raised or lowered pitches and/or "clue chords" (major–minor seventh chords, diminished seventh chords, six-four chords, or augmented sixth chords). These signs tell us what to expect. Once in the new tonal region, we can usually look for a cadence—and we can assume the final chord of this cadence to be I or V.

How does the music cross the tonal border? Does it slip gently across, as common chord modulations are likely to do? Does it cross more overtly, as do chromatic tonal shifts? Perhaps the music darts across the border disguised as an enharmonic common chord.

When a chord at the tonal border is a German sixth chord, a dominant seventh chord, or a diminished seventh chord, it is well to keep the "e-word" (enharmonic) in mind. Think of every V^7 as a potential Gr6 or $++^4_3$, and consider how every diminished seventh chord would function with each of its other chord members as the root. Often, the "secret lives" of these chords are the key to understanding a modulation.

▶ *For assignments on "the secret lives of chords," turn to Workbook Chapter 23, assignments 3A–3G.*

DO YOU KNOW THESE TERMS?

- chromatic modulation
- common chord modulation
- chromatic pivot
- enharmonic diminished seventh chord
- enharmonic German sixth chord
- enharmonic pivot

CHAPTER TWENTY-FOUR

Harmonic Extensions and Chromatic Techniques

TRIADIC EXTENSIONS: CLIMBING THE OVERTONE SERIES

From the tenth century to the twentieth, Western harmony has ascended the harmonic series. From the open-fifth chanting of Guido's day to full acceptance of the triad in the later Middle Ages, from the extension of the triad to include sevenths in the Baroque era to the further accretions—ninths, elevenths, and thirteenths—in the nineteenth century, each addition to the vocabulary scaled the next higher rung on the overtone ladder.

KEY CONCEPTS IN THIS CHAPTER

- Triadic Extension
- Linear Chromaticism
- Harmonic Sequence

EXAMPLE 24-1

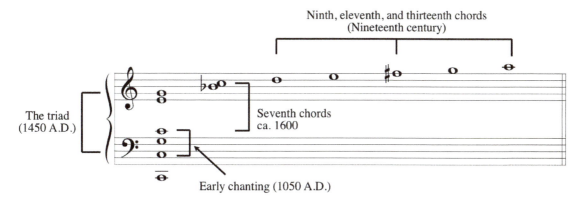

THE RISE OF THE NINTH

The Dominant Ninth Chord

A **ninth chord** is a five-member sonority in which a third above the chord seventh creates a ninth above the root. Though many different ninth chord types can be formed this way, only a few have been widely assimilated into the vocabulary. In the eighteenth and nineteenth centuries, the most common were the **dominant ninth chords**.

EXAMPLE 24-2

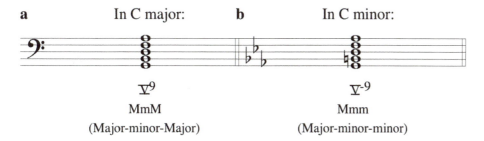

Notes:

1. The **dominant-major ninth**, shown in a, contains a major ninth above the root of a major–minor seventh chord (MmM).

2. The **dominant-minor ninth**, shown in b, contains a minor ninth above the root of a major–minor seventh chord (Mmm).

3. Roman numeral symbols for a and b are V⁹ and V⁻⁹, respectively. Common lead-sheet symbols are G9 and G7–9 or G7♭9.

In art music, dominant ninth chords, like dominant seventh chords, typically behave in only one way—as a dominant—making it possible to refer to them by function ("dominant ninth") rather than by structure ("major–minor–major ninth" and so on). Both the ninth and seventh can usually be analyzed as downward-stepping nonchord tones.

Common Voicings

Example 24-3 shows some common voicings and resolutions. All but d are in root position, a reflection of actual practice.

EXAMPLE 24-3 Arrows = resolution of 7th, 9th, and LT

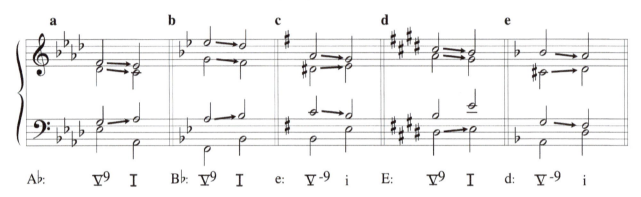

Note:

In four-voice settings, the chord fifth is omitted.

EXAMPLE 24-4 Chopin: Etude, op. 10, no. 3

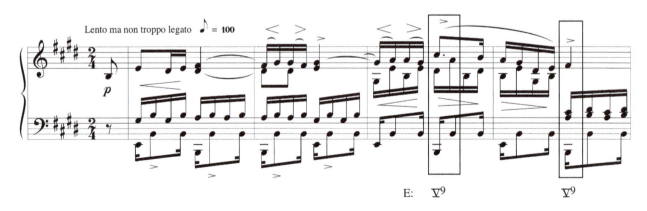

Notes:

1. As in this example, the fifth is frequently omitted. Here is the chord of m. 3, beat 2:

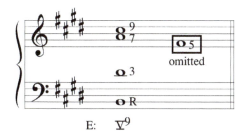

2. In m. 3, the ninth (C♯) immediately resolves stepwise, in the manner of an appoggiatura. The seventh (A) resolves to G♯ in m. 4.

When the ninth resolves as it does in Example 24-4, you may wonder whether to analyze the harmony as a true ninth chord or as a seventh chord with a nonharmonic tone. Although either analysis is often valid, we can apply the same guideline to ninth chords as we did to seventh chords:

> *A ninth as long as the chord should belong to the chord.*

In Example 24-5, the ninths appear not to resolve. This fact, along with their prominence, justifies their analysis as chord members.

EXAMPLE 24-5 Tchaikovsky: Lenski's Aria from *Eugene Onegin* (act 2, scene 2)

continued

EXAMPLE 24-5 *continued*

Notes:

1. Three dominant-minor ninth chords appear in the passage. Their lack of an immediate or obvious resolution reflects the progressive liberation of dissonance at the pens of nineteenth-century composers.

2. One V^{-9} (m. 96) is in first inversion.

Inverted Ninth Chords

As with altered dominants, inversions of ninth chords are usually not indicated in the chord symbols because the symbols become unwieldy. Although ninth chords can be found in all inversions, the ninth is rarely, if ever, on the bottom of the chord and rarely in a lower position than the chord root.

CONCEPT CHECK

Add key signatures, voice the following ninth chords for soprano, alto, tenor, and bass, and resolve them: F9; D–9; V^9 in A♭; V^{-9} in A.

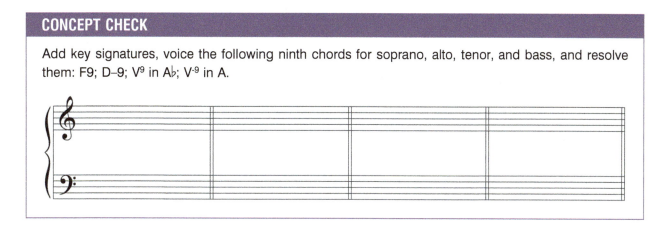

Secondary Dominant Ninth Chords

Dominant ninth chords can tonicize just as effectively as dominant seventh chords.

EXAMPLE 24-6 Puccini: "Che gelida manina" from *La Boheme* (act 1)

REVIEW AND REINFORCEMENT_____

Do you see a large-scale arpeggiation at work in Example 24-6?

CONCEPT CHECK

Does the ninth of the V⁹/V in Example 24-6 resolve? In Example 24-7, one secondary dominant ninth chord and its resolution have been identified. Identify all others.

EXAMPLE 24-7 Tchaikovsky: *Romeo and Juliet* 🔊

Db: V⁻⁹/iii

➤ *Assignment 1A in Workbook Chapter 24 can be completed now.*

Other Ninth Chords

After dominant ninth chords, the most common types are the **major ninth chord** (MMM) and **minor ninth chord** (mmM). Although rare in the nineteenth century, these chords are common in jazz. Example 24-8 shows their diatonic forms in major and minor keys.

EXAMPLE 24-8

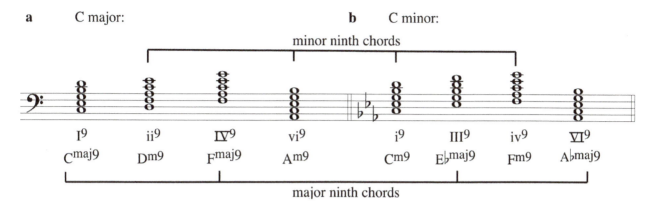

a   C major: **b**   C minor:

Note:

An alternative symbol for "maj9" is "M9."

As with the dominant ninth chords, these chords are found most often in root position, and even in inversions, the ninth is normally voiced higher than the root. It might or might not resolve downward.

EXAMPLE 24-9a Burt Bacharach and Hal David: "What the World Needs Now Is Love" 🔊

Note:

All three of the ninth chord types shown in Example 24-8 are present in Example 24-9a, along with the dominant ninth chord and a less common type (mMM). Traditional resolution of the ninth is not a priority in this vernacular style.

A summary of the ninth chords present in Example 24-9a follows:

EXAMPLE 24-9b

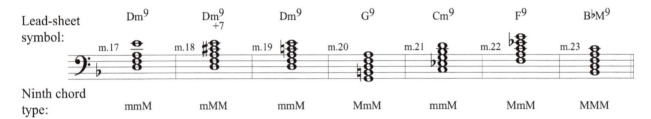

We'll return to nondominant ninth chords in Chapter 28.

Eleventh Chords

Eleventh chords result when a third is positioned atop the ninth. These chords are found only occasionally in the nineteenth century, almost always as a dominant (V^{11}). They are almost never complete; the eleventh usually replaces the third.

EXAMPLE 24-10

The upper members of this chord can be disposed in any way. However, even more often than with ninth chords, the root remains the lowest tone. Possible voicings include:

EXAMPLE 24-11

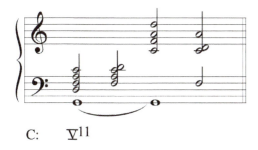

Wagner often spins long cables of dominant harmony in which the individual melodic strands intertwine to produce eleventh chords. The process often occurs over a pedal point that serves as the chord's root, as in Example 24-12.

EXAMPLE 24-12 Wagner: "Wahn! Wahn!" (*Die Meistersinger von Nürnberg*) (act 3, scene 1)

Like nondominant ninth chords, nondominant eleventh chords were as rare in the nineteenth century as they are common in jazz. They are prevalent in the music of Debussy, Ravel, and some other twentieth-century composers and as such will be considered in Chapter 28. The most common eleventh chord, aside from the V^{11}, is the "minor eleventh," which can have the diatonic functions shown in Example 24-13. (When stacked as shown you can see why these chords are sometimes called "tall chords.")

EXAMPLE 24-13

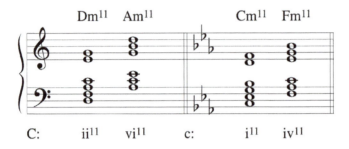

Note:

Eleventh chords can be complete or incomplete. They almost always appear in root position, and though often stacked as shown, the upper members can be disposed in other ways.

EXAMPLE 24-14 Hart and Webber: "All I ask of you" (from *Phantom of the Opera*) 🔊

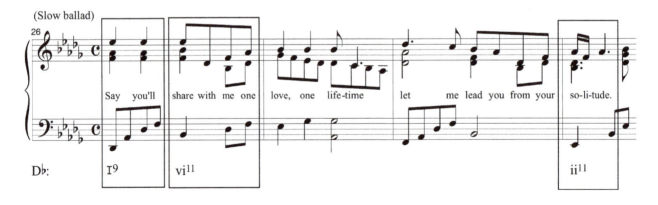

CONCEPT CHECK

Add lead-sheet symbols to Example 24-14. On the blank staff below, construct the boxed chords in simplest position, blackening the omitted chord tones.

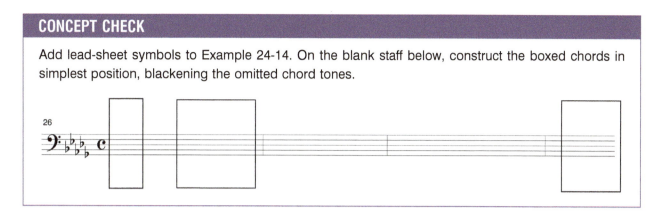

Example 24-15 contains ninth and eleventh chords as well as altered chords recently discussed.

EXAMPLE 24-15 Joe McBride: "Secret Rendezvous"

Notes:

1. Ninth and eleventh chords are shown stacked in simplest structure on the extra staff.

2. The iii$^{\sharp 9}$ is so marked because the ninth (F$\sharp$) is a chromatically raised pitch in C.

REVIEW AND REINFORCEMENT

In the empty measure above, fill in the missing chord and supply its Roman numeral symbol. Referring back to Examples 24-8 and 24-13, add lead-sheet symbols above each measure. Note: The first chord is the topic of the next paragraph.

Thirteenth Chords

The thirteenth chord represents the ultimate extension of the triad. A complete thirteenth chord contains all seven tones of the scale. Such structures are truly rare. Like ninth and eleventh chords, the thirteenth chord most often appears as a root-position dominant. In nineteenth-century music, the chord is incomplete, with either the eleventh or, more often, the third present (never together). In four-voice settings, the chord members critical to its identity are the root, third, seventh, and thirteenth. These are the members present in the V^{13} that begins Example 24-15. It (a) and other possible voicings are shown below.

EXAMPLE 24-16 From Ex. 24–15

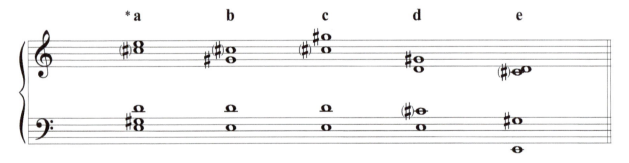

*In example a: $\underline{V}^{-13}$ (with C natural) or $\underline{V}^{13}$ (with C sharp)

Three of these chord members are tendency tones—the third (the leading tone), the seventh, and the thirteenth. The lowered thirteenth (C♮ in Example 24-16) is enharmonically the same pitch as a raised fifth (B♯). The spelling reflects the resolution and determines whether the chord should be analyzed as V^{-13} or V^{7+5}.

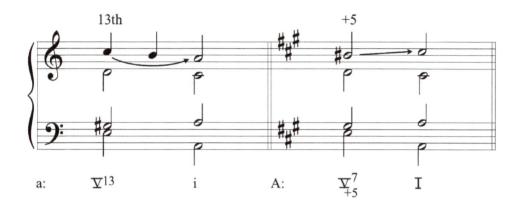

In nineteenth-century music, the thirteenth topples down to the tonic, either directly (a) or stepwise through the fifth of the dominant (b).

EXAMPLE 24-17

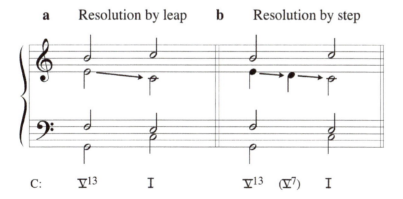

Example 24-18 contains both resolutions.

EXAMPLE 24-18 Chopin: Nocturne, op. 32, No. 1 🔊))

Note:

In both cases, the chord members present are the root, the third, the seventh, and the thirteenth. In both cases, the thirteenth resolves downward—by leap in m. 1, by step in m. 7.

CONCEPT CHECK

Look again at Example 24-4. Can you locate a dominant thirteenth chord? How does the thirteenth resolve?

▶ *For assignments on triadic extensions, turn to Workbook Chapter 24, assignments 1A–1F.*

LINEAR CHROMATICISM

Most chromatic harmonies are linear (melodic) at the core. When more than one chord member is altered—but not at the same time—the chord undergoes a *gradual* identity change that has been called **chord mutation** because the harmonies *evolve*. Because harmonies generated in this way are byproducts of the voice leading, they are often nonfunctional. Roman numeral labeling may be uninformative and needlessly confusing.

Chopin's Adventure

If Chopin was not the first major composer to experiment with chords' mutability, he produced the most renowned examples of the technique. Example 24-19a shows how a chromatic descent by each voice generates familiar chords that behave in unfamiliar ways—the V^7/V does not resolve to V, the vii^{ø7}/VI does not resolve to VI, and so on.

EXAMPLE 24-19a Chopin: Mazurka, op. posth. 68, no. 4 a) Analysis by Roman numeral 🔊

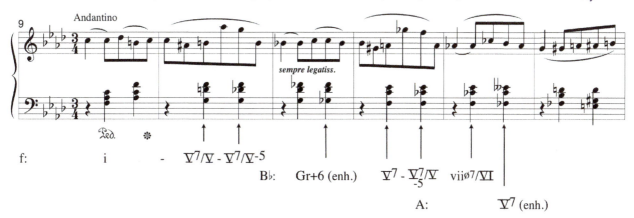

EXAMPLE 24-19b A better way

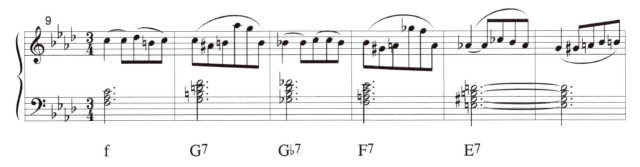

f   G7   G♭7   F7   E7

Notes:

1. In many cases, only a single pitch change occurs between the chords.

2. Each voice of the texture, including the melody, descends chromatically. If each voice moved downward *at the same time*, descending dominant seventh chords would result: G7–G♭7–F7–E7, as shown in b. Lead-sheet symbols such as these are probably more informative than Roman numerals.

3. Example 24-19b shows both the harmonic essence of the passage and the voice leading.

The next example is particularly well known.

EXAMPLE 24-20 Chopin: Prelude, op. 28, no. 4

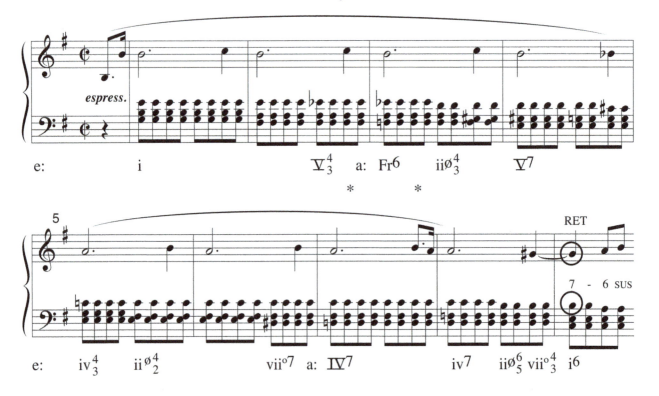

Note:

1. Asterisks indicate Roman numerals that are enharmonic interpretations of the notated chords.

2. As in the previous passage, each voice in the left-hand accompaniment descends the chromatic ladder, although not in synchronization. Unlike Example 24-19, many of the harmonies generated still function in traditional ways. Measures 1 and 2 and mm. 5 and 6 make perfect functional sense in e, while mm. 3 and 4 and mm. 7 and 9 are understandable in a.

➤ *For assignments on linear chromaticism, turn to Workbook Chapter 24, assignments 2A–2C.*

HARMONIC SEQUENCE

Harmonic sequence was introduced earlier. It rates an encore here because of its prominence in music of the nineteenth century and beyond. In Example 24-21, the linear chromaticism in the left-hand part generates a tonicizing chord group that is repeated sequentially, tonicizing first C, then B, and finally B♭ (without ever sounding the tonicized chord).

EXAMPLE 24-21 Chopin: Mazurka, op. 17, no. 4

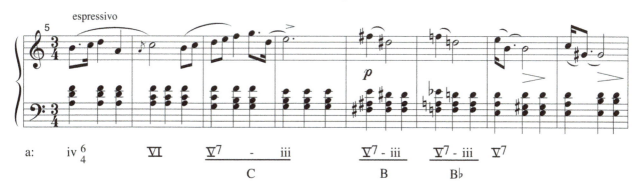

EXAMPLE 24-21a Chord mutation in mm. 7-11

Usually, a harmonic sequence is generated when each voice of the texture forms a melodic sequence, as in the next example.

EXAMPLE 24-22 Chopin: Nocturne, op. 48, no. 2 🔊

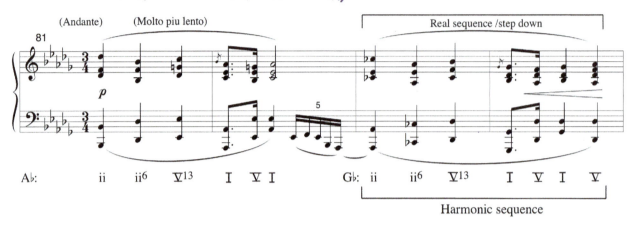

CONCEPT CHECK

Which members of the V¹³ chords in m. 81 and m. 83 are present? How does the thirteenth resolve?

Example 24-23 contains seventh, ninth, eleventh, and thirteenth chords in a two chord harmonic sequence (somewhat inexact) that descends the circle of fifths.

EXAMPLE 24-23 David Foster, Jay Graydon, and Jim Champlin: "After the Love Has Gone"

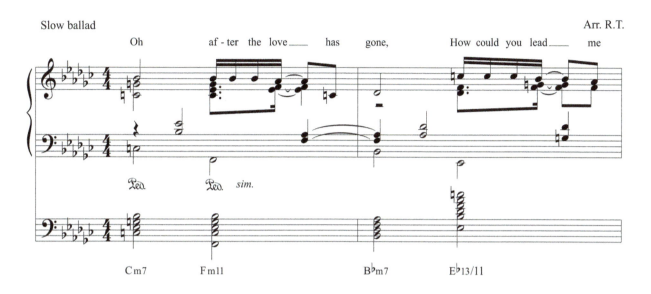

Example 24-24 shows the sequential passage that forms the basis for an entire movement. Shorter sequences are embedded within longer ones

EXAMPLE 24-24 Saint-Saëns: Trio in E Minor, op. 92 (third movement) 🔊

CONCEPT CHECK

Although in a different key and meter, and although it contains melodic chromaticism not present in Example 24-22, Example 24-24 is similar to it in some fundamental ways. Explain this. Provide a complete harmonic analysis. Identify the largest-level sequence and the embedded sequences within.

➤ *For assignments on harmonic sequence, turn to Workbook Chapter 24, assignments 3A–3C.*

⊕ CODA

At the beginning of Part Seven, the nineteenth century was credited with an expansion of the harmonic practice that comprised both new vocabulary and new syntax. Everything discussed in Part Seven falls into one or the other of these categories. The triadic extensions described in this chapter represent additions to the *vocabulary*—that is, new chords (similar to new words). The linear and sequential processes spawned new *syntax*—that is, new chord order (analogous to word order). Collectively, these innovations are the harmonic stuff and substance of nineteenth-century music. Triadic extension and linear chromaticism in particular set the stage for further innovation by Claude Debussy and other Classical composers as well as jazz innovators in the twentieth century. These are described in Part Nine.

DO YOU KNOW THESE TERMS?

- chord mutation
- dominant-major ninth chord
- dominant-minor ninth chord
- eleventh chord
- harmonic sequence
- linear chromaticism
- major ninth chord
- minor ninth chord
- thirteenth chord

Form

PART EIGHT

Every work of art has a **form**, which is the manner in which it fills the dimension it occupies. A work of visual art exists complete and intact, and the eye can behold it at a single glance. Not so, music, which unfolds over a time span.

In Chapter 9, we encountered melodic form—phrases, periods, phrase groups, and double periods. Important in determining our analysis were cadences and the similarity and contrast present. Cadences determined whether phrases combined to form larger units, and we deployed letter names (a, a′, b, and so on) to describe the phrase relationships.

Part Eight deals with larger forms—the structures created by periods and such in combination. The same factors—cadences and musical similarity and contrast—are operative at this level, determining the number of sections, their relationship to one another, and whether the overall form has a continuous or sectional nature.

Chapter 25 offers several ways of approaching form. It introduces some principles and processes that have been used widely by composers for hundreds of years and then examines these principles and processes in short works from the art music, jazz, and popular repertoires. Chapters 26 and 27 introduce sonata form and rondo—larger forms important in much concert music.

CHAPTER TWENTY-FIVE

Binary and Ternary Forms

KEY CONCEPTS IN THIS CHAPTER

- Musical Processes
- Repetition and Variation
- Binary Form
- Rounded Binary Form
- Ternary Form

THREE WAYS OF LOOKING AT FORM

In a poem bearing the same name, Wallace Stevens counted "Thirteen Ways of Looking at a Blackbird." There may or may not be that many ways of looking at musical form, but three are worthy of our attention. One is through examination of a work's motivic content. Another addresses the similarity and contrast that create a work's sectional divisions. A third considers the musical processes a composer has employed. All three ways seek to understand how a composer's three basic choices—to repeat, to vary, or to create—have shaped the music in question.

Motivic Analysis

To repeat, to vary, or to create: We can look at every section of music, every passage, in fact every musical moment, and characterize it as a repetition of something, a variation/extension/development of something, or something completely new. Attempts to understand a complete composition as an outgrowth of these choices can be called **motivic analysis**. Example 25-1 can be understood, albeit a bit simplistically, in this way.

EXAMPLE 25-1 Brahms: Waltz, op. 39, no. 3 🔊

C = Create   V = Vary   R = Repeat

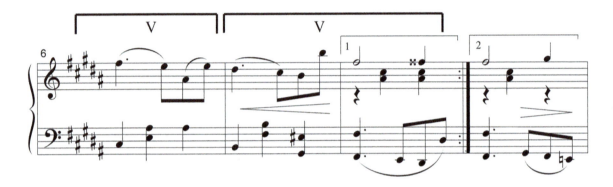

Note:

After composing two measures, Brahms elected to *vary* his melodic idea to conform to new harmonies (mm. 3 and 4). In m. 5, he *repeated* the rhythmic pattern of m. 1 but *created* a new melodic contour. Next, he chose to *vary* that material by stating it in sequence (m. 6) followed by a modified sequence (m. 7). Brahms' final compositional choice was to *repeat* the entire eight-measure phrase.

Similarity and Contrast

The second approach to form identifies and compares the sections into which a work may be divided. At the most basic level, these sections are defined by two things: (1) cadences and (2) the similarity or contrast present in the music.

Example 25-2 shows the rest of the Brahms Waltz.

EXAMPLE 25-2 Brahms: Waltz, op. 39, no. 3

Notes:

1. The two halves are obviously more alike than dissimilar.

2. The element most important in defining the form is the cadence in m. 9. It divides the piece into two parts. The second most important element is probably the melody itself, which, while motivically similar throughout, is nevertheless different enough in mm. 10–17 that we do not hear it as a mere repetition of mm. 1–9.

CONCEPT CHECK

In what specific ways is the melody of the second half related to that of the first? Which of the three composer choices—repetition, variation, or creation—generated m. 10? Name a non-melodic feature of the first half that persists in the second half. Compare the two halves from the standpoint of harmonic rhythm. Besides melody and cadences, which musical elements—register, rhythm, texture, harmonic rhythm, articulation, dynamics, tempo—help to distinguish the sections? Which play *no* role?

Musical Processes

At any point in any composition, the music is likely to be doing one of five things: (1) setting the stage for what's to come (preparatory process), (2) stating a theme (thematic process), (3) moving from one section, mood, tonality, tempo, and so on to another (transitional process), (4) preparing for or extending a cadence (cadential process), (5) developing a musical idea (developmental process).

Each of these musical processes has distinct qualities that affect the listener in different ways. Short works such as the Brahms Waltz, and most popular music as well, do little beyond stating a melody (the thematic process), perhaps with extended endings (the cadential process). More complex works are likely to exhibit the other processes as well. The musical examples in ensuing parts of this chapter employ three of these processes—the thematic, transitional, and cadential—which are exemplified in an elementary way in Kuhlau's Sonatina, op. 20, no. 1.

The **thematic process**: This typically involves full-blown melodies that display a unified mood, tonality, and tempo. The thematic process usually features complete phrases and periods with well-defined contours, varied but uncomplicated rhythms, and clear cadences. *Note, however:* The cadences themselves, necessary phrase-defining elements in *all* melodies, do not constitute the cadential *process*, as will be described shortly.

EXAMPLE 25-3 Kuhlau: Sonatina, op. 20, no. 1 (first movement) Thematic Process

Note:

Contrasting four-measure phrases are punctuated by clear cadences (both half cadences). Contours are distinctive, rhythms are simple, and the tonality is stable.

The transitional process: A common element is a change in tonality. Tonally, the term transition describes movement *away from* the tonic and retransition describes movement *back to* the tonic. Because transitional passages often connect themes, they typically lack a strong melodic character of their own, instead making ample use of scales, arpeggios, and sequences.

EXAMPLE 25-4 Kuhlau: Sonatina, op. 20, no. 1 (first movement) Transitional Process 🔊

Note:

Composed entirely of arpeggiations in the bass, the passage can be viewed as a melodic "non-event" that connects the thematic passage shown in Example 25-3 with the next thematic passage. A mode change (m. 12) precedes a V/V (mm. 14–15) that sets up a new tonality, the dominant.

The **cadential process:** Cadences are present within *all* the processes. However, it is the build-up to or extension of a cadence that constitutes the *cadential process*, and it can be quite lengthy. *Approach* to a cadence usually happens through a prolonged dominant or pre-dominant, and *extension* usually involves a prolongation of the final cadence chord—either I or V. Repeated cadential harmonies and short melodic figures are common.

EXAMPLE 25-5 Kuhlau: Sonatina, op. 20, no. 1 (first movement) Cadential Process 🔊

Note:

The passage is a prolonged G in both the bass and the "melody"—a repeated and extended authentic cadence in the dominant (G). Like the transition in Example 25-5, it is a melodic non-event, an extended G major scale over a repeated half cadence, with accents that create a large-scale arpeggiation (LSA) in mm. 28 and 29. Unlike the transition, it does not modulate but remains tonally anchored.

Kuhlau's Sonatina op 20, no. 1, from one of his earliest sets, illustrates the thematic, transitional, and cadential processes in their most elemental form. At the pens of greater composers such as Mozart and later composers such as Beethoven, the processes are often more complex—more complex but fundamentally the same.

CONCEPT CHECK

Identify the musical process in each of the following passages and explain the reasons for your choices.

EXAMPLE 25-6a Mozart: Piano Sonata, K. 332 (first movement)

EXAMPLE 25-6b

EXAMPLE 25-6c 🔊

▶ *For assignments, turn to Workbook Chapter 25, assignments 1A–1C.*

STATEMENT AND RESTATEMENT (AA′)

Immediate, exact repetition, while a frequent composer choice, is rarely reflected when describing music's form. Although the children on the bus may sing "One Hundred Bottles of Beer on the Wall" 100 times (until no bottles remain), the song's form is described simply as "A"—not AAAA . . . and so on. Our topic here, then, is actually "statement and *varied* restatement." This is designated A A′.

The simplest form of statement-varied restatement is the parallel period, shown in Example 25-7.

EXAMPLE 25-7 Chopin: Prelude, op. 28, no. 7

Notes:

1. The two phrases, a (mm. 1–8) a' (mm. 9–16), form a parallel period—*parallel* because they are rhythmically identical and built from the same idea, and *period* because only the second (final) cadence is conclusive.

2. Only one musical process is present—the thematic. Virtually all characteristics of the thematic process (see p. 456) are on display.

3. A high point is reached in m. 12, created through a crescendo, a rise to the highest pitch, and the only chromatic harmony (V⁷/ii) of the piece.

Example 25-8 is a longer, more complex example of varied restatement. The A section comprises several phrases: a (mm. 1–8) followed by its exact repetition (mm. 9–16), and b (mm. 17–24) followed by a cadential extension (mm. 25–28) and retransition (mm. 30–34).

EXAMPLE 25-8 Clementi: Sonatina, op. 36, no. 1 (Vivace) 🔊

Notes:

1. A′ begins at m. 35, identical to A for the first 16 measures. Its b phrase is altered to remain in the home key of C, then repeated exactly, and the repetition is followed by a cadential extension (mm. 67–70). A complete diagram of the form looks like this:

A					A′				
a	a	b	ext.	retrans.	a	a	b′	b′	ext.
m. 1	m. 9	m. 17	m. 25	m. 29	m. 35	m. 43	m. 51	m. 59	m. 67

2. Three processes are present: thematic (mm. 1–24 and 35–59), cadential (mm. 25–28 and 67–70), and transitional (mm. 29–34). The cadential extensions both occur over a tonic pedal point–G at mm. 25–28 and C at mm. 67–70.

3. Example 25-8 shows how all three compositional choices—to repeat, vary, or create—can be invoked at different levels.

Example 25-8 is considerably longer and more complex than Example 25-7. Still, both are based on the same principle—statement and varied restatement (A A′). Example 25-8 clearly divides into two parts—because of its length and the elaborate cadential preparation in mm. 30–34—whereas Example 25-7 is better viewed as a one-part form.*

* It is possible to view the form of Example 25-8 in other ways. Your instructor may choose to discuss these alternatives later.

THE CODA

The term "coda" has been used to designate the concluding paragraphs in most chapters of this book. It came up in a musical context in Chapter 19 (The Fugue). When a cadential extension occurs at the end of a piece, be it a fugue, a sonata, or a song, that extension is often called a coda. Codas vary in length, from the five-measure coda in Example 25-8 to the gargantuan 129 measures that end the first movement of Beethoven's Fifth Symphony. Despite their length or musical style, all codas follow what might have been a piece's concluding cadence and embody to a great extent the cadential process.

Example 25-9 contains features that are typical in codas.

EXAMPLE 25-9 Beethoven: Piano Sonata, op. 13 (second movement) 🔊

Coda: (Prolongs the cadence
chord-I-of m. 64)

continued

EXAMPLE 25-9 *continued*

Note:

The cadential process begins where the thematic process ends, in m. 66. From this point forward, the music scarcely departs from the tonic in repetitive melodic statements, first in eight-beat patterns, then in four-beat patterns, over V^7–I harmonies.

STATEMENT AND CONTRAST (AB)

AA' forms can be described as binary or unitary, depending on the strength of the cadential separation between parts. Statement followed by contrast creates a two-part (binary) form. As with melodic phrases, the difference between A A' and A B resides *in the degree of contrast* between the sections. In the latter, the composer's choice is not to repeat or vary, but to create something new. Even so, because composers usually seek ways to tie their ideas together, relationships between the sections are common.

Three commonly found harmonic/tonal plans are:

EXAMPLE 25-10a

Section:	A		B	
Cadence:		AC or HC		AC
Tonality:	I	I	I	
	i	i	i	

EXAMPLE 25-10b

Section:	**A**		**B**		
Cadence:		AC			AC
Tonality:	I	$\underline{V}$	$\underline{V}$	I	
	i	v or III	v (III)	i	

EXAMPLE 25-10c

Section:	**A**		**B**		
Cadence:		AC			AC
Tonality:	I	$\underline{V}$	Various	I	
	i	v or III	Various	i	

Sectional versus Continuous Forms

The main differences in the foregoing plans are tonal. a remains in a single key. If its A section ends in a perfect authentic cadence, it is termed a sectional binary form, meaning the first section could stand alone. If its A section ends in a half cadence, it is termed a continuous binary form, meaning the first section relies on the second for completion. Plans b and c modulate by the end of the first section and, by definition, are continuous. Plans b and c differ in their return to the tonic in the second section; b does so directly, whereas c explores other tonalities first.

Symmetric versus Asymmetric Forms

Look ahead to Example 25-11. It differs in two significant ways from the preceding forms. First, B (mm. 8–24) is vastly longer than A, creating an asymmetric rather than symmetric binary form. Second, B cannot be viewed as a varied repetition of A. Even though Bach continued to draw upon the piece's opening motive, B is substantially different. Bach clearly opted to create rather than to vary or repeat after m. 8.

This is a visual representation of the form:

A		B			
a	b	c	d	e	f
m. 0	m. 4	m. 8	m. 12	m. 16	m. 20

CONCEPT CHECK

1   Which harmonic/tonal plan shown above does Example 25-11 most closely resemble?

2   Locate all examples of the opening motive in the B section. Which processes—thematic, cadential, or transitional—are present? In what ways does this work differ from the Brahms Waltz, op. 39, no. 3 (Example 25-2)? In what sense is it similar?

EXAMPLE 25-11 J. S. Bach: French Suite, no. 5 (Gavotte)

STATEMENT-CONTRAST-RESTATEMENT (ABA)

The restatement of original material following a contrast can be exact (A B A) or varied in any number of ways (A B A'). One of the most common ways to alter the returning material is to shorten it, although lengthening it is also possible. The principle of statement-contrast-restatement has been mined extensively. It became the basis for myriad Romantic character pieces and operatic arias, and countless popular songs.

EXAMPLE 25-12 Beethoven: Sonata, op. 14, no. 2 (second movement) 🔊))

continued

EXAMPLE 25-12 *continued*

Notes:

1. The overall form is A(m. 1) B(m. 9) A′(m. 13).

2. The music following the four-measure B is equal to A in length. However, four of these measures (mm. 17–20) follow what might have been the final cadence (m. 16) and sound like a cadential extension. The actual repeated material is a mere two measures (mm. 13–14).

3. B contrasts with A and A′ in its legato articulation and its initially higher register.

4. The texture is homophonic throughout.

5. The thematic process dominates.

Here is a visual representation of the form:

A	B	A′	ext.
a	b	c	a′
m. 1	m. 5	m. 9	m. 13	m. 17
I	I to V	I (IV) I	I

Consider Example 25-12 in light of the three choices available to Beethoven. In mm. 1–2 he *created* an idea. At mm. 3–4 and 5–6 he *varied* it. He then *varied* m. 6 to form mm. 7 and 8. At m. 9, Beethoven *created* a new idea that he *varied* in mm. 10 and 11 (modified sequences). He *repeated* his opening at mm. 13–14, then *created* anew up to the cadence at m. 16. He again *created* in mm. 17–19, after which he *repeated* the cadence of m. 16.

REVIEW AND REINFORCEMENT

Example 25-12 teems with secondary functions. How many can you identify?

EXAMPLE 25-13 Paul Desmond: "Take Five"

continued

EXAMPLE 25-13 *continued*

Example 25-13 is typical of hundreds of American popular songs and jazz standards. The B section, called a bridge in popular terminology, functions like the B section in many classical forms. It "bridges" the A and its return with a brief allusion to another tonality and leads *via* half cadence back to the (usually) shortened restatement.

In both Examples 25-12 and 25-13, B ends with a half cadence that leads smoothly back to the original music. When A' is a *shortened* return, as it is in Example 25-12, the piece sounds like it's in two sections rather than three:

		Inconclusive Cadence
Section 1	Section 2	
A	B	A'
I	V	- I

The inconclusive cadence at the end of B has much to do with producing this effect. A special name—rounded binary—has been given to the resulting form to distinguish it from a true ternary form. As the name suggests, the second section is "rounded off" by the brief return of original material. However, the return of material alone is not enough to create a third section.

The so-called **32 bar form** (A A B A') of Example 25-13 and hundreds of jazz and popular standards is typically rounded binary. When only the melody and lead-sheet symbols are given, the music is usually shown in this format:

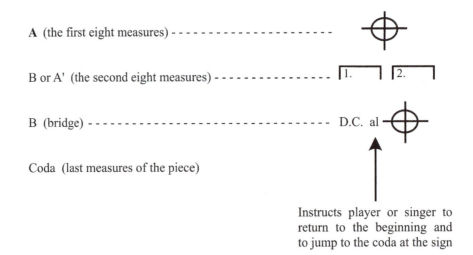

A (the first eight measures) -

B or A' (the second eight measures) - - - - - - - - - - - - - -   1.   2.

B (bridge) - D.C. al

Coda (last measures of the piece)

Instructs player or singer to return to the beginning and to jump to the coda at the sign

In Example 25-14, B ends with a decisive cadence in its own key and is followed by a *complete* restatement of A. Because of these two factors, we hear three separate and distinct sections. The form is **ternary** (three-part) rather than binary: A B A.

EXAMPLE 25-14 Schumann: *Kinderszenen*, op. 15 no. 6 🔊

continued

EXAMPLE 25-14 *continued*

This is what the form looks like:

EXAMPLE 25-14a

A		B		A	
a	a	b	c	a	a
m. 0	m. 4	m. 8	m. 13	m. 15	m. 20
I	I	IV	IV	I	I
Section 1		Section 2		Section 3	

CONCEPT CHECK

Look again at Bach's Invention no. 6 (pp. 320–322). Is its form A A', A B, A B A', or A B A? Why?

Rounded Binary versus Ternary Form

As Example 25-14 illustrates, the differences between rounded binary and ternary forms reside in elements beyond the cadence structure. Typical characteristics of the full ternary include:

1. An A section that ends harmonically closed without modulating.

2. A strongly contrasting B that's harmonically self-contained (that is, it begins and ends in its own key, which is different from A).

3. A complete return of original material.

When appearing together, these elements create the sense that B is a self-contained section distinct from A and A'.

Following is a graphic summary of the differences between the forms. It also shows their typical tonal structure. The "barlines" indicate points where strong cadential divisions occur.

ROUNDED BINARY

| A | | B | A' | Shortened return |

I - x | x - I

TERNARY

| A | | B | | A | Full return |

I - I | x - x | I

➤ *For assignments on binary and ternary forms, turn Workbook Chapter 25, assignment 2A.*

⊕ CODA

What divides a piece into sections? It's usually a strong cadence, musical contrast, or both. In *both* rounded binary and ternary forms, a divisional cadence (conclusive or inconclusive) separates A from the following B. The cadence separating B from the returning A may be divisional or not and is often the deciding factor in determining whether we hear two or three sections.

Or not! When the choice between rounded binary or ternary is unclear, consider this:

> *The harder a distinction is to see,*
>
> *The less significant it's apt to be.*

To put it another way: It's less critical to distinguish a rabbit from a hare than a bronco from a bear. If it's possible to regard a piece as one form or the other, chances are the distinguishing factors are slight and more than one viewpoint is sustainable. In these cases, identifying the form might be less important than understanding why (or why not) it might be viewed as such. Such issues are best reserved for advanced levels of study. For now, simply be aware that the principle of statement-contrast-restatement governs *both* rounded binary and ternary forms.

DO YOU KNOW THESE TERMS?

- asymmetric
- binary
- coda
- continuous forms
- rounded binary
- sectional forms
- symmetric
- ternary

CHAPTER TWENTY-SIX

Sonata Form

A HISTORY IN BRIEF

Establishment, Departure, and Return

The origins of sonata form can be traced to Baroque dance movements such those discussed in Chapter 25, especially the rounded binary form. Recall that three tonal events took place: (1) establishment of the tonic followed by a modulation to a secondary key (usually the dominant); (2) an area of harmonic instability; (3) a return of the tonic.

KEY CONCEPTS IN THIS CHAPTER

- Cadential process
- Developmental process
- Exposition
- Tonic-Dominant Polarity
- Transition and Retransition
- Recapitulation
- Coda

EXAMPLE 26-1

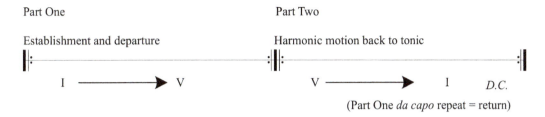

Part One   Part Two

Establishment and departure   Harmonic motion back to tonic

I ⟶ V   V ⟶ I   *D.C.*

(Part One *da capo* repeat = return)

Over time, distinctive thematic material came to mark the two tonal areas of Part One, and the beginning of Part Two was given over to developing the themes' potential and exploring additional tonalities. The resulting harmonic instability of this area was balanced by an extended return of the intact themes but remaining in the tonic, thereby reconciling the tonal conflict of Part One and providing a satisfying sense of closure.

Over the years, musicians began to observe consistencies in these compositions that led to the theoretical description of sonata form. While studying sonata form, think of it not as a mold into which composers poured their ideas but rather as a general way of proceeding. Each example of the form differs from others in ways that make it unique.

MOZART: "EINE KLEINE NACHTMUSIK" (FIRST MOVEMENT)

The Exposition

The **exposition** involves the establishment of two tonal areas (tonic and dominant) that consist of **primary thematic material** and **secondary thematic material** respectively. The thematic process may begin immediately or follow an **introduction** that is typically in a slow tempo.

Primary Tonality and Theme

In "Eine kleine Nachtmusik," the primary theme (mm. 1–18) begins without introduction. It consists of four phrases that form a double period. While all are four-measure phrases "at heart," the second (b) is extended to six measures and the fourth (c') is truncated to three measures. While listening to this part of the movement, take note of its tonal stability and strong melodic identity.

EXAMPLE 26-2 *Eine kleine Nachtmusik* (Primary thematic/tonal area)

Notes:

Phrase a= mm. 1–4 ending with half cadence

Phrase b= mm. 5–10 ending with imperfect authentic cadence

Phrase c= mm. 11–14 ending with imperfect authentic cadence

Phrase c'= mm. 15–17 ending with perfect authentic cadence

Transition

The primary thematic area is usually followed by a **transition**, characterized by an increase in rhythmic activity and tonal instability. The transition typically involves a modulation to the dominant, or in minor keys, to the relative major (III). In "Eine kleine Nachtmusik," the transition begins in m. 18 with a dramatic *sforzando* and increased rhythmic activity in the lower strings. A modulation to D major occurs in m. 21 and the transition ends with a half cadence in m. 27.

EXAMPLE 26-3 *Eine kleine Nachtmusik* (transition)

Secondary Tonality and Theme

A new and often contrasting theme marks the secondary tonal area, or "polar key." In "Eine kleine Nachtmusik," as in much of Mozart's music, the new theme is quieter and more lyrical. Note, incidentally, the more polyphonic interplay between the upper and lower strings. This theme consists of a parallel period (mm. 28–35) followed by a contrasting period that repeats from measures 43 through 50.

EXAMPLE 26-4 *Eine kleine Nachtmusik* (Secondary thematic/tonal area)

Closing Area

The exposition usually concludes with a closing area, in which the *cadential process* described in Chapter 25 prevails. If this material has a strongly thematic character, it's called a **closing theme**. If it's purely cadential, it is more often termed a **codetta**.

In "Eine kleine Nachtmusik," a short cadential extension (mm. 51–55) follows an elided cadence (mm. 51) and wraps up the exposition in the dominant, D major.

EXAMPLE 26-5 *Eine kleine Nachtmusik* (Codetta) ◀))

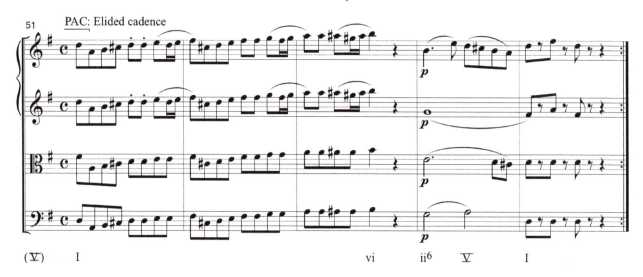

Development

The **developmental process** involves the manipulation of musical ideas presented earlier. These ideas may be combined contrapuntally. Thematic fragmentation, unstable harmonies, rapid modulation, and increased textural complexity are common. One idea, one dynamic level, or one texture may quickly yield to the next, creating a capricious quality. In developmental passages, change is the one constant, and it is often dramatic.

In "Eine kleine Nachtmusik," the development begins with a restatement of the opening fanfare-like motive. Then followed by tonicizations of D Major, C Major, A Minor, and G minor, during which the thematic material beginning at m. 35 is stated sequentially.

EXAMPLE 26-6 *Eine kleine Nachtmusik* (Development) 🔊

D: I   V   V/ii   CM: I   V   I

V   I   am: V   i   gm: V   VI

Retransition

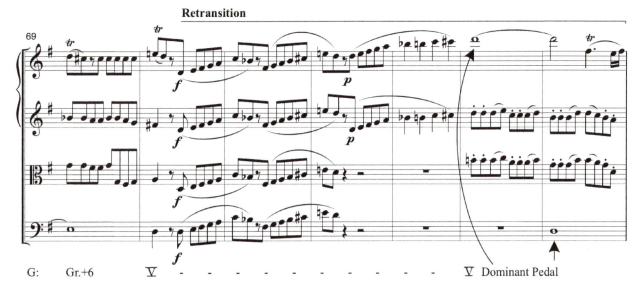

G: Gr.+6   V - - - - - - - - - - V Dominant Pedal

Retransition

"Retransition" literally means "moving back to." At the end of the development, a harmonic preparation for the returning tonic usually occurs. This often occurs over a dominant pedal point or other **dominant prolongation**. In "Eine kleine Nachtmusik," the retransition occurs in mm. 70–75. (See Example 26-6.)

Recapitulation

The most significant aspect of a recapitulation (or "return") is the re-establishment of the tonic. Typically, the primary and secondary themes return in the same order but may undergo some revision with some phrases shortened, lengthened, or omitted altogether. The most significant change is that the secondary thematic area is heard in the *tonic* instead of the dominant, often necessitating changes in the transitional area. Composers have dealt with that passage in the following ways:

- Transposition: The transition may be simply transposed so that it remains in the tonic.

- Recomposition: The transition may be rewritten in part or in whole, to exclude the original modulation.

- Repetition: If the original transition did not modulate, then it may simply be repeated.

- Omission: The transition may be omitted entirely.

In "Eine kleine Nachtmusik," the primary thematic material is restated, followed by a transition partially repeated and slightly recomposed to end on a half cadence in G rather than in D.

EXAMPLE 26-7 *Eine kleine Nachtmusik* (Recapitulation) 🔊

continued

EXAMPLE 26-7 *continued*

The secondary thematic material follows, in the home key of G but otherwise unchanged.

EXAMPLE 26-8 *Eine kleine Nachtmusik* (Recapitulation continues) 🔊

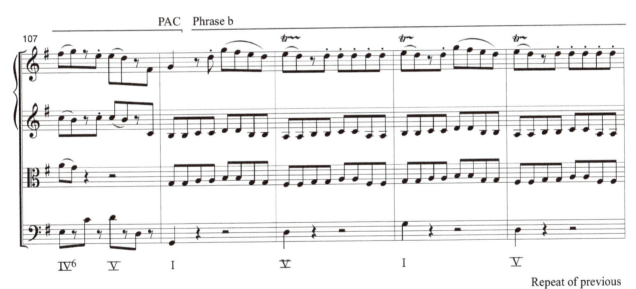

Repeat of previous period (phrase b & c

continued

EXAMPLE 26-8 *continued*

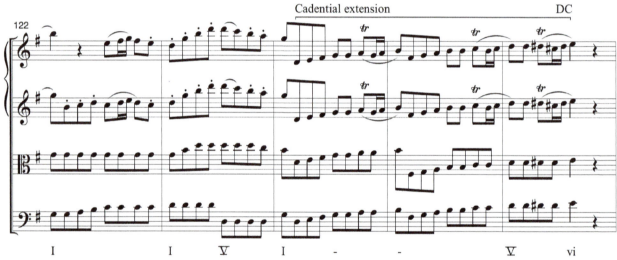

Coda

The coda is the final bit of cadential music in a sonata-form movement. If present, it typically occurs after the cadence that terminates the closing area—*the cadence that otherwise would end the movement*. Its length can vary considerably, but in most cases, the musical process is cadential throughout, never straying very far from the tonic, which it prolongs.

EXAMPLE 26-9 *Eine kleine Nachtmusik* (Coda)

In order to see a more concise picture of this sonata form, a reduction analysis showing the fundamental "middle ground" bass and harmony of each of the three sections (exposition-development-recapitulation) is shown in Example 26-10. The notation reflects the melodic hierarchy described in Chapter 7 and demonstrates melodic and harmonic interdependence; half-notes show the most fundamental harmonies (background); stemmed quarter notes show supporting tones; and un-stemmed notes are dependent on resolution. Un-stemmed noteheads reduced in sized demonstrate interior voice leading in the foreground. Slurs show resolution and arpeggiation. Roman numerals on the upper level show the principal harmony while the lower level Roman numerals demonstrate the fundamental background harmony. Double measure numbers show music that is repeated in various locations (12/24: this music occurs both in measures 12 and 24).

EXAMPLE 26-10a

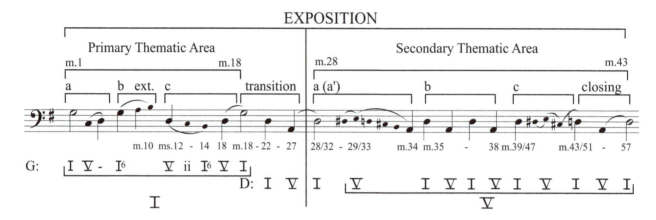

EXAMPLE 26-10b

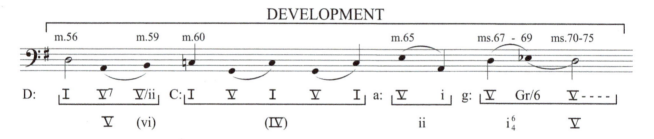

EXAMPLE 26-10c

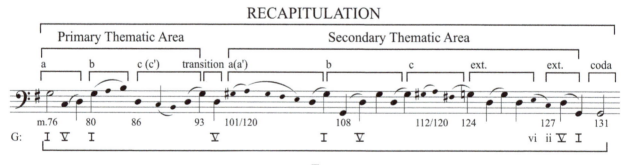

SUMMARY OF "EINE KLEINE NACHTMUSIK" (FIRST MOVEMENT)

The exposition . . .

begins without introduction in G major.

- The primary theme is a double period.

- The secondary theme (in D, the dominant) begins in m. 28, comprises two symmetrical periods (contrasting and parallel) with a repetition of the second, and ends with a short closing section.

The development . . .

begins with a statement of the opening phrase in the dominant, and immediately takes on a developmental character (harmonic fluctuation and thematic fragmentation).

- E minor is tonicized in m. 59 (note the leading-tone D♯), but a deceptive resolution effects an abrupt modulation to C major (m. 60).

- Fragments of the thematic material from m. 35 and beyond are heard in C, A minor (note the leading-tone G♯ in m. 65), and G minor (suggested by its dominant in measure 67 and the continuing presence of B♭ and E♭ through m. 71).

- The mode changes quickly to G major in m. 74 when the B♭ changes to B natural in a cadential six-four chord (mm. 74–75).

- Compared to the exposition, the development is relatively short with only three keys explored and two themes heard.

- The retransition (m. 70) is equally brief.

The recapitulation . . .

begins exactly like the exposition.

- Since the recapitulation remains in the home key, the transition is altered—shortened by two measures, the last two cleverly rewritten to introduce the secondary thematic area in the tonic.

- The secondary thematic area and **closing section** are almost exact transpositions of the original passages from the exposition.

The coda . . .

Any music that is **added** after the completion of repeated music signals the end of the recapitulation and the beginning of a closing section known as the **Coda**. It is a cadential extension that may or may not use thematic/motivic material.

ADDITIONAL PIECES FOR STUDY

Beethoven: Piano Sonata, op. 10, no. 1 (first movement)
(Turek/McCarthy: *Theory for Today's Musician* Workbook)
Haydn: Piano Sonata H. XVI:37 (first movement)
(Turek/McCarthy: *Theory for Today's Musician* Workbook)
Mozart: Piano Sonata K. 332 (first movement)
(Turek: *Analytical Anthology of Music*, McGraw-Hill, 1992)
Haydn: String Quartet, op. 20, no. 5 (first movement)
(Turek: *Analytical Anthology of Music*, McGraw-Hill, 1992)
Beethoven: String Quartet, op. 18, no. 1 (first movement)
(Turek: *Analytical Anthology of Music*, McGraw-Hill, 1992)
Beethoven, Piano Sonata, op. 53 (first movement)
(Turek: *Analytical Anthology of Music*, McGraw-Hill, 1992)
Mendelssohn, Octet for Strings, op. 20 (first movement)

DO YOU KNOW THESE TERMS?

- closing area
- codetta
- developmental process
- dominant prolongation
- exposition
- primary thematic/tonal area
- recapitulation
- retransition
- secondary thematic/tonal area
- transition

CHAPTER TWENTY-SEVEN

The Rondo

KEY CONCEPTS
IN THIS CHAPTER

- Episode and Refrain

- Rondo form

PERSPECTIVE

Refrain and Episode

Along with sonata form, another popular format for extended movements in the Classical period and beyond was the **rondo**. Rondos are of two principal types—the five-part (A–B–A–C–A) and the seven-part (A–B–A–C–A–B–A). Both types can be found with a second B refrain in place of C. Seven-part rondos with a developmental C episode resemble sonata form and are thus called **sonata rondos**.

The rondo principle involves a theme that recurs as a **refrain** interspersed with digressions called **episodes**. Refrains and episodes may be linked by transitions (from refrain to episode) and retransitions (from episode to refrain), and the piece or movement may end with a coda. In the classical style, refrains are often folk-like melodies with balanced phrases that produce symmetrical periods. While episodes tend to be in related keys and may display developmental features, the refrain typically remains in the tonic and undergoes very little transformation. This makes it the most stable and immediately recognizable feature of the form and an anchor that keeps the music from drifting into remote tonal waters. The intervening episodes ("B" and "C") are harmonically explorative, often in mediant relationships to the refrain.

In this study, we'll consider a **five-part rondo**, the second movement of Beethoven's "Pathétique" Sonata, op. 13. This staple of piano literature closely parallels the norms in the treatment of the form in the middle and later Classical period.

BEETHOVEN: "PIANO SONATA", OP. 13, (SECOND MOVEMENT)

The Refrain (A)

The theme in this movement is a beautifully lyric melody marked "Adagio cantabile," consisting of two four-measure contrasting phrases, the first ending with a half cadence, the second ending with a perfect authentic cadence. The eight-measure period is repeated an octave higher with textural enhancement in the alto.

EXAMPLE 27-1 Beethoven: Piano Sonata, op. 13 (refrain) 🔊))

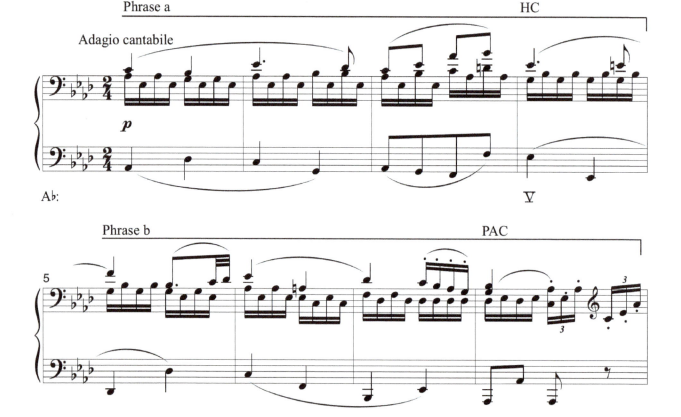

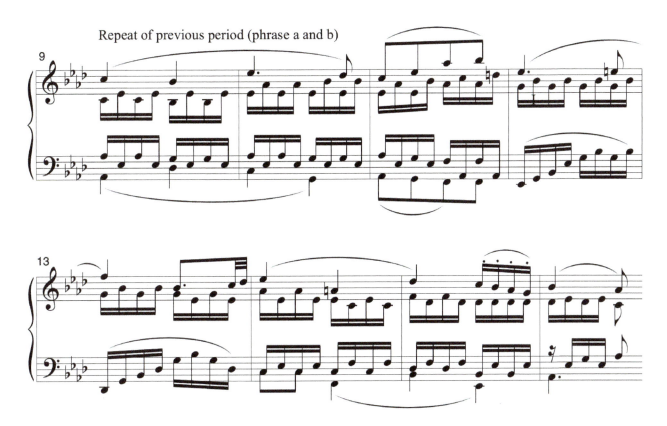

Repeat of previous period (phrase a and b)

The First Episode (B)

We've encountered the term episode in our study of the fugue. Here, as there, the episode's function is to provide a digression (tonal and otherwise). Episodes may be rhapsodic and even developmental, consisting of scalar passages, motivic fragments, and arpeggiations.

This episode is thematic. Its structure differs from the refrain. A single seven-measure phrase begins abruptly in the relative minor (a tonal shift) and modulates to the dominant E flat followed by a two-measure cadential extension (m. 23–25). The extension, repeated, becomes a retransition, returning to the home key at the very last moment at the end of m. 28.

EXAMPLE 27-2 Beethoven: Piano Sonata, op. 13 (first episode) 🔊

REVIEW AND REINFORCEMENT

The tonal shift to F minor that begins this episode is a special type of modulation discussed in Chapter 23. Do you recall its name?

The Second Refrain (A′)

The return of the refrain is an exact restatement of the first eight measures, labeled A′ because the second eight measures are not present. It leads directly to the second episode. (Refrains are often abbreviated and sometimes varied, but almost always remain in the tonic.)

EXAMPLE 27-3 Beethoven: Piano Sonata, op. 13 (second refrain)

The Second Episode (C)

The second episode is the longest of the movement and also the most rhythmically active, introducing a new element—the sixteenth note triplet. It provides the most distant tonal digression, beginning without transition in the parallel minor (A♭ minor) and modulating to E. It ends with a three-measure retransition (mm. 48–50) to the final refrain.

EXAMPLE 27-4 Beethoven: Piano Sonata, op. 13 (second episode) 🔊

REVIEW AND REINFORCEMENT_____

The modulation from A♭ minor to E major in mm. 41–44 may seem complex, but it is actually quite logical, and we've discussed this process before. Refer back to an earlier Beethoven example in Chapter 23 (Example 23-5), and discuss the similarities in the way this modulation is accomplished (Think enharmonically).

The Third Refrain (A″)

Beethoven provides a complete restatement of the theme, retaining and enhancing the triplet accompaniment introduced in the C episode to create a sense of continuity and growth.

EXAMPLE 27-5 Beethoven: Piano Sonata, op. 13 (third refrain) 🔊))

continued

EXAMPLE 27-5 *continued*

The Coda

A seven-measure coda follows the third refrain. A clear example of the cadential process, it prolongs the tonic of m. 66 through a repeated V^7-I harmonic progression. Notice how the pattern first unfolds over two measures (mm. 67–68 and mm. 69–70) and is then compressed into four beats (mm. 70–71, 71–72, and 72–73).

EXAMPLE 27-6 Beethoven: Piano Sonata, op. 13 (coda)

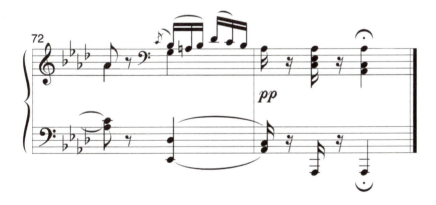

Summary

This movement is a concise five-part major-key rondo with episodes in the relative minor and parallel minor, no transitions from refrain to episode, and brief retransitions (mm. 27–28 and mm. 48–50) from the episodes to the refrains. A diagram comparing the form of this movement to a "fully loaded" five-part rondo follows.

a   Five-part rondo with all elements present

Intro.	A	tr.	B	ret.	A	tr.	C	ret.	A	Coda

b   Beethoven Piano Sonata op. 13 (second movement)

Section:	A	B	ret.	A	C	ret.	A	Coda
Measure:	1	17	27	29	37	48	51	66
Length:	16mm.	12mm.		8mm.	14mm.		16mm.	8mm.
Tonality:	A♭	f-E♭		A♭	a♭-E		A♭	A♭

tr. = transition;   ret. = retransition

A graphic reduction of the bass line similar to that in Chapter 26 is shown below with a background harmonic analysis for the refrain and first episode. As previously discussed, the second episode demonstrates the most far-reaching harmonic excursion of the movement.

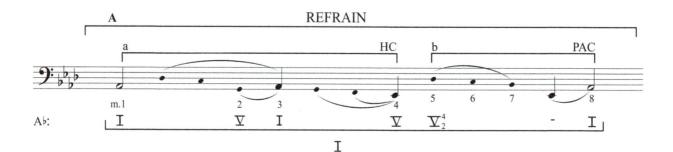

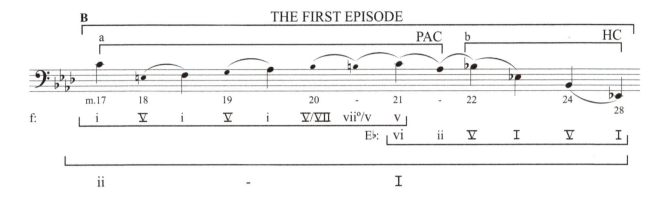

THE FIRST EPISODE

THE SECOND EPISODE

Key: ___ ___ ___ ___ ___ ___ ___ ___ ___ ___ ___ ___ ___ ___ ___ ___ ___ ___

CONCEPT CHECK

Give a complete harmonic analysis of the second episode by filling in the blanks under **c**. Also, provide a phrase and period analysis.

➤ *For assignments on rondo form, turn to Workbook p. 339.*

DO YOU KNOW THESE TERMS?

- episode
- refrain
- rondo

Music in the Twentieth Century and Beyond

Although art music in the twentieth century represented, in many important respects, the continuation of past practices, much of it reflected an unprecedented reassessment of the nature and function of melody, harmony, rhythm, form, sound, and even the meaning of music. The reassessment led to a rift between art music and popular music—a schism that grew into a chasm. It lasted for the better part of the century, but toward its end, musicians from both sides (art and popular) began to approach the cleft and peer across.

A sizable catalogue of new techniques was introduced to music by a relatively small group of twentieth-century composers. Chapter 28 considers some of the more important innovations in harmonic vocabulary and syntax, chiefly by Claude Debussy. Chapter 29 examines these and other techniques in music that sounds less traditionally tonal, focusing on works by Igor Stravinsky and Béla Bartók. Chapters 30 and 31 take a look at music that represents a complete break with traditional conceptions of harmony and tonality, principally through the music of two of the twentieth century's acknowledged musical leaders, Arnold Schoenberg and Anton Webern.

Chapter 32 is devoted to the harmonic principles of jazz. Because this music informs much of the vernacular music of our everyday lives, a basic understanding of it is essential to all musicians—critical, in fact, for today's composer, arranger, and music educator. The space limitations of this book and the time limitations of the theory course mandate that we be selective in the topics we include here. Those versed in jazz may lament, for example, the omission in this chapter of the octatonic scale and its extensive versatility. This and other standard jazz techniques must remain the province of jazz theory textbooks.

A discussion of jazz must include the blues, which has had an equally profound impact on American music, and so Chapter 33 gives an overview of blues form and melodic/harmonic practices.

We, the authors, believe that any graduate of a college music program should be capable of writing a song, no matter how basic. Chapter 34 provides a basis for composing songs in popular styles, with ample references to existing works.

CHAPTER TWENTY-EIGHT

Syntax and Vocabulary

KEY CONCEPTS IN THIS CHAPTER

- Nonfunctional Harmonic Syntax

- Planing

- Modality

- New Melodic and Harmonic Building Blocks

SYNTAX

STRUNG WHICH ORDER IN TOGETHER TO SYNTAX REFERS THE ELEMENTS ARE. *Is that clear?* How about now: **Syntax** refers to the order in which elements are strung together. In grammar, meaning depends not only on word *choice* but on word *order*. In music, meaning depends not only on chord *choice* but on chord *order* (and much more).

During a 20-year period, Claude Debussy (1862-1918) virtually rewrote the rules of harmonic succession, creating music in which nonfunctional relationships became the norm.

Question: What is harmonically unusual about this passage?

EXAMPLE 28-1 Debussy: *Pour le Piano* (Sarabande), mm. 37–38

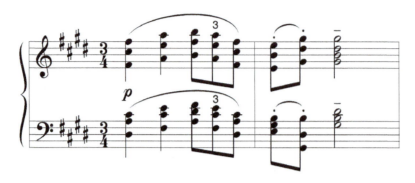

Answer: Other than the chords themselves, which are quite familiar, almost everything. Let's begin at the end—the cadence. By either major or minor standards, it's unusual—in C♯, a half cadence that ends on a *minor* dominant, or in E a cadence on iii. Leading to this point is a gathering of seventh chords that seem uncertain of their function. The first two—in E, a vii°⁷ followed by a ii⁷ (a retrogression)—set the tone.

A little further along, we encounter this:

EXAMPLE 28-2 Debussy: *Pour le Piano* (Sarabande), mm. 9–10

Again, familiar chords bump against one another in odd ways, producing a nonfunctional string of chromatic and diatonic-third relationships: A–F♯–d♯–A–F♯–d♯.

Planing

Debussy was the great liberator of the triad, freeing it from an obligation to behave in prescribed ways. However, freedom can lead to chaos. Debussy's control—as was Chopin's and Liszt's—was linear.

Planing refers to the parallel melodic motion of two or more musical lines. In Debussy's music, we can distinguish two types:

1. Diatonic planing: Each line moves in parallel motion with the others, by intervals of the same numeric value but not necessarily the same quality. Like a tonal sequence, the precise intervallic motion is conditioned by the key so that the music remains diatonic.

EXAMPLE 28-3 Debussy: *Pour le Piano* (Sarabande), mm. 37–38

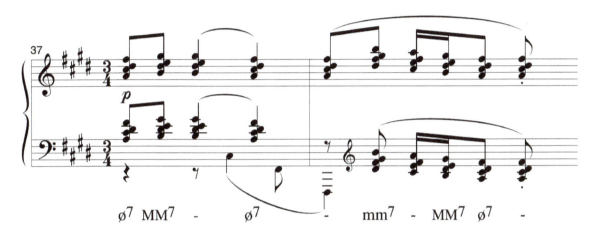

2. Chromatic planing: This is a bolder type in which each melodic line moves by *precisely* the same size interval, yielding a chromatic series of identical harmonic structures that conform to no particular key.

EXAMPLE 28-4 Debussy: *Pour le Piano* (Sarabande), mm. 11–12

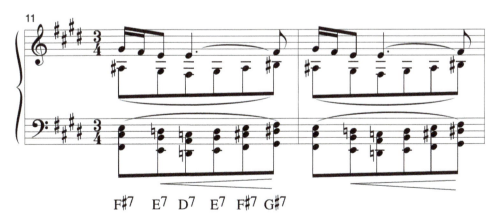

CONCEPT CHECK

On the staff below, show both diatonic and chromatic planing (first chord given) beneath the given melody notes.

EXAMPLE 28-5

The Nonfunctional "Dominant Seventh"

The natural behavior of the dominant seventh chord is tonicization within the context of functional tonality. Each chord formed beneath the melody in Example 28-4 is a Mm7 chord. However, these chords are nonfunctional, and the shorthand name we've been using—"dominant-seventh"—suggests a function they do not perform.

Perhaps following Debussy's lead, other composers ventured into new syntactic realms, relating traditional chords in non-traditional ways.

CONCEPT CHECK

Compare Examples 28-6 a, b, and c. What kinds of harmonic structures are featured in each? Which type of planing—diatonic or chromatic—is present in each?

EXAMPLE 28-6a Debussy: *Pour le Piano* (Sarabande), mm. 56–57

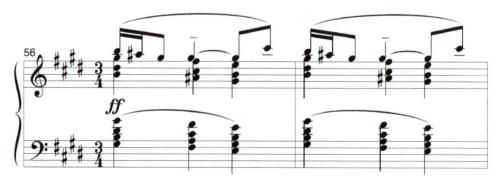

EXAMPLE 28-6b Richard Rodgers: "Slaughter on Tenth Avenue" 🔊

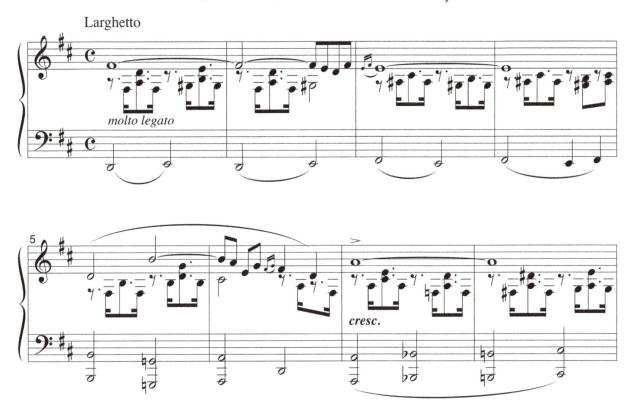

EXAMPLE 28-6c Prokofiev: Classical Symphony, op. 25 (third movement) 🔊

CONCEPT CHECK

Which type of planing appears in Example 28-6d? To which of the preceding passages in Example 28-6 does it seem most similar harmonically? Why?

EXAMPLE 28-6d John Fogerty: "Proud Mary"

The Augmented Triad

Long the stepchild of functional harmony, the augmented triad found a home in Debussy's music. Again, he tethered its use to planing. Passages such as the next are less tonally anchored than the preceding ones owing to the tonal ambiguity of the augmented triads in the right-hand part.

EXAMPLE 28-7 Debussy: "Minstrels" (*Preludes*, Bk. I, no. 12) mm. 37–43

Modality

Debussy's fascination with the Church modes probably helped inform his approach to syntax since modally based music predated major–minor tonality and its associated harmonic functions. In Chapter 1 the Church modes were compared to the major and minor scales. A quick review:

EXAMPLE 28-8a

Major modes

Ionian (major scale):	C	D	E	F	G	A	B
Lydian:	C	D	E	**F♯**	G	A	B
Mixolydian:	C	D	E	F	G	A	**B♭**

Minor modes

Aeolian (natural minor scale):	C	D	E♭	F	G	A♭	B♭
Dorian:	C	D	E♭	F	G	**A**	B♭
Phrygian:	C	**D♭**	E♭	F	G	A♭	B♭

Notes:

1. Boxes enclose the modal inflection—the single pitch difference between each mode and the major or natural minor scale.

2. Only one of the modes—Lydian—retains the leading tone and is therefore capable of producing a *major dominant*.

Look again at Examples 28-3 and 28-6a. In the first, the $\hat{5}$–$\hat{1}$ motion in the bass creates the feeling that F♯ is the tonal center, suggesting Dorian mode.

EXAMPLE 28-8b F♯ Dorian

The melodic cadence on G♯ in the second perhaps implies Aeolian mode.

EXAMPLE 28-8c G♯ Aeolian

During the seventeenth century, Renaissance modal practice gradually gave way to functional harmonic syntax. Three hundred years later—in a bit of irony, perhaps—functional harmonic syntax fell victim to Debussy's use of the modes.

Each mode has a distinctive character, and composers have used them to produce particular affects (emotional states).

EXAMPLE 28-9a Carlos Chavez: Ten Preludes (no. 1)

EXAMPLE 28-9b Ralph Turek: "Carnival Days" (from *Songs for Kids*)

Notes:

1. a is E Phrygian. The mood is tinged with melancholy. The second degree a half step above the **final** ("tonic") gives Phrygian the darkest aura of any mode. Do you recall the lachrymose sound of the Neapolitan? Formed on the lowered second scale degree, it's diatonic in the Phrygian mode.

2. b is C Lydian. The mood is playful. Because it is the only mode to retain the leading tone, and because the raised fourth degree acts as a leading tone to the dominant as well, Lydian is the brightest mode.

CONCEPT CHECK

Name the mode suggested in the following passage:

EXAMPLE 28-10 Miles Davis: "So What?"

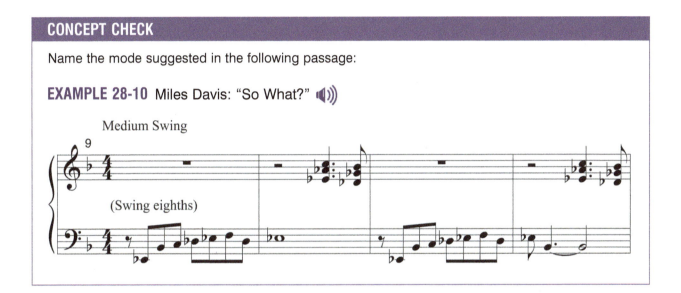

Modal Cadences

Modal cadences are two chord phase endings that contain modal inflections. As with tonal cadences, the final chord is likely to be heard as tonic or dominant, even though the chord succession leading to the cadence may be nonfunctional. Debussy's music is filled with such moments.

EXAMPLE 28-11a Debussy: "Hommage a Rameau" (*Images*, Book I)

EXAMPLE 28-11b Debussy: "Les collines d'Anacapri" (*Preludes*, Bk. I, no. 5)

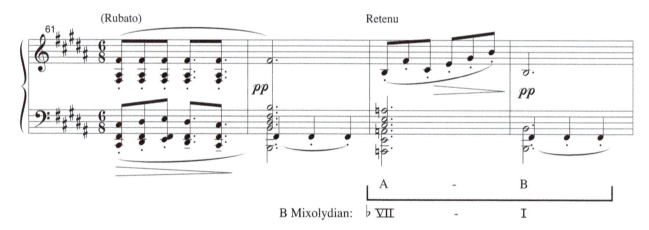

CONCEPT CHECK

Using Example 28-8 as a reference, identify the mode suggested by the following cadences. Assume the second chord to be the mode's *final* ("tonic") in each case. Add the Roman numeral symbols that would describe each cadence. Identify the tone that constitutes the modal inflection in each cadence.

EXAMPLE 28-12

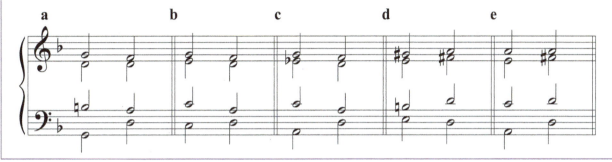

▶ *For assignments on syntax, turn to Workbook Chapter 28, assignments 1A–1F.*

NEW MELODIC AND HARMONIC STRUCTURES

The following melodic passage appears in Debussy's "Sarabande":

EXAMPLE 28-13 Debussy: *Pour le piano* (Sarabande), mm. 63–66

The melody consists of five different pitches that huddle around G♯. Here are the pitches placed in the form of a scale:

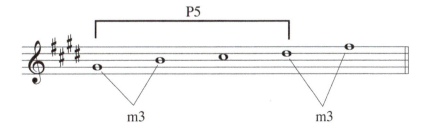

Pentatonic Scales

In the broadest sense, any five-tone scale is a **pentatonic scale**. The types most commonly used by composers have characteristics identical to the preceding one:

- They contain no half steps (thus no leading tones).

- They contain no more than two whole steps in succession.

These two characteristics assure two others:

- A minor third occurs at two points.

- No tritones are present.

With no leading tone, any pitch in this scale might be made to sound like a tonic by sheer emphasis, registral placement, and so on. In practice, composers have favored the two pitch arrangements that allow a major or minor triad to be constructed above the lowest tone.

EXAMPLE 28-14

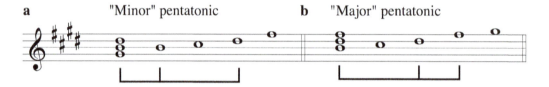

CONCEPT CHECK

Write the pitch material found in Example 28-15. What scale is this? Which pitch sounds like a "tonic?" Why?

EXAMPLE 28-15 Debussy: "Voiles" (*Preludes*, Book I, no. 2) 🔊

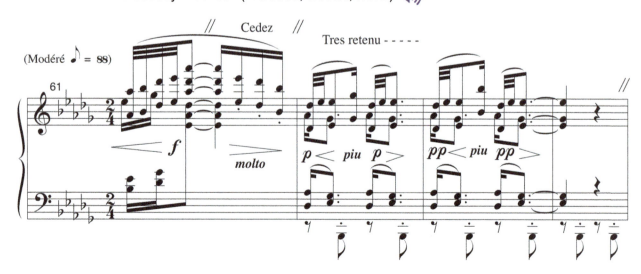

Melody and harmony are often woven with the same thread on Debussy's loom. That "thread" may be a mode or other type of scale. Examples 28-15 and 28-11a are cases in point.

Quartal and Quintal Harmonies

A structure inherent in the pentatonic scale is the **quartal harmony**—a stack of fourths. In the pentatonic scale, all the fourths are perfect. Each note of the scale is a member of a quartal harmony that can be built from the pitches in the scale.

EXAMPLE 28-16

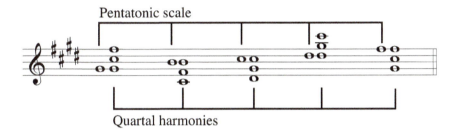

The entire pentatonic scale can be stacked to form an extended quartal harmony:

A quartal harmony can be restacked as a **quintal** harmony—a stack of fifths. The sounds are intrinsically related. However, to distinguish them, we'll use the following symbols: $Q^{(4)}$ = Quartal; $Q^{(5)}$ = Quintal. We might further refine the symbols to show the chord "root"—that note above which the others stack as fourths or fifths.

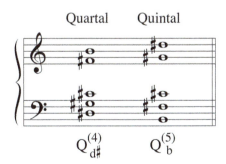

It might not always be clear whether a chord is better analyzed as quartal or quintal. In some structures, one interval or the other will be more prominent:

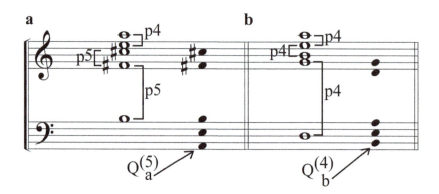

Note:

In a, the P5s on the bottom of the chord argue for a quintal analysis. In b, P4s are clearly more evident.

In other cases, either analysis may be possible.

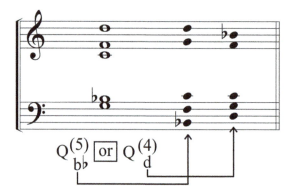

Where *neither* the P4 nor the P5 are prominent in a pentatonic chord, use of the symbol Q is probably arbitrary and needless.

CONCEPT CHECK

Stack the following chords as fourths or fifths and symbolize in an appropriate manner:

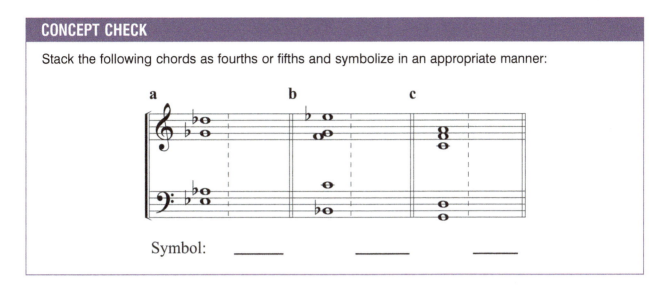

Symbol: _____   _____   _____

The middle section of Debussy's "Sarabande" features quartal harmonies moving in parallel motion (planing) beneath a partly pentatonic melodic line.

EXAMPLE 28-17 Debussy: *Pour le Piano* (Sarabande), mm. 23–28

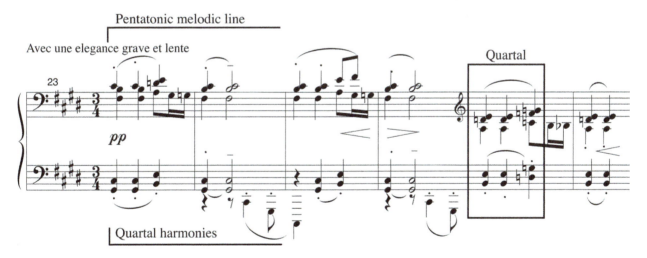

CONCEPT CHECK

In Example 28-18, mm. 16–19 contain complete pentatonic harmonies that can be analyzed as either quartal or quintal. In the empty measures provided, stack the chords both ways and symbolize them accordingly.

EXAMPLE 28-18 Hindemith: *Ludus Tonalis* (Fugue no. 5) 🔊))

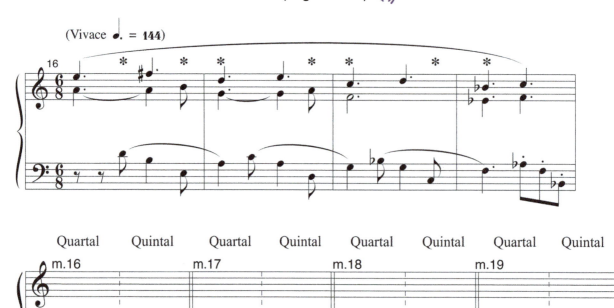

Symbol: ____ ____ ____ ____ ____ ____ ____ ____

▶ *Assignments 2A, 2C, and 2E in Workbook Chapter 28 can be completed now.*

Whole-Tone Scale

Debussy used other scalar patterns as a basis for his pitch material, among them the whole-tone scale—a succession of six whole steps.

EXAMPLE 28-19

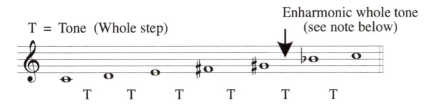

Notes:

The enharmonically spelled whole tone is a necessity at some point in the whole-tone scale. It can occur between any two pitches, such as F♯–A♭, or A♯–C, and so on.

Regarding the whole-tone scale:

1. There are no half steps in the whole-tone scale (hence the name) and therefore no leading tones.

2. The whole-tone scale contains six rather than seven pitches. One letter name must be omitted in its spelling, so that one of the whole tones is spelled enharmonically.

3. The scale may be transposed upward by half step only once before the pitch content of the original is duplicated.

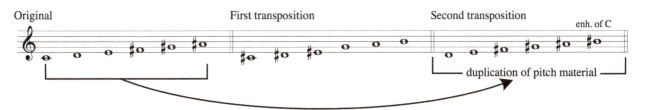

4. Only one of the four basic triad types can be formed—the augmented triad. It can be constructed on every degree of the scale.

5. The whole-tone scale contains abundant tritone relationships but no possibilities for their resolution.

Perhaps Debussy was intrigued by this scale's lack of leading tones and tonic-dominant relationships. Example 28-20 show the opening of "Voiles," a ternary form in which the outer sections are based melodically and harmonically on a single transposition of the whole-tone scale. (Example 28-15 was from the middle of this prelude, which by contrast is constructed entirely on the pentatonic scale.)

EXAMPLE 28-20 Debussy: "Voiles" (*Preludes*, Bk. I no. 2) 🔊

Other Scales

Other scales make occasional appearances in Debussy's music. One such scale comprises two identical tetrachords. It might be viewed as a Phrygian mode with raised third and seventh degrees.

EXAMPLE 28-21a W= Whole step; H= Half step

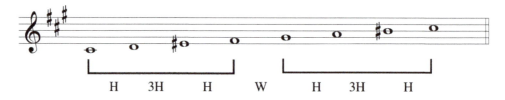

EXAMPLE 28-21b Debussy: "Soiree dans Grenade" (*Estampes*, no. 2)

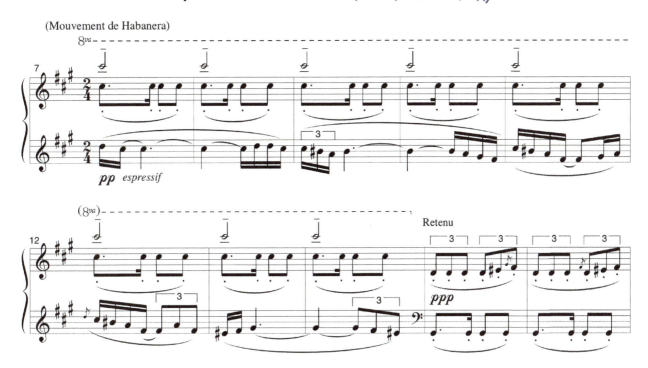

A scale that has been used more extensively throughout the century is the **octatonic scale**. This eight-tone scale comprises alternating half steps and whole steps, with several features that have appealed to composers. Chief among them are its limited transpositional capabilities. It can be transposed only twice before the pitch content of the original is duplicated. The first and fourth lines in Example 28-22 illustrate this.

EXAMPLE 28-22

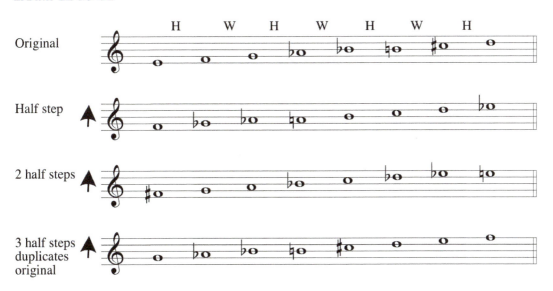

Example 28-23a illustrates characteristics of the octatonic scale that result from its symmetrical interval structure. A major triad can be formed starting on every other pitch. This is true also of a minor triad, a diminished triad, and a "dominant seventh" chord. A diminished seventh chord can be formed beginning on *every* pitch.

EXAMPLE 28-23a

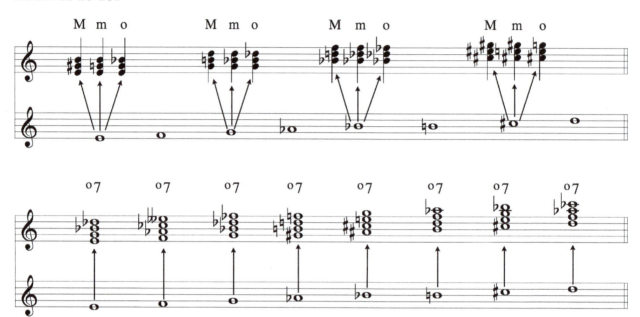

EXAMPLE 28-23b Debussy: "Feuilles mortes" (*Preludes*, Bk. II, no. 2)

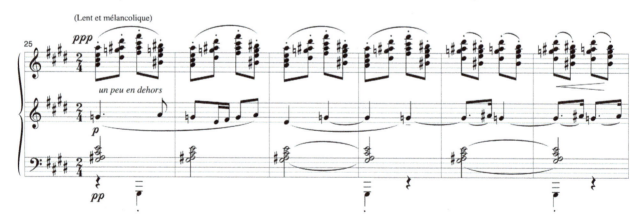

Ravel, Scriabin, Stravinsky, and Messiaen are prominent among twentieth-century composers who have employed the octatonic scale. We'll encounter it again in Chapter 29.

▶ *For assignments on new melodic and harmonic structures, turn to Workbook Chapter 28, assignments 2A–2G.*

⊕ CODA

Claude Debussy was a countercultural fellow. Caught in the rising Wagnerian tide and the general mania for things German that deluged his native land, he swam vigorously against the current and found his way to a distant shore. Some of his comments are anecdotal. After attending a performance of Wagner's "Ring," he reportedly said, "My God, how tiresome these people in skins and helmets become by the fourth night . . ." In the middle of an orchestra concert, he reportedly whispered to a friend, "Let's go, it's beginning to develop."

Debussy's "distant shore" provided solid footing for the likes of Stravinsky, Bartók, Copland, George Crumb, Bill Evans, and countless film composers. The music represented in the next two chapters—indeed, much of the music of the twentieth century—follows either the way pointed by Wagner or the way pointed by Debussy.

DO YOU KNOW THESE TERMS?

- Church modes
- final
- modal cadences
- modality
- octatonic scale
- pentatonic scale
- planing
- quartal
- quintal
- syntax
- whole-tone scale

CHAPTER TWENTY-NINE

New Tonal Methods

PERSPECTIVE

The musical examples in this chapter create a musical language through techniques identical or similar to Debussy's. However, they sound less traditionally tonal. Whether a piece asserts or lacks a pitch center is a question that may elicit different answers from different listeners. Some of the examples in this chapter might seem more at home in Chapter 30, and vice versa, depending on who's doing the listening.

NEW TONAL VENTURES

Quartal Harmonies

We noted Debussy's occasional use of quartal harmonies in Chapter 28. Paul Hindemith integrated them more fully into his harmonic vocabulary. In Hindemith's music, triadic harmonies surface mainly at cadences, with more complex harmonies residing in phrase interiors. In Example 29-1a, the melody rests on a largely quartal cushion formed by the lower voices, two or three of which move in parallel motion for the greater part of the phrase. Béla

KEY CONCEPTS IN THIS CHAPTER

- Quartal and Quintal Harmonies
- Polychords
- Polytonality
- Bimodality
- Dual Modality
- Ostinato
- Implied Polymeter

Bartók, too, was attracted to the rootless sound of quartal harmonies. Example 29-1b is more straightforward in its use of these sounds.

EXAMPLE 29-1a Hindemith: "Un cygne", from *Six Chansons* (1939)

EXAMPLE 29-1b Bartók: *Fourteen Bagatelles, op. 6, no. 11* (1908)

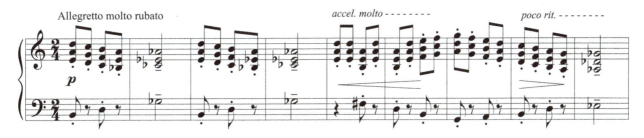

Quartal harmonies owe their unique sound largely to their lack of tritones and minor seconds. The effect is mildly dissonant, and a "rootless" quality from the stacking of equidistant intervals. (Recall that the diminished seventh chord and the augmented triad heard *in isolation* are likewise rootless.) However, as explained in Chapter 28, quartal and quintal harmonies can be stacked in other ways.

EXAMPLE 29-2

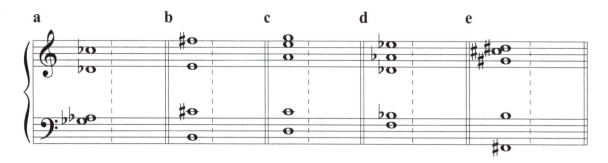

REVIEW AND REINFORCEMENT

Stack the harmonies of Example 29-2 in either fourths or fifths and symbolize them in the manner described in Chapter 28.

Polychords

Polychords are harmonies that can be heard as two (rarely more) discrete chords. To be heard this way requires some spatial separation and/or timbral distinction (dissimilar sound sources). The absence of common tones between the component chords also aids in separating the sounds. The chords may be of the same or different type. Although no widely accepted way of symbolizing these structures exists, a possibility is to indicate the component structures, as shown in Example 29-3.

EXAMPLE 29-3

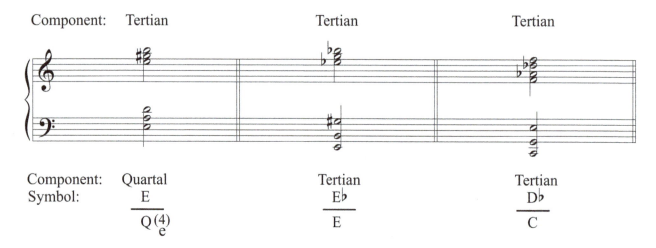

Notes:

1. The upper and lower components of each polychord are separated by an octave or greater distance. Although this much registral separation does not always occur, it helps to render the component chords aurally distinct.

2. The upper and lower components share few if any common tones. Polychords can be even more distinct when played by contrasting sound sources, such as oboes and trombones.

Polychords are perhaps more interesting in theory than they are common in practice. In some cases, they can be analyzed alternatively as extended triads or mixed-interval chords. Few musical examples are as overtly polychordal as Example 29-4a. Example 29-4b is less clearly polychordal but more typical.

EXAMPLE 29-4a William Schuman: *Three Score Set*, second movement (1943) 🔊

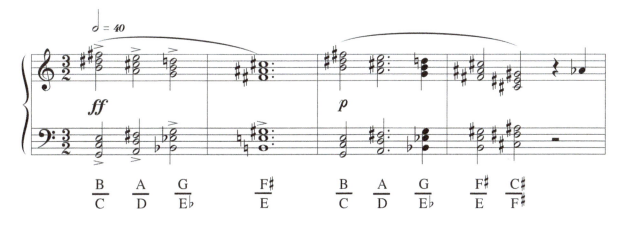

EXAMPLE 29-4b Vincent Persichetti: *Harmonium, op.* 50, no. 3 (1959) 🔊

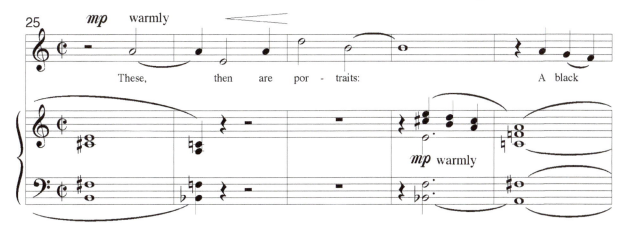

continued

EXAMPLE 29-4b *continued*

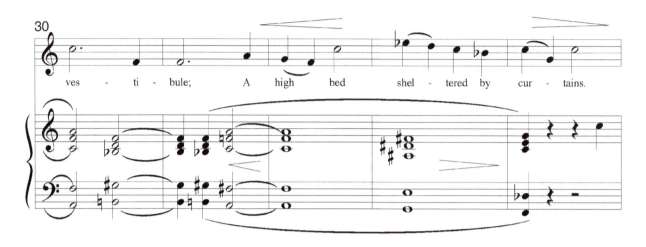

Note:

In **b**, the complete triads in the right-hand part seem to provide the harmonic basis for the melody while the left-hand part consists mostly of sixths that follow their own course. Analysis as polychords (the left hand as incomplete triads) seems a logical way to analyze the passage.

CONCEPT CHECK

In a manner similar to Examples 29-3 and 29-4, add chord symbols that reflect the polychordal components in the passage that follows. Besides the polychords, what other compositional technique is employed in the passage?

EXAMPLE 29-5 Honegger: Symphony No. 5, first movement (1950)

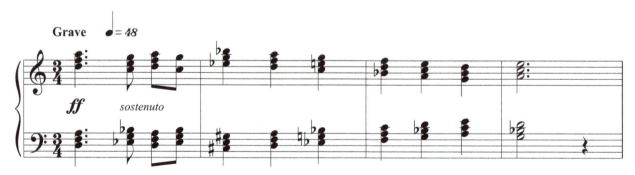

Polytonality

Polytonality suggests that two (or more) tonalities exist simultaneously in a passage. The technique has been used to a limited extent, possibly because it's difficult to project multiple tonal centers effectively without keeping the harmonic structure extremely elementary. Examples 29-6a and b, like the previous examples, illustrate both more and less straightforward applications of the technique.

EXAMPLE 29-6a Ravel: "Blues" (Sonate pour Violon et Piano, second movement (1897))

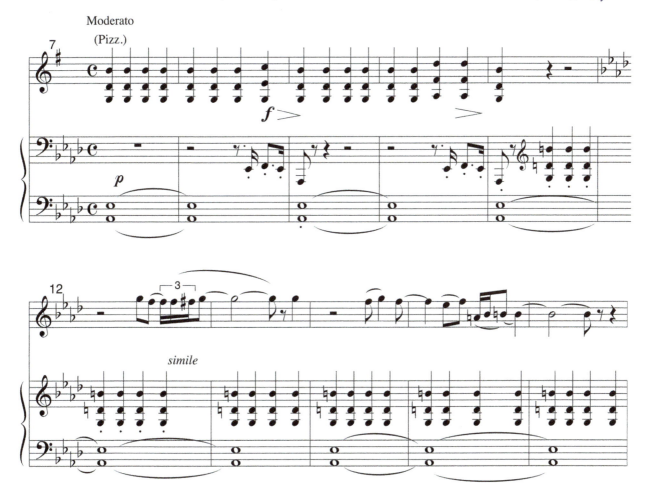

Note:

G major is juxtaposed against A flat major. Even where the violin key signature changes to A♭, that part is still in G. F♮ and later B♭ are the "blue notes" (to be discussed in Chapter 32) in that key.

EXAMPLE 29-6b Stravinsky: *The Rite of Spring,* "The Sacrifice" (1913)

Note:

Casting aside enharmonic spellings reveals alternating triads in the Piano I—D♯m and C♯m—with D♯ sounding vaguely like the final in D♯ Phrygian. This occurs over a Piano II part solidly anchored in D minor (with G♯). Example **b** is somewhat less overt in its polytonality than Example a.

Bimodality/Dual Modality

Perhaps a more accurate term than polytonality for the Stravinsky passage is **bimodality**—
the use of two modes simultaneously. When both modes are centered on *the same* final,
the term "dual modality" is preferred by some.

EXAMPLE 29-7 Bartók: "Major and minor," no. 59 (from *Mikrokosmos* vol. II)

Pandiatonicism

Pandiatonicism is the use of pitch material diatonic to a given scale or mode with few
or no chromatic pitches. For the most part, functional harmonic relationships are not
present, so that any diatonic pitch can occur against any other diatonic pitch. Because of
this pitch equality, harmonic tension is minimized, and cadences are often produced more
by rhythmic means than harmonic. Often the texture is polyphonic, and the harmonies
show little consistency because they are the mere byproducts of the moving lines.

EXAMPLE 29-8a Ned Rorem "The Air Is the Only" from *Poems of Love and the Rain* (1962)

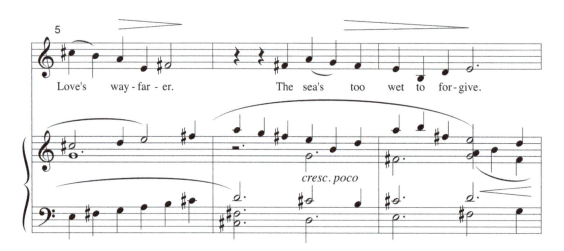

Notes:

1. The passage is purely pandiatonic in D.

2. Each line is independent, although related (note the loose imitation between the voice and the upper piano line and the imitation that begins in the lowest piano line in m. 6).

3. The harmonic structures formed on downbeats show little consistency, but seconds are prominent, reflecting the largely stepwise lines.

4. There is little sense of tension and resolution. The pitches owe greater allegiance to the lines in which they reside than to a harmonic hierarchy.

EXAMPLE 29-8b Dello Joio: Piano Sonata, no. 3, first movement (1949) Variation IV

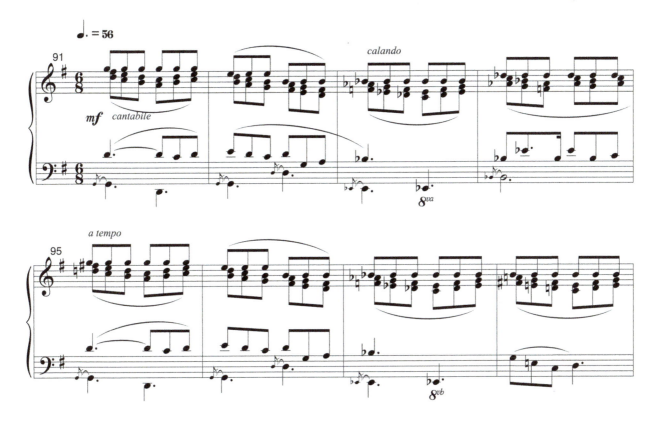

Note:

Pandiatonicism can range from purely to partly so. This passage is pandiatonic alternately in G and A♭ (or E♭ Dorian if you interpret the bass as $\hat{1}$ and $\hat{5}$). Because of the tonic-dominant feel of the bass, the passage has a stronger sense tonal focus than a.

STRAVINSKY AND BARTÓK

Igor Stravinsky

During a nearly 60-year compositional ride, Igor Stravinsky (1882–1971) traveled practically every important musical byway, from Russian post-Romanticism and Neoclassicism to serialism and free atonality (these latter to be covered in Chapter 30). Although his methods (and his country of residence) changed, his Russian roots remained close to the surface.

"The Rite of Spring"

Stravinsky's "Rite of Spring," a depiction in music and dance of an ancient Russian fertility ritual, contains at some point every technique we've discussed, often in a distilled and subtle guise. Although its first performance met considerable hostility, "Le Sacre du Printemps" has come to be regarded as a masterpiece of twentieth-century music. Excerpts appear below.

EXAMPLE 29-9a Stravinsky: *The Rite of Spring* (Introduction)

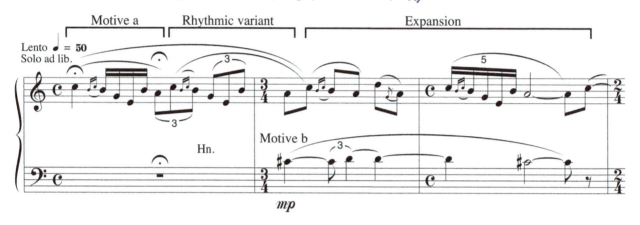

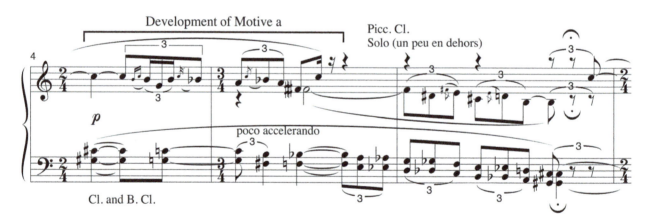

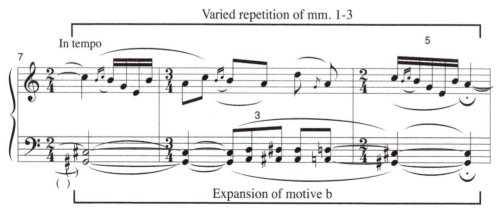

Notes:

1. The opening bassoon melody might be viewed either as C major pentatonic or A minor pentatonic with an added B.

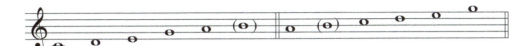

Stravinsky's approach to melodic development—repeating small fragments, adding minor pitch and rhythm changes at each repetition—is illustrated here.

2. Stravinsky sets a chromatic motive centered on C♯ against the prevailingly diatonic bassoon solo to create a vaguely bitonal quality. This motive grows into parallel-moving lines (planing) at m. 4 that descend an octave to land once more on C♯ in m. 7.

EXAMPLE 29-9b Stravinsky: *The Rite of Spring* ("Spring Rounds")

One of Stravinsky's favorite compositional techniques—the ostinato, a repeating melodic/rhythmic pattern (from the same root word as "obstinate")—provides the foundation for this passage.

Béla Bartók

Béla Bartók (1881–1945) pursued a multifaceted career as a composer, concert pianist, and ethnomusicolgist. His interest in the folk music of his native Hungary is evident in his own compositions. Although a catalogue of his techniques would be remarkably similar to one compiled for Stravinsky, Bartók's music has an individuality that owes much to the character of his native folk music and to his more traditional approach to development and counterpoint.

"Boating" (from *Mikrokosmos* Book V)

In his *Mikrokosmos*, a six-volume set of 153 piano pieces of graded difficulty, we have a compendium of nearly all Bartók's techniques.

EXAMPLE 29-10 Bartók: "Boating" from *Mikrokosmos*, vol. V (1939)

continued

EXAMPLE 29-10 *continued*

Analysis

Form: Two major dividing points are articulated by identical means, producing a ternary or rounded binary form:

Section:	A	B	A'	(Coda)
Measures:	1-23	24-34	35-47	43-47

Both divisions are articulated by a momentary pause preceded by a *ritardando* and *diminuendo*, followed by an *a tempo* and texture change.

The principal element of contrast in the B section is the exchange of right- and left-hand material.

EXAMPLE 29-11

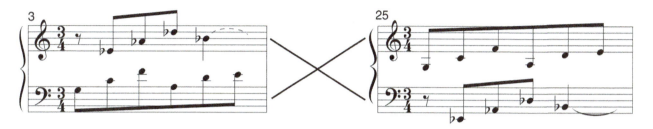

Measure 35 marks the beginning of the A'. It is far from a literal restatement of the first section. The right-hand part is an octave higher, and the melody is compressed. The final five measures sound cadential and might be called a coda.

PENTATONIC MELODY

In A, a pentatonic melody, using the pitches E♭, G♭, A♭, B♭, and D♭ (the black keys on the piano) appears as the upper voice. It begins with a quartal motive related to the left-hand accompaniment (refer to Example 29-11 above).

CONCEPT CHECK

Note the extent of the melodic repetition in the first 14 measures. How is the opening phrase expanded? Compare this to Stravinsky's melodic process.

MODALITY

Measures 15–23 contain entirely white-key pitches in the upper voice: A B C D E F G. The focal pitch appears to be A since the melody begins and ends on that pitch and returns to it numerous times. The mode suggested is A Aeolian.

In B, the black key pentatonic melody appears fragmented in the lower voice. In A', this melody, still compressed, returns to the upper voice.

HEMIOLA

Throughout the piece, a hemiola is produced by the gently rocking accompaniment that suggests a 6/8 meter.

EXAMPLE 29-12

The melody sounds as if it is metrically at odds with this pattern. Together, the melody and its accompaniment create an implied polymeter—two different but simultaneous sounding meters notated in a single meter signature.

HARMONY AND TONALITY

The most obvious harmonic feature is the quartal accompaniment that at first functions as an ostinato.

EXAMPLE 29-13

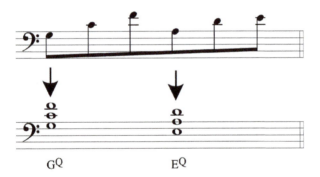

At m. 15, the left-hand ostinato yields to a string of arpeggiated quartal harmonies over a bass that descends almost a complete octave to A. The completion of this descent occurs in m. 24 as the upper voice takes over the ostinato pattern, again on G. The third section also begins on G, suggesting that pitch as the overall tonal center.

EXAMPLE 29-14

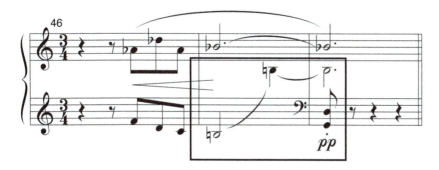

Together, the two hands produce a polytonal effect, black keys against white keys throughout.

REVIEW AND REINFORCEMENT

Page back through this chapter and take note of the number of examples that contain planing. This is one indication of Debussy's influence on the generation of composers who followed him.

⊕ CODA

As you played and studied the music in this chapter, it may have struck you that most if not all of it is triadic, quartal, scalar, or modal at its core. What else is possible? A few composers have experimented with "clusters," as harmonies built of seconds are called. But the larger answer to the question, "What else is possible?" resides in the music we'll consider next, in Chapter 30.

DO YOU KNOW THESE TERMS?

- Bimodality
- Implied polymeter
- Neoclassicism
- Ostinato
- Pandiatonicism
- Polychord
- Polytonality

CHAPTER THIRTY

Non-Serial Atonality

PERSPECTIVE

The music we've studied to this point embodies a principle held sacrosanct for hundreds of years —that music must be organized around tonal centers. In the early twentieth century the Austrian composer, Arnold Schoenberg (1874–1951), faced what he considered the impasse of traditional tonality due to the high degree of chromaticism reached at the end of the nineteenth century. He sought a music in which pitches would not be members of a tonal hierarchy but rather would be equally important within the chromatic total.

If Debussy was the great liberator of the triad, Schoenberg was the great liberator of dissonance, treating all harmonic combinations as equally viable. His music garnered a huge following and influenced practically every composer of art music in the twentieth century. Yet, his methods have not proven to hold the future of all music. Composers have been finding ways back to various aspects of tonality, and Schoenberg's methods are taking an appropriate place in the musical mainstream among those already available.

KEY CONCEPTS IN THIS CHAPTER

- Pitch Class Sets
- Set Type
- Mod 12
- Index Numbers
- Normal Order
- Best Normal Order
- Prime Form
- Interval Class Vector
- Set Class

ATONALITY

Tools and Terminology for Analysis

For better or worse, Schoenberg's early style has been dubbed "atonal," meaning without tonal center. This music might better be termed "pantonality," as it distributes tonal significance more equitably among the chromatic total than does traditional tonal music. A process and corresponding terminology have been developed for its analysis.

1. **Octave and enharmonic equivalence**: Absence of traditional harmonic function in this music permits pitches of the same note name in any octave or enharmonic spelling in any octave to be considered identical.

2. **Pitch class** (PC): Any given pitch and all its octave transpositions and enharmonic spellings belong to the same pitch class. Pitch class incorporates both octave equivalence and enharmonic equivalence.

In Example 30-1 all notes are the same pitch class.

EXAMPLE 30-1 All notes are the same pitch class

3. **Pitch class interval** (PCI): The number of semitones (half steps) between two pitch classes. A pitch class interval is represented by an uppercase letter I with a superscript numeral indicating the number of semitones between the two pitch classes. A table of traditional interval and pitch class intervals labels is listed below:

$$m2 = I^1, M2 = I^2, m3 = I^3, M3 = I^4, P4 = I^5, Aug.4/dim.5 = I^6$$

$$P5 = I^7, m6 = I^8, M6 = I^9, m7 = I^{10}, M7 = I^{11}, P8 = I^{12}$$

4. **Ordered pitch class interval**: A pitch class interval designated by its exact semitone content and by its contour with a plus (+) for ascending contour, or a minus (–) for descending contour. Such designations refer to intervals as they are found in the "surface" of a composition (exactly how the composer wrote them):

EXAMPLE 30-2

$$I^{+22} \qquad I^{-22}$$

5. **Unordered pitch class interval**: The shortest distance between two pitch classes without reference to its contour:

EXAMPLE 30-3a

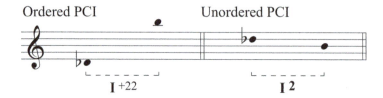

6. **Modulo 12 (Mod 12)**: In atonal music, 12 is a crucial number since Western music is a 12-note system and atonality seeks equity within the chromatic total. In Mod 12, compound intervals are converted to their simple equivalents and the shortest distance between two notes can be found by applying simple arithmetic. For example, intervals larger than an octave "wrap around" the octave (12 half steps) like a clockface, meaning $12 = 0$, $13 = 1$, $14 = 2$ and so on. Thus, any interval larger than 12 (any compound interval) can be reduced to its simple equivalent by subtracting 12:

$$I^{18}-(\text{Mod } 12) = I^6$$

EXAMPLE 30-3b

Any two intervals that add up to 12 (0 Mod 12) are considered to be **complements**, such as a perfect fourth—I5 and a perfect fifth—I7 ($5 + 7 = 12$). In other words, an interval and its inversion are complementary and span 12 semitones (an octave).

7. **Interval class (IC)**: An interval class is the smallest distance between two pitch classes. Thus, the interval class of any interval is its smallest complement. For example, the interval class of the perfect fifth from C4 to G4 (7 half steps) is that of its complement, the perfect fourth (C4 to G3), which is the shortest distance between the two pitch classes (5 half steps). Likewise, a major sixth (9 half steps) is an interval class 3—the complement ($12 - 9 = 3$). No interval class exceeds 6 semitones or I6 since a larger interval will invert to a smaller complement.

EXAMPLE 30-4

Note:

All are interval class 3, meaning they can be re-arranged to span three half steps

---

8. **Index numbers**: Index numbers are integers affixed to each pitch class, making it possible to analyze intervals with simple arithmetic. It is analogous to "fixed-Do" solfege where, in this case, pitch class "C" is identified by the fixed integer zero (C = 0), C-sharp/D-flat = 1, D = 2, and so on. The index table is listed below (enharmonic equivalents apply):

    C = 0, D♭ = 1, D = 2, E♭ = 3, E = 4, F = 5, F♯ = 6, G = 7, A♭ = 8,
    A = 9 B♭ = 10, B = 11

    To find the distance of ascending intervals such as E^4 (4) to B-flat^4 (10), the first index integer is subtracted from the second, yielding the numeral of the interval, 10–4 = I^6. For descending intervals, the second index integer is subtracted from the first, B-flat^4 (10) to E^4 (4), 10–4 = I^6. For intervals that cross "C zero," 12 (Mod 12) is added to the smaller index integer. For example, to find the interval descending from E-flat^4 (3) to B^3 (11), add 12 (Mod 12) to 3 (3 + 12 = 15). The interval calculation, then, is 15 – 11 = I^4.

9   **Ordered pitch class set**: An ordered pitch class set is *a collection of pitch class intervals* as they are heard in a musical composition or in the "surface" of the music. An ordered pitch class set forms the basis of an atonal work's pitch organization. It is thus similar to a motive, with this important difference: a motive is usually a melodic/*rhythmic* unit, while a pitch class set is a melodic/*harmonic* unit that can appear in any rhythmic pattern, in any melodic order, in any transposition, and with its pitch class in any octave and any spelling. It can appear as a melodic figure, a single harmony, or a partly melodic and partly harmonic figure.

EXAMPLE 30-5

Ordered Sets:

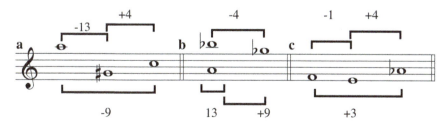

Note:

While the pitch class sets in a, b, and c contain different pitch classes, the pitch class interval content for all is the same (as shown in Example 30-6).

10 **Unordered pitch class sets**: The result of analyzing ordered sets to find commonality among them. Atonal set analysis concerns itself with interval content, so a pitch class set can be reordered, inverted, or transposed and still be identified as belonging to a single distinct set.

EXAMPLE 30-6

Ordered Sets:

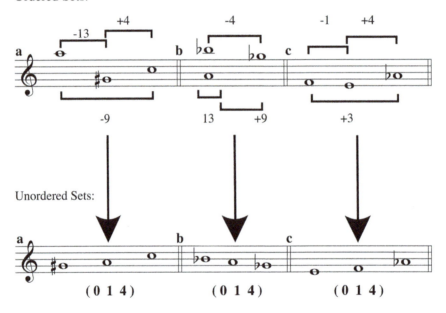

Unordered Sets:

11. **Set names**: A means of naming sets according to the number of pitch classes they contain (the above sets are called "tetrachords"). Since Western music is based on 12 pitch classes, sets are usually arranged in divisions of 12; 3-note, 4-note, and 6-note sets. However, they can be found in any numerical arrangement, typically one through nine with the following names:

- Dyad (2-note set)
- Trichord (3-note set)
- Tetrachord (4-note set)
- Pentachord (5-note set)
- Hexachord (6-note set)

- Septachord (7-note set)
- Octachord (8-note set)
- Nonachord (9-note set)

CONCEPT CHECK

Using index numbers for the first two given pitches in each example below, determine the size of each interval. The first example is done for you.

(add Mod 12 to a PC in a higher octave group

Index: 8   6
Inverval: (+12) = I10   ___   ___ ___ = I ___   ___ ___ ___ = I ___   ___ ___ ___ = I ___

Unorder the trichord in example a and the tetrachord in example b below. Try to keep the smallest interval at the beginning of the set.

Ordered Sets

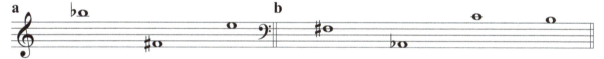

Unordered Sets

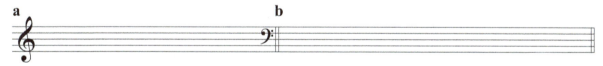

SET ANALYSIS

Schoenberg's Early Atonality

The following passage, from one of Schoenberg's earliest atonal compositions, demonstrates a trichord set in several of its transformations (bracketed or enclosed).

EXAMPLE 30-7 Schoenberg: *Klavierstücke*, op. 11, no. 1

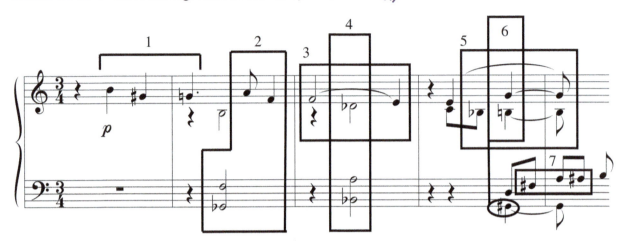

CONCEPT CHECK

Play each of the bracketed/enclosed note groups and observe their aural similarity. This is because they all have identical interval class structure. They all contain an interval class 1, an interval class 3, and an interval class 4.

---

1. pitch class set: B–G♯ = IC 3; G♯–G = IC 1; B–G = IC 4

2. pitch class set: G♭–F = IC 1; G♭–A = IC 3; F–E = IC 4

3. pitch class set: F–D♭ = IC 4; D♭–E = IC 3; F–E = IC 1

4. pitch class set: B♭–A = IC 1; B♭–D♭ = IC 3; A–D♭ = IC 4

5. pitch class set: B♭–B = IC 1; B♭–G = IC 3; B–G = IC 4

6. pitch class set: G♯–B = IC 3; G♯–G = IC 1; G–B = IC 4

7. pitch class set: F♯–A = IC 3; A–A♯ = IC 1; F♯–A♯ = IC 4.

The melodic-harmonic engine driving Schoenberg's "Klavierstücke", op. 11, no. 1 is a consistent pitch class trichord, each containing an interval class 1, interval class 3, and an interval class 4. At this point, the question is often asked if Schoenberg was aware of these details when composing. Although it's certain that he was, it is likely that he used a mixture of theoretical awareness and intuition, sculpting both melodic lines and harmonies from selected intervals according to the dictates of his ear.

▶ *Assignment 1A and 1B in Workbook Chapter 30 can be completed now.*

Normal Order

Set analysis begins with finding the **normal order** of a pitch class set—the ascending order that yields the smallest interval from the lowest pitch, known as the **reference pitch**, to the highest pitch. To find the normal order, use the first pitch in the set as a reference pitch and organize the set in ascending order within one octave. Note the set's **ambitus**—the range from the reference pitch to the highest pitch. Next, perform a **gap rotation** by identifying the two pitch classes with the largest gap. Use the second pitch in the gap as a new reference pitch and reorder the set ascending from that pitch. Continue gap rotation, comparing the ambitus of each ordering to the previous one. The order that yields the smallest ambitus is the set's **normal order**. The process is shown below.

EXAMPLE 30-8

The Ordered set   Unordered sets

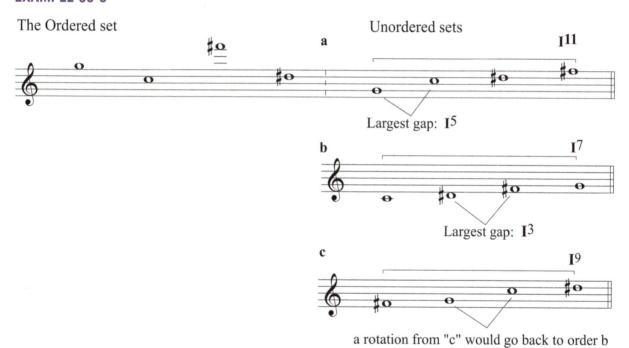

- The set is organized in ascending order within an octave (order a in Example 30-8).

- The set's ambitus in a is I^{11}. The largest gap occurs between the pitch classes g and C. To perform the first gap rotation, the second pitch class in the gap—C—becomes the next reference pitch, yielding b, where the set's ambitus is I^7.

- For the next rotation, two competing gaps are equal—C–D♯ and D♯–F♯. In such a case, give preference to the gap followed by the smaller interval, in this case, D♯–F♯, since it is followed by the g, a semitone above the F♯. This rotation yields c, which has an ambitus of I^9.

- Since set order b has the smallest ambitus (I^7) from the reference pitch C, order b is normal order of the set.

SET TYPE

The **set type** is identified by a numeric list (with or without parentheses) of the set's semitone content measured from the reference pitch (= 0) to each successive pitch class in the set.

EXAMPLE 30-9

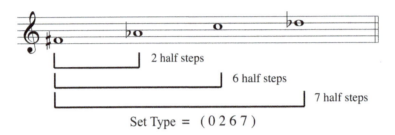

Set Type = (0 2 6 7)

CONCEPT CHECK

Find normal order for each of the pitch class sets below and give their set types.

EXAMPLE 30-10

Best Normal Order

A set might be further distilled to its most compact identity. This involves finding its **best normal order** by inverting it and then reorganizing it in ascending order. Unlike triad inversion in tonal music, when a pitch class set is inverted, every upward interval is replaced by a downward interval of the same size. Known as **melodic inversion**, it's like doing pushups on a mirror. Keep in mind, however, that the set may already be in best normal order. You'll find out by comparing the set type of the inversion with the set type of the original. The one with the smallest intervals packed closest to the left is the **best normal order**.

Through inversion, the pitch classes C–D♯–F♯–G (Example 30-11a) become C–A–F♯–F (Example 30-11b). Remember that the pitch class changes in b are irrelevant since the sole objective of inversion is to determine interval content. When the set is placed back in ascending order (c), the set type changes:

EXAMPLE 30-11

a: Normal Order   **b**: Inversion

(0   3   6   7)

c: Resulting Set from Inversion

(0   1   4   7)

It's necessary to choose one of these pitch class sets to represent best normal order. This can be done by comparing the interval content of set types in a and c. c is best normal order since it begins with the smaller interval "01" as opposed to a, which begins with "03."

Other Ways

You might see other ways of determining best normal order such as choosing the set with the lowest sum of all the intervals in the set type: (0 3 6 7) = 16 (pitch class set a) compared to (0 1 4 7) = 12 (indicating that pitch class set c is best normal order). A quick way to find the set type of the inversion is to subtract all the integers in the set type from its highest integer starting with that integer: In this case, $7 - 7 = 0$, $7 - 6 = 1$, $7 - 3 = 4$, and $7 - 0 = 7$: (0 1 4 7).

Prime Form

Best normal order is the process of placing the pitches of a pitch class set in their most compact order. Once the best normal order has been determined, we give it a name—its set type. This numerical expression of the pitch class set's best normal order is known as its prime form. Thus, the best normal order of the set in Example 30-11 are the pitch classes F, F♯, A, C. The prime form is 0 1 4 7 (parentheses are not necessary in displaying prime form). You might think of prime form as atonal music's "chord symbol" or a kind of figured bass, although it's more than that. It's the label used to refer to all melodic and harmonic units that have the same intervallic content and therefore is an indispensable tool for discovering the harmonic unity that underlies an atonal work.

EXAMPLE 30-12 Schoenberg: "Nacht" from *Pierrot Lunaire*

Inversional Symmetry

In seeking a pitch class set's best normal order, you might find that the inversion of its normal order yields an identical set type. This condition is known as **Inversional Symmetry** or **Inversional Equivalence** (also known as **"Invariance"**). An inversionally symmetrical set is analogus to a palindrome such as "MOM," or "DAD." Such a set is demonstrated in the hexachord below:

EXAMPLE 30-13 Inversional Symmetry

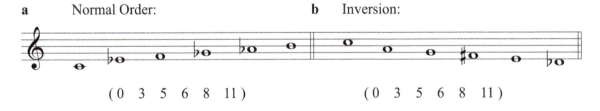

a   Normal Order: **b**   Inversion:

(0   3   5   6   8   11)   (0   3   5   6   8   11)

c   Set Resulting from Inversion:

(0   3   5   6   8   11)

CONCEPT CHECK

Create three tetrachords that are inversionally symmetrical.

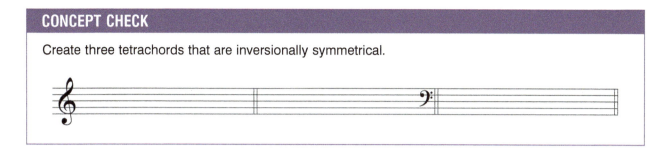

The Interval Class Vector

While some atonal compositions are based on a single prime form set, others appear to be based on two or more. Closer analysis may reveal that the sets are related on a deeper intervallic level than their prime forms indicate. This is important to understanding the harmonic unity in such works, especially in works where rhythmic motives play a minor role. A tool useful in this regard is the **Interval Class Vector** or **Interval Vector**. A set's interval vector reveals the total of all intervals heard in the interior of a melodic figure or sonority in a kind-of "score board."

The **interval vector** (IC vector) contains six numerals that indicate the number of times each interval class occurs in a set—hence, its limitation to six numerals. The first numeral indicates the number of times interval class 1 occurs, the second, the number of times interval class 2 occurs, and so on. The interval vector differs from prime form in that all interior intervals are accounted for, not just those measured ascending from the reference pitch.

You can think of a vector analysis as creating a set type from every pitch class in the set, beginning with the bottom pitch class followed by the same analysis from every successive pitch class in the set. In creating an interval class vector, any interval higher than I6 is inverted to its smaller complement.

EXAMPLE 30-14

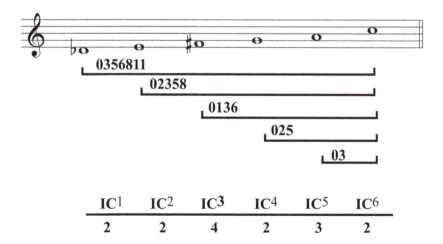

IC^1	IC^2	IC^3	IC^4	IC^5	IC^6
2	2	4	2	3	2

The analysis is placed between two arrows: < 2 2 4 2 3 2 >

The complete analysis of this hexachord is:

Prime Form: 0 3 5 6 8 11 Interval Vector: < 2 2 4 2 3 2 >

The Z Relationship

In our discussion of the interval vector, we discovered that pitch collections can have similarities in the way they sound despite having different prime forms. In fact, sets having differing prime forms can be found to have identical interval vectors. Such sets bear the **Z relationship**. In Example 30-15 below, the two tetrachord gestures 0 1 4 6 and 0 1 3 7 might appear to have only an I1 in common. But analyzing them vectorally (for their interval vectors) demonstrates that they share the interval vector < 1 1 1 1 1 1 >. Therefore, the prime forms 0 1 4 6 and 0 1 3 7 demonstrate **the Z relationship**.

EXAMPLE 30-15

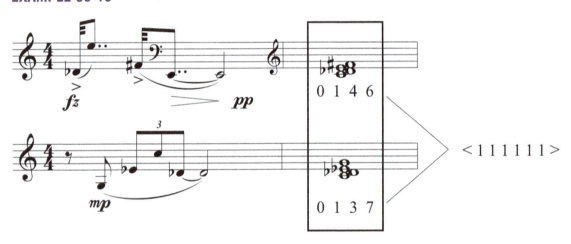

CONCEPT CHECK

Place the following set in best normal order, and construct its interval class vector:

EXAMPLE 30-16

APPLICATIONS TO ANALYSIS

The two opening gestures (set "Y" and set "Z") in Daniel McCarthy's "Visions and Apparitions" (for flute, vibraphone and percussion) demonstrate a high degree of unity. We can simply compare the prime forms to observe immediate similarities but a comparison of the vectors reveals greater similarity. In Example 20-18b, we'll concentrate on creating the interval class vector for set "Z."

EXAMPLE 30-17 Daniel McCarthy: *Visions and Apparitions* (second movement) 🔊

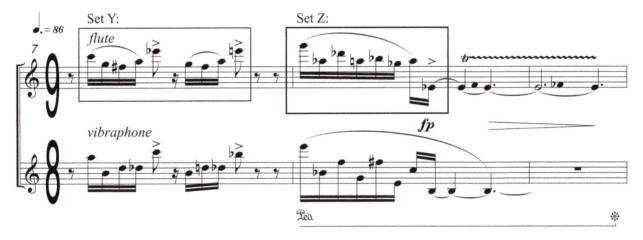

EXAMPLE 30-17a Set Z in prime form

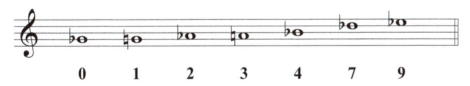

Using set types to determine the interval class vector of Set Z:

1. Create 6 set types, one beginning on each successive pitch in the "Z" collection— first from G♭, then from G, then from A♭, and so on.

2. Scan the 6 sets and count the times each number appears. For example, the number "1" appears in 4 of the set types and thus "4" becomes the first number of the interval class vector, meaning an interval class 1 is formed among 4 pairs of pitch classes (G♭–G, G–A♭, A♭–A, A–B♭). The number "2" occurs in 4 of the set types as well and thus becomes the second number in the vector.

3. CAUTION: For set integers higher than 6, the complement is entered in the vector so that the number 9 is tallied in the vector as an interval class 3, 8 is entered as an interval class 4, and 7 is entered as an interval class 5.

EXAMPLE 30-18

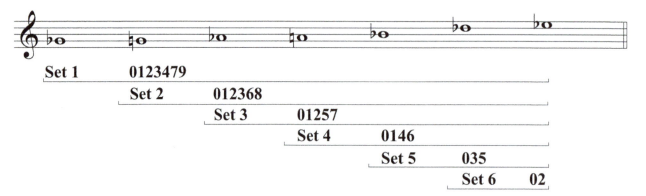

Set 1	0123479
Set 2	012368
Set 3	01257
Set 4	0146
Set 5	035
Set 6	02

Set Z interval class vector:

IC^1,	IC^2,	IC^3,	IC^4,	IC^5,	IC^6
4.	4.	4.	3.	4.	2

When comparing the prime forms of Y [0 1 3 4 6 9] and Z [0 1 2 3 4 7 9], some surface similarities are obvious—both have an ambitus of I9 and both begin with an I1, for example. We can further see that both contain an I3 and I4. The distinction seems to be that set Y has an I6 while Z has I7 and no tritone (I6). But their vectors reveal further similarities.

While Set Z appears not to contain an I6 in its prime form, the interval relationship between I1 and I7 reveals that a tritone does exist in its interior (7 − 1 = 6). This is where the vector analysis is most revealing. The vector of each set shows an identical number of tritones (I6) and similar occurrences of I3 and I4. It also demonstrates dissimilarity. Set Z is the more dissonant of the two with I1 and I2 occurring twice as much as Y.

IC vector for Set Y: < 2 2 5 2 2 2 >

IC vector for Set Z: < 4 4 4 3 4 2 >

Hints for Analysis

1. Consider identifiable melodic-rhythmic figures. Sets most likely involve three or four pitch classes, because in general, the larger the set, the less useful it is as a unifying device per se. Most of the repertoire in this textbook uses the "set" of all 12 pitch classes, but that alone serves no unifying or organizing purpose in the music.

2. Sets containing six or seven pitch classes may actually be a combination of smaller sets.

3. Create the set classes (in prime form) of all sets you identify, and mark their occurrences at various key points in the work—beginnings, endings, important section changes, and so on.

4. As in tonal music, consider pedal points and ostinatos apart from the rest of the texture.

5. Remember that the order of the pitch classes in a set is not very significant. Interval relationships are what provide unity and pitch organization in this music.

Set and Superset

The 0 1 4 trichord is integral to David S. Bernstein's "Three Silhouettes for Guitar." The set is heard at the beginning (G–B♭–B) and several times throughout the piece without transposition. However, larger sets occur that contain 0 1 4 with added intervals. These expansions are known as **supersets**. For example, measure three opens with a 0 1 4 trichord but the addition of the F natural expands the trichord into a 0 1 2 4 tetrachord. Another superset expands 0 1 4 on beat 3 of measure six into a 0 1 4 5 8 pentachord.

EXAMPLE 30-19 David S. Bernstein: *Three Silhouettes for Guitar* (second movement)

CONCEPT CHECK

In mm. 7 and 8, what set is formed by the lower line (stem-down notes)? How does the music above this line relate to the original set? Analyze the superset on beat 1–2 in measure 10.

Another Way

Despite the numerical bent of this chapter, there is nothing wrong with understanding and describing music such as Example 30-22 in traditional musical terms, as long as you remember that traditional harmonic function does not apply. For example:

- "Three Silhouettes for Guitar" features major and minor thirds and the minor second clashes that result from their combination.

- Sets constructed of perfect fourths and fifths and the major seconds and minor thirds that attend their combination—i.e., (0 2 7) and (0 2 5 7)—can produce a mildly dissonant, opening-sounding music reminiscent of Copland.

- Sets containing only major seconds, major thirds, and tritones, such as (0 2 6), can produce music with many "dominant-ninth-sounding" sonorities reminiscent perhaps of Debussy.

CONCEPT CHECK

The opening of the second movement of Daniel McCarthy's "An American Girl," ("II. Siobhan in Colonial Williamsburg") uses two distinct types of "harmonies." For example, mm. 1, 5–6, and 10–11 may be analyzed by traditional methods while the remaining measures could be analyzed as sets. Describe the music in both ways.

EXAMPLE 30-20 Daniel McCarthy: *An American Girl*, (second movement) 🔊

SUMMARY OF TERMINOLOGY

- Enharmonic equivalence: Any notes of the same pitch are equivalent regardless of spelling (p. 549).

- Octave equivalence: Enharmonically spelled notes are also equivalent regardless of octave (p. 549).

- Pitch class: A singular pitch and its enharmonic and octave equivalents (p. 549).

- Pitch class interval: The semitone distance between two pitch classes (p. 549).

- Ordered pitch class interval: The exact semitone distance and contour between two pitch classes as written in the surface of a composition (p. 550).

- Unordered pitch class interval: The shortest distance between two pitch classes (p. 550).

- Modulo 12: A modular arithmetic system of integers where the semitones in a pitch class interval and its inversion (complement) equal the sum of 12 (p. 550).

- Complement: The inversion of a pitch class interval, which, added to the original interval, equals Mod 12 (p. 550).

- Index numbers: Fixed integers given to every pitch class from which arithmetic interval calculations are made: i.e.; D♯ (integer 3) ascending B♭ (integer 10) = I7 (p. 551).

- Interval class: The shortest semitone distance between two pitch classes (p. 550).

- Pitch class set: A collection of pitch classes (pp. 551–552).

- Set type: A list of numerals given to a set demonstrating its semitone content from the lowest pitch class to each successive pitch class (p. 556).

- Normal order: A pitch class set in ascending order with the smallest distance from the lowest to highest pitch class (p. 555).

- Melodic inversion: A set that is reordered in reverse intervalic contour (p. 556).

- Best normal order: A normal ordered set with the smallest intervals packed to the left (p. 556).

- Prime form: The set type for best normal order (p. 557).

- Inversional symmetry (invariance): A pitch class set that has the same set type for both normal order and its inversion (p. 558).

- Interval vector: A six-digit analysis for occurrences of all interval classes in a set (p. 559).

- Z relationship: Two sets of differing prime forms with identical interval vectors (p. 559).

- Set class: The hierarchical ordering of pitch class sets developed by Allen Forte (p. 556).

CHAPTER THIRTY-ONE

Serial Atonality

SERIALISM

The Evolution of an Idea

Feeling that non-serial atonality lacked the organizing power to sustain larger musical works, Schoenberg developed the aggregate chromatic pitch class system known as 12-tone or serial composition. His approach to this method was gradual, as can be seen in Example 31-1, Schoenberg's last composition using a freely atonal approach—in his words, "composing with the notes of the motive."

KEY CONCEPTS IN THIS CHAPTER

- 12-Tone Row/Series
- Row Variation/ Transposition
- Row Matrix
- Derived Set
- Hexachordal Symmetry
- Aggregate
- Segmentation
- Discrete/Non-discrete Sets
- Indexing

EXAMPLE 31-1a Schoenberg: *Fünf Klavierstücke*, op. 23, no. 4 mm. 1–3 🔊

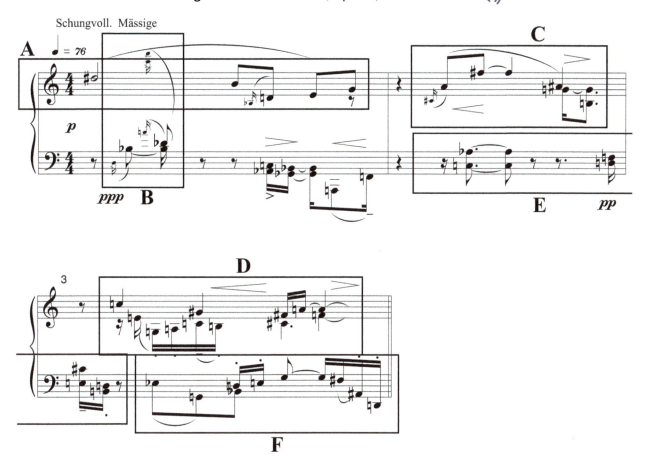

EXAMPLE 31-1b mm. 24–26 🔊

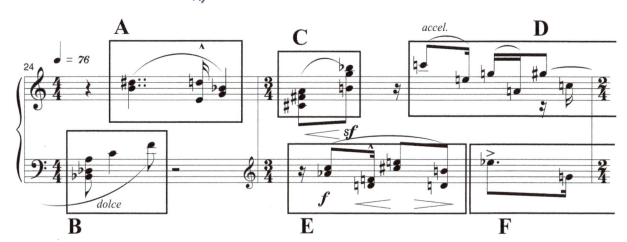

continued

EXAMPLE 31-1b *continued*

(D)

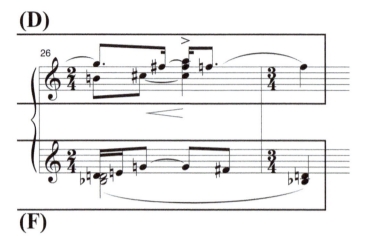

(F)

Notes:

1. A comparison of the two passages (Box A to Box A, Box B to Box B, and so on) reveals some concern for preserving the ordering of pitch classes and also a tendency to use all 12 pitch classes in close succession, two techniques basic to the 12-tone method.

2. The 0 1 4 5 set and its subsets—0 1 4 and 0 1 5—are embedded in the majority of the melodic figures, imparting a similarity to them that also unifies the piece as a whole.

Certain techniques basic to the 12-tone method are present in Schoenberg's treatment of sets in his earlier works, with this important difference: Ordering is the essence of a 12-tone row's identity. As we discuss the method, it may be helpful to think of the row as a "theme" that is subject to all the traditional techniques of development.

Basic Tenets of the 12-Tone Method

Schoenberg set forth the following "rules," then proceeded to break every one (so much for theory):

1. The pitch material for a composition is derived from a discrete ordering of all 12 pitch classes.

2. No pitch class is to be sounded out of order.

3. No pitch class is to be repeated (except for immediate repetition) until all other members of the row have been sounded.

A composer can decide how strictly or casually to apply these principles. Beyond that, flexibility resides in the method as follows:

1. A pitch class can appear in any octave.

2. The row can appear in any or all of four basic forms. The superscript numeral indicates the semitone level of transposition; in this case, no transposition.

    Prime (P⁰): the original series

    Retrograde (R⁰): The series in reverse order

    Inversion (I⁰): The series in melodic inversion

    Retrograde Inversion (RI⁰): The reverse order of the inversion

    A row and its four basic transformations, called row forms, are shown in Example 31-2.

EXAMPLE 31-2

P_0

R_0

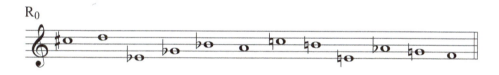

I_0

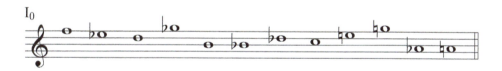

RI_0

3. Any of the four row forms (series) can be transposed to begin on any pitch.

EXAMPLE 31-3 (Prime series transposed one half step higher)

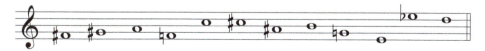

4. The members of the row may be assigned any durational value and may be used in any rhythmic or harmonic configuration.

5. One or more forms of the row may be used simultaneously. For example, one row form may provide the melodic line while another provides a subsidiary line or supporting harmonies, or the same row may be distributed between both the melody and its supporting harmonies.

CONCEPT CHECK

Write the series indicated by the row form and transposition based on the prime row given below:

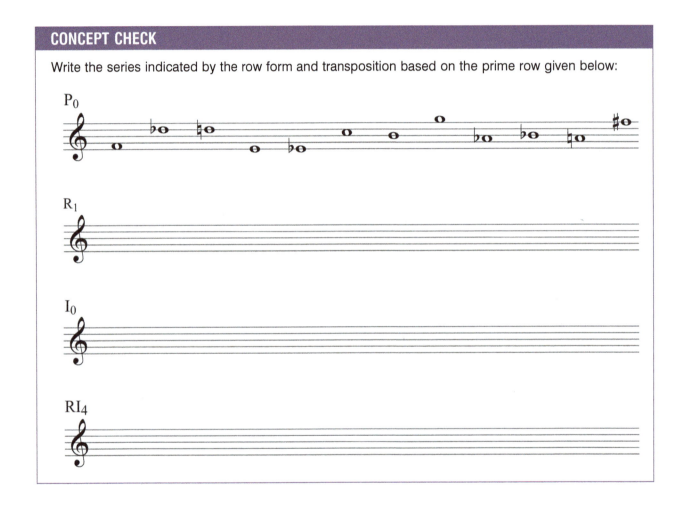

Example 31-4a shows the beginnings of two possibly very different compositions based on the P0 series of Example 31-2 and a single transformation. As you can see, the 12-tone method can be used to produce any kind of music the composer wishes to create while providing a "built-in" means of unification. Order numbers indicate each pitch's position in the series.

EXAMPLE 31-4a Ralph Turek: *Three by Twelve* (first movement) 🔊

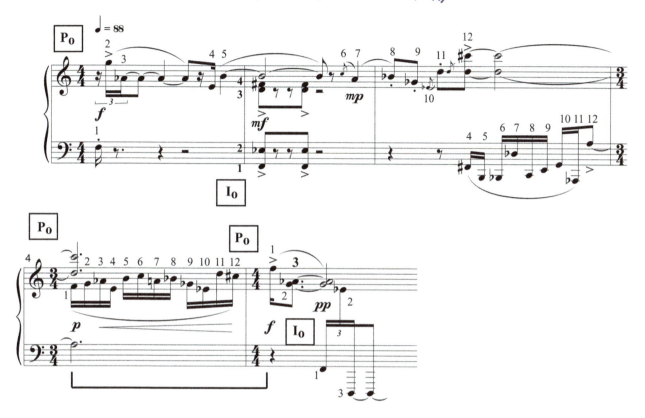

Row Deployment:

m. 1:   P0 is distributed between the right-and left-hand parts.

m. 2:   The melodic line is a continuation of P0. The first four pitches of I0 occur in the left-hand part as a chord. (Note its immediate repetition.)

m. 3:   The left-hand part is a continuation of I0. The right hand completes P0.

m. 4:   A new P0 statement takes place "inside" a sustained harmony by members of both P0 and I0.

m. 5:   The right-hand part begins a new P0 statement. The left-hand part begins a new I0 statement.

EXAMPLE 31-4b Ralph Turek: *Three by Twelve* (second movement) 🔊

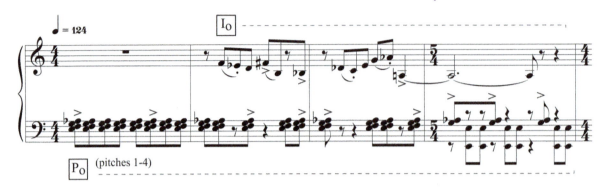

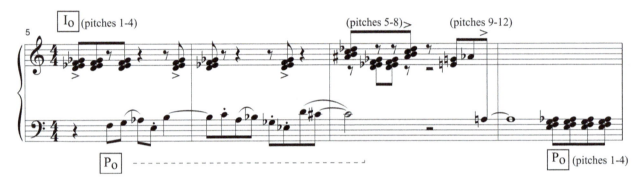

Row Deployment:

mm. 1–4: The first four pitches of P0 occur vertically in the left-hand part as a rhythmic pedal point. The right-hand part contains a complete linear statement of I0.

mm. 5–6: The first four pitches of I0 occur vertically in the right-hand part as a rhythmic pedal point. The left-hand part contains a complete linear statement of P0.

THE MATRIX

Composers routinely use the prime, retrograde, inversion, and retrograde inversion forms of their rows in multiple transpositions (P11, I7, R4, RI9, and so on), making it difficult to recognize row variations in analysis. In order to aid identification, theorists use a **matrix**, which orders the pitch classes of all the rows and their transpositions into a "grid."

Constructing a Matrix

To construct a matrix, construct a table of 48 squares, 12 in a row from left to right and 12 in a column from top to bottom. In the top row, enter the note names of the P0 row form from left to right. In the left column from top to bottom, enter the note names of the I0 row form. Since both P0 and I0 share the same note name at the beginning of the row, they share the same note name at the upper left-hand corner of the matrix.

For this matrix, we'll use the series (row) from Example 31-2.

EXAMPLE 31-5

F	G	A♭	E	B	C	A	B♭	F♯	E♭	D	C♯
E♭											
D											
F♯											
B											
B♭											
D♭											
C											
E											
G											
A♭											
A											

Notice that the second row begins on E♭—ten semitones above the F that begins P0. Therefore, the prime row form beginning on E♭ is labeled P10. (Row forms are indexed above (not below) P0.)

Since the first note of P10 (E♭) is one step lower than the first note of P0, the P10 row form can be completed by entering every note one full step lower than the note directly above it. Although this seems to be the easiest way to complete a row form, errors can compound, so be sure to check you accuracy. Similarly, the third prime row form, beginning on D, now named P9, is one semitone lower than the row directly above it, P10. Each note of P9 will thus be one half step lower than the corresponding note of P10. (You are free to spell pitches enharmonically.)

If you proceed correctly, the beginning note of P0 and I0 appearing at the top left corner of the matrix—in this case, F—will run diagonally through the matrix from the top left corner to the bottom right corner, as the arrow indicates.

EXAMPLE 31-6

I₀ (above first column)

P0	F	G	Ab	E	B	C	A	Bb	F#	Eb	D	C#	R0
P10	Eb	F	F#	D	A	Bb	G	Ab	E	C#	C	B	R10
P9	D	E	F	C#	Ab	A	F#	G	Eb	C	B	Bb	R9
	F#	G#	A	F	C	C#	Bb	B	G	E	D#	D	
	B												
	Bb												
	Db												
	C												
	E												
	G												
	Ab												
P4	A	B	C	G#	Eb	E	C#	D	Bb	G	F#	F	R4

RI₀ (below first column)

CONCEPT CHECK

Complete the matrix above following the steps just described. You might first add the note F on the diagonal dotted line all the way down. This will serve as a check for you as you complete each row form.

Indexing the Matrix

Once the matrix is complete, all rows running left to right are labeled P for "prime" forms (not to be confused with the term used for the prime form of a set), indexed with a subscript numeral indicating its transposition in semitones above the first pitch above the initial pitch of P0. All columns running from top to bottom are labeled I forms (inversion), indexed according to the distance in semitones of the first pitch above the initial pitch of I0. For example, columns 1 (beginning on F) and 2 (beginning on G) are labeled I0 and I2, respectively. Rows running from right to left are labeled R forms (retrograde) and columns running from bottom to top will be labeled RI forms.

Retrogrades share the same index number with their corresponding prime form, and retrograde inversions share the same index number with their corresponding inversion. (The retrograde of P7 will be R7, and the retrograde of I4 will be RI4, and so on.)

IDENTIFYING THE ROW: SEGMENTATION

Schoenberg wrote his "Fourth Quartet" in 1936, shortly after moving to Los Angeles, where—in an irony of the first magnitude—he resided only blocks away from Igor Stravinsky, a composer whose music was a universe removed from his own.

You may wonder if this work's prime series first unfolds linearly in the first violin or vertically throughout the ensemble. Actually, the series unfolds both ways. In our analysis, we can use traditional musical sensibilities to detect the prime series.

Composers' approaches to the 12-tone method have ranged from strict to casual. Schoenberg himself was fond of **segmentation**—using segments of the row, such as trichords (three-note segments), tetrachords (four-note segments), or hexachords (six-note segments) in a manner similar to the fragmentation of the themes and subjects in earlier music.   Since the trichord orientation permeates the opening of this composition both melodically and harmonically, a trichord analysis should be revealing.

EXAMPLE 31-7 Schoenberg: Fourth String Quartet, op. 37 (first movement) 🔊

continued

EXAMPLE 31-7 *continued*

The texture is clearly homophonic, with an accompanied melody in Violin I that comes to an end in measure six. Since this phrase forms an **aggregate**—a chromatic total—we might suspect that this is the row. The accompaniment (violin II, viola, and cello) consists of nine pitches segmented into three trichords that form an aggregate with each trichord of the melody in violin I. Thus, the prime series is sounding both melodically and harmonically, overlapping in the first six measures. It is illustrated below with its transformations.

EXAMPLE 31-8

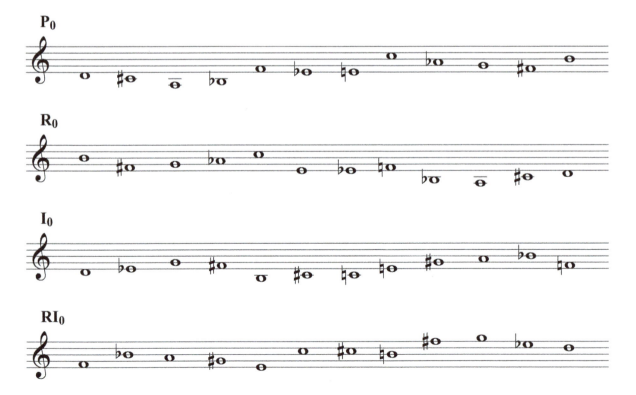

The series' trichord orientation is particularly interesting since its beginning and ending trichords are identical: 0 1 5. This creates a "palindromic" symmetry in the connection of any row with a subsequent transformation. However, even though the interior trichords 027 and 048 are distinct from the outer 015s, they are all connected by a semitone, a strong intervallic feature of 0 1 5.

EXAMPLE 31-9

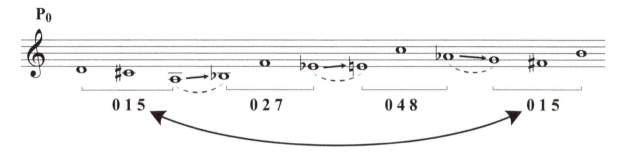

HEXACHORDAL SYMMETRY

The quartet reveals a deeper organization of row segmentation. The two hexachords in the series (see Examples 31-7, 31-8, and 31-9) have identical prime forms—in this case, 0 1 4 5 6 8. In this way, even though the second and third trichords are not symmetrical (027 and 048) the larger harmonic or melodic unit hexachord solidifies harmonic unity within the composition.

EXAMPLE 31-10

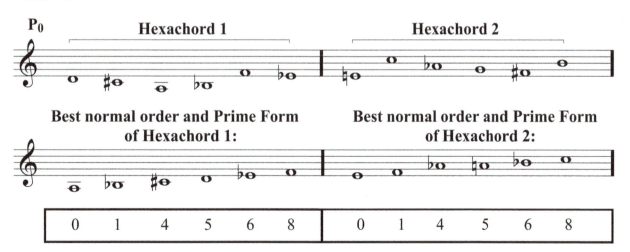

It may have occurred to you that a row can itself have a pronounced effect on the melodic and harmonic character of music based on it. This is true, and for that reason, composers have not been casual in choosing their rows. In the foregoing Schoenberg example we looked at the properties of contiguous sets, or sets that equally divide the row such as four trichords or three tetrachords. Such sets are known as **discrete sets**. However, composers may exploit the sounds of **non-discrete** or overlapping sets (sets that do not divide the series by three, four, or six non-overlapping units).

Such is the case in "Quaderno Musicale di Annalibera" by Luigi Dallapiccola. In the series illustrated below, Dallapiccola exploits triadic sonorities in one **non-discrete** (a) and three **discrete** (b–c–d) trichords.

EXAMPLE 31-11 Dallapiccola: 12-tone row used in *Quaderno Musicale di Annalibera*

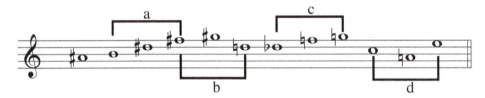

Note:

With a major triad, two implied ninth chords, and a minor triad (bracketed) obtainable from adjacent row members, you'd expect this row to produce music that sounds different from Schoenberg's Quartet. And you'd be correct.

EXAMPLE 31-12 Dallapiccola: *Quaderno Musicale di Annalibera* (Simbolo) 🔊))

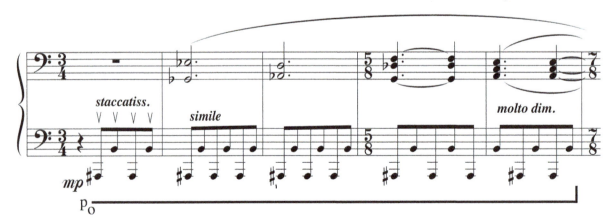

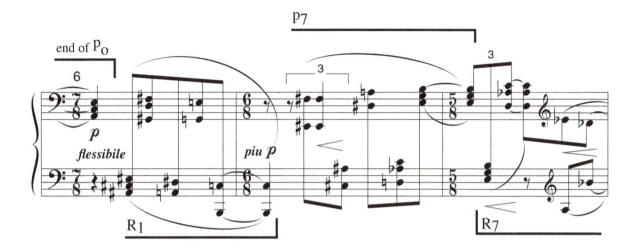

Notes:

1. The row is deployed in such a way that triads and seventh chords predominate.

2. The row members are voiced in such a way that the BACH motive—B (=B♭) A C H (=B)*—or its transposition, retrograde, or inversion is heard melodically at the top of the texture (hence the subtitle "symbol"). For example, the highest notes in mm. 2–5 are E♭–D–F–E: a transposition of B♭–A–C–B.

3. The row members are consistently segmented (2 + 2 + 2 + 3 + 3 or the reverse), lending harmonic and rhythmic uniformity.

The German use of the letter B to symbolize B♭ and H to symbolize B natural has its origins in medieval times when the symbols b and h stood for "soft B" (B♭) and "hard B" (B♮) respectively.

HINTS FOR ANALYSIS

How does one determine whether a piece is a 12-tone work? Following these steps should help:

1. Examine both the individual lines and textural changes for evidence of row changes, as well as at beginnings of phrases and sections.

2. Examine prominent harmonic structures for random pitch duplication that might suggest the work may not be serial.

3. If one passage fails to reveal insights, turn your attention to other passages

4. If segmentation is employed extensively, you may find melodic lines and harmonic figures of less than 12 pitches. The work may even appear to be set-based. Discovering the row can be especially challenging in such works.

5. For all possible rows that you discover, construct the other three forms—R, I, and RI—and look for these.

CONCEPT CHECK

Complete a matrix for the row in Example 31-11.

1. Can you find two additional identical nondiscrete trichords in this series?
2. Find two nondiscrete tetrachords of 0146 and 0157.

EXAMPLE 31-13

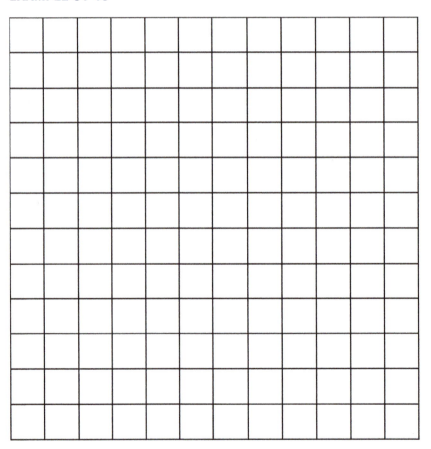

THE DERIVED SET

Another type for row symmetry exists in the **derived set** or **derived row**, in which all discrete trichords or tetrachords of a series produce the same prime form. In Anton Webern's "Concerto for Nine Instruments,", op. 24, his highly motivic style generated a trichord derived set of 0 1 5 as you can see and hear from the very beginning:

EXAMPLE 31-14

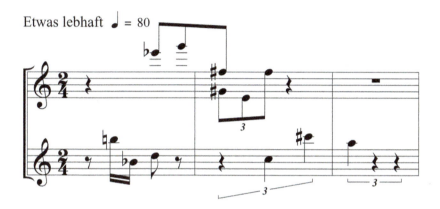

An examination of the row demonstrates Webern's segmentation of the series into four discrete trichords of 0 1 5, coinciding with his highly motivic writing in rhythmic groupings of threes:

EXAMPLE 31-15

⊕ CODA

Like a mountain road, the music of the twentieth century has followed a tortuous path, plunging forward into new musical terrain and then turning back into styles and techniques of the past. For example, Schoenberg's "Klavierstücke", op. 11, no. 1 (Example 30-5), a work still "modern" in its relentless dissonance and renunciation of harmonic tradition, was composed nearly 20 years before Ravel's triadic and tonal Violin Sonata (Example 29-6a). Talk about a flashback!

The century's musical pluralism has rendered the terms "contemporary" and "modern" musically meaningless. Moreover, their chronological significance is only relative, because what is contemporary today will become less so tomorrow. Virtually all musical styles and techniques are open for exploration today, making familiarity with them all the more important for today's musician.

DO YOU KNOW THESE TERMS?

- 12-tone row
- aggregate
- derived set
- discrete/non-discrete sets
- hexachordal symmetry
- indexing
- row forms
- segmentation
- serialism
- the matrix

CHAPTER THIRTY-TWO

Harmonic Principles in Jazz

KEY CONCEPTS IN THIS CHAPTER

- Triadic Extension
- Chord Substitution
- The Turnaround
- Tritone Equivalence
- Implied Lines
- Auxiliary Chords

WHAT'S THE DIFFERENCE?

Jazz has transcended its genre, and today its influence is everywhere—in popular music, film, and concert music. A musician's training today is incomplete without an exposure to it. Versatile performers are able to approximate the style when required. Composers who hope to make a living at their trade are at a disadvantage if they cannot write in the style. And music educators must be able to relate to the many offshoots of jazz that appeal to their students.

Key to any understanding of jazz is an understanding of its harmonic structure. This chapter introduces the basics of mainstream jazz harmony, organized under three broad headings. Much that you've already learned applies, but there are differences, too. Perhaps most important is the omnipresence of triad extensions—sevenths, ninths, and thirteenths. Jazz treats these triad extensions as chord members in good standing that do not necessarily require resolution.

What This Chapter Can't Do

This chapter can't turn you into a jazz player. Only a superb ear, a natural affinity for the style, and years of study and practice can do that.

What This Chapter Can Do

What this chapter can do is lay a foundation for further study and equip you with a basic harmonic vocabulary and an arsenal of representative techniques. This will enable you to produce harmonizations and arrangements in the jazz style and to talk knowledgably about the music.

EXTENDING THE TRIAD

The Basic Seventh Chords (A Review)

Few things are as daunting as a comprehensive table of jazz harmonies. In truth, the myriad symbols are but extensions and alterations of the five basic seventh chord types you already know—the MM7, the Mm7, the mm7, the om7, the oo7—along with another chord that, for consistency, we'll call the mM7.

Why not, then, just use the symbols for these six chord types? Actually, "real books" (they were previously called "fake books," but there was nothing fake about them) and lead sheets generally do. But extensions and alterations can color a basic harmony in very different ways. Play and listen to the different D7 chords in Example 32-1. All have the root, third, and seventh in the left-hand part. The right-hand part contains the extensions.

EXAMPLE 32-1

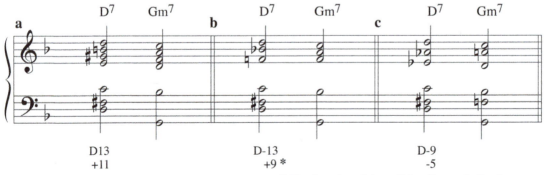

* The flatted tenth is traditionally symbolized enharmonically as a sharp nine.

As a keyboardist or guitarist, which do you play? As a saxophonist, how do the different alterations affect your improvisation? One reason for more elaborate symbols is to promote agreement when there are multiple chord instruments in a rhythm section (such as piano and guitar) about which extensions and which alterations to use. Another reason is to reflect the precise harmonic structures used in an arrangement, so that the pianist, guitarist, or soloist doesn't use a chord variant at odds with the written parts.

The matter is almost moot in a small combo such as a piano trio with melody instrument. In such groups, the players may agree on only certain nonstandard harmonies in advance. Whether or not they do, skillfull players listen carefully to one another and interact spontaneously, and the occasional clashes go mostly unnoticed.

The Extended Seventh Chord

Here, then, are the six basic seventh chords, with common extensions and just a few of the many ways to voice the larger chords that result. The chart reflects some of the disparity displayed in the symbolization of the bigger jazz chords. The good news: You will more often encounter and use the basic seventh chord symbols on the left than the more unwieldy symbols on the right.

EXAMPLE 32-2a

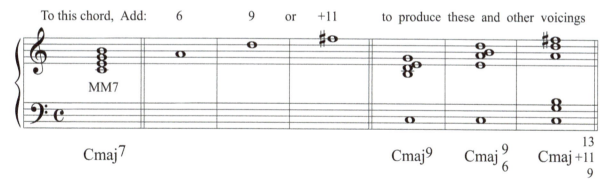

EXAMPLE 32-2b

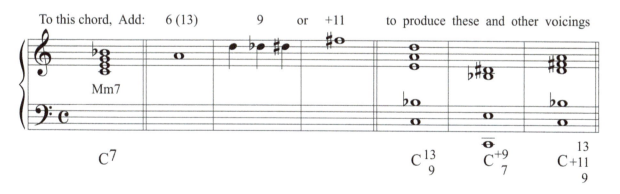

EXAMPLE 32-2c

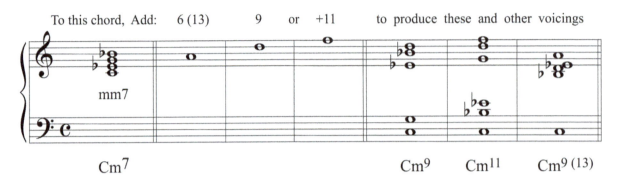

EXAMPLE 32-2d

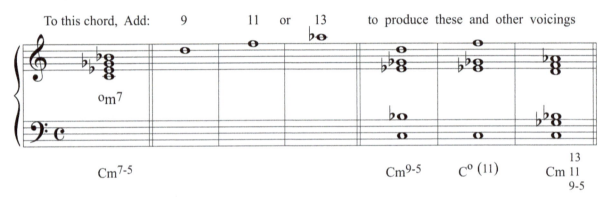

EXAMPLE 32-2e

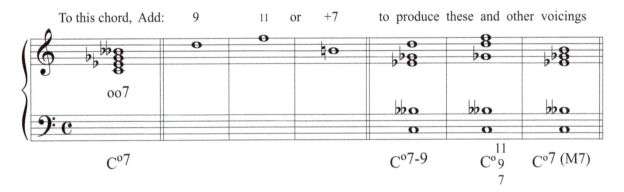

EXAMPLE 32-2f

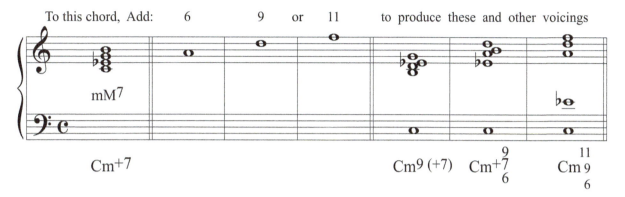

Regarding extended chord symbols:

1. The various ways of expressing the triadic extensions are in common use.

2. All extensions listed for a given basic chord are compatible—they can be used together—with one exception: A ninth used together with either its raised or lowered form produces a seldom-used dissonance. (Try playing a C7, as in **b**, and add both D and D♯, or D and D♭, and you'll hear why.)

3. The raised ninth (+9 or ♯9) normally appears over one chord only—the dominant seventh (as in **b**). It is often spelled as a lowered third (♭3), especially when it moves downward to the ♭9.

this is often spelled like this

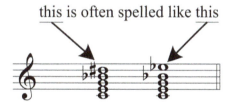

4. The omission of a chord fifth is normally not indicated in a symbol.

5. A "9" or "11" alone (Cm9 or Cm11) signifies a major ninth or perfect eleventh above the root. It also implies the inclusion of the seventh. If the seventh is to be omitted from a ninth chord or larger, it is common practice to use the symbol for the simple triad along with "add _," such as Cm^add9, which suggests this:

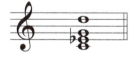

6. Regarding the V⁷:

    As in art music, the V⁷ chord (b) can contain an altered fifth (♯5 or ♭5), which may be spelled enharmonically. The ♭5 is enharmonically the same pitch as the +11. However, the +11 typically occurs as an extension above the fifth and resolves upward, whereas the ♭5 typically replaces the unaltered fifth and may resolve downward.

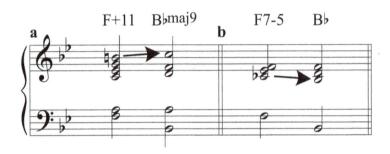

Over a dominant seventh chord, only two pitches—the major seventh and perfect eleventh–are widely treated as incompatible (such as B and F over a C7), and even the eleventh can be used if the third is omitted.

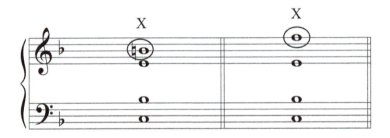

The eleventh is usually omitted from the V¹³, and if present, is augmented (for example in a G13, C♯).

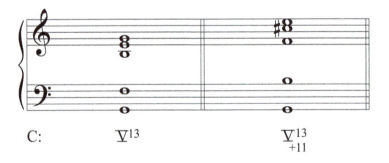

7. All the chord symbols can exist as "slash chords" (Cm7/B♭, for example), to indicate a bass note other than the root.

General Guideline

Complete chord symbols can be unwieldy. In general, if you use a basic symbol, a jazz player will know what to do with it. Use complete symbols only to promote agreement among players.

CONCEPT CHECK

From the six basic seventh chords, choose the one that forms the basis for each of the following extended harmonies, and write it in simplest position next to the larger chord:

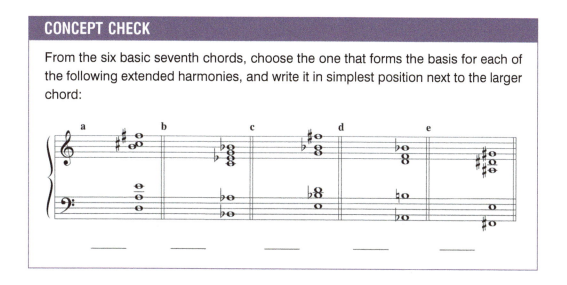

▶ *Assignment 1A in Workbook Chapter 32 can be completed now.*

Melodic Implications

The preceding point no. 2 has the following melodic ramifications:

Each seventh chord with its extensions, placed within a single octave, constitutes potential scalar material for melodies or melodic improvisation based on it.

EXAMPLE 32-3a

EXAMPLE 32-3b

EXAMPLE 32-3c

Note:

The scales in a and b are actually the Lydian and Dorian modes respectively. Perhaps inspired by George Russell's 1953 jazz theory book *The Lydian Chromatic Concept of Tonal Organization*, some jazz teachers emphasize the compatibilty of the Church modes with certain altered and extended harmonies (particularly Dorian with the mm. 7, Lydian with the MM. 7, Mixolydian with the Mm. 7).

CONCEPT CHECK

Provide the basic seventh chord symbols for Example 32-4. At mm. 2 and 4, the melody note is an extended chord member. Because of this, the extension should be reflected through a more complete chord symbol. Do so. At m. 6, the melody note E (on beat 2) is an embellishing tone. What type is it?

EXAMPLE 32-4 Vince Guaraldi: "Christmas Time Is Here"

Voicing

Example 32-2 provided some sample voicings. While there's no such thing as an inherently "wrong" spacing in jazz, the principles are those you learned in Part Four:

1. Space intervals wider near the bottom of the chord.

2. Except where needed in a bass line or inner voice, keep elevenths and thirteenths in the higher reaches. On the piano, this effectively means placing those chord members in the right-hand part. For guitar, this can mean playing only the upper reaches of the chord, omitting the root entirely (except in solo guitar work).

3. Double chord members only for a fuller sound, special effects, or to reinforce a melodic line.

Two common voicing "templates" are:

Template 1	Template 2
Other chord Members	Other chord Members
7	5
R	R

Sample root-position voicings of a Cm7 chord, some with ninth, eleventh, and/or the thirteenth, follow. All use either template 1 or 2. This helps to keep the texture transparent.

EXAMPLE 32-5a Template 1 (Root and seventh on bottom)

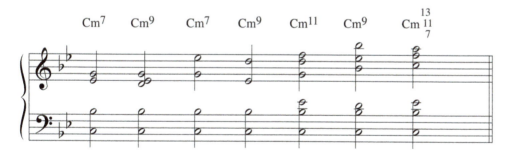

EXAMPLE 32-5b Template 2 (Root and fifth on bottom)

CONCEPT CHECK

Notate the complete symbol for each chord in Example 32-5b. Keeping the root in the bass, redistribute the other chord members. Play the chord and listen carefully to the effect. Now, look again at Example 32-4. For each chord, tell whether it conforms to template 1, template 2, or neither.

▶ *Assignment 1F in Workbook Chapter 32 can be completed now.*

Jazz voicings display much greater variety than can be suggested by two templates. In his solo piano rendering of "Everything Happens to Me," Clare Fischer shows in the first four measures a fondness for both ninths and tenths in addition to fifths and sevenths at the bottom of his voicings. At the same time, he shows just how far beyond the basic seventh chords a jazz rendition is likely to venture.

EXAMPLE 32-6 Tom Adair/Matt Dennis: "Everything Happens to Me" as performed by Clare Fischer (trans. by Bill Dobbins) 🔊

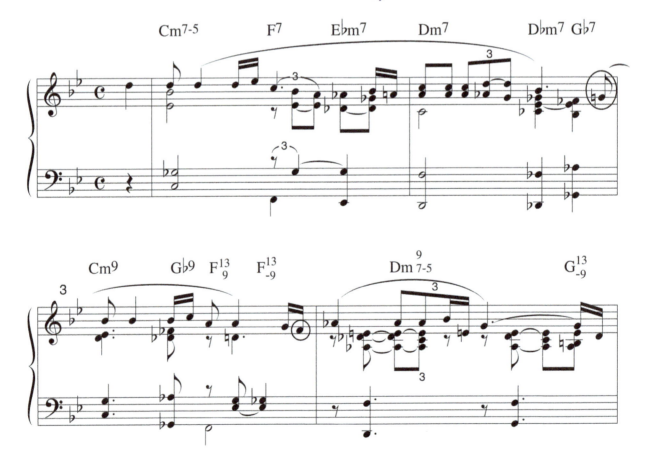

Note:

Only basic symbols are given above mm. 1–2. The more complete symbols are given above mm. 3–4, for comparison. Notice the occasional clashes between melody and harmony (circled), an accepted byproduct of the music's improvisatory nature.

➤ *For assignments on extending the triad, turn to Workbook Chapter 32, assignments 1A–1G.*

CHORD SUBSTITUTION

Why Substitute?

Chord substitution results when jazz players seek to vary commonplace harmonic patterns. Because the search for new interpretations is ongoing, chord substitution has grown into the 800-pound gorilla of jazz harmonization. The most basic substitution involves creating secondary dominants.

Tonicization

EXAMPLE 32-7 Barbera/Hanna/Curtin: "Flintstones Theme" (based on chord changes to George and Ira Gershwin's "I Got Rhythm")

a Basic harmonies

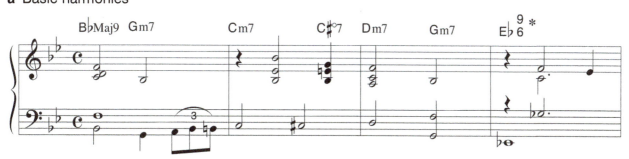

*5th and 7th omitted, 6th added

continued

b mm. 5–8 with tonicizations 🔊

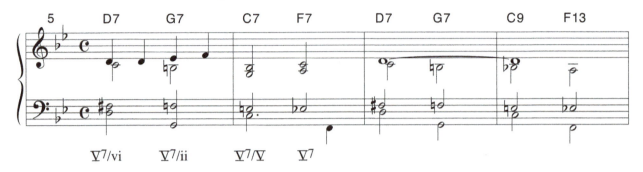

Note:

In **b**, the dominant (F7) in m. 6 has been tonicized by the chord preceding it. That chord, in turn has been tonicized by its predecessor. And that chord likewise has been tonicized, creating a chain of dominant seventh chords that spiral downward by fifth (D7–G7–C7–F7). The pattern is then repeated. This lends harmonic variety by changing a pattern (B♭Maj7–Gm7–Cm7) that has already been heard in mm. 1–2.

REVIEW AND REINFORCEMENT

Provide a Roman numeral analysis of Example 32-7.

Recall that a tonicization can be elaborated by preceding the tonicizing V with its own pre-dominant. Expanded tonicization is one of the most fundamental jazz techniques.

EXAMPLE 32-8 Barbera/Hanna/Curtin: "Flintstones Theme" (Bridge) 🔊

a Basic harmonies (with abbreviated chord symbols)

continued

b With expanded tonicizations 🔊

Note:

In **b**, each V⁷ has been prefaced by a pre-dominant—Am7–D7, Dm7–G7, Gm7–C7, Cm7–F7—creating a sequence of tonicizing chord groups.

REVIEW AND REINFORCEMENT_____

Only basic seventh chord symbols are shown in b even though some alterations and extensions are present. Show the complete chord symbols at: m. 10, beat 2_____ m. 12, beat 4_____, m. 16, beat 4_____. Using Roman numerals, show the tonicizing chord groups present in the passage. (Refer back to Example 16-4a if you've forgotten how to do this.)

➤ *Assignments 2A and 2B in Workbook Chapter 32 can be completed now.*

Tritone Equivalence

Another common chord substitution involves tritone-related chords. This might seem odd to you. After all, the tritone is the most distant of tonal relationships. Right? Well, yes and no. Consider Example 32-9.

EXAMPLE 32-9

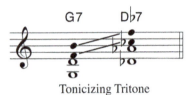

Tonicizing Tritone

Note:

The two chords have the tonicizing tritone in common—f, and b (=C♭). The two notes exchange functions: TI (B) becomes FA (C♭), and vice versa.

Now notice what happens if we create identical altered forms for both chords:

EXAMPLE 32-10

Notes:

1. Lowering the fifth of each chord gives them identical pitch content, each an enharmonic inversion of the other.

2. This renders the two tritone-related chords interchangeable. Jazz players have extended the principle to include any two dominant seventh chords—with or without extensions and alterations—that are tritone-related. In circle of fifths progressions, the substitution can create a chromatic descending bass line.

The Turnaround

In Example 32-7, the harmonic pattern surrounding the melodic cadence pitch at mm. 7–8 is called a turnaround—a pattern that leads back to the beginning. Chains of secondary V⁷s are common turnarounds. Jazz players are expected to know many such patterns. We'll learn how to create turnarounds.

Examples 32–11 a–d show the evolution of several standard turnarounds through simple tonicization followed by tritone substitution. Notice that each progression has a logic that propels it toward the tonic by a slightly different route.

EXAMPLE 32-11a Basic progression

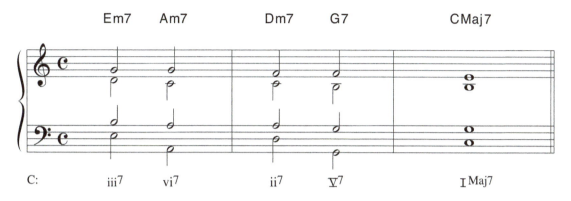

EXAMPLE 32-11b Simple tonicization (chain of secondary Vs)

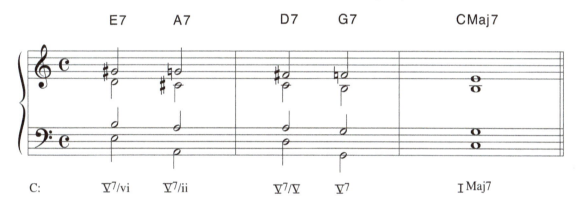

EXAMPLE 32-11c Tritone substitution for first and third chords of **b**

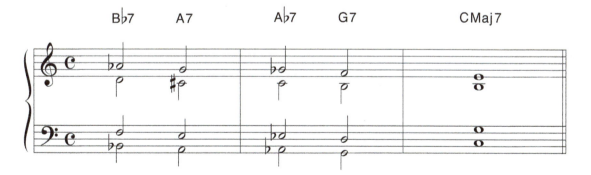

EXAMPLE 32-11d Tritone substitution for second and fourth chords of **b**

EXAMPLE 32-11e Tritone substitution for all four chords of **b**

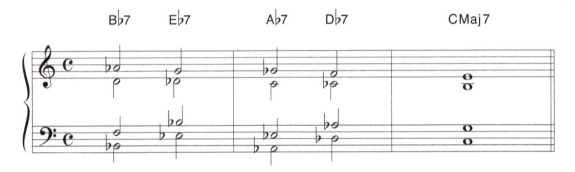

Notes:

1. Both a and b are circular-fifth progressions. b is achieved by changing each chord of a into a V^7 of the following chord (V^7/vi–v^7/ii–v^7/V).

2. c and d are produced by substituting tritone-related dominant seventh chords to every other chord in b. c approaches the dominant (G7) by chromatic motion, while d approaches the tonic (C maj7) by chromatic motion.

3. e is the result of tritone substitution for every chord in b. This produces a complete circular-fifth progression a tritone removed from the original.

Let's apply this to the turnaround in m. 8 of a jazz classic.

EXAMPLE 32-12a Wolf and Landesman: "Spring Can Really Hang You Up the Most"
(m. 8 = turnaround: corresponds to Example 32-11**a**) 🔊

Arr. R.T.

EXAMPLE 32-12b

EXAMPLE 32-12c

CONCEPT CHECK

1   In Examples b and c, the melody notes on beats 1 and 3 constitute extensions of the basic seventh chords. Identify those extensions.

2   Provide the complete lead-sheet symbols for Example 32-12 a, b, and c. For a, place a chord symbol on every beat.

Let's return to "The Flintstones Theme" and apply tritone substitution to the chain of secondary dominants in mm. 5–8 (see Example 32-7b).

EXAMPLE 32-13 Barbera/Hanna/Curtin: "Flintstones Theme" 🔊

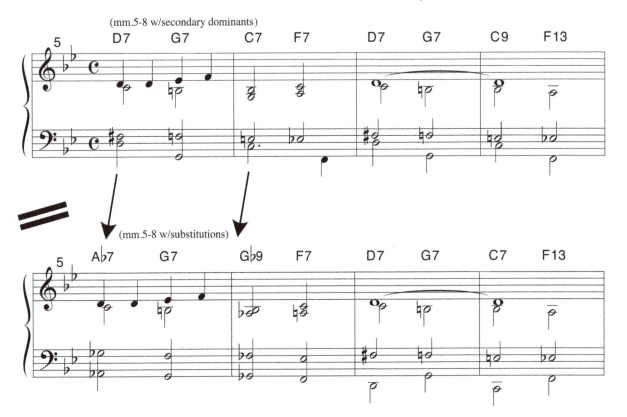

Note:

The following tritone substitutions have been made: in m. 5, A♭7 for D7, and in m. 6, G♭9 for C7. This creates a chromatic descending bass line and eliminates repetition of the pattern D7–G7–C7–F7 (see Example 32-7b).

Substitution Guideline

Melody notes permitting, a tritone substitute can replace any V^7 or any chord that can be turned into a secondary V^7.

Arthur Hamilton's classic ballad, "Cry Me a River," teems with such opportunities: mm. 2 and 3 (Cm7–Fm7), m. 3 (Fm7–B♭7), mm. 3 and 4 (B♭7–E♭maj7), m. 4 (G7), mm. 5–6 (C7–F9), m. 6 (F9), and mm. 7–8 (B♭7–E♭maj7). Not all of the possible substitutions will sound well with this melody, but those that will are shown in boldface in Example 32-14, as basic dominant ninth chords (unextended, unaltered).

EXAMPLE 32-14 Arthur Hamilton: "Cry Me a River"

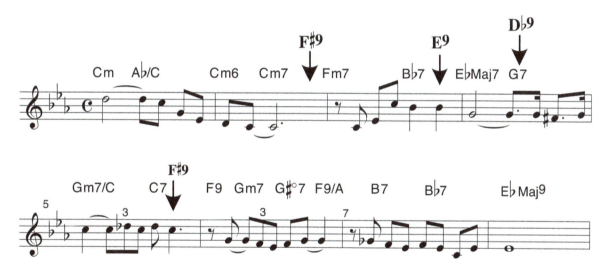

CONCEPT CHECK

Name the alteration that the melody note would represent in each substitute (boldface) chord. How would you change the chord symbol to reflect this alteration?

The substitutions shown in Example 32-14 are incorporated in the following piano rendering.

EXAMPLE 32-15 Arthur Hamilton: "Cry Me a River"

Arthur Hamilton: "Cry Me a River"

The first of the substitute chords has been respelled enharmonically, a more appropriate spelling in E♭. Enharmonic spelling of chords, practically the rule in jazz, can be a barrier to understanding harmonically complex passages

CONCEPT CHECK

Notate the rest of the chords of Example 31-15, in simple position on the staff below.

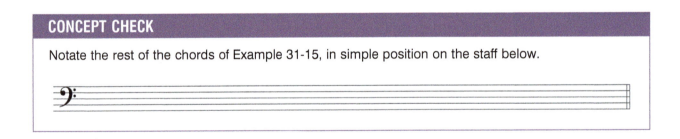

▶ *Assignments 2C–2F on Workbook pages 412–413 can be completed now.*

Expanded Tritone Substitution

An expanded tritone substitution is similar to an expanded tonicization—the predominant to the tritone substitute is added, creating a tritone-related ii–V.

EXAMPLE 32-16

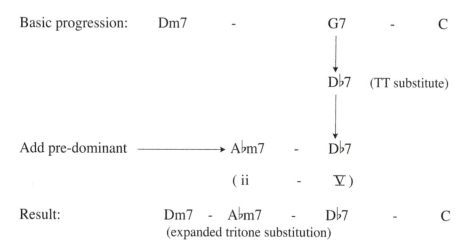

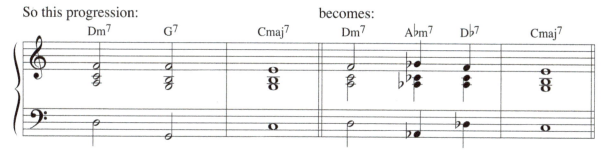

Let's return to the turnaround patterns shown in Example 32-11 c and d to see how this sounds.

EXAMPLE 32-17a This . . .

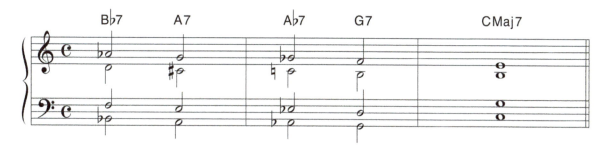

EXAMPLE 32-17b becomes this . . .

EXAMPLE 32-17c and this . . .

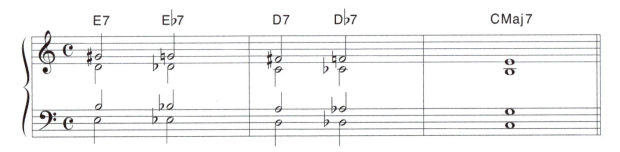

EXAMPLE 32-17d becomes this . . .

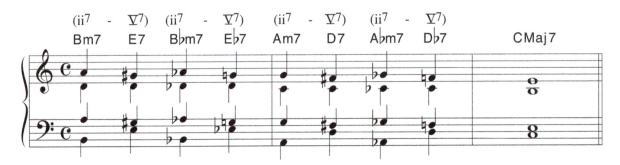

The popular song repertoire written between roughly 1900 and 1950—the standards, as they're called—provides jazz artists with simple melodies for reharmonization much like the chorale did for J. S. Bach in his day. With each new harmonization, a song acquires new interest and vitality. Reharmonization has done much to keep this music alive.

➤ *For assignments on chord substitution, turn to Workbook p. 410.*

IMPLIED LINES

Today's arranger essentially part-writes his or her way through a series of lead-sheet symbols much like you've done with the figured bass. The goal is the same: to create attractive melodic lines that, collectively, produce the given harmonies. Much of an arrangement's appeal depends on the quality of those melodic lines.

Reading between the Chords

Because lead-sheet symbols are somewhat less efficient at showing linear motion than were figured bass symbols, arrangers and players must learn to spot implied lines.

EXAMPLE 32-18a Typical lead-sheet appearance

EXAMPLE 32-18b Actual chords and implied line

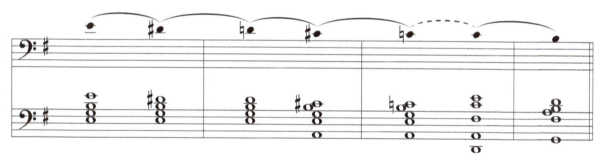

Granted, this line is nothing but a chromatic descent. However, it can serve as the basis for a countermelody (given to the saxophones in the following arrangement).

EXAMPLE 32-18c 🔊

Here are the changes for the first two measures of "Cry Me a River," as they appear in one popular "fake book:"

Cm   A♭/C | Cm6   Cm7

Implied in this succession is the line: G–A♭–A–B♭. In Example 32-19, this line has been placed in the bass (although it could have been situated in a middle voice as well). It lends melodic interest and logic to what is essentially a prolonged C minor harmony.

EXAMPLE 32-19 Arthur Hamilton: "Cry Me a River"

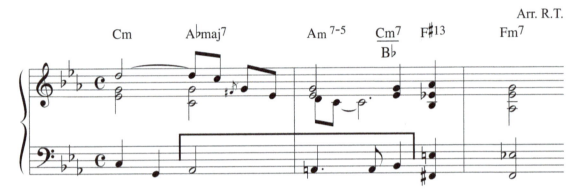

How does one recognize implied lines? One clue is a series of repeated chords, especially ones containing several different extensions or alterations. The alterations usually form the implied line. Example 32-20 shows a pattern used to embellish a minor triad over several measures, a pattern so common that the implied line is recognizable to jazz musicians at 50 paces.

EXAMPLE 32-20

Example 32-21 shows this pattern at work.

EXAMPLE 32-21 Leon Russell: "This Masquerade" 🔊

Note:

The implied line—F–E–Eb–D—has been added to the top voice of the left-hand part (bracketed).

Patterns such as the foregoing seem almost to dictate a scalar line. Not all patterns do. Even so, melodic lines—scalar or otherwise—can be fashioned out of almost any progression. That's one definition of part writing.

▶ *Assignment 2B on Workbook p. 417 can be completed now.*

You've already learned that nothing enhances a passage like an interesting bass line. And you know this is often achieved through passing tones and inversions. Compare the bass line suggested by the lead-sheet symbols in Example 32-22a with the more purposeful one in the piano arrangement that follows it.

EXAMPLE 32-22a Paul Webster and Johnny Mandel: "A Time for Love"

EXAMPLE 32-22b Piano arrangement of a 🔊

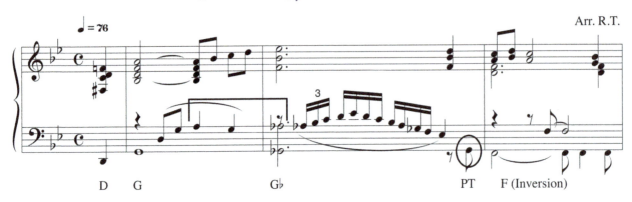

A nearly stepwise bass (shown beneath the music) is attained through use of passing tones and inversion. Notice also the inner-voice scalar line (bracketed). This is not to say you should do this at every opportunity. The practice can become manneristic and predictable. Usually a mixture of bass patterns—some by step, some by circle of fifths, some by thirds, and so on—is most effective.

Auxiliary Chords

Jazz makes extensive use of auxiliary chords—passing chords and neighbor chords to fill the intervals between principal harmonies, appoggiatura chords to accentuate those harmonies, and so on. Like nonchord tones, these often involve motion by step or half step between, into, or away from the principal harmonies.

EXAMPLE 32-23a Johnny Mercer and Harold Arlen: "My Shining Hour"

EXAMPLE 32-23b Song in piano rendition 🔊

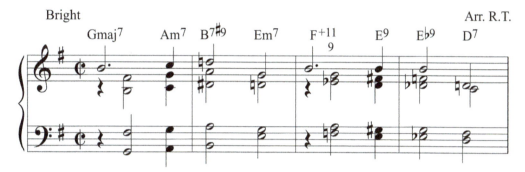

Note:

In m. 2, the Em7 (vi7) has been pushed to the second beat and preceded by its dominant (B7). In m. 1, a diatonic passing chord (Am7) has been inserted between the GMaj7 and B7.

REVIEW AND REINFORCEMENT

Refer back to Example 32-23b and explain the chord substitutions in mm. 3–4. All result from two processes—tonicization and tritone substitution. It may help to work backward from the final D7.

Example 31-24 shows a song with basic chord symbols as it would appear in a fake book and a piano accompaniment that incorporates auxiliary chords.

EXAMPLE 32-24a Charles Fox and Norman Gimbel: "Killing Me Softly" 🔊

I heard he sang a good song, I heard he had a style,

And so I came to see him to lis - ten for a while.

EXAMPLE 32-24b Song with piano accompaniment

Note:

Chords have been added at the points marked with an asterisk.

What kinds of chords should one add? An easy-to-remember technique that works much of the time has been used here:

Use an auxiliary chord of the same type as the chord it embellishes or connects.

Preceding the first lead-sheet chord in m. 1 f the preceding example—B♭m7—are Cm7 and Bm7. And the A♭maj7 in m. 3 has been preceded by an Amaj7.

Added Practice: Examine the remaining auxiliary chords in Example 32-24 and describe their types. What chord symbol would you use in m. 2 (beats 1–2)?

⊕ CODA

Jazz harmonization is endlessly fascinating, and the processes can seem fascinatingly endless. It helps, though, to remember that it reduces largely to this: extending, substituting, and adding chords. As Bach and his contemporaries had a vocabulary and set of procedures for harmonizing melodies, so does today's jazz musician.

While jazz scoring is beyond the scope of this text, a generalization is not. Arranging consists largely of three techniques: (1) harmonization, (2) creation of secondary lines, (3) voicing the harmonies and orchestrating the lines. We've addressed these techniques, but only in an introductory way. If the topic interests you, you should consider a course in jazz arranging.

➤ *For assignments on implied lines, turn to Workbook p. 416.*

DO YOU KNOW THESE TERMS?

- appoggiatura chord
- auxiliary chord
- expanded tritone substitution
- extended tonicization
- implied lines
- neighbor chord
- passing chord
- standards
- triadic extension
- tritone-related chords
- tritone substitution

CHAPTER THIRTY-THREE

The Blues

PERSPECTIVE

Few things musical are as uniquely American or as timeless as the blues. Born and nurtured in the nineteenth-century rural South, the blues migrated North and into the cities in the early twentieth century, undergoing a process of maturation and refinement that continues to the present day. The term blues means different things to different people—"a style of music, a type of performance, a musical form, (or) a state of mind."[1] It can mean the gritty vocal style of Muddy Waters, the weeping guitar lines of B.B. King, the frenetic music in the 1980 cult movie *The Blues Brothers*, and much more.

THE BLUES THEN AND NOW

What Is "The Blues?"

When musicians—particularly jazz musicians—use the term "blues," they are usually referring to a

---

1 Tirro, Frank, *Jazz: A History*. New York: W.W. Norton & Company, Inc. 1993.

repeating harmonic pattern that serves as the basis for a succession of melodic, rhythmic, and textural variations (improvised or written). Today's musician should have a working understanding of this form.

The origin of the blues was vocal—a rhymed couplet with the first phrase repeated, yielding the three-phrase structure a a' b:

EXAMPLE 33-1

Text phrase A (voice) . . . . Response (guitar)

I

Text phrase A (voice) . . . . Response (guitar)

IV   I

Text phrase A (voice) . . . . Response (guitar)

V   I

The music was, from its beginning, improvisatory, and the guitar "response" that punctuated each vocal phrase may have initially allowed the singer time to think up the next lyrics. Three chords were used—the primary triads—all open-string, easily playable chords in the key of E.

As it evolved from unwritten practice to a notated one, the form settled into this 12-measure pattern:

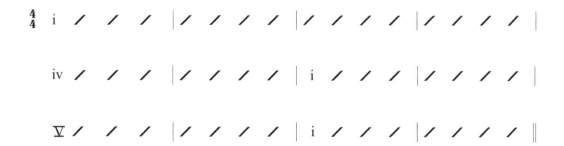

Here, then, even after more than a century of evolution, is the **12-bar blues** in near-pristine form, in the key of F. (Sixteen and 24 bar variants will be discussed later.)

EXAMPLE 33-2 Tracy Chapman: "Give Me One Reason"

	"Give me one reason to stay here, And I'll turn right back around"	Instrumental fill
a	mm. 1-2	mm. 3-4
	F^7 **$B\flat^7$**	F^7 ($F^7 = \underline{V}^7/\underline{IV}$)

	"Give me one reason to stay here, And I'll turn right back around"	Instrumental fill
a'	mm. 5-6	mm. 7-8
	$B\flat$	F^7

	"Said I don't want to leave you lonely, You got to make me change my mind"	Instrumental fill
a	mm. 9-10	mm. 11-12
	C^7 **$B\flat^7$**	F^7 C^7

Notes:

1. The *lowered seventh* present above each root imparts a dominant seventh quality to each chord. The blues and its offspring are the only Western vernacular music in which the Mm7 is routinely divorced from its function as a dominant in need of resolution.

2. Three chords (in boldface) have been added to the basic blueprint—at m. 2, m. 10, and m. 12. These were but the first of many subsequent additions.

Adding the IV^7 in m. 10 creates both a retrogression following the V^7 of m. 9 and a plagal motion with respect to the coming I. The plagal motion is common in popular music and blues-inflected music, particularly in its musical relative, Gospel.

EXAMPLE 33-3 Oscar Peterson: "Hymn to Freedom" (transcribed from *Oscar Peterson: Paris Jazz Concerto*, Europe I #71044, April 25, 1964)

➤ *Assignment 1A in Workbook Chapter 33 can be completed now.*

The Basic Blues Today

Despite the persistence of more or less pure forms, the blues has acquired over the years an expanded harmonic vocabulary, largely through the chord-extension and substitution techniques detailed in Chapter 32. Example 33-4 shows one way the blues might be played today. Chord choices and voicings vary from one performer to the next. The bass (played by a bassist rather than the keyboardist) is improvised and thus changes upon repetition.

EXAMPLE 33-4 12-Bar Blues (Typical) 🔊))

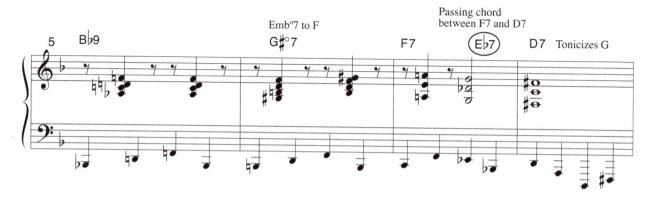

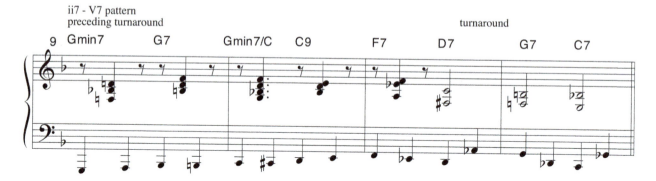

How did the harmonic pattern shown in Example 33-2 evolve into this? First of all, today, a ninth and/or thirteenth is an option on each and every chord in the blues pattern. As for the other chords, the biggest change involves tonicization. Working backward from the final bar:

Tonicization

In mm. 11 and 12:

The C7 in the original blues has been tonicized by G7 in m. 12. The G7 in turn has been tonicized by D7 in m. 11 to create a four chord turnaround (F7–D7–G7–C7).

In mm. 9 and 10:

A ii–V succession (Gm7–C9) now precedes the F7 of m. 11.

The Gm7 of m. 9 is tonicized by the D7 of m. 8.

Substitution accounts for other chords:

Substitution

In m. 4:

The B9 is a tritone substitute. (See Examples 32-9 and 32-10 to review this technique.)

In m. 6:

An embellishing o7 to the F7 of m. 7 has been added, creating a chromatically rising bass (B♭–B–C) in mm. 5, 6, and 7.

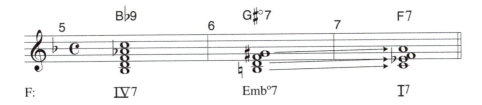

In m. 7:

A passing chord (E♭7) has been inserted between the F7 of m. 7 and the tonicizing D7 of m. 8. Here are the three chords, voiced to show more clearly the passing function of the E♭7:

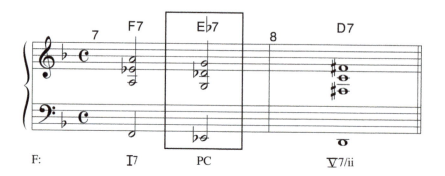

Now let's look at one further elaboration of the blues pattern. The essential changes are bracketed.

EXAMPLE 33-5a 12-Bar Blues with Further Substitution 🔊

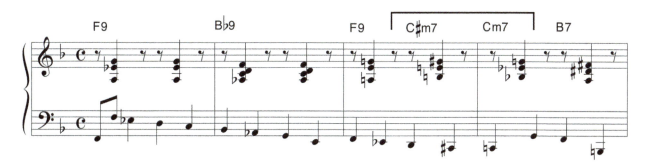

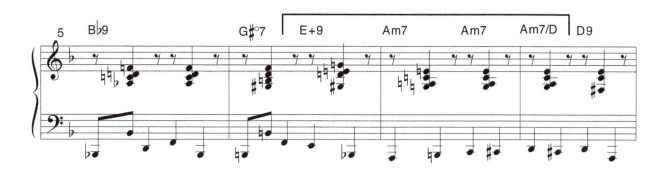

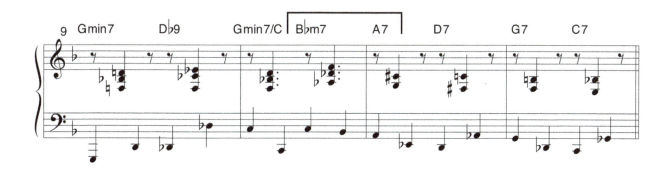

Tonicizing Chord Groups

Comparing Example 33-5 to Example 33-4:

In m. 4 and 5:

Recall that B7 is a tritone substitute for F7.

Preceding the original F7 of m. 4 with a Cm7 to create a tonicizing chord group (ii7–V^7):

$$\text{B}\flat: \qquad \text{ii}^7 \qquad \underline{\text{V}}^7$$

and then substituting the tritone-related B7 for the F7 produces:

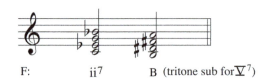

$$\text{F:} \qquad \text{ii}^7 \qquad \text{B (tritone sub for}\,\underline{\text{V}}^7)$$

a chromatic descending chord succession to the subdominant B♭ in m. 5 (Cm7–B7–B♭9).

In m. 3:

The C♯m7 is an auxiliary chord to the Cm7:

EXAMPLE 33-5b Aux. = Auxiliary chord: Upper voices in this chord look like neighbor tones.

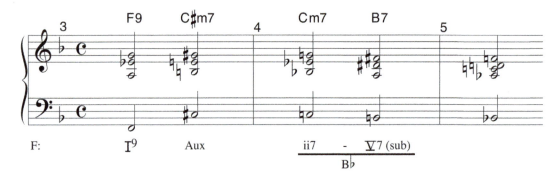

In mm. 6–8:

The D9 in m. 8 is preceded by Am7 (m. 7) to create another ii7–V group (Am7–D9), and the Am7 is tonicized by the E7+9 of m. 6.

m.6	m.7	m.8
E7+9	|Am^7	|Am^7/D D^9|
$\underline{\text{V}}^7$/iii	iii^7	
	ii^7	$\underline{\text{V}}^9$
	ii	

In m. 9:

The D♭9 is a tritone substitute for G7 (which is a stand-in for Gm7).

In m. 11 and 12:

The A7 tonicizes the D7 that tonicizes the G7 that tonicizes the C7 (a circle of fifths).

In m. 10:

An auxiliary B♭m7 precedes the A7 of m. 11.

Here's a rhythmic simplification of Example 33-5, with analysis illustrating the foregoing points.

EXAMPLE 33-6

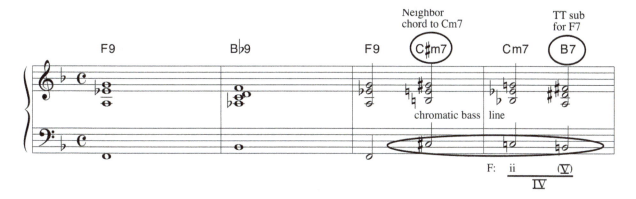

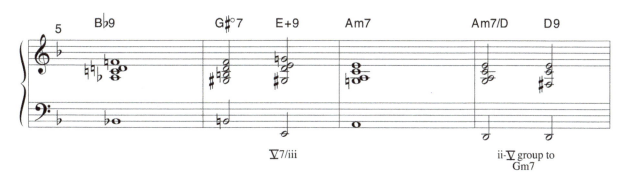

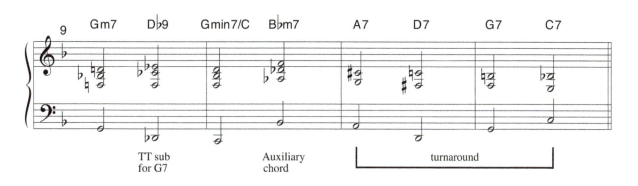

As you can see, the blues pattern tolerates endless tinkering, most of it involving tritone substitution and/or the addition of tonicizing chord groups. One thing leads to another, and you might wonder: At what point is the blues no longer the blues? The harmonic pilings that support the form are the prolonged I in mm. 1–4, the turn toward IV (or various substitutes) in m 5, the turn toward V (or various substitutes) in m. 9, and the return to I (or its substitutes) in m. 10—in other words, the structure shown in Example 10-1. The position of these goal chords defines the blues harmonically but do not alone constitute the blues, which is also defined by melodic and rhythmic features discussed in the next section of this chapter.

Minor-Key Blues

The minor-key blues appears to have a history as old as the major-key form. The principal difference lies in the tonic and subdominant harmonies, which are minor rather than major. Following are the goal chords:

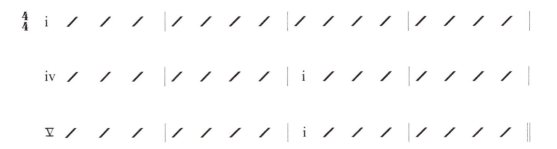

It also seems that the minor blues has been generally subject to less extensive harmonic elaboration. A fairly typical contemporary minor blues pattern follows.

EXAMPLE 33-7 Standard Minor Blues 🔊))

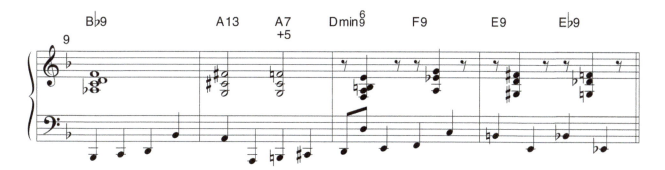

In m. 4:

A secondary dominant precedes the iv of m. 5 (D+9 = V+9/iv).

In m. 6:

An altered dominant (V^{7+5}) leads back to i.

In m. 9:

The B♭9 is a tritone substitute for a V^7/V (E7). Either of these chords leads logically to the (V^{13}) of m. 10.

In m. 8:

The F9 is a secondary dominant to the tritone substitute B♭9 of m. 9 (F9 = V^9/VI leading to VI in m. 9).

➤ *For assignments, turn to Workbook Chapter 33, assignments 1A–1D.*

BLUES MELODIC PRACTICE

Blues melodies are heavily laced with **blue notes**—pitches, most notably the third and seventh scale degrees, slightly flatter than their equal-tempered counterparts. These inflected pitches add a "bluesy" touch to any jazz or popular piece they happen to grace.

Blue Notes and Pentatonicism

The origin of blue notes is wrapped in the faded years of the nineteenth-century rural South, but theories exist. One attributes the pitch discrepancies to the differences between African untempered scales and the Western equal-tempered scale. Another possibility involves the **pentatonic** scale, which was a clear presence in nineteenth-century hymns and folk song. Sung over the primary triads in a major key, this scale might have resulted in out-of-tune notes that became the blue notes.

EXAMPLE 33-8

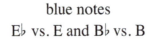

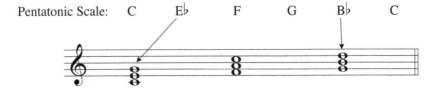

Notes:

1. E♭ sung over I and B♭ sung over V produce clashes that may have created the blue notes.

2. The blue notes, positioned atop the I7 and V⁷, produce the chords today symbolized as C7♯9 and G7♯9. The customary spelling of the ♯9 as a flatted third has much to do with the blue notes in these chords.

Blue Note Scales

One of the most common **blue note scales**, found in dozens of tunes and **riffs**, coincides with this pentatonic scale with one additional blue note—the raised fourth (flat fifth) degree:

    Pitch: C E♭ F F♯ (G♭) G B♭ C

Transposed to B♭, it appears in all but the final two measures of Horace Silver's "Cookin' at the Continental."

EXAMPLE 33-9 Horace Silver: "Cookin' at the Continental" (Scale: B♭ D♭ E♭ E F A♭ B♭) 🔊

Blue Note Scales in Minor Keys

The blue note scale works equally well for both major and minor blues. In major blues, such as Example 33-9, it represents a type of mode mixture. In minor, $\hat{2}$ loses some of its color, evaporating into the minor tonic, whereas $\hat{4}$ creates a poignant friction when it rubs against either the fifth of the tonic or the root of the subdominant.

EXAMPLE 33-10

blue notes
B♭ vs. B and G♭ (F♯) vs. F and G

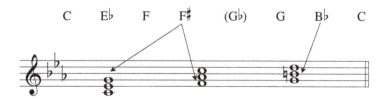

EXAMPLE 33-11 Lew Brown and Ray Henderson: "The Thrill is Gone" (This transcription is a melodic and rhythmic simplification based on multiple recordings of B.B. King performances.) (Scale: B D E F F♯ A B)

> *For assignments on blues melodic practice, turn to Workbook Chapter 33, assingments 2A–2D.*

Blues Variants

The blues has traditionally been a proving ground for jazz artists. Perhaps because of this and because of its elemental character, it has adapted to many passing styles. It can readily rock, and it waltzes well in either $\frac{3}{4}$ or $\frac{9}{8}$. In a choir robe, it can yank a congregation from the pews. It has been adapted by Miles Davis, Bill Evans, Denny Zeitlin, and others to fit the structure of the Church modes (beyond the scope of our study). In addition, the blues comes in other lengths. Most popular are the 16-bar blues and the 24-bar blues; the latter is usually a rapid-tempo version of the 12-bar blues, with each harmony doubled in length.

Example 33-12 is a 16-bar minor blues with a purely pentatonic melody over a rock beat. It's a piece steeped in the past. Like the earliest blues, it contains only three chords. However, VI has been substituted for iv in the second phrase, and a harmony of stacked fourths (symbolized as Dm7) stands in for V.

EXAMPLE 33-12 Herbie Hancock: "Canteloupe Island" (transcribed from *Empyrean Isles: Herbie Hancock,* BLP 4175 Blue Note Records, Inc.)

The accompanimental pattern has roots in early blues guitar, where the primary triads were elaborated through a stepwise rocking motion from the fifth of each chord to the seventh and back:

EXAMPLE 33-13 *Hancock,* BLP 4175 Blue Note Records, Inc.

This pattern became important in the boogie-woogie piano style, and it shows up repeatedly in blues arrangements, where it is sometimes referred to as a "Greek shuffle."

EXAMPLE 33-14 Jerry Leiber and Mike Stoller: "Kansas City" 🔊))

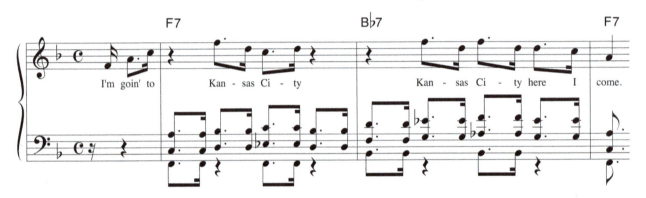

⊕ CODA

This chapter stops far short of describing all the variants of the blues that have been written or recorded. No form has been as influential in the history of jazz. Many of the harmonic techniques discussed in Chapters 28 and 29 have been employed by composers and jazz players to wrap the blues, in all its formats (12-bar, 16-bar, 24-bar), in ever-new packaging. The blues train has been chugging on for over a century now, picking up harmonic freight all along the way. It's doubtful that it will stop anytime soon.

DO YOU KNOW THESE TERMS?

- 12-bar blues
- blue note scales
- blue notes
- blues
- riff
- walking bass

CHAPTER THIRTY-FOUR

Shaping a Song

KEY CONCEPTS IN THIS CHAPTER

- Text Setting/ Declamation

- Melody/Non-Harmonic Tones

- Harmonic Accompaniment

- Verse/Chorus/Bridge

PERSPECTIVE

Song and Dance

Did early man sing first or dance first? Only early man knows, and "he's" not talking. However, it seems safe to assume that all music is either song- or dance-derived. Song is common to all cultures, and the compositional concerns that govern its writing have changed little over the years. We'll examine those concerns in the context of modern-day popular music and then apply the principles to the composition of a song.

When setting out to write a song, what element should you consider first: melody, lyrics, or accompaniment? The answer is, whatever inspires you—it doesn't matter. However, it's important to understand how the individual elements of a song—melody, lyrics, rhythms of the lyrics, and harmonic accompaniment—interact.

LYRICS

The unique challenge of song writing involves the words, known as the **text** or **lyrics**. In popular song, the lyrics are either created by the composer of the music or by a collaborator called a "lyricist." Lyrics can be composed for existing music, music can be composed for existing lyrics, or music and lyrics can be composed concurrently. Lyrics more often precede the music or are created concurrently and indeed usually determine many aspects of the music.

When a composer fashions a melody to suit the lyrics, the process is called **text setting**, and when a singer performs the music, her delivery is referred to as her **declamation**. Among concerns are form, the rhythm of the words, and musical ways of reflecting or enhancing their meaning.

Words and Rhythm

Setting a text to rhythms that go against the natural flow of the lyrics can cause a song to sound awkward and detract from a good melody with well-written harmonies. A good practice, therefore, is to recite the lyrics several times in a speaking voice and then mark the syllables you've stressed or elongated and note your natural cadences. This is called **scansion**.

This has been done for the first two lines of text from the song, "Looking for Cool" (the Bridge and Chorus)"

> I tried to **act** as **cool can**, but **I** couldn't **get** it,
> I tried to **show** her **I'm** a **man**, but **she** wouldn't **let** it!
> And I wasn't cool! You're not cool and you know it!
> Looking for Cool!

When you speak a text aloud, consider where you might place pick-up notes, down beats, syncopations, and so forth. You might hear "I tried to . . ." as pick-ups, and the words "act" and "show" having the emphasis of downbeats. ". . . act as cool can," and "show her I'm a man," might suggest a mild syncopation.

Listen to the melody, rhythm, and harmony of this song in Example 34-1. Would you have used some differing rhythms, or stressed different words? There are no absolutely right or wrong ways. However, notice that the accentuation in the two first lines is parallel, enabling a second phrase that is rhythmically similar to the first. Setting rhythmically similar text phrases to similar rhythms enhances a song's cohesiveness.

EXAMPLE 34-1 Daniel McCarthy: "Looking for Cool" (Funk)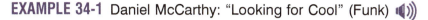

I tried to act as co-ol can___ but I di-dn't get it,   I tried to

show her I'm a man___ but she wou-ldn't let it!   and I was-sn't cool!___

and you're-not cool__ and you know it!

loo-king for cool

a - roo!_____ so cool!___

loo-king for cool_____ a - roo!_____ so cool!___

REVIEW AND REINFORCEMENT

Name the cadences that occur in mm. 19–21 and mm. 27–29.

Natural sounding text setting generally entails granting less emphasis to less important words—articles such as "the," prepositions such as "of," or conjunctions such as "and," placing accented syllables and more significant words in stronger metric positions or on higher pitches, placing musical cadences at the ends of grammatical units such as phrases and clauses, and so on.

> **CONCEPT CHECK**
>
> Here's a lyric. Use the symbol ´ to indicate accented words and syllables. It'll help if you recite the lines.
>
> "Maybe I should have saved those leftover dreams,
> Funny, but here's that rainy day; . . ."
>
> Example 34-2a shows these lines set to a melody. How closely does the melody match your accentuation?

EXAMPLE 34-2a Jimmy Van Heusen and Johnny Burke: "Here's That Rainy Day"

Notes:

1. The two text phrases (punctuated by a comma and a semicolon) end with melodic cadences.

2. The words "maybe," "leftover," "funny," and "rainy," are positioned metrically so that the accented syllable is on a stronger beat than the unaccented.

3. Both "maybe" and "funny" are set with a half note on their second syllable, seeming to invite a reflective pause.

4. The quarter notes in m. 2 and m. 6 closely parallel the even rhythm of the lyrics as they normally would be spoken.

Words and Meter

QUESTION: What is rhythmically different about these two sets of lyrics?

a. "This old man, he played one; he played knick-knack on my thumb . . ."

b. "The days of wine and roses laugh and run away like a child at play . . ."

ANSWER: Lyric a is clearly metric, easily recitable in four measures of 4/4 time. (Try it.) Lyric b gives no hint of meter.

Nevertheless: A non-metric lyric can be set in a metric way by skillful and sensitive manipulation of the text's natural rhythm. Example 34-2b shows how Henry Mancini did this.

EXAMPLE 34-2b Henry Mancini: "The Days of Wine and Roses"

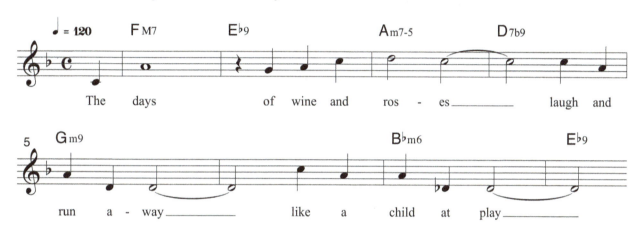

Mancini squeezed this lyric into two 4-measure phrases by: 1) greatly lengthening two words ("days" and "roses"); 2) setting two 5-syllable phrases ("laugh and run away") and ("like a child at play") in musically parallel fashion; and 3) by creating pauses of the requisite duration at the phrase endings.

MELODY AND HARMONY

Motive and Sequence

Often a motive becomes the springboard from which an entire melody can be launched. This is true of Example 34-3 (notwithstanding the sentiment expressed by the lyrics), where the arpeggiation of a seventh chord (bracketed) begins every phrase unit in the first part of the verse.

EXAMPLE 34-3 Billy Joel: "The Longest Time"

If you said good-bye to me to-night, There would still be mu-sic left to write.

What else could I do? I'm so in-spi-red by you That has-n't hap-pened for the long-est time.

As in earlier times, sequence is a powerful way to develop a song. Lines of text that are obviously parallel lend themselves well to sequential treatment. Consider this lyric:

> "A multi-colored tapestry
> Sunlight on a restless sea
> A portrait than can never be
> You and me."

The three rhyming lines of equal length beg for a sequential treatment, such as this:

EXAMPLE 34-4 Ralph Turek: "You and Me"

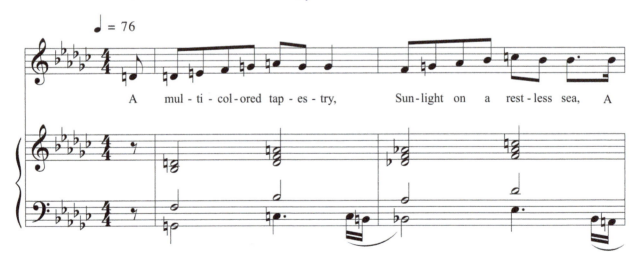

A mul-ti-col-ored tap-es-try, Sun-light on a rest-less sea, A

Some of the most successful melodies in the popular genre involve repetition or modified repetition of phrases. The melody in Example 34-5 avoids any sense of repetition, and partly because of this, it is distinctly unmemorable. Can you name other features of this melody that may make it so?

EXAMPLE 34-5

Notes:

1. There are too many differing rhythms—no motivic patterns are established.
2. There are too many leaps of various intervals.
3. No key is established.
4. It implies no discernible harmonic structure. Harmonization would be difficult at best.

Extracting a Melody from a Harmonic Pattern

There are two ways to write melodies: 1) write the melody first and fashion the harmonic accompaniment to fit it; 2) write chord progressions and extract melodic lines from the harmonies. Example 34-6 illustrates the latter process.

The song is in C major beginning with two phrases of a three-phrase period, the first ascending scale-wise from G3-to-G4, the second descending to A3. This melody was fashioned out of an unusual chord succession beginning on IV, followed by two diatonic submediant chords (vi and iii), and ending with a borrowed subtonic ($\flat$VII). Note that several of the initial notes at each chord change are chord sevenths:

EXAMPLE 34-6 Daniel McCarthy: "One Fine Day" (Ballad) 🔊

Just when my fear reached an ex - treme_____ God took me to a place of dreams!

For a very brief melodic idea, the harmonic support might comprise no more than two chords. Regardless, the melodic idea should imply those chords clearly. In Example 34-7 partial arpeggiations are embellished by lower neighbors.

EXAMPLE 34-7

For a very brief melodic idea...

CONCEPT CHECK

See how many variations of this melodic idea you can compose. You might change its pitch level, its contour, its rhythm, or a combination of these. Begin with modest changes, gradually moving farther from the original idea, but be sure that each variation still implies the given harmonies clearly.

Example 34-7 might be continued to produce the modulating period shown or it might continue in many other ways:

EXAMPLE 34-8

Notes:

1. The harmonies are based on a circular-fifth model, first in C, then in the chromatically third-related key of A.

2. The phrases are not very complicated. Complexity is not required for a melody to be effective. Nor need it be avoided.

The motive of Example 34-7 was borrowed from a song by Michel Legrand, written for the 1971 movie *Brian's Song*, concerning the untimely death of Chicago Bears running back, Brian Piccolo.

EXAMPLE 34-9 Michel Legrand: "The Hands of Time" (Theme from *Brian's Song)*

Notes:

1. The initial motive at a is repeated with an octave shift of its ending at b. (Notice how that simple octave shift of one note changes the effect of the four measures.)

2. At c and d, the first half of the motive is repeated in sequence, a third lower at each repetition.

3. The half cadence in mm. 7 and 8 enhances the flow by paving the way for the next phrase.

4. The song has its harmonic basis in the stepwise descending bass line discussed in Chapter 5 (see Example 5-17 on page 74).

1   Add Roman numeral analysis to Example 34-9.

2   Adapt one of the variations you created for Example 34-7 to one of the harmonic patterns previously used on p. 72 or one of your own to create a two-phrase group or two-phrase period.

HARMONIC MODELS, FORMS, AND STYLES

We'll now study the integration of harmonic models, form and style in several songs.

> *Harmony: Diatonic Mediants*
> *Form: Verse*
> *Style: Rhythm and Blues Ballad*

The most common chord progressions in popular songs involve the use of the tonic, subdominant, and the dominant. "Long Ago" (Example 34-10) avoids this pattern. The 4-phrase verse is built on a recurring succession of three descending mediants. A verse is a recurring section of music, usually at the beginning of a song, which is repeated with different lyrics at each repetition.

EXAMPLE 34-10 Daniel McCarthy: "Long Ago" (Verse) 🔊

When I looked at her   I ne ver knew that she'd e-ver lie   I thought I fi-na-ly found a love____that

ne-ver could di-e____   and tru-sting her__ came ea - si - ly, - but then came a   day,   when

she got mad   and turned a - round   and just walked a-wa-y____

REVIEW AND REINFORCEMENT

What is harmonically unusual about the end of the verse? Would you term this a period?

Harmony: Mode Mixture/Secondary Function
Form: Bridge
Style: Rhythm and Blues Ballad

A device that can add harmonic color to your song is mode mixture (modal borrowing). The bridge to "Long Ago" (Example 34-11) is supported by a borrowed subdominant. Recall from our study of the fugue that a bridge is connective music. In popular song it is often heard only once or twice, in the middle or near the end. Harmonically, it often features the harmonies that are the most distant from tonic. The following bridge is a three-phrase period:

2 (a) + 2 (b) + 2 (c):

EXAMPLE 34-11 Daniel McCarthy: "Long Ago" (Bridge) 🔊

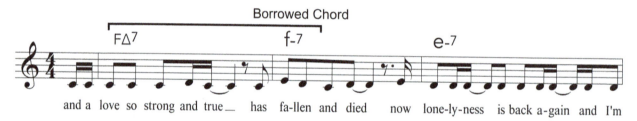

Harmony: Modality (Dorian) and Ostinato
Form: Chorus
Style: Funk

The use of the "Church Modes" (Dorian and Phrygian are most common) in ostinato patterns has proven to be a solid "canvas" for vocal melodies. In the chorus of the funk tune, "Humpti Dumpti," a "snap and pop" bass provides an ostinato that supports E Dorian harmonies. A chorus is a section of a song that follows the verse and repeats each time to the same lyrics.

EXAMPLE 34-12 Daniel McCarthy: "Humpti Dumpti" (Chorus)

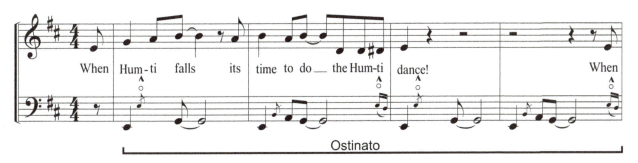

Harmony: Chromatic Mediant/Dorian Mode
Form: Bridge
Style: Funk

Perhaps less common is the use of the chromatic mediant. In the "Bridge" from "Humpti Dumpti" (Example 34-13) the chord "changes" begin on the subdominant and move to a minor chord on the raised sixth degree. This chromatic mediant relationship (a minor to c-sharp minor) is diatonic in E Dorian.

EXAMPLE 34-13 Daniel McCarthy: "Humpti Dumpti" (Bridge)

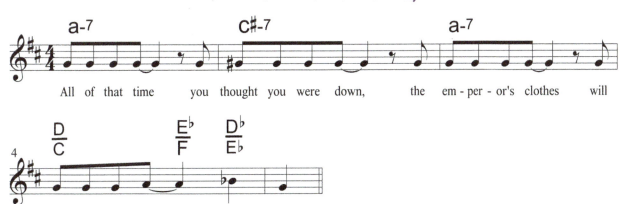

"Rock" is arguably the most enduring pop style. Its harmonic resources have changed over the years, but one thing hasn't—its rhythmic drive. Guitar-based rather than keyboard and synth-based (as in Funk and R&B), its harmonic basis has deep roots in the blues. This can be heard in the music of its early performers such as Elvis Presley, The Beatles, The Rolling Stones, and Led Zeppelin.

In Example 34-14, the verse is sung with only drums as accompaniment. The voice alternates with a unison riff—a single-line motive played by the entire band in a manner that might be likened to the ritornello in a Baroque Concerto Grosso.

In the verse, the alternating unison riff and unaccompanied vocal is a three-phrase period (a–a'–b) in E Dorian.

EXAMPLE 34-14 Dave McCarthy: "Close Your Eyes" (Verse)

SONG WRITING THEN AND NOW

Example 34-15 compares a contemporary popular song with a jazz standard from 1967. Beyond substantial harmonic and melodic differences, the pieces reflect changes in song writing methods that have occurred over time. Today, lyrics and music are often worked out by a single performing artist, using the ear rather than a music pen or notation software. The notated form of the song often comes into being after the fact by way of transcription from a recording, possibly by a second party. In earlier times, a lyricist and composer worked in tandem to create and fully notate a song prior to its recording by a third party.

EXAMPLE 34-15a Alan and Marilyn Bergman and Michel Legrand: "You Must Believe in Spring"

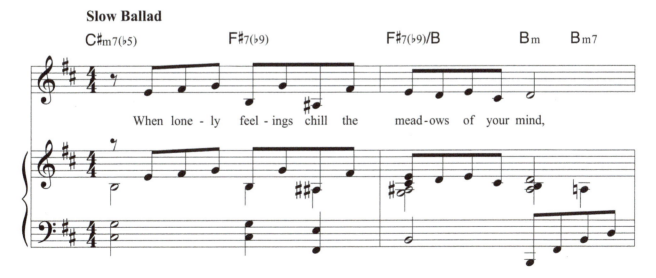

continued

EXAMPLE 34-15a *continued*

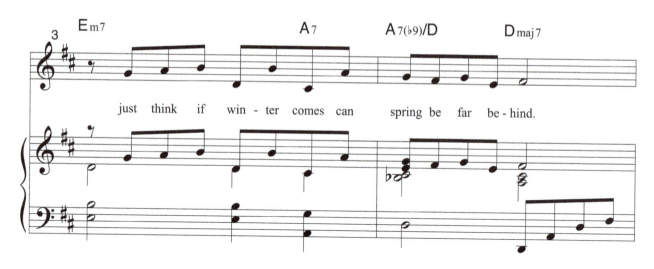

Notes:

1. All two-syllable words are placed rhythmically so that the accented syllable falls on the downbeat, reflecting the normal accentuation of the spoken phrases.

2. Both phrases are punctuated by an elongated note and an authentic cadence.

3. The melody is sequential, reflecting the parallel nature of the text phrases, and the harmonic structure is traditional, based on the circle of fifths.

EXAMPLE 34-15b Adele Adkins: "Someone Like You"

Notes:

1. The melody approximates the probable rhythm of a spoken delivery. Recite these phrases: "I heard . . .," "settled down . . .," "found a girl . . .," "married now . . ." Does the cadence of your speech not correspond to the musical rhythms?

2. The pitch structure of the melody is less complex than Example 34-15a (it's simply a five-note descending motive repeated four times), but the rhythmic structure is more complex.

3. The apparent rhythmic complexity of the melody is probably due to the transcriber's efforts to reproduce the singer's precise rhythmic nuances. Such nuances do not appear in published songs where the notated music precedes the performed version.

➤ *For assignments on text and melody, turn to Workbook p. 431.*

⊕ CODA

Songs vary widely in harmonic and melodic sophistication. This in itself has little to do with quality, since beauty can reside in both simplicity and complexity. More important is a tune that "connects" and strikes a balance between unity and variety, and a plan (whether it be harmonic, melodic, rhythmic or something else) that provides enough variety to sustain interest.

DO YOU KNOW THESE TERMS?

- bridge
- chorus
- declamation
- lyrics
- riff
- syllabic
- text
- text setting
- verse

APPENDIX A

Pitch

PITCH AND ITS NOTATION

Question: Why does a hummingbird hum? Answer: It doesn't. That "humming" is caused by its wings, which flap up to 70 times a second. Anything that moves back and forth that rapidly—in fact, anything that oscillates more than 16 times per second—produces a pitch.

Pitch is how high or low a tone sounds, and it's the ear's response to frequency—rate of vibration. The higher the frequency of flapping wings, vibrating strings, or other things, the higher we perceive the pitch to be.

The Staff and its Clefs

Until the advent of recording, only two ways of preserving music existed—word-of-mouth (oral tradition) and music notation (written tradition). The latter is central to the training of musicians. Pitches are notated on a five-line **staff** using one of four **clefs**: treble, bass, alto, or tenor. Example A1-1 shows middle C—the C closest to the middle of the piano keyboard—in each clef.

EXAMPLE A1-1

Treble clef

Alto clef

continued

EXAMPLE A1-1 *continued*

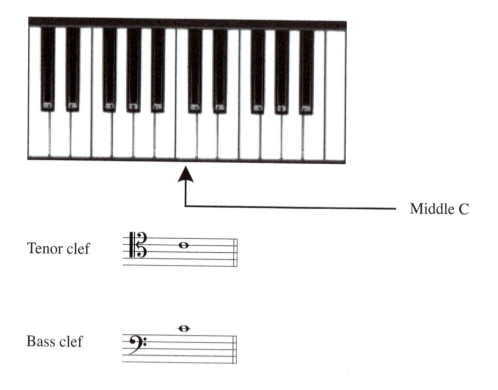

Tenor clef

Bass clef

Ledger Lines

Because a five-line staff cannot conveniently accommodate all the pitches playable by most instruments, we extend the staff through **ledger lines**—short horizontal lines drawn through the stems and heads of notes too high or low to be located directly on the staff.

EXAMPLE A1-2

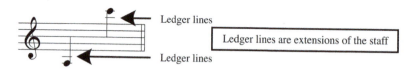

Ledger lines

Ledger lines are extensions of the staff

Ledger lines

Octave Designation

Pitches of the same letter name but in different registers are said to be in different **octaves**. If we count up eight white keys from middle C—counting middle C as one—we again reach the note C, but an octave higher. The most common way of distinguishing pitches in various octaves is shown in Example A1-3, starting with the lowest C on the piano keyboard. All pitches between C1 and C2 are given the numeric suffix "1," all pitches between C2 and C3 the numeric suffix "2" and so on.

EXAMPLE A1-3

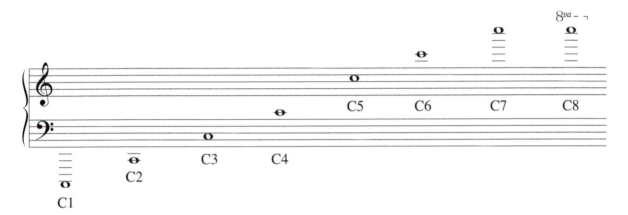

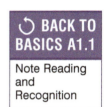

In Example A1-3, the mark above the C8 is an **ottava sign**. It is a way to show this pitch without using an unreadable number of ledger lines. The abbreviation, 8va, above a note directs that the note be played an octave higher. Likewise, the symbol 8va bassa beneath a note or passage directs that it be played an octave lower. The term *loco* cancels either instruction.

↻ **BACK TO BASICS A1.1**

Note Reading and Recognition

EXAMPLE A1-4

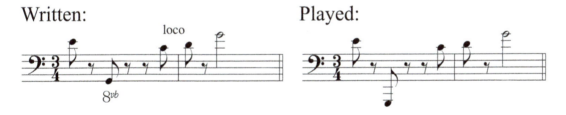

Another way to avoid excessive ledger lines is to use a different clef. Alto clef is used chiefly for viola parts. Tenor clef is used on occasion for the cello, bassoon, and trombone. These are instruments that sometimes play in a register that would require the constant use of ledger lines in either treble or bass clef.

EXAMPLE A1-5a Melody notated in treble clef requires many ledger lines *below* the staff

EXAMPLE A1-5b Same melody notated in bass clef requires many ledger lines *above* the staff

EXAMPLE A1-5c Same melody notated in alto clef requires fewer ledger lines

CONCEPT CHECK

Re-notate the melody of Example A1-5 in tenor clef.

THE HALF STEP AND WHOLE STEP

↻ **BACK TO BASICS A1.2**

Note Identification

The interval—that is, the difference in pitch—between any white key on the piano and an adjacent black key is a **half step**, the smallest interval normally used in Western music. However, there is no black key between E and F, nor between B and C. These are the only two half steps that occur between white keys. Between any two other adjacent white keys the interval is a **whole step**, which is equal to two half steps.

EXAMPLE A1-6

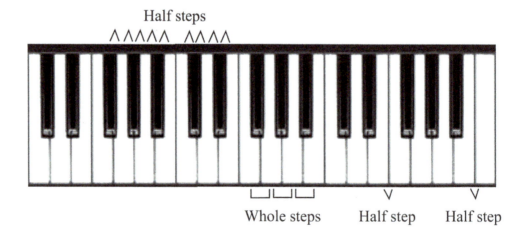

Flats and Sharps

The black keys share the letter names of the white keys immediately above or below them. However, a symbol is added to indicate that its pitch is to be higher or lower than that of the white key. This is called chromatic alteration and the symbols used are the following:

flat	♭	A symbol that indicates a pitch is to be lowered by a half step.
sharp	♯	A symbol that indicates a pitch is to be raised by a half step.
double flat	♭♭	A symbol that indicates a pitch is to be lowered by two half steps.
double sharp	×	A symbol that indicates a pitch is to be raised by two half steps.
natural	♮	A symbol that cancels the effect of a preceding chromatic alteration and restores the original, unaltered pitch.

Note:

A flat or a sharp can be used to cancel the effect of a preceding double flat or double sharp, restoring the note to its single flatted or sharped pitch. Normally, you will see this accomplished by ♮♭ or ♮♯.

Enharmonics

The black keys of the piano can be designated using either flats or sharps. Different spellings of the same sounding pitch are called **enharmonic equivalents**.

EXAMPLE A1-7

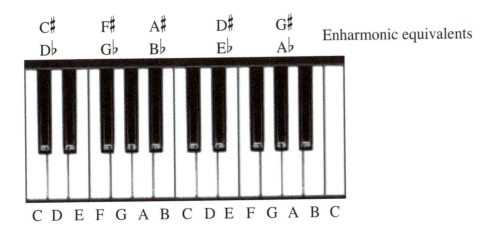

Enharmonic equivalents

CONCEPT CHECK

Notate the following pitches enharmonically:

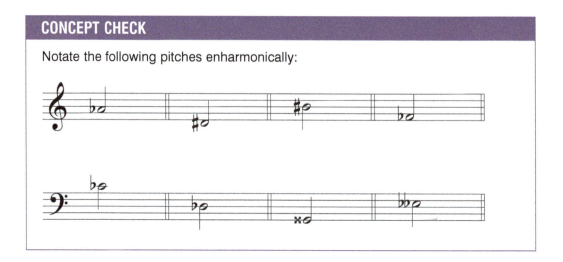

↻ BACK TO
BASICS A1.3

Enharmonic
Pitch
Recognition

Using enharmonic equivalents, the interval between a white key and an adjacent black key can be spelled enharmonically two ways, i.e., G–G♯ or G–A♭. When the same letter name is used (G–G♯), the interval is called a **chromatic half step**. When adjacent letter names are used, the interval is called a **diatonic half step**.

CONCEPT CHECK

Identify the half steps as diatonic or chromatic. Then notate the diatonic half steps as chromatic half steps and vice versa.

EXAMPLE A1-8

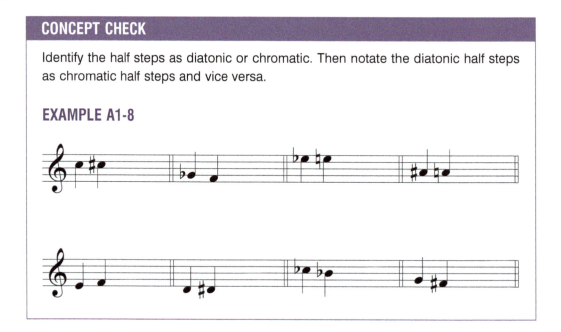

Flats, sharps, naturals, and so on appearing before a pitch to indicate its temporary chromatic alteration are called accidentals. By tradition, an accidental affects all recurrences of the pitch prior to the occurrence of a bar line—a vertical line extending from the top to the bottom of the staff. However, it does not affect that pitch in any other octave.

EXAMPLE A1-9

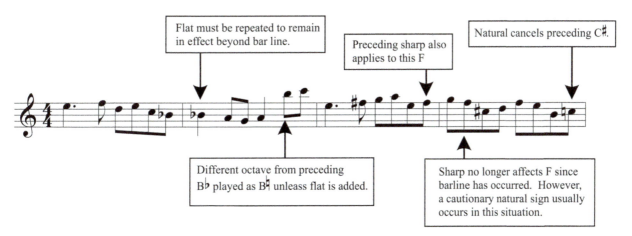

Flat must be repeated to remain in effect beyond bar line.

Preceding sharp also applies to this F

Natural cancels preceding C♯.

Different octave from preceding B♭ played as B♮ unless flat is added.

Sharp no longer affects F since barline has occurred. However, a cautionary natural sign usually occurs in this situation.

In general, when a pitch is preceded by a sharp, the next pitch will be higher, and when a pitch is preceded by a flat, the next pitch will be lower, as shown in Example A1-8.

Intervals are discussed in greater detail in Chapter 2: Intervals.

➤ *For assignments on pitch and its notation, turn to Workbook p. 435.*

↺ **BACK TO BASICS A1.4**

Diatonic and Chromatic Half Steps

SCALES AND KEYS

A scale is the arrangement, in ascending or descending order, of the pitch material upon which a composition is based. All 12 pitches of the octave so arranged constitute a **chromatic scale**.

EXAMPLE A1-10 Sharps Used Ascending; Flats Used Descending

The Major Scale

A **major scale** can be played between any two Cs, using only the white keys.

EXAMPLE A1-11

It is the succession of half steps (h) and whole steps (w)—w–w–h–w–w–w–h—not the pitches per se, that defines the scale. It is possible (if not historically precise) to see this succession as two intervallically identical four-note segments, called **tetrachords**, separated by a whole step:

	Lower tetrachord					Upper tetrachord			
w		w		h	**W**	w		w	h

Lower tetrachord   Upper tetrachord

w   w   h   **W**   w   w   h

Whole step (**W**) separates two identical tetrachords

When we attempt to construct a major scale starting on G, the fifth degree of C major—again using only white keys—the interval succession changes, and the scale is no longer a major scale. To correct the interval pattern, the seventh degree must be raised.

EXAMPLE A1-12

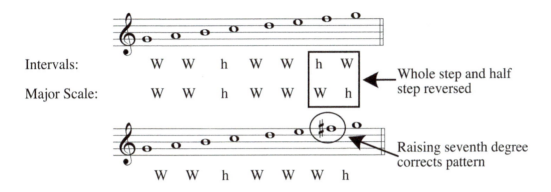

Intervals: W   W   h   W   W   h   W   Whole step and half
                                            step reversed

Major Scale: W   W   h   W   W   W   h   ← Whole step and half
                                            step reversed

                                            Raising seventh degree
                                            corrects pattern

W   W   h   W   W   W   h

If we then try to construct a new major scale beginning on the fourth degree of the C major scale—F—a different alteration is required, this time to preserve the interval pattern of the lower tetrachord. A flat must be added to the fourth degree.

EXAMPLE A1-13

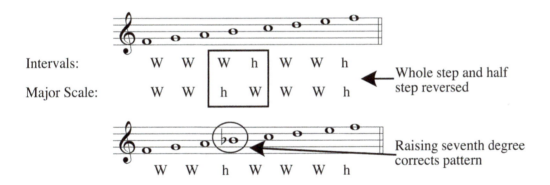

Intervals: W   W   W   h   W   W   h   Whole step and half
                                            step reversed

Major Scale: W   W   h   W   W   W   h   ← Whole step and half
                                            step reversed

                                            Raising seventh degree
                                            corrects pattern

W   W   h   W   W   W   h

Rewriting a scale at a different pitch level is called **transposition.** Continuing to transpose the major scale by beginning on the fifth degree of each new scale necessitates raising the seventh degree each time in order to preserve the interval succession in the upper tetrachord.

EXAMPLE A1-14

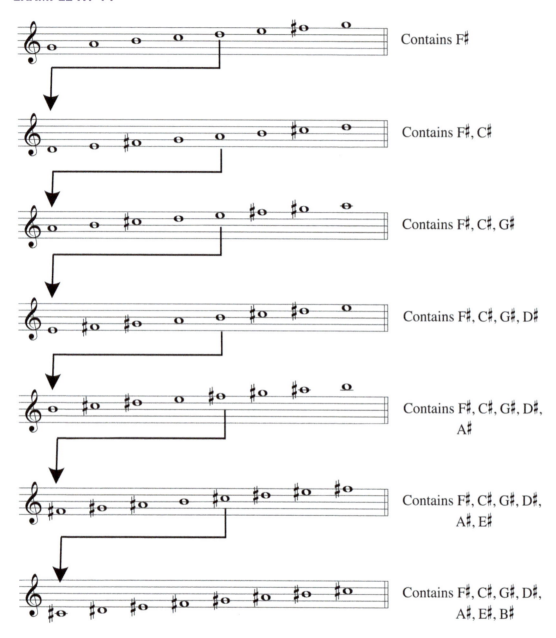

Contains F#

Contains F#, C#

Contains F#, C#, G#

Contains F#, C#, G#, D#

Contains F#, C#, G#, D#, A#

Contains F#, C#, G#, D#, A#, E#

Contains F#, C#, G#, D#, A#, E#, B#

If we continue to transpose the major scale by starting on the fourth degree of each new scale, a flat must be added to the fourth degree each time.

EXAMPLE A1-15

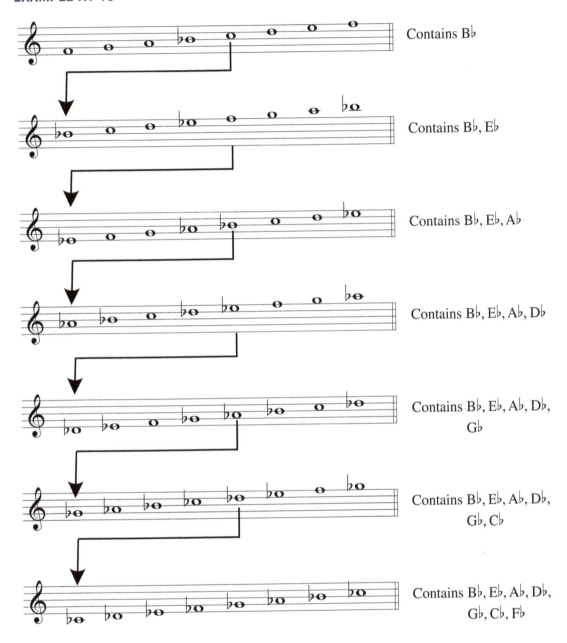

Contains B♭

Contains B♭, E♭

Contains B♭, E♭, A♭

Contains B♭, E♭, A♭, D♭

Contains B♭, E♭, A♭, D♭, G♭

Contains B♭, E♭, A♭, D♭, G♭, C♭

Contains B♭, E♭, A♭, D♭, G♭, C♭, F♭

The first note of a major scale is called the **tonic**. It is the pitch of greatest stability and the end-point of most compositions that have that scale as their basis.

⟳ **BACK TO BASICS A1.5**

Major Scale Spelling and Recognition

Key Signatures

The sharps or flats of the scale on which a piece is based, placed at the beginning of each staff, is called a **key signature**. There is a precise order and manner of placement for the sharps and flats of a key signature.

EXAMPLE A1-16a Sharps

Note:

Axis slants downward to right for all clefs but tenor.

EXAMPLE A1-16b Flats

Note:

Axis slants upward to right for all clefs.

The names of the major scales and their key signatures are arranged in a "circle of fifths" below.

EXAMPLE A1-17

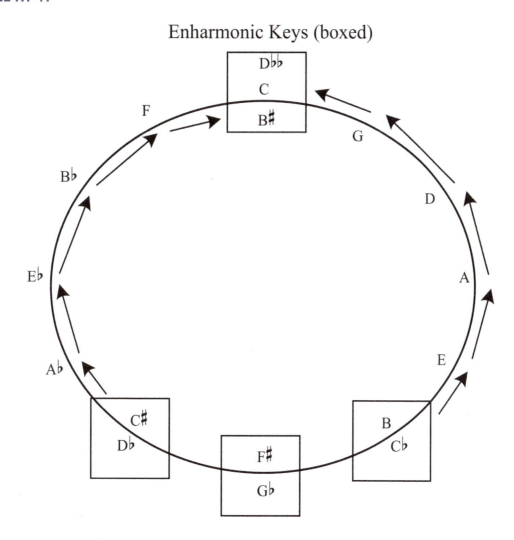

Enharmonic Keys (boxed)

Notice that moving in both directions around the circle brings us to the same scale, spelled enharmonically two different ways. The arrows show that continuing to add sharps or flats leads back to the original pitch or key, spelled enharmonically. Keys directly across the circle from each other (i.e., in the one o'clock and seven o'clock positions) are in the most remote possible relationship, sharing only one common tone. On the other hand, keys adjacent to each other are in the closest possible relationship, containing six common tones.

↻ BACK TO
BASICS A1.6

Major-Key
Signatures

Relative Major and Minor

Every major scale has a relative minor—that is, a scale that shares the same key signature. To find a major scale's relative, count upward to the sixth degree. This is the tonic of the relative minor.

EXAMPLE A1-18

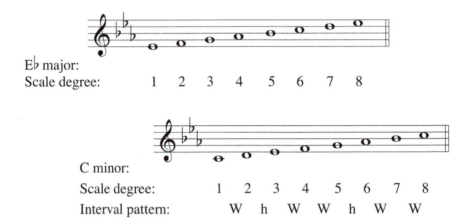

E♭ major:
Scale degree: 1   2   3   4   5   6   7   8

C minor:
Scale degree: 1   2   3   4   5   6   7   8
Interval pattern: W   h   W   W   h   W   W

Note:

The interval pattern of the minor scale differs from its relative major, but its pitch content is identical. Just as genetic factors define our relatives, it's identical pitch content that makes a major and minor scale relatives.

Example A1-19 lists the relative major and minor scales for keys up to seven sharps and flats.

EXAMPLE A1-19

Major key:	Relative minor key:	Key signature:
C	a	
G	e	1 sharp
D	b	2 sharps
A	f♯	3 sharps
E	c♯	4 sharps
B	g♯	5 sharps
F♯	d♯	6 sharps
C♯	a♯	7 sharps
C♭	a♭	7 flats
G♭	e♭	6 flats
D♭	b♭	5 flats
A♭	f	4 flats
E♭	c	3 flats
B♭	g	2 flats
F	d	1 flat

Enharmonic Equivalents

Minor Scale Forms

The form of the minor scale that uses the precise pitch content of its relative major is called the **natural minor scale**. The next example is from a well-known song that is constructed entirely upon the natural minor scale.

EXAMPLE A1-20 "God Rest Ye Merry Gentleman"

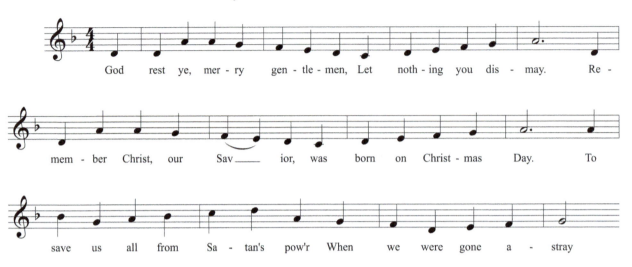

See Example 3-8 on p. 39 for another natural minor passage.

The natural minor form is seen in actual practice much less often than the following two altered forms. The **harmonic minor scale** contains a raised seventh degree.

EXAMPLE A1-21a D Harmonic Minor Scale

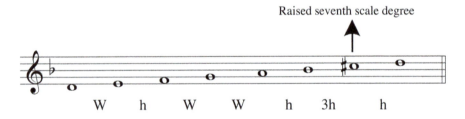

EXAMPLE A1-21b J. S. Bach: Fugue no. 2 from *The Well-Tempered Clavier*, (Book I)

C harmonic minor form

The harmonic minor form of the scale was favored for harmonic structures (hence the name). But the extra large interval (three half steps) between the sixth and seventh degrees was considered awkward to sing. The importance of vocal music led to a different form, the **melodic minor scale**, which was favored for melodic lines. In it, the sixth and seventh degrees are raised in ascending passages and returned to their natural minor state in descent.

EXAMPLE A1-22a D melodic minor scale

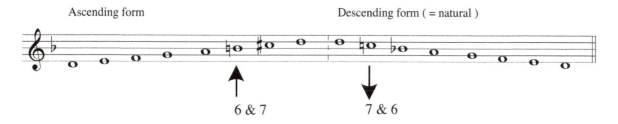

EXAMPLE A1-22b Haydn: "Hungarian Rondo"

G melodic minor form

Note:

The raising of the sixth and/or seventh degrees in a minor key requires the use of accidentals. In b, raising E♭ to E♮ in m. 70 eliminates the extra large interval E♭-F♯ of the harmonic minor form. The E♭ is preserved in m. 68 because it descends (to D on beat two).

In all three minor scale forms, the lower five notes (the lower pentachord) are identical. It is in their upper four notes (the upper tetrachord) that they differ, and the difference can be stated as a principle:

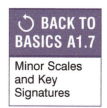

↻ **BACK TO BASICS A1.7**

Minor Scales and Key Signatures

The Melodic Minor Principle

1. $\hat{7}$ is usually raised when moving upward to the tonic ($\hat{8}$), and if $\hat{6}$ precedes, it too is raised.

2. $\hat{6}$ is usually lowered when moving downward to $\hat{5}$, and if $\hat{7}$ precedes, it too is lowered.

Note:

A caret (^) above a numeral will be used in this book to designate a scale degree.

CONCEPT CHECK

Apply the melodic minor principle to the following E minor passage:

EXAMPLE A1-23

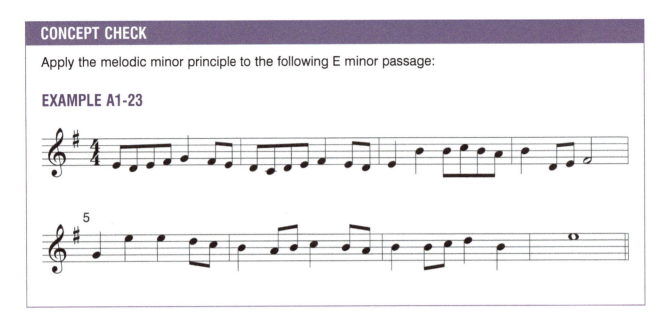

A minor scale that shares the same key signature as a major is termed its relative minor. When instead it shares the same tonic, it is called the **parallel minor**.

EXAMPLE A1-24

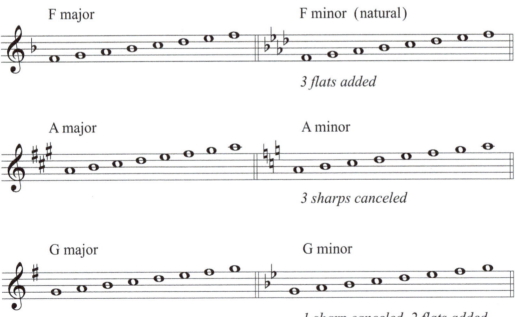

F major   F minor (natural)

3 flats added

A major   A minor

3 sharps canceled

G major   G minor

1 sharp canceled, 2 flats added

The single most important difference between a major scale and its parallel minor is $\hat{3}$, which is a half step lower in all forms of the minor scale. The parallel minor of a given major scale is always three keys removed—in the direction of more flats (or fewer sharps).

▶ *For assignments on scales and keys, turn to Workbook p. 440.*

DO YOU KNOW THESE TERMS?

- chromatic half step
- chromatic scale
- clef
- diatonic half step
- double flat
- double sharp
- enharmonic equivalent
- flat
- half step

- harmonic minor
- key signature
- ledger line
- major scale
- melodic minor principle
- natural
- octave
- ottava sign

- parallel minor
- pentachord
- relative minor
- sharp
- staff
- tetrachord
- transposition
- whole step

Rhythm

ELEMENTS OF THE PROPORTIONAL SYSTEM

Rhythm constitutes the durational aspects of music's sounds and silences, along with their accentual patterns. The symbols of rhythmic notation—notes and rests—are proportional, meaning their values are not fixed but are relative to one another.

Note	Rest	Name and relative duration
‖o‖	▪	***Breve***: found only occasionally; the longest value expressible by a single shape
𝅝	▬	***Whole note****:* the longest single note in general use; half the value of the breve, twice the value of the half note
𝅗𝅥	▬	***Half note***: half the value of the whole note, twice the value of the quarter note
𝅘𝅥	𝄽	***Quarter note****:* half the value of the half note, twice the value of the eighth note
𝅘𝅥𝅮	𝄾	* ***Eighth note***: half the value of the quarter note, twice the value of the sixteenth note
𝅘𝅥𝅯	𝄿	* ***Sixteenth note***: half the value of the eighth note, twice the value of the thirty-second note
𝅘𝅥𝅰	𝅀	* ***Thirty-second note***: half the value of the sixteenth note; the smallest value in common use

* When more than one of these note types appear in succession, the flags are often replaced by beams:

𝅘𝅥𝅮 𝅘𝅥𝅮   becomes   ♫   and   𝅘𝅥𝅯 𝅘𝅥𝅯 𝅘𝅥𝅯 𝅘𝅥𝅯   becomes   ♬♬

and so on.

Other durations are made possible through use of the following:

The tie: a curved line connecting adjacent notes of the same pitch, binding them into a single duration.

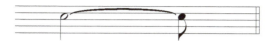

Notes:

1. Ties connect noteheads—not stems—but do not touch them. Traditionally, the longer value precedes the shorter value in any tied combination.

2. Rests are never tied.

The dot: The augmentation dot extends the duration of the note or rest it follows by half the value. A second dot adds half the value of the first dot.

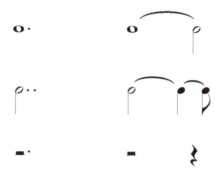

Most music moves along at a steady pace commonly measured by the beat—the durational value that sets toes tapping and fingers snapping. It's usually what the conductor indicates through arm motions. **Tempo** is the speed of the beat. Composers began to include tempo indications in their scores during the eighteenth century, when Italian was the most widely used language among musicians. Most common tempo expressions are thus Italian (such as Allegro for "fast").

Accent is the emphasis placed on certain notes. A tonal accent is the emphasis that occurs when a pitch is notably higher than the surrounding pitches. An agogic accent is stress by means of longer duration. A dynamic accent places emphasis on a note by playing it more forcefully than the surrounding notes.

Of these, the dynamic accent (represented by markings such as >, ^, and *sfz*) is no doubt the most familiar to you.

► *For drill and assignments on proportional notation, turn to Workbook p. 449.*

METER AND MEASURE

In Example A2-1, the tonal and agogic accents create a pattern of strong (S) and weak (w) beats (quarter note = beat).

EXAMPLE A2-1 Brahms: Wiegenlied, op. 49, No. 4, Tonal (T) and Agogic (A) accents

This regular pattern is called a metric pattern. Meter is the grouping together of two or more beats by means of accents. A measure constitutes one complete cycle of the metric pattern, beginning on an accented beat. The following are normal accentual patterns for measures containing two, three, or four beats:

1 2   1 2 3   1 2 3 4

Measures are separated from each other by bar lines.

EXAMPLE A2-2

As evident from Example A2-2, musical works need not commence with the first strong beat of a pattern. A weak-beat beginning is called an **anacrusis** (more informally, an up-beat, or pick-up).

In Example A2-2, the sign following the key signature is a **meter signature**. Its upper number tells how many of the note values expressed by the lower number are contained within a measure. The lower number indicates a note value that may or may not be the beat, depending on whether the meter is simple or compound.

Simple Meters

A meter signature with an upper number of 2, 3, or 4 is simple. In **simple meters**, the beat divides into two parts. The note value expressed by the lower number is the note value that receives the beat. The upper number indicates how many beats are contained within a measure.

2. Signifies two beats in a measure

4. Signifies that the quarter note = the beat

EXAMPLE A2-3a **2** Signifies two beats in a measure; **4** Signifies that the quarter note = the beat

Division of beat
into two parts

Meter Classification: Simple duple

3. Signifies three beats in a measure

8. Signifies that the eighth note = the beat

EXAMPLE A2-3b **3** Signifies three beats in a measure; **8** Signifies that the eighth note = the beat

Division of beat
into two parts

Meter Classification: Simple triple

4. Signifies four beats in a measure

2. Signifies that the half-note = the beat

EXAMPLE A2-3c **4** Signifies four beats in a measure; **2** Signifies that the half note = the beat

Division of beat
into two parts

Meter Classification: Simple quadruple

Compound Meters

Any meter signature with an upper number that is a multiple of three—for example, 6, 9, and 12—is **compound**. In **compound meters**, the beat divides into three parts. The note value expressed by the lower number is not the note value that receives the beat but rather the value representing the three-part division of the beat. Put another way, it takes three of this note value to equal one beat.

6. Signifies six eighth note equivalents in a measure

8. Signifies that the eighth note = one-third beat

EXAMPLE A2-4a **6** Signifies six eighth note equivalents in a measure; **8** Signifies that the eighth note = one-third beat

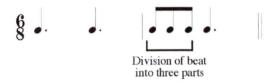

Division of beat
into three parts

Meter Classification: Compound duple

9   Signifies nine quarter note equivalents in a measure

4. Signifies that the quarter note = one-third beat

EXAMPLE A2-4b **9** Signifies nine quarter note equivalents in a measure; **4** Signifies that the quarter note = one-third beat

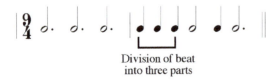

Division of beat
into three parts

Meter Classification: Compound triple

Note:

In compound meters, the note value that receives the beat will always be a dotted note, because only dotted values are equal to three of the next smaller value.

CONCEPT CHECK

Transcribe the $\frac{6}{8}$ pattern of Example A2-4 into $\frac{6}{4}$. Transcribe the $\frac{9}{4}$ pattern to $\frac{9}{8}$ and $\frac{9}{16}$.

Two metric symbols warrant mention at this point. This symbol

is often used to represent $\frac{4}{4}$, and this symbol

is used to represent $\frac{2}{2}$ (also called **alla breve**).

Rhythm and Meter in Conflict

Conflict between rhythm and meter creates musical interest. Three cases are:

Borrowed divisions: A note value that normally divides into two parts (simple) is divided into three parts (compound), and vice versa.

EXAMPLE A2-5a Three-part division of beat (quarter note) where two-part division is the norm

EXAMPLE A2-5b Four-part division of beat (dotted quarter note) where three-part division is the norm

EXAMPLE A2-5c Three-part division of half note where two-part division—into two quarter notes—is the norm

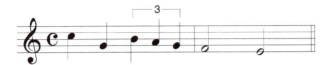

Notes:

1. An Arabic numeral is added to indicate the number of notes in the borrowed division.

2. When note values are not connected by a beam, a bracket can be used with the numeral for clarity.

3. The note value used for the borrowed division is that used for the normal division.

Syncopation: A normally unaccented part of a beat or measure is accented. A common means of accentuation is duration. In $\frac{4}{4}$ meter, the first and third beats are normally stronger than the second and fourth beats. Therefore, a longer duration on the second or fourth beat is a syncopation.

EXAMPLE A2-6

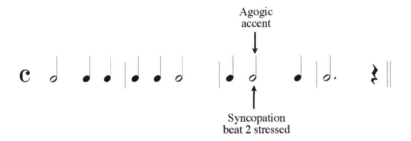

In $\frac{3}{4}$, the first beat is stronger than either the second or third. Therefore, longer durations on the second or third beat produce syncopation.

Syncopation can also occur within a beat. Since the first part of any beat (the downbeat) is stronger than any other part, a longer duration that begins anywhere but the downbeat can create syncopation.

EXAMPLE A2-7

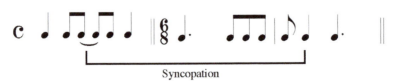

A particular type of syncopation, called **hemiola,** involves the rhythmic ratio 3:2. It most often occurs when three equal-value notes are played in the time of two equal-value notes.

EXAMPLE A2-8

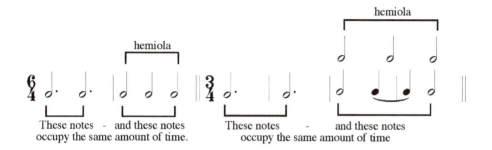

In Example A2-9, syncopation is created on the third beat of m. 1 and m. 4. This is a result of the hemiola between the bass line, which steadfastly maintains a feeling of $\frac{3}{4}$, and the melody, which alternately sounds like $\frac{3}{2}$ (mm. 1–2 = ♩♩♩) and $\frac{3}{4}$ (m. 3 = ♩♩♩). Note the juxtaposition of *two three-beat groupings* in the bass and *three two-beat groupings* in the melody.

EXAMPLE A2-9 Mozart: Symphony no. 40, K. 550 (third movement)

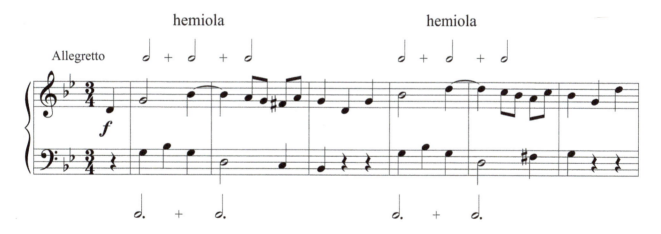

▶ *For drill and assignments on meter and measure, turn to Workbook p. 451.*

NOTATING RHYTHM

Modern music publishers adhere to fairly uniform practices regarding the notation of rhythm. The guiding principle is: Be as concise as possible while clearly reflecting the meter. This is achieved through the proper use of dots, ties, beams, and rests.

1. Dots and ties

   a. A dot may follow any type of note, as long as it does not create a value too long for the measure and it does not obscure the beat for too long a period. Otherwise, the dotted value should be replaced by a tied value.

EXAMPLE A2-10

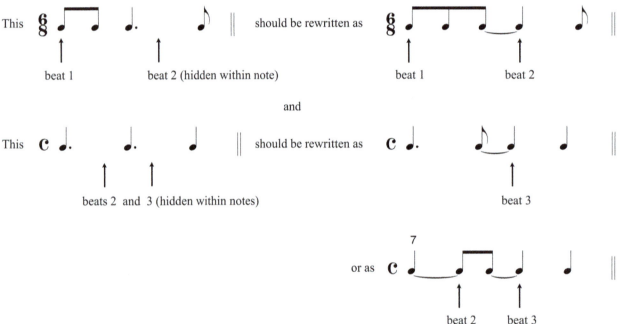

EXAMPLE A2-11 Double-dotted values are rare in actual practice

In compound meters, double-dotted notes are not used.

2. Beams

    a. Beams should not cause confusion about where the beats occur in the measure.

EXAMPLE A2-12

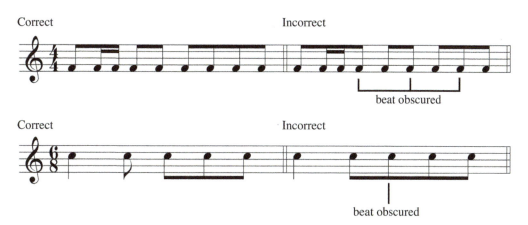

    b. In 4/4, beams usually do not span the second and third beats.

EXAMPLE A2-13

    c. All notes within a beat that can be beamed should be beamed.

EXAMPLE A2-14

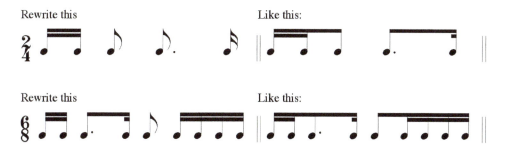

General Guideline: *Except where a commonly used single note value is available, it is always acceptable to notate your music so that an imaginary bar line could be placed just before each and every beat.*

3. Rests

    a. Rests are never tied.

    b. As with note values, rests should not cause confusion about where the beat is.

EXAMPLE A2-15

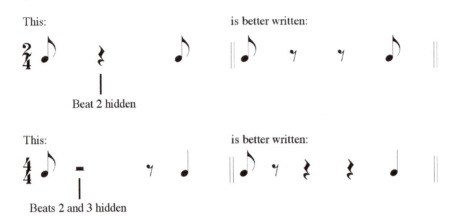

c. In simple meters, two rest values are preferred to dotted rests, except for values smaller than a quarter rest. However, in compound meters, dotted rests are common because they represent the beat or a multiple of it.

EXAMPLE A2-16

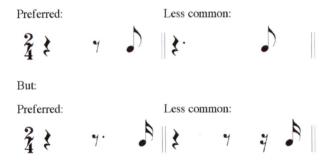

d. Two quarter rests are preferred to a half rest in 3/4.

e. Whole rests may be used to indicate an empty measure, regardless of the meter signature. The rest is placed in the center of the measure.

↻ **BACK TO BASICS A2.1**

Notation

➤ *For drill and assignments on notating rhythm, turn to Workbook p. 454.*

DO YOU KNOW THESE TERMS?

- agogic accent
- anacrusis
- augmentation dot
- borrowed division
- compound meter

- dynamic accent
- hemiola
- measure
- meter
- proportional notation

- simple meter
- syncopation
- tie
- tonal accent

Lead-Sheet Symbols

The symbol for a given chord may vary from one published source to the next. Jazz and popular musicians become familiar with these variants. The symbols in this appendix, among those commonly used in lead sheets and "real books" include some of these inconsistencies. Most of the symbols are extensions of those for the five basic seventh chords you already know, and they can usually be employed when those chords are indicated. The following principles govern their use:

1. Both ♭ and–are used to indicate a lowered chord member C7♭5 or C7–5); both ♯ and + are used to indicate a raised chord member (C7+5 or C7♯5).

2. The symbols M, Maj, MA, and (triangle) all mean "major." The symbols m, min, MI and–all mean "minor."

3. The use of a 9, 11, or 13 alone normally implies inclusion of all lower extensions as well (i.e., Cm11 implies inclusion of the seventh and ninth). The notation "add" is often used to show individual upper extensions where the lower extensions are not desired (Cm (add 11)).

4. Major ninth chords (i.e., CMaj9), minor ninth chords (Cm9), and dominant ninth chords (C9) are built on seventh chords of the same type (CMaj7, Cm7, or C7).

5. The symbol 9 indicates a major ninth above all seventh chords unless otherwise specified (–9, or b9). The dominant seventh chord (C7) is the only seventh chord above which the minor ninth is common.

6. The eleventh (11) normally is chromatically raised above major seventh and dominant seventh chords and diatonic above minor seventh, half-diminished seventh, and diminished seventh chords.

7. A sixth (6) and thirteenth (13) are the same pitch. However, the thirteenth is included above a seventh chord, while the sixth is added to a simple triad.

8. The appropriate ninth and/or eleventh and/or sixth or thirteenth can normally be added to any seventh chord.

Examples on C with Typical Symbol

Seventh Chord • Extensions or Alterations

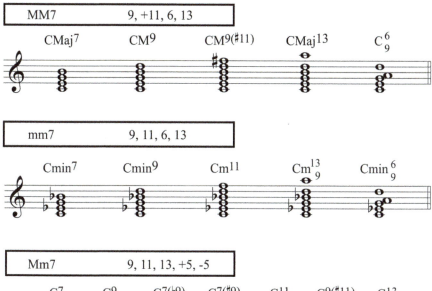

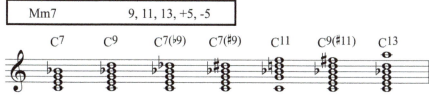

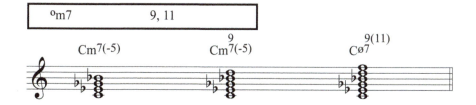

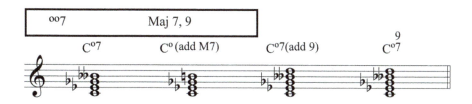

Part Writing Guidelines

A Melodic Principles

1. Range: Each voice should remain within its range.

2. Interval structure: Each line should be basically conjunct (the bass may be less so), with large leaps less common and leaps larger than a third usually approached and left by step.

3. Nondiatonic intervals: Avoid these.

4. Leading tone and chromatic tones: Resolve these, especially when in an outer voice.

B Voicing

1. Spacing: Allow no more than an octave between the soprano and alto or between the alto and tenor.

2. Doubling:

    General Guide: The bass may be doubled unless it is the leading tone or another tendency tone (a chromatic pitch or a chord seventh, for example).

    Root Position and Second Inversion: The bass is the preferred doubling in root position and second inversion major and minor triads.

3. First Inversion: Doubling in first inversion triads is often determined by melodic considerations, but in general the soprano is the preferred doubling.

C Chord Connection

1. Outer voices: Move the outer voices in contrary or oblique motion as often as possible.

2. Consecutive perfect consonances: Avoid moving perfect fifths, perfect octaves, or perfect unisons to another such interval in the same two voices on successive beats.

3. Voice crossing and overlap: Avoid this.

4. Common tones: Retain common tones between two chords in the same voice. When common tones are not present between two chords, move the upper voices contrary to the bass if possible

5. First Inversion: Use first inversion to improve the melodic character of the bass. Try to leave the doubled tone in contrary motion.

6. Second Inversion: Restrict second inversion to only the cadential I, the passing V or I, the pedal IV or I, and arpeggiated I, IV or V.

7. Nonchord tones: Adding nonchord tones to the texture should not affect the basic voice leading.

D Final Word

When a part writing problem seems insurmountable, one of the following options may still be available:

*   Change the structure or inversion of the chord.

*   Use optional doubling.

*   Change the harmony.

*   Change the melody.

Glossary

A Capella: Normally referring to choir music sung without instrumental accompaniment.

Accent: Emphasis placed on a particular note through metric placement, dynamic level, articulation, duration, or register.

Accidental: A sign placed before a note to indicate a temporary raising or lowering of its pitch or a cancellation of a previous accidental.

Acoustics: The study of the physical properties of musical sound.

Agogic accent: Emphasis placed on a particular note by virtue of its longer duration than the surrounding notes.

Alla breve: Literally ("according to the breve"), a synonym for "cut time" ($\frac{2}{2}$).

Altered chord: A harmony that contains pitches not diatonic in the key in which it appears.

Altered dominant: A dominant or dominant seventh chord with a raised or lowered fifth.

Altered pre-dominants: Chromatic harmonies, including the Neapolitan sixth chord and augmented sixth chords, that progress to the dominant with a heightened tendency to resolve owing to the altered tone.

Alto: 1) A female voice type with an approximate range from G3 to D4. 2) The term normally used to refer to the second highest musical line in a multi-voiced composition.

Anacrusis: Literally "before the crusis (beat)," an upbeat or pick-up to the ensuing measure.

Answer: In a fugal exposition, the imitation of the subject at the level of the dominant.

Antecedent: In a period, the first of the phrases, ending without a sense of completion and requiring a consequent phrase to bring about a resolution.

Anticipation: An embellishing tone usually found at cadences, in which one voice, usually the soprano, resolves to its cadence pitch ahead of the other voices.

Appoggiatura: An embellishing tone approached by leap and resolved to a metrically weaker pitch by step, usually in the opposite direction of the leap.

Appoggiatura chord: A nineteenth-century harmony in which several of the chord members resemble appoggiaturas in that they are approached by leap and resolved by step. The true chord can be found at the point of their resolution.

Arpeggiated six-four chord: A second inversion triad, most often a tonic or dominant, that results when the chord is outlined by the lowest voice of the texture.

Arpeggio, arpeggiation: The melodic outlining of a chord in a single voice.

Art song: Music composed for concert performance by a trained singer accompanied by piano.

Asymmetric: In melody, a period or phrase group in which the phrases are of unequal length. A binary form in which the second part is longer or shorter than the first part.

Atonality: The term given to music that contains neither traditional tonal references nor a pronounced sense that one pitch possesses greater stability than all the others and thus constitutes the tonal center.

Augmentation: A contrapuntal device in which a melodic/rhythmic figure appears in longer note values than its original form.

Augmentation dot: A sign that, placed after a note or rest, extends its duration by one-half the undotted value.

Augmented sixth chord: A group of altered predominant chords commonly found in eighteenth- and nineteenth-century music, characterized by an augmented sixth interval formed by the bass (a half step above the dominant) and the raised fourth scale degree (a half step below the dominant). Specific types are the Italian, French, and German sixth chords.

Augmented triad: A three-note chord built of major thirds in which the highest member is an augmented fifth above the root.

Authentic cadence: The harmonic formula V–I (or V–i in minor keys) that creates a conclusive point of punctuation and repose at the end of a musical thought.

Auxiliary chord: Any chord that is heard as a neighbor chord or passing chord to another.

Bar line: A vertical line that extends from the top to the bottom of the staff and separates the measures.

Bass: 1) A male voice type with an approximate range from E 2 to C4; 2) The term normally used to refer to the lowest voice of a multiple-voice texture.

Beat: The basic durational unit in a piece of music.

Bimodality: The use of two modes simultaneously in a composition or a portion thereof. Typically, one voice or musical line is in one mode while another is in a different mode.

Binary: Any musical form that divides into two basic parts, usually designated A B. The form was extremely popular during the Baroque era, used almost exclusively in the instrumental suites of that period.

Blue notes: In jazz, the slightly flat third, seventh, and sometimes fifth scale degrees. They fall outside the equal-tempered major scale, lying somewhere between the diatonic scale degrees and their chromatically lowered forms.

Blue note scales: Scales combining blue notes with some or all of the pitches of the major scale, such as C D E♭ E F G A B♭ C.

Blues: An indigenous form of black American folk music combining African melodic practices and simple Western harmonies in strophic forms that has been and continues to be an influence in jazz, rock, and even symphonic music.

Borrowed division: The use of a simple division of the beat in a compound meter, or the reverse—a compound division of the beat in a simple meter.

Borrowed harmonies: The altered chords that result from the process of modal borrowing (see "modal borrowing"). The chords most often used in this way are the ii°, ii°⁷, iv, vii°⁷, and ♭VI—all diatonic in a minor key but borrowed for use in the parallel major key.

Bridge: 1) In a fugal exposition, a short passage linking the end of the answer with the next entry of the subject, often serving to modulate from the dominant back to the tonic. 2) In popular music, a short section, usually in a different tonality, which separates the initial statement of the main melody and its return.

Cadence: A point of melodic and/or harmonic repose, often created through a slowing or pause in motion and serving as a punctuation between phrases.

Cadential elision: A process in which the end of one phrase and the beginning of the next phrase coincide, thereby avoiding a cadential separation between the two.

Cadential extension: The lengthening of a musical phrase upon repetition through a restatement or expansion of its cadence.

Cadential process: Music that either prepares for or extends a cadence.

Cadential six-four chord: A metrically strong second inversion tonic triad preceding the dominant at a cadence, and in fact best analyzed as a dominant with nonchord tones a fourth and sixth above the bass.

Chain suspension: A series of suspension figures in which the resolution of one suspension becomes the preparation for the next.

Change of mode: In a musical composition, the shift from a major key to its parallel minor or the reverse.

Changing tone: A two-note embellishment involving the pitches a step above and below a more important tone and its repetition.

Chorale: A hymn tune that originated in the Lutheran Church during the sixteenth century, comprising several stanzas of verse sung to the same music.

Chord: A single musical sound comprising three or more different pitches (not counting octave duplications).

Chordal mutation: A gradual and subtle chord change, in which one member of the harmony changes at a time, often generating unusual harmonic successions in the process.

Chromatic: A term referring to music, intervals, or pitches not confined to the pitch material of a given scale or mode.

Chromatic modulation: A change of tonal center involving no common chords, usually signaled by a diatonic pitch moving to a chromatically altered pitch in one or more voices.

Chromatic pivot: The pivotal chord in a chromatic modulation. It usually serves a recognizable function in both keys. However, its function in at least one of the keys is chromatic, and in this way it differs from a common chord, which functions diatonically in both keys.

Chromatic-third relationship: Two chords with roots a third apart, in which one chord contains a chromatic alteration of one or both common tones. The term also refers to two tonalities in which the tonics are in a chromatic-third relationship.

Church modes: A set of scales that formed the basis of much medieval and Renaissance music, predating and eventually evolving into our major and minor scales.

Clef: A sign placed at the left side of a staff to indicate which lines and spaces represent the various pitches.

Closely related keys: The five tonalities that differ from a given tonality by no more than one flat or sharp—thus the relative major or minor, the dominant and its relative key, and the subdominant and its relative key.

Coda: An extension of the ending of a composition, which helps to create a convincing close by prolonging and reaffirming the tonic.

Common chord: In a modulation, a chord diatonic in both the old and new keys that serves as the pivotal point in the modulation.

Common chord modulation: Also called "pivot chord modulation," a change of tonality aided by a chord diatonic in both keys that acts as a pivot between the two.

Common practice period: The period in musical history, roughly 1650–1900, in which composers used functional tonality as the harmonic basis of their music.

Common tones: The pitches shared between two chords in any harmonic relationship.

Compound interval: Any interval exceeding the octave in size.

Compound meter: A meter in which the primary division of the beat is into three parts.

Conjunct: Melodic motion involving stepwise intervals.

Consecutive perfect consonances: A succession of perfect fifths, perfect octaves, or perfect unisons between the same two voices, considered objectionable practice in strict part writing.

Consequent: The final phrase of a period, which, due to its more conclusive cadence, provides a greater sense of completion than the preceding (antecedent) phrase(s).

Consonance: Two or more pitches that, when sounded together, produce a sense of stability and repose.

Continuo: The name given to the figured bass line in Baroque-era compositions or the group of instruments that plays the figured bass (usually a keyboard instrument and a melodic bass instrument, such as the viola da gamba).

Contrary motion: The movement by two voices from one tone to the next in the opposite direction.

Contrasting period: Phrases in antecedent-consequent relationship that are composed of different material and differ in general character.

Counterexposition: In a fugue, a group of subject-answer entries in the tonic, usually appearing immediately after the exposition or separated from the exposition by a brief episode.

Countermelody: A secondary melody set as counterpoint against a principal melody. The term is used more in popular music and jazz arrangements than in art music.

Countermotive: A distinctive counterpoint that appears more or less consistently against the principal motive in an invention.

Counterpoint: Music consisting of two or more melodic lines heard simultaneously but displaying a certain degree of independence (of contour and rhythm).

Countersubject: A counterpoint that is employed frequently against the subject or answer in a fugue, providing a contrasting idea and additional material for development.

Deceptive cadence: A two chord formula punctuating a musical thought, in which the dominant moves to any chord but the tonic. The chord most often substituted for the expected tonic is the submediant.

Development: A section of a musical work where a musical idea is worked out and its potential realized through various compositional devices such as imitation, inversion, rhythmic variation, and so on.

Developmental process: The musical process involved in working out a musical idea. It usually involves rapid tonal changes, abrupt shifts in tempo, dynamics, texture, and unstable harmonies with infrequent resolutions.

Diatonic: A term referring to music or intervals confined to the pitch material of a given scale or mode.

Diatonic-third relationship: Two chords whose roots lie a third apart and which contain two common tones, as in I–vi, I–iii, i–VI, and so on.

Diminished seventh chord: The chord formed by the addition of a diminished seventh above the root of a diminished triad. It most often occurs on the leading tone of a minor key, as a vii°⁷.

Diminished triad: A three-note chord formed when a minor third is stacked above a minor third, the highest note forming a diminished fifth against the root.

Diminution: The restatement of a melodic/rhythmic figure in shorter note values.

Disjunct: Melodic motion involving intervals larger than a whole step.

Dissonance: The effect of two or more pitches sounding together that produce a sense of instability and desire for resolution.

Dominant: The functional name given to the fifth degree of a scale and to the triad formed on this pitch.

Dominant seventh chord: The seventh chord type formed on the fifth scale degree, consisting of a major triad with a minor seventh above its root. Because this type of seventh chord appears diatonically only on the dominant, it is simply called the dominant seventh chord.

Dominant-major ninth chord: The harmony formed when a third is placed above the seventh of a major-key dominant seventh chord, forming a major ninth above the chord root.

Dorian: One of six Church modes that predated and led to the major and minor scales, viewable today as a natural minor scale with a raised sixth degree.

Double period: Four phrases in which the final phrase ends more conclusively than the preceding three. The phrases may be similar (called a parallel double period) or dissimilar (called a contrasting double period).

Doubling: In four-part writing, reinforcing one of the members of a triad by including it in two of the voices.

Doubly augmented fourth chord: A German sixth chord with the mediant respelled enharmonically as a supertonic to reflect its upward resolution to the third of a major tonic six-four chord.

Dynamic accent: Emphasis placed on a particular note by virtue of its performance at a louder level or with a more emphatic articulation than the surrounding notes.

Eleventh chord: A chord formed by the addition of a third above the ninth in a ninth chord.

Embellishing diminished seventh chord: A fully diminished seventh chord that functions not as a leading-tone chord but as an auxiliary chord, usually to the tonic or dominant. The seventh of this chord is a common tone with the root of the embellished chord.

Embellishing tone: A pitch that serves as a connection between or decoration of the more important pitches of a melodic line.

Enharmonic: A term referring to different spellings of the same pitch or interval.

Enharmonic change of mode: A shift to the parallel major or minor key accompanied by an enharmonic respelling of that key, as in G♭ major to F♯ minor.

Enharmonic diminished seventh chord: A diminished seventh chord used enharmonically, usually in a modulation, so that a chord member other than its root functions as the new root.

Enharmonic equivalence: Two pitches, intervals, or chords that sound the same but are spelled differently.

Enharmonic German sixth chord: See Doubly Augmented Fourth Chord.

Enharmonic pivot: A chord which, at the point of a modulation, is diatonic in the old key and, respelled enharmonically, diatonic in the new key.

Entry group: In a fugue, two or more statements of the subject in immediate or near-immediate succession, in a manner similar to the exposition but appearing at later points in the fugue.

Episode: In a fugue, a short passage in free counterpoint that separates those sections containing complete statements of the subject. The material of an episode may be derived from the subject or countersubject or may use unrelated material, but by definition, an episode does not contain a complete statement of the subject.

Equal temperament: A system of tuning the octave such that every half step is slightly smaller than its acoustically pure counterpart so that the 12 half steps of our chromatic scale fit into the octave. It is the system by which the modern keyboard and fretted instruments are tuned.

Escape tone: An embellishing tone approached by step and left by leap.

Expanded tritone substitution: In jazz, the substitution of a harmony or group of harmonies a tritone removed from the original harmony. It most often occurs with dominant seventh-based chords or with ii–V tonicizations.

Exposition: The first section of a fugue, in which each voice enters in turn with a statement of the subject or its answer.

Extended tonicization: A common procedure in jazz, wherein a secondary predominant is added before a secondary dominant to create a secondary ii–V motion to a tonicized chord.

Fifth relation: Two chords whose roots are related to each other by the interval of a fifth, as C and G.

Figured bass: A notational method in general use for keyboard instruments during the seventeenth and eighteenth centuries. Numbers beneath the pitches of the bass line indicate the intervals to be added above the line, and thus indicate the harmonies as well.

Final: The central tone of a mode, usually the tone upon which melodies in the mode end.

Form: The shape of a musical work as created by cadences, the similarity and contrast of the musical elements, and the interaction of the musical processes.

Fragmentation: A technique wherein small portions of a melodic idea are heard in isolation and used in sequences, imitation, or other developmental ways.

French sixth chord: An augmented sixth chord consisting of the half step above the dominant (in the bass), the half step below the dominant (in an upper voice), the tonic, and the second scale degree.

Frequency: The rate of a periodic vibration, usually expressed as a number of cycles per second, which directly affects our perception of pitch.

Fugue: A contrapuntal composition for a fixed number of voices (usually two to five) in which a subject, stated by all voices in turn at the beginning, recurs at various points in a variety of tonalities and contrapuntal textures.

Functional tonality: A term describing the system by which the chords of a major or minor key are related to each other and to the tonic.

Fundamental: The lowest (and usually the loudest) tone in a harmonic series, produced by a string or air column, vibrating in its entire length.

Gamut: G on the bottom line of the bass clef, the lowest note in Guido's hexachord system. Generally refers to the entire range of a pitch system.

German sixth chord: An augmented sixth chord consisting of the half step above the dominant (in the bass), the half step below the dominant (in an upper voice), the tonic, and the third scale degree.

Grand staff: The combined treble- and bass-clef staves on which keyboard music is notated.

Ground bass: Short, repeated bass line, usually four to eight measures long, that form the basis of many Baroque-era works.

Half cadence: Most commonly, a harmonic cadence ending on the dominant triad.

Half step: The smallest interval normally used in Western music and the smallest interval on the piano.

Half-diminished seventh chord: The chord formed by the addition of a minor seventh above the root of a diminished triad. This chord appears diatonically on the leading tone of a major key and the supertonic of a minor key.

Harmonic minor: The natural minor scale with the seventh degree raised by one half step. It is the form most often the harmonic basis of music in minor keys.

Harmonic rhythm: The rate of chord change, or the series of durational patterns formed by the chord changes in a musical work.

Harmonic sequence: The repetition of a harmonic pattern at a different pitch level.

Harmonic series: In a complex waveform, the spectrum of frequencies that are whole-number multiples of the fundamental. This series of frequency components is responsible for a sound's timbre, or tone quality.

Harmonics: Frequencies above a given fundamental that form whole-number ratios with it, coloring the basic sound.

Harmony: The effect produced by the simultaneous sounding of several discrete pitches.

Hemiola: A particular type of 3:2 rhythmic ratio involving successive or simultaneous divisions of the quantity six in two ways—as two groups of three units and as three groups of two units.

Hexachord: (1) Any six adjacent notes of different pitch (excluding octave duplications). (2) A collection of six pitches, usually comprising a segment of a 12-tone row. (3) The basis of Guido's organization of the pitch gamut of his day into overlapping six-note groups.

Homophony: A texture in which individual voices having neither melodic nor rhythmic independence.

Hypermeasure: Measures that exhibit a regular pattern of accentuation in the same way that the beats within a measure do, creating a higher-level metric organization.

Hypermeter: A large level of metric structure created by a regular pattern of accented and unaccented measures. Many folk songs exhibit a hypermetric structure that mirrors their meter. For example, in $\frac{4}{4}$, measures that group into fours with the first and third measures of each group accented.

Imitation: The restatement in close succession of a melodic figure by a different voice.

Imperfect consonance: Traditionally, thirds and sixths, which were considered less pure and simple than octaves, unisons and fifths but more pleasing to the ear than seconds and sevenths.

Implied harmony: The chords suggested by a single melodic line or by a combination of lines in which all members of the harmony are not heard. The chords are aurally inferred either from the intervals generated by the lines or from the chords outlined in one of the lines.

Implied lines: In popular styles, melodic lines or scalar patterns suggested by the lead-sheet symbols.

Implied polymeter: Music in two different meters sounding simultaneously but notated in a single meter signature.

Incomplete neighbor: The name preferred today for an unaccented appoggiatura.

Index number: A subscript placed after the letters P, R, I, or RI to indicate the transposition level of a row form. P and I forms are indexed according to their first pitch while R and RI forms are indexed according to their last pitch. In this way, a P form and its corresponding retrograde have the same index number, as do an I form and its corresponding retrograde (RI).

Inharmonics: Frequency components of a sound that do not exist in whole-number ratios to the fundamental frequency. These components impart a dissonant quality to the sound.

Interlude: In the broadest sense, any kind of musical insertion. In song, it usually refers to the instrumental passages that separate or connect the verses.

Interval: The musical distance between two pitches.

Interval class: The smallest possible distance between two pitch classes. This means any interval comprising one to six half steps along with its inversion, its compound forms (those larger than an octave), and enharmonic spellings, symbolized by a number from 1 to 6 to indicate the number of half steps spanned.

Invention: The name given to two sets of short keyboard studies by J. S. Bach, in two and three voices respectively. In these studies, a short idea (motive) is developed in a continuous imitative counterpoint featuring various contrapuntal devices.

Inversion: (1) Octave transposition of one of the pitches of an interval so that the lower pitch becomes the higher and vice versa. (2) Any position of a triad or seventh chord in which the root is not the lowest tone.

Invertible counterpoint: Counterpoint constructed in such a way that the lower part may become the higher part and vice versa through transposition of one or both lines.

Italian sixth chord: An augmented sixth chord containing the half step above the dominant (in the bass), the half step below the dominant (in an upper voice), and the tonic.

Key: The scale and tonic that predominate in a musical work, reflected by the key signature.

Key signature: An inventory of the flats or sharps used consistently in a composition or in a section of a composition, grouped together and placed immediately after the clef sign at the beginning of each staff.

Large-scale arpeggiation: Broken triad formations created by the more important pitches in a melody, which are normally nonadjacent pitches, so that the arpeggiation unfolds over a prolonged time span.

Lead sheet: In popular music and jazz, the representation of the music through a melody along with chord symbols placed above it to guide musicians in their melodic and harmonic interpretation.

Leading tone: The functional name given to the major or minor scale degree one half step below the tonic, or to the triad formed on this pitch.

Ledger line: Short horizontal lines representing an extension of the staff, drawn through the stems of notes too high or too low to be placed directly on the staff.

Linear chromaticism: Chromatic harmonies formed as the byproducts of chromatic melodic motion.

Lydian: One of six Church modes that predated and led to the major and minor scales, viewable today as a major scale with a raised fourth degree.

Major: The mode based on the major scale and its seven diatonic chords.

Major ninth chord: A five-member sonority extending a major triad with the addition of a major seventh and major ninth above the root (symbolized MMM9).

Major seventh chord: The chord formed by the addition of a major seventh above the root of a major triad. It most often is found on the subdominant in a major key (IV^7) and on the submediant and mediant (VI^7 and III^7) in a minor key.

Major triad: A three-note chord consisting of two intervals above its root—a major third and a perfect fifth—and appearing as the tonic, dominant, and subdominant of a major-key work.

Measure: One complete cycle of the accentual pattern in a given meter.

Mediant: The functional name given to the third degree of a major or minor scale, or to the triad formed on this pitch.

Melodic inversion: Turning a melodic figure "upside down" so that its contour and interval structure are a mirror of the original form, with upward steps and leaps becoming downward steps and leaps of the same size, and vice versa.

Melodic minor: The natural minor scale with the sixth and seventh degrees raised by one half step in ascent. In descending passages, the sixth and seventh degrees usually are those of the natural minor scale. It is the form most often the basis for minor-key melodies.

Melodic tonality: The tendency of a melody to define its tonal center by emphasizing one certain pitch in various ways.

Meter: A regularly recurring pattern of strong and weak pulses that forms the background on which the many rhythms of a piece of music are imposed.

Metric shift: A type of syncopation involving the temporary but extended displacement of the primary accent of a measure.

Minor: The mode based on the minor scale and its diatonic chords.

Minor ninth chord: A five-member chord extending a minor triad with the addition of a minor seventh and major ninth above the root (symbolized mmM9).

Minor seventh chord: The chord formed by the addition of a minor seventh above the root of a minor triad. It is most often found on the supertonic of a major key and the subdominant of a minor key.

Minor triad: A three-note chord consisting of two intervals above its root—a minor third and a perfect fifth—and appearing as the tonic and subdominant in a minor-key work.

Mixolydian: One of six Church modes that predated and led to the major and minor scales, viewable today as a major scale with a lowered seventh degree.

Modal borrowing: A process involving the brief and occasional use of a harmony called a "borrowed harmony" from the parallel major or minor mode.

Modal cadence: A harmonic pattern containing an inflection characteristic of one of the Church modes.

Mode: See Church modes

Mode mixture: A general procedure wherein the harmonic resources of the parallel major and minor modes are combined. It includes modal borrowing and change of mode.

Modulation: The process of changing tonal centers.

Motive: A short melodic/rhythmic idea that serves as the basis for an invention or, through its frequent occurrence, lends unity to any composition.

Motivic analysis: Analysis that seeks to understand how all elements of a musical composition relate to each other by identifying motivic similarities among sections, subsections, phrases, and so on.

Musica ficta: Literally "made music," pitch alterations that were made by performers, usually to create half steps to important tones. Musica ficta was partially responsible for the evolution of major–minor tonality from the older system of Church modes.

Musical process: The collective functioning of the musical elements to create a sense that a passage is serving one of several purposes—stating a theme, developing an idea, changing tonality, mood, or character, prolonging a cadence, and so on.

Natural minor: A seven-tone scale with the interval pattern of whole step, half step, whole step, whole step, half step, whole step, whole step, identical to the Aeolian mode.

Neapolitan sixth chord: A major triad with the lowered supertonic as its root, most often serving a pre-dominant harmonic function in minor keys.

Neighbor chord: A harmony made up of neighbor tones to the members of the preceding and following chords.

Neighbor tone: An embellishing tone occurring stepwise between a more important pitch and its repetition.

Nonchord tone: The term used to describe embellishing tones when they occur in a harmonic context and are not members of the prevailing harmony.

Nondominant seventh chord: Any seventh chord that functions neither as a V (dominant) nor as a viio (leading-tone chord).

Normal order: The arrangement of the pitches of a set from lowest to highest, so that the first and last pitch span the smallest possible interval.

Oblique motion: The movement by one voice from one tone to a different tone while a second voice remains on the same tone.

Octatonic scale: Literally, a scale of eight tones. The name has been appropriated for a scale used by Debussy and others that consists of eight alternating whole and half steps.

Octave: A term referring to the interval spanned by 12 half steps, from a given pitch to the next higher or lower pitch of the same latter name. The frequency ratio between two such pitches is 2:1.

Order number: A number indicating the positions (from one to 12) occupied by the notes of a 12-tone row.

Ottava sign: A symbol (8va) that, placed above a pitch, directs that it be performed an octave higher than written.

Overtone: Any of the harmonics occurring above a fundamental frequency.

Pandiatonicism: The use of pitch material from a given scale or mode, with few or no extraneous pitches and lacking the usual functional harmonic and melodic relationships.

Parallel major–minor: A major and minor scale or key sharing the same tonic.

Parallel motion: The movement by two voices from one tone to the next in the same direction and by the same number of steps or half steps.

Parallel period: Phrases in antecedent-consequent relationship, the last beginning with the same or similar material as the first but ending more conclusively.

Parallel perfect consonances: The movement of two voices from one perfect consonance to another of the same type. Considered objectionable practice in strict four-part writing. (Also called "consecutive perfect consonances.")

Part writing: Composing or arranging for multiple voices so that each voice forms a melodic line that fits together with the other voices to produce a harmonic structure.

Passing chord: A harmony whose tones can be viewed as passing tones between chord members in the preceding and following chords.

Passing six-four chord: A second inversion triad, usually a dominant or tonic, in which the motion of the individual voices through the doubled chord tone (the fifth) resembles a passing tone. The resulting chord becomes, in effect, a passing chord.

Passing tone: An embellishing tone occurring stepwise between two more important tones of different pitch.

Pedal point: A pitch that is sustained or repeated while the other voices of the texture change pitch, creating dissonances against it.

Pedal six-four chord: A second inversion triad, usually a subdominant or tonic, in which the bass line remains stationary prior to and following the chord itself, resembling a pedal point.

Pedal tone: On a wind instrument, the fundamental tone of the harmonic series produced by the instrument vibrating in its whole aspect. Usually not part of the normal playing range, pedal tones are those that are overblown to produce the notes in the normal playing range.

Pentachord: Any consecutive five pitches.

Pentatonic scale: An ascending or descending pitch collection that consists of five tones to the octave, most often containing no half steps and no more than two whole steps in succession.

Perfect authentic cadence: A V–I harmonic pattern in which the tonic appears in the highest voice on the final chord and the two chords are in root position.

Perfect consonance: The designation given by early theorists to intervals having the simplest frequency ratio, specifically, the perfect fourth, perfect fifth, perfect unison, and perfect octave.

Period: Two phrases, sometimes three, that are perceived as a unit because the final phrase ends more conclusively than the preceding phrase(s), providing a greater sense of completion.

Permutation: Any reordering of the pitches of a set or 12-tone row.

Phrase: A melodic unit, typically four to eight measures long, which expresses a more or less complete musical thought.

Phrase extension: A means of expanding a phrase upon repetition by adding material to its beginning, middle, or end.

Phrase group: Two or more phrases that, although not forming a period, are nevertheless related and convey a sense that they belong together.

Phrygian: One of six Church modes that predated and led to the major and minor scales, viewable today as a minor scale with a lowered second degree.

Phrygian cadence: A type of half cadence, found only in minor, comprising the chords iv6–V.

Picardy third: The major tonic triad that often ends a minor-key movement in the Baroque era.

Pitch: The sensation of highness or lowness attributed to a musical tone, the result of a periodic waveform's frequency.

Pitch class: A term used in set theory to denote a single pitch along with all of its octave duplications and enharmonic spellings.

Pitch class interval: The interval formed by two pitch classes.

Pitch class set: A collection of pitch class intervals in any order.

Plagal cadence: A conclusive cadence involving two chord formula IV–I (or iv–in minor keys).

Planing: Two or more voices moving together in parallel motion, generating intervals or harmonies of the same general or specific type.

Polychord: Two or more harmonic structures sounding simultaneously but perceivable as discrete chords.

Polyphony: A texture consisting of lines that are melodically and rhythmically independent.

Polytonality: Music suggesting the simultaneous presence of more than one tonal center.

Postcadential: Referring to extensions that occur after a cadence has been completed and thus prolong the effect of its final chord.

Postlude: In song, the instrumental conclusion following the last vocal phrase.

Power chords: In rock music, the perfect fifths usually produced on the guitar's fifth and sixth strings.

Precadential: Referring to extensions that occur in the approach to a cadence, often prolonging the effect of its first chord.

Pre-dominant: Chords that normally proceed directly to the dominant—the subdominant and the supertonic. According to a more recent view, one of only three harmonic functions, the other two being tonic and dominant.

Prelude: In song, a short instrumental introduction that precedes the vocal entrance and serves to set the mood or to establish an accompaniment pattern. It is usually a manifestation of the preparatory process.

Preparatory process: The collective functioning of the musical elements in a way that sets the style or mood of the music to come.

Prime: In 12-tone music, the original form of the 12-tone row.

Prime form: The expression of the best normal order for a set and its inversion. Prime form assigns the first (lowest) pitch the number "0" and the remaining pitches numbers that correspond to their distance in half steps above the lowest pitch.

Progression: The strongest type of harmonic motion, in which each chord moves to the next closest chord to the tonic, as measured in descending-fifth root movements. Harmonic progression generates a satisfying feeling of forward momentum in music.

Proportional: A term referring to the rhythmic aspect of our notation system, in which durational values are not absolute but are fixed only in relationship to one (i.e., a half-note is half as long as a whole note, and so on).

Quartal: A chord built of superposed fourths.

Quintal: A chord built of superposed fifths.

Ragtime: A highly syncopated style of piano music, mainly African-American in origin, in vogue in the United States at the turn of the twentieth century and one of the forerunners of jazz.

Range: The distance spanned by the highest and lowest pitches of a melodic line.

Real: Referring either to sequences or imitation that constitute exact intervallic repetitions of a preceding idea.

Realize, realization: The term describing what a performer does when he or she plays a figured bass line, filling out the chords and adding embellishments as the style requires.

Recapitulation: Generally, any restatement of originally heard material near the end of a musical work. More specifically, the return of the exposition material in a sonata-form movement following the development section.

Relative major–minor: A major and minor scale pair sharing the same key signature but not the same tonic.

Repetition: A type of harmonic motion in which a chord is repeated or moves to another chord of the same class (i.e., pre-dominant to pre-dominant).

Resolution: The motion from a tone or chord to another tone or chord of greater stability.

Retardation: An upward-resolving suspension.

Retrograde: A row transformation involving the reversal of the pitch order.

Retrograde inversion: In 12-tone music, the statement of the melodically inverted row in retrograde.

Retrogression: A harmonic motion in which each chord moves to a new chord more distant from the tonic as measured in ascending-fifth root movements, such as a supertonic to a submediant.

Rhythm: A term referring generally to the temporal aspects of music—the duration of its sounds and silences.

Root: In a triad or seventh chord, the note above which the others can be arranged as a stack of thirds.

Root position: Any arrangement of the tones of a chord in which the root appears as the lowest pitch.

Rounded binary: A two-part form in which the second part is "rounded off" by a (usually abbreviated) restatement of initial material, symbolized A|BA'.

Row form: In 12-tone works, one of the four basic aspects of a 12-tone row—prime, retrograde, inversion, or retrograde inversion.

Scale: An inventory of the pitches that form the basis of a musical composition, arranged in ascending or descending order.

Second relation: Two chords whose roots are a second apart.

Secondary dominant, secondary function: Chords that momentarily serve as dominants with respect to a temporary tonic.

Secondary leading tone: In a secondary dominant or leading-tone chord, the note that serves momentarily as the leading tone to the root of the tonicized chord.

Segmentation: A technique in which a 12-tone row is divided consistently into fragments—usually trichords, tetrachords, or hexachords—that are treated similarly to the motives in a theme.

Sensitive tones: The least stable tones in a scale or key, each usually separated by a half step from a member of the tonic triad and displaying pronounced inclination to resolve to that pitch. (Also called "tendency tones.")

Sequence: A melodic or harmonic pattern repeated in close succession at a pitch level other than the original.

Set: A collection of pitch classes that serves as the basis for an atonal work.

Set type: A way of describing the interval content of a pitch class set. The pitch classes are placed in ascending order in the closest possible position, the lowest (first) pitch is assigned the number "0," and the other pitches are assigned numbers indicating the number of half steps between them and the first pitch.

Seventh chord: A four-note chord formed when a seventh above the chord root is added to a triad.

Similar motion: The movement by two voices from one tone to the next in the same direction but by a different interval.

Simple interval: An interval spanning an octave or less.

Simple meter: A meter in which the primary division of the beat is into two parts.

Single entry: In a fugue, an isolated statement of the subject, as opposed to statements occurring in groups.

Six-four chord: A second inversion triad.

Solmization: The act of singing melodic lines using a system of syllables developed by Guido where each syllable corresponds to a scale degree (do, re, mi, fa, sol la, ti).

Song form: A term that describes the ABA (ternary) form applied to a song.

Soprano: 1) A voice type with an approximate range from C4 to G5. 2) The term normally used to refer to the highest musical line in a multi-voiced vocal or choral composition.

Spacing: The manner in which the notes of a chord are distributed among the various voices of the texture.

Staff: A set of five horizontal lines, on and between which the musical notes are written. In conjunction with a clef sign, it indicates the pitches of the notes appearing on it.

Standards: The term applied to popular songs written in the earlier part of the twentieth century that have withstood the passage of time and continue to be performed and recorded.

Step progression: The stepwise connection of important (usually nonadjacent) pitches in a melody that contribute to its sense of overall direction.

Stretto: A feature often found in the later parts of a fugue involving overlapping statements of the subject in two or more voices.

Strophic: A formal structure in which all verses of a song are sung to the same music.

Structural tone: The most important pitches in a melodic line, which usually serve as goal tones around, toward and from which the other tones move.

Subdominant: The functional name given to the fourth degree of a major or minor scale, or to the triad formed on this pitch.

Subject: A melodic idea that serves as the basis for a fugue, presented initially in each voice in turn and subsequently restated at various points in a variety of textures and tonalities.

Submediant: The functional name given to the sixth degree of a major or minor scale, or to the triad formed on this pitch.

Subtonic: The functional name given to the lowered seventh degree of a minor scale, or to the triad formed on this pitch.

Supertonic: The functional name given to the second degree of a major or minor scale, or to the triad formed on this pitch.

Suspension: The dissonance created when one voice in a texture of two or more voices is delayed in its downward stepwise motion from one tone to the next.

Symmetric: Periods in which the antecedent and consequent phrases are roughly of equal length. Forms characterized by correspondence on both sides of their midpoint, such as an ABA in which both A sections are the same length.

Syncopation: The shift in accentuation to a normally unaccented part of a beat or measure.

Syntax: The way harmonies are strung together to form harmonic patterns.

Tempo: The speed of the beat.

Tendency tone: See "Sensitive tones."

Tenor: (1) A male voice type with an approximate range from C3 to G4. (2) The term normally used to refer to the third highest musical line in a multi-voiced composition, below the alto and above the bass.

Ternary: Any musical form dividing into three basic parts.

Tertian: Referring to chords constructed of thirds.

Tetrachord: A four-note segment of a scale or mode.

Text setting: In song, the fashioning of a melody to suit the words.

Texture: The density and complexity of the musical fabric of a work, determined by the number of lines, their degree of independence, the complexity of the harmonies, the instrumentation, the degree of rhythmic animation, and other factors.

Thematic process: The collective functioning of the musical elements to create passages that are mainly melodic, with strongly contoured and identifiable phrasing, clear cadences, and stable harmonies.

Third relation: Two chords whose roots are related by the interval of a third.

Thirteenth chord: A chord formed by the addition of the 13 above an eleventh or ninth chord.

Tie: A curved line connecting two adjacent notes of the same pitch, binding them into a single sound equal to their combined durations.

Timbre: A term referring to the quality of a musical tone (tone color), which is determined in part by its overtone content.

Tonal: A term used to describe music in which a particular pitch is endowed with a feeling of greater importance and finality than the other pitches.

Tonal accent: Emphasis on a particular pitch by its placement in a register different from the pitches that surround it.

Tonal sequence: A sequence in which the quality of certain intervals is changed, usually to remain diatonic in the key of the original statement.

Tonic: The first and most stable pitch of a given major or minor scale and the pitch for which the scale is named.

Tonic-dominant axis: The polar tones around which many tonal melodies are organized, comprising important high and low points and goals for the melodic gestures.

Tonicize, tonicization: A process whereby a chord other than the tonic is caused to sound temporarily like a tonic by being preceded and supported by its own dominant (or dominant seventh chord) or leading-tone chord.

Tonicizing chord group: A group of chords (most commonly ii–V) that function most clearly with respect to a secondary tonic and thus enhance its momentary status as a tonic.

Tonicizing tritone: The interval comprising the two sensitive tones (fa and ti) in any secondary dominant seventh chord or secondary leading-tone triad. It is their strong tendency to resolve that creates the tonicizing effect.

Transitional process: Passages that signal a change in musical condition, i.e., from subdued to agitated, from soft to loud, from fast to slow, from one tonality to another, and so on.

Transposition: The process of rewriting a scale, or a passage based on a scale, at a different pitch level, in a different key.

Triad: A three-note chord in which two of the notes can be arranged as a third and fifth above the lowest note (the root).

Triadic extension: Any triad above which additional thirds have been stacked.

Trichord: A three-note segment of a scale, mode, or 12-tone row.

Tritone: A musical interval comprising three whole steps that splits the octave precisely in half. It is normally spelled as a diminished fifth or augmented fourth.

Tritone-related chords: In jazz, substitute dominant or dominant-seventh chords that are used instead of the original chord. The substitutes are root-related to the originals by a tritone.

Tritone substitution: See tritone-related chords.

Turnaround: In jazz, a chord pattern that leads back from the end of a phrase or period to its beginning.

12-tone method: A method of composing in which a 12-tone row and its various transformations serves as a basis for the composition.

Voice: The generic term for any musical line.

Voice crossing: A motion between two voices in which the lower voice moves above the upper voice momentarily, or conversely, the upper voice moves below the lower voice. Considered objectionable practice in strict four-voice writing.

Voice leading: The process of leading each voice in a multi-voiced texture to its next tone in such a way that pleasing melodic lines and chord voicings result.

Voice overlap: An exceptional part writing practice in which a voice is moved above the preceding pitch of a higher voice or *below* the preceding pitch of a lower voice.

Voicing: The manner in which a chord is spaced and doubled.

Walking bass: In jazz, bass lines that move at a regular pace (which usually corresponds with the beat) through the harmonies in largely scalar lines.

Whole step: An interval comprising two half steps.

Whole-tone scale: A six-note scale made up entirely of whole tones.

Credits

Index

period
  contrasting 150
  defined 148
  double 155
  parallel 149
phrase, phrases
  and cadences 144
  antecedent 148
  consequent 148
  defined 142
  length of 143
  phrase group 151
  relationships among 146
Phrygian half cadence 83
Phrygian mode 9, 515
pitch class 549
pitch class set 551
pivot chord 284
plagal cadence 82
planing 510
polychord 532
polyphony *see* counterpoint
polytonality 535
popular music
  cadences in 87
  musical form in 474
  seventh chords in 238–240
postcadential extensions *see* extension,
    cadential
precadential extensions *see* extension,
    cadential
pre-dominants
  and chord substitution 271, 596
  and circle of fifths 69
  defined 69
  and modulation 290
  and tonicizing chord groups 271–275
preparatory process 456
primary triads 61
prime *see* twelve–tone method, row
    forms
prime form 557
progression 70

quartal harmonies 521, 531
quintal harmonies *see* quartal harmonies

ragtime 269
range 102
ranges, voice 170
real answer *see* fugue
real sequence *see* sequence
recapitulation 486
refrain 496
relative major and minor 660
repetition
  in functional harmony 70

in melody 105
in phrasing 146
resolution
  of suspension 129
retardation 129
retransition
  defined 457
  in sonata form 486
retrograde *see* twelve-tone method, row
    forms
retrograde inversion *see* twelve-tone
    method, row forms
retrogression 72
rhythm
  notation of 674
  proportional 666
roman numeral symbols 60
rondo 477
  analysis of Beethoven Piano Sonata,
    op. 13 (III) 496–504
  cadential process in 502
  episode in 497
  refrain in 496
  retransition in 499
  thematic process in 496–497
root-position triads
  chord connection guidelines 213,
    681
  in fifth relationship 197
  in second relationship 199
  in third relationship 198
rounded binary form 457
  vs. ternary form 459
row forms 542
rule of chromatics 286, 289

scalar motion
  bass patterns 72
  and implied lines 605
  and transitional process 457
scales
  blue notes 624
  evolution of 8
  in melodies 113
  octatonic 527
  pentatonic 420
  whole tone 524
secondary dominants
  and chord substitution 593
  and harmonic sequence 260–261
  in jazz and popular styles 264
  and part writing 255–257
  and tonicization 245–248
secondary dominant seventh chord 252
secondary function
  and chromatic lines 261
  defined 247

and harmonic sequence 264
in jazz and popular styles 268
and melody harmonization 279
and part writing 258
in ragtime 269
secondary leading tone 249
secondary leading-tone seventh chord
    256
secondary leading-tone triad 257
second inversion
  arpeggiated six-four chord 223
  cadential six-four chord 219
  defined 38
  and part writing 218–223
  passing six-four chord 220
  pedal six-four chord 223
  six-four chords compared 226
  six-four chord variants 224
second relationship 199
segmentation 575
sensitive tones
  defined 170
  and part writing 186–190, 228
  and secondary function
    258–259
  and seventh chords 227
sentence 146
sequence
  in Bach's inventions 319, 323
  defined 107
  in fugues 328
  harmonic 264, 445
  real 108
  tonal 108
  and transitional process 441
serialism 566
set *see* pitch class set
set type 556
seventh chords
  basic jazz seventh chords 584
  and chain suspensions 238
  classification of 40
  defined 40
  dominant-functioning 228
  embellishing diminished seventh chord
    395
  extensions of 585
  figured bass notation of 55
  incomplete 236–238
  inversion of 42, 65
  jazz voicing in 591
  lead-sheet notation of 47
  nondominant 234
  and part writing 227
seventh, delayed resolution 232
seventh, unresolved 232
sharp symbol 651

Index of Musical Examples

Audio Playlist

Example	Composer	Title
2-4	Gordon/Gruska	"Friends and Lovers"
2-7	Schumann	"Träumerei" from *Kinderszenen*, op. 15
3-1	Hancock	"Maiden Voyage"
3-4	Traditional	"Prayer of Thanksgiving"
3-8	Tchaikovsky	*Romeo and Juliet*
3-9	Traditional	"A Prayer of Thanksgiving"
3-12	Bach	*Brandenburg Concerto* No. 2 (I)
3-16	Bach	Prelude No. 1 (from *WTC* I)
4-1	Holyfield/House	"Could I Have this Dance?"
4-3	Holyfield/House	"Could I Have this Dance?"
4-5	Curtis/Becaud	"Let it Be Me"
4-6	Bach	"Ich steh' mir einem fuss im Grabe" (from *Cantata* 156)
4-7	Handel	"For unto us a Child is born" (from *Messiah*)
5-2a	Folk hymn	"Amazing Grace"
5-3	Folk hymn	"Amazing Grace"
5-10a	Bach	French Suite in D minor (Menuett II)
5-10b	Mozart	Rondo, K. 494
5-10c	Kosma and Mercer	"Autumn Leaves"
5-13	Jacobs/Casey	"Those Magic Changes" (from *Grease*)
5-16a	Davis/Gordy/Hutch/West	"I'll Be There"
5-16b	Bach	French Suite, no. 5 (Gavotte)
5-17	Handel	Concerto Grosso, op. 6, no. 12 (II)
5-19a	Bach	"Wachet auf" (from *Cantata* 140)
5-19b	Hendrix	"Hey Joe"
5-20	Posner/Levine/Luke/Hindlin	"Sugar"
6-2	Mozart	Piano Sonata, K. 332 (I)
6-3	Scubert	Ständchen"
6-6b	Spiritual	"Michael, Row the Boat Ashore"
6-7a	Beethoven	Piano Sonata, op. 26 (I)
6-7b	Mendelssohn	*Kinderstück*, op. 72, no. 1

Example	Composer	Title
6-7c	Veracini	Sonata No. 3 for Violin and Continuo
6-8a	Beethoven	Piano Sonata, op. 7 (III)
6-8b	Swift/Max/Martin/Schuster	"We Are Never Getting Back Together"
6-10a	English folk song	"Scarborough Fair"
6-10b	Hendricks/Timmons	"Moanin'"
6-11	Nunn/Webber	"Memory"
6-12	Sondeim/Berstein	"Maria"
6-13	Beethoven	Piano Sonata op. 22 (II)
6-14	Schumann	"Volksliedchen" (No. 9 from *Album for the Young*, op. 68)
6-16	Bach	"Herz und Mund und Tat und Leben" (from *Cantata* 147)
6-20	Chopin	Nocturne, op. 37, no. 1
6-21	Chopin	Etude, op. 10, no. 3
7-1a	Key/Smith	"The Star-Spangled Banner"
7-1b	Old English Air	"America"
7-4a	Mozart	Piano Sonata, K. 331 (III)
7-4b	Schumann	*Kinderszenen*, no. 6 ("An Important Event")
7-4c	King	"You've Got a Friend"
7-5	Bergman/Legrand	Theme from *Summer of '42*
7-6	Chopin	Mazurka, op. 68, no. 3
7-9b	Rundgren	"Can We Still Be Friends?"
7-10a	Beethoven	Piano Sonata, op. 10, no. 1 (I)
7-10b	Rodgers/Hammerstein	"Do-Re-Mi" (from *The Sound of Music*)
7-11	Beethoven	"Für Elise" (from *Albumblatt*)
7-12	Joel	"The Longest Time"
7-13	Wagner	*Die Meistersinger von Nürnburg* (Prelude)
7-14	Handel	"Alla Hornpipe" (from *Water Music*)
7-23	Rachmaninov	Symphony No. 2 (II)
8-4	Rossini	*Petite Messe Solonnelle* ("Kyrie")
8-6	Mendelssohn	Overture to *The Hebrides*, op. 26
8-7a	Mozart	Piano Sonata, K. 279 (I)
8-7b	Mozart	Piano Sonata, K. 283 (I)
8-8	Rodgers/Hammerstein	"Some Enchanted Evening" from *South Pacific*
8-9	Chopin	Valse, op. 69, no. 2
8-10	Wade/Reading	"Adeste Fidelis"
8-13	Beethoven	Piano Sonata, op. 27, no. 2 (II)
8-15	DeVorzon/Botkin	"Nadia's Theme" (from *The Young and the Restless*)
8-16	Wagner	*Tristan und Isolde* (act 2, scene 2)
8-17	Mozart	Piano Sonata, K. 331 (I)
8-18	Tchaikovsky	"Arabian Dance" (from *The Nutcracker*)
8-19	Bach	"Herz und Mund und Tat und Leben" (Chorale from *Cantata* 147)
8-20a	Evans	"Turn Out the Stars (*Bill Evans at Town Hall*-Verve 6-8683)
8-20b	Bricusse/Newley	"Pure Imagination (*Willy Wonka and the Chocolate Factory*)
8-21	Brahms	Symphony, no. 2 op. 73 (I)
8-22	Van Halen	"Jump"
8-24	Debussy	"Clair de Lune" (from *Suite Bergamasque*)
9-3a	Mozart	*Eine kleine Nachmusik*, K. 525 (I)
9-3b	Chopin	Prelude, op. 28, no. 20

Example	Composer	Title
9-4	Bach	"Herz und Mund und Tat und Leben: (Choral, *Cantata* 147)
9-5	Zaret/North	"Unchained Melody"
9-6	Mozart	Piano Sonata, K. 283 (II)
9-7	Toplady/Hastings	"Rock of Ages"
9-9	Mozart	Piano Sonata, K. 311 (II)
9-10a	Kuhlau	Sonatina, op. 55, no. 4 (II)
9-10b	Rimsky-Korsakov	*Scheherazade* (III)
9-11	Debussy	"Clair de Lune" (from *Suite Bergamasque*)
9-13	Chopin	Mazurka, op. 7, no. 1
9-15a	Beethoven	Piano Sonata, op. 26 (I)
9-15b	Chopin	Fantaisie-Impromptu, op. 66
9-16	Goffin/King	"Will You Love Me Tomorrow?"
9-17	Mozart	Piano Sonata, K. 309 (I)
9-18a	Mozart	"Durch Zärtlichkeith und Schmeicheln" (no. 8 from *Die Entführung aus dem Serail*)
9-18b	Haydn	Piano Sonata, H. XVI: 34 (I)
9-19	Bergman/Grusin	"It Might Be You" (theme song from *Tootsie*)
10-14	Bach	French Suite, no. 2, Menuet
11-1	Sondheim/Berbnstein	"Somewhere" (from *West Side Story*)
11-4	Weiss/Peretti/Creatore	"Can't Help Falling in Love"
11-8a	Copland	*Fanfare for the Common Man*
11-8b	Keys	"If I Ain't Got You"
11-13	Fawcett/Naegeli	"Blest be the Tie"
12-10	Bach	"Ermuntre dich, mein schwacher Geist"
12-11	Elvey/Alford	"Come, Ye Thankful People Come"
13-2	Bach	"Schmücke dich, o liebe Seele"
13-4	Bach	"Wo sol lich fliehen hin"
13-5	Bernstein	"One Hand, One Heart" (from *West Side Story*)
13-10	Bach	"Schaut, ihr Sünder"
13-11a	Beethoven	Seven Variation on "God Save the King" (Theme)
13-11b	Beethoven	"God Save the King" (Theme: Ending "**b**")
13-13	Beethoven	Symphony, no. 9 (fourth movement)
13-14	Faber/Henry/Walton	"Faith of Our Fathers"
13-15	Bach	"Valet will dir geben"
13-16	Elvey	"Come, Ye Thankful People Come"
13-18	Baring-Gould/Sullivan	"Onward, Christian Soldiers"
13-19	Spiritual	"Michael, Row the Boat Ashore"
13-20a	Beethoven	Piano Sonata, op. 26 (I)
13-20b	John/Rice	"Can You Feel the Love Tonight?" (from *The Lion King*)
14-3a	Bach	"Für deinen Thron tret'ich hiermit"
14-3b	Bach	"Christ lag in Todesbanden"
14-3c	Bach	"Gott lebet noch"
14-3d	Bach	"Wach' auf, mein Herz"
14-5	Traditional Dutch air	"Prayer of Thanksgiving"
14-6	Beethoven	Piano Sonata, op. 10, no. 1 (third movement)
14-8	Bach	"Das neugeborne Kindelein"
14-9	Corrigan	"Cockles and Mussels"
14-10	Bach	"O Ewigkeit, du Donnerwort"
14-12	Purcell	*Ode for St. Cecilia's Day*

Example	Composer	Title
14-13	Rodgers/Hammerstein	"Climb Ev'ry Mountain" (*The Sound of Music*)
14-15a	Edmonds	"I Said I Love You"
14-15b	Mozart	Rondo, K. 494
14-16	Wickham/Napier-Bell/ Donaggio/Pallavicini	"You Don't Have to Say You Love Me"
14-17a	Delange/Mills/Ellington	"Solitude"
14-18	Davis	"Tune up"
15-1	Bolton	"All Through the Night"
15-2	Bareillis	"She Used to Be Mine"
15-4	Traditional	"Come, Ye Thankful People, Come"
15-6a	Lennon/McCartney	"The Long and Winding Road"
15-6b	Beethoven	Symphony, no. 1, op. 21 (I)
15-7b	Harris	"Don't Know Why"
15-9	Mozart	Piano Sonata, K. 284 (III)
15-10	Schumann	*Kinderszenen*, no. 6 ("An Important Event")
15-12	Beethoven	String Quartet, op. 18, no. I (III)
15-14	Schubert	Impromptu op. 142, no. 3
15-16	Evans	"Waltz for Debby"
15-17	Kuhlau	Sonatina, op. 55, no. 5 (I)
15-18a	Bach	Prelude, no. 11 from *WTC*, Book I
15-18b	Handel	Concerto Grosso, op. 6, no. 1 (Allegro)
16-1	Fosdick/Poulton	"Aura Lee"
16-2a	Joplin	"The Sycamore (A Concert Rag)"
16-2b	Peterson	"Hymn to Freedom"
16-3	Cetera	"If You Leave Me Now"
16-4b	Scaggs	"We're All Alone"
16-5a	Davis	"Tune Up"
16-5b	Young	"Stella by Starlight"
16-7a	Bricusse/Newley	"Pure Imagination"
16-7b	MacDonald/Abrams	"Minute by Minute" (from *The Doobie Brothers: Minute by Minute*, Warner Bros. Reva. Inc-3192-3)
16-9a	Portnoy/Angelo	"Where Everybody Knows Your Name" (theme from *Cheers*)
16-9b	Rice/Webber	"I Don't Know How to Love Him" (*Jesus Christ Superstar*)
16-10	Scottish Air (Words by Robert Burns)	"Auld Lang Syne"
16-11		"Auld Lang Syne"
16-12		"Auld Lang Syne"
17-1a	Bach	"Wach auf, mein Herz"
17-1b	Follese/Delaney	"The Way You Love Me"
17-1c	Dehr/Gilkyson/Miller	"Greenfields"
17-2	Mozart	Symphony, no. 40 in G minor, K. 550 (III)
17-3	Anonymous	Minuet (from the *Notebook for Anna Magdalena Bach*)
17-8	Chopin	Mazurka, op. 56, no. 1
17-9a	Schubert	"Kennst du das Land"
17-9b	Bernstein	"Tonight" (from *West Side Story*, act 1, no. 7)
17-10	Brahms	"Erinnerung," op. 63, no. 2
17-11	Mozart	Piano Sonata, K. 310 (I)
17-12a	Brahms	*Variations on a Theme of Robert Schumann*, op. 9
17-12b	Schubert	Symphony, no. 8 (I)
17-13	Bach	"Helft mir Gott's Güte preisen"

Example	Composer	Title
18-3a	Bach	French Suite, no. 3 (Minuet)
18-3b	Bach	Two-Part Invention, no. 13, BWV 784
18-7	Williams	"One Barrel Chase" (from *Jaws*)
18-8	Bergman/Legrand	"How Do You Keep the Music Playing?"
18-9	Rodgers and Hart	"My Romance" (as performed by the Jack Schantz Quartet, Interplay Recordings, 1993)
18-10	Bergman/Legrand	"How Do You Keep the Music Playing?"
18-11	Burke/Haggart	"What's New?"
18-12a	Bach/Crüger	"Nun danket alle Gott"
18-12b	Bach/Crüger	"Nun danket alle Gott"
18-14	Bach	Two-Part Invention, no. 1, BWV 772
18-15	Bach	Two-Part Invention, no. 6 in E Major, BWV 777
19-5	Bach	*The Well-Tempered Clavier*, Book I, BWV 861 (Fugue No. 16)
19-6	Bach	*The Well-Tempered Clavier*, Book II, BWV 885 (Fugue No. 16)
19-7	Bach	*The Well-Tempered Clavier*, Book II, BWV 881 (Fugue No. 12)
19-8	Bach	*The Well-Tempered Clavier*, Book I, BWV 847 (Fugue No. 2)
19-9	Bach	*The Well-Tempered Clavier*, Book I, BWV 861 (Fugue No. 16)
20-1	Legrand	"The Summer Knows" (from The Summer of '42)
20-2	Mozart	Piano Sonata, K. 332 (II)
20-3	Beethoven	Piano Sonata, op. 26 (II)
20-6a	Brahms	"Die Mainacht"
20-6b	Tchaikovsky	"Waltz of the Flowers" (from *The Nutcracker*)
20-6c	O'Sullivan	"Alone Again, Naturally"
20-8a	Sager/Hamlisch	"Nobody Does It Better"
20-8b	Bricusse/Williams	"Can You Read My Mind?" (from the Move *Superman*)
20-9	Weiss/Thiele	"What a Wonderful World"
20-11	Schubert	"Kennst du das Land"
20-14a	Beethoven	Piano Sonata, op. 14, no. 1 (III)
20-14b	Brahms	Symphony, no. 3, op. 90 (II)
20-14c	Williams	*Star Wars* (main theme)
20-15	Haydn	Piano Sonata, H. XVI: 34 (I)
20-17	Dvořák	New World Symphony, op. 95 (Largo)
21-3	Beethoven	Piano Sonata, op. 27, no. 2 (I)
21-5b	Verdi	"Stride la vampa!" from *Il Trovatore* (act 2, scene 1)
21-7	Mozart	Piano Sonata, K. 280 (II)
21-8	Chopin	Valse, op. 64, no. 2
21-9	Gounod	"Marcha Funebre de un Volatin"
21-10	Kusik/Rota	"Speak Softly Love" (Theme from *The Godfather*)
21-12	Bach	*The Well-Tempered Clavier*, Book I, BWV 844 (Prelude no. 1)
21-13	Beethoven	Thirty-Two Variations on an Original Theme in C Minor, Wo0.80
21-18a	Schubert	Sonatina for Piano and Violin, op. posth. 137, no. 2
21-18b	Mozart	String Quartet, K. 421 (III)
21-18c	Chopin	Etude, op. 10, no. 3
21-22	Joplin	"The Sycamore"
21-23	Monk	"'Round Midnight"

Example	Composer	Title
21-24	Schumann	"Am leuchtenden Sommermorgen" (no. 12 from *Dichterliebe*, op. 48)
22-2a	Beethoven	Sonata, op. 28 (III)
22-2b	Chopin	Nocturne, op. 27, no. 1
22-4	Dello Joio	Piano Sonata, no. 3 (I)
22-5	Schubert	"Die Liebe hat gelogen"
22-6a	Beethoven	Bagatelle, no. 8, op. 119
22-6b	Wolf	"Gebet" (No. 28 from *Mörike Songs*)
22-6c	Rogers	"Some Enchanted Evening" (from *South Pacific*)
22-6d	Joplin	"Pleasant Moments" (Ragtime Waltz)
22-10a	Haydn	String Quartet, op. 76/4 (I)
22-10b	Tchaikovsky	Symphony, no. 6, op. 74 (I)
22-11	Schubert	Moments musical No. 6 from *Sechs Moments Musicaux*, op. 94 (D.780)
22-12a	Mahler	"Rheinlegendchen" (from *Des Knaben Wunderhorn*)
23-1	Brahms	"Wie Melodien zieht es mir," op. 105, no. 1
23-3	Beethoven	Piano Sonata, op. 10, no. 1 (I)
23-4a	Beethoven	Trio, op. 1, no. 1 (IV)
23-4b	Smith/Bernard	"Walking in a Winter Wonderland"
23-4c	Beethoven	Sonata for Violin and Piano op. 24 (II)
23-5a	Brahms	Quintet, no. 1, op. 88
23-5b	Liszt	Consolation, no. 2
23-6	Schubert	"Sehnsucht"
23-9	Tchaikovsky	Onegin's Aria from *Eugene Onegin*
23-10	Chopin	Fantasy in F Minor, op. 49
23-12	Brahms	Ballade, op. 10, no. 4
23-13	Beethoven	Piano Sonata, op. 13 (I)
23-14	Beethoven	Piano Sonata, op. 13 (I)
23-16	Beethoven	Symphony, no. 5, op. 67 (II)
23-17	Liszt	Consolation, no. 2
24-4	Chopin	Etude, op. 10, no. 3
24-5	Tchaikovsky	Lenski's Aria from *Eugene Onegin* (act 2, scene 2)
24-6	Puccini	"Che gelida manina" from *La Boheme* (act 1)
24-7	Tchaikovsky	*Romeo and Juliet*
24-9	Bacharach/David	"What the World Needs Now Is Love"
24-12	Wagner	"Wahn! Wahn! *Die Meistersinger von Nürnberg)* (act 3, scene 1)
24-14	Hart/Webber	"All I Ask of You" (from *Phantom of the Opera*)
24-15	McBride	"Secret Rendezvous"
24-18	Chopin	Nocturne, op. 32, no. 1
24-19	Chopin	Mazurka, op. posth. 68, no. 4
24-20	Chopin	Prelude, op. 28, no. 4
24-21	Chopin	Mazurka, op. 17, no. 4
24-22	Chopin	Nocturne, op. 48, no. 2
24-23	Foster/Graydon/Champlin	"After the Love Has Gone"
24-24	Saint-Saëns	Trio in E Minor, op. 92 (III)
25-1	Brahms	Waltz, op. 39, no. 3
25-2	Brahms	Waltz, op. 39, no. 3
25-3	Kuhlau	Sonatina, op. 20, no. 1 (I)
25-4	Kuhlau	Sonatina, op. 20, no. 1 (I)
25-5	Kuhlau	Sonatina, op. 20, no. 1 (I)

Example	Composer	Title
25-6a	Mozart	Piano Sonata, K. 332 (I)
25-6b	Mozart	Piano Sonata, K. 332 (I)
25-6c	Mozart	Piano Sonata, K. 332 (I)
25-7	Chopin	Prelude, op. 28, no. 7
25-8	Clementi	Sonatina, op. 36, no. 1
25-9	Beethoven	Piano Sonata, op. 13 (II)
25-11	Bach	French Suite, no. 5 (Gavotte)
25-12	Beethoven	Piano Sonata, op. 14, no. 2
25-13	Desmond	"Take Five"
25-14	Schumann	*Kinderszenen*, op. 15, no. 6
26-2	Mozart	*Eine kleine Nachmusik* (I), Exposition, First Thematic Area
26-3	Mozart	*Eine kleine Nachmusik* (I), Exposition, Transition
26-4	Mozart	*Eine kleine Nachmusik* (I), Exposition, Second Thematic Area
26-5	Mozart	*Eine kleine Nachmusik* (I), Exposition, Codetta
26-6	Mozart	*Eine kleine Nachmusik* (I), Development
26-7	Mozart	*Eine kleine Nachmusik* (I), Recapitulation, First Thematic Area/Tran.
26-8	Mozart	*Eine kleine Nachmusik* (I), Recapitulation, Second Thematic Area
26-9	Mozart	*Eine kleine Nachmusik* (I), Coda
27-1	Beethoven	Piano Sonata, op. 13 (II), Theme A (Refrain)
27-2	Beethoven	Piano Sonata, op. 13 (II), Episode B
27-3	Beethoven	Piano Sonata, op. 13 (II), Refrain
27-4	Beethoven	Piano Sonata, op. 13 (II), Episode C
27-5	Beethoven	Piano Sonata, op. 13 (II), Refrain
27-6	Beethoven	Piano Sonata, op. 13 (II), Coda
28-6b	Rodgers	"Slaughter on Tenth Avenue"
28-6c	Prokofiev	Classical Symphony, op. 25 (III)
28-6d	Fogerty	"Proud Mary"
28-7	Debussy	"Minstrels" (*Preludes*, Bk. I, no. 12)
28-9a	Chavez	Ten Preludes (no. 1)
28-9b	Turek	"Carnival Days" (from *Songs for Kids*)
28-10	Davis	"So What?"
28-11a	Debussy	"Hommage a Rameau" (*Images*, Book I)
28-11b	Debussy	"Les collines d'Anacapri" (*Preludes*, Bk. I, no. 5)
28-15	Debussy	"Voiles" (*Preludes*, Bk. I, no. 2)
28-17	Debussy	*Pour le piano* (Sarabande)
28-18	Hindemith	*Ludus Tonalis* (Fugue, no. 5)
28-20	Debussy	"Voiles" (*Preludes*, Bk. I, no. 2)
28-21b	Debussy	"Soiree dans Grenade" (*Estampes*, no. 2)
28-23b	Debussy	"Feuilles mortes" (*Preludes*, Bk. II, no. 2)
29-1a	Hindemith	"Un cygne," from *Six Chansons* (1939)
29-1b	Bartók	*Fourteen Bagatelles*, op. 6, no. 11 (1908)
29-4a	Schuman	*Three Score Set*, (II) (1943)
29-4b	Persichetti	*Harmonium*, op. 50, no. 3 (1959)
29-5	Honegger	Symphony No. 5, (I) (1950)
29-6a	Ravel	"Blues" Sonate pour Violon et Piano (II)
29-6b	Stravinsky	*The Rite of Spring*, "The Sacrifice" (1913)
29-7	Bartók	"Major and minor," no. 59 (from *Mikrokosmos* vol. II)

Example	Composer	Title
29-8a	Rorem	"The Air Is the Only" (from *Poems of Love and the Rain*)
29-8b	Dello Joio	Piano Sonata, no. 3 (I), Variation IV
29-9a	Stravinsky	*The Rite of Spring* (Introduction)
29-9b	Stravinsky	*The Rite of Spring* ("Spring Rounds")
29-10	Bartók	"Boating" from *Mikrokosmos*, vol. V (1939)
30-7	Schoenberg	*Klavierstücke*, op. 11, no. 1
30-12	Schoenberg	"*Nacht*" from *Pierrot Lunaire*
30-17	McCarthy	*Visions and Apparitions* (II)
30-19	Bernstein	*Three Silhouettes for Guitar* (II)
30-20	McCarthy	"Siobhan In Colonial Williamsburg" from *An American Girl* (II)
31-1a	Schoenberg	*Fünf Klavierstücke*, op. 23, no. 4
31-1b	Schoenberg	*Fünf Klavierstücke*, op. 23, no. 4
31-4a	Turek	*Three by Twelve* (I)
31-4b	Turek	*Three by Twelve* (II)
31-7	Schoenberg	Fourth String Quartet, op. 37 (I)
31-12	Dallapiccola	*Quaderno Musicale di Annalibera* (Simbolo)
32-4	Guaraldi	"Christmas Time is Here"
32-6	Adair/Dennis	"Everything Happens to Me"
32-7a	Barbera/Hanna/Curtin	"Flintstones Theme"
32-7b	Barbera/Hanna/Curtin	"Flintstones Theme"
32-8a	Barbera/Hanna/Curtin	"Flintstones Theme"
32-8b	Barbera/Hanna/Curtin	"Flintstones Theme"
32-12a	Wolf/Landesman	"Spring Can Really Hang You Up the Most"
32-13	Barbera/Hanna/Curtin	"Flintstones Theme"
32-15	Hamilton	"Cry Me a River"
32-18c	Turek	Medium Latin
32-21	Russell	"This Masquerade"
32-22b	Webster/Mandel	"A Time for Love"
32-23b	Mercer/Arden	"My Shining Hour"
32-24a	Fox/Gimbel	"Killing Me Softly with His Song"
33-3	Peterson	"Hymn to Freedom"
33-4	Typical	12-Bar Blues
33-5	with Further Substitutions	12-Bar Blues
33-7	Standard	Minor Blues
33-9	Silver	"Cookin' at the Continental"
33-12	Hancock	"Canteloupe Island"
33-14	Leiber/Stoller	"Kansas City"
34-1	McCarthy	"Looking for Cool"
34-3	Joel	"The Longest Time"
34-4	Turek	"You and Me"
34-6	McCarthy	"One Fine Day"
34-10	McCarthy	"Long Ago" (Verse)
34-11	McCarthy	"Long Ago" (Bridge)
34-12	McCarthy	"Humpti Dumpti" (Chorus)
34-13	McCarthy	"Humpti Dumpti" (Bridge)
34-14	McCarthy (Dave)	"Close Your Eyes"
34-15	Adkins	"Someone Like You"